TypeScript 5 Design Patterns and Best Practices

Build clean and scalable apps with proven patterns and expert insights

Theofanis Despoudis

‹packt›

TypeScript 5 Design Patterns and Best Practices

Group Product Manager: Kaustubh Manglurkar

Publishing Product Manager: Bhavya Rao

Book Project Manager: Arul Viveaun S

Senior Editor: Shreya Sarkar

Technical Editor: K Bimala Singha

Copy Editor: Safis Editing

Indexer: Hemangini Bari

Production Designer: Jyoti Kadam

DevRel Marketing Coordinator: Nivedita Pandey

First published: September 2021

Second edition: February 2025

Production reference: 2041125

Published by Packt Publishing Ltd.

Grosvenor House

11 St Paul's Square

Birmingham

B3 1RB, UK.

ISBN 978-1-83588-322-8

www.packtpub.com

To my wonderful daughters, Sofia and Eleni. This book is for you, with the hope that you always pursue your dreams and never stop learning.

– Theofanis Despoudis

Contributors

About the author

Theofanis Despoudis lives in Ireland, where he works as a senior staff software engineer for WP Engine. He is the co-author of *The React Workshop* and *Advanced Go Programming in 7 Days*, and maintains many open source projects on GitHub.

Theofanis works extensively with Faust.js, a Next.js framework written in TypeScript, and is actively developing a next-generation Headless WordPress toolkit leveraging TSDocs. He is also passionate about experimenting with AI technologies and exploring their applications in modern development workflows.

I am deeply grateful to those who have supported and encouraged me along this journey, especially my editor Shreya Sarkar; book project manager, Arul Viveaun S; publishing product manager, Bhavya Rao; and the technical reviewers, Dr. Sanjay Krishna Anbalagan and Sunil Raj Thota, whose insights and dedication have been invaluable to the completion of this book.

About the reviewers

Dr. Sanjay Krishna Anbalagan earned his Master's degree and Ph.D. in Computer Science, specializing in data visualization, from the University of Massachusetts Lowell. He has worked at Cengage Learning and is currently employed at Amazon Web Services (AWS). With a strong focus on data visualization, Dr. Anbalagan contributes his expertise to advance the field through innovative solutions and research.

Sunil Raj Thota is a seasoned software engineer with extensive experience in web development and AI applications. Currently working in the Amazon QuickSight team, Sunil has previously contributed to significant projects at Yahoo Inc., enhancing user engagement and satisfaction through innovative features at Yahoo and AOL Mail. He has also worked at Northeastern University as a research assistant and at MOURI Tech as a senior software engineer, optimizing multiple websites and leading successful project deployments. Sunil co-founded ISF Technologies, where he championed user-centric design and agile methodologies. He has also contributed to the books *AI Strategies for Web Development* and *The Art of Micro Frontends*. His academic background includes a master's in analytics from Northeastern University and a bachelor's in electronics and communications engineering from Andhra University.

Table of Contents

Part 1: Introduction to TypeScript 5

1

2

TypeScript Core Principles 45

Part 2: TypeScript Core Design Patterns

3

Creational Design Patterns 85

4

Structural Design Patterns   131

5

Behavioral Design Patterns for Object Communication   179

6

Behavioral Design Patterns for Managing State and Behavior   209

Part 3: Advanced TypeScript Concepts and Best Practices

7

Functional Programming with TypeScript   241

8

Reactive and Asynchronous Programming   287

9

Developing Modern and Robust TypeScript Applications   317

10

Anti-Patterns and Workarounds   349

11

Exploring Design Patterns in Open Source Architectures   369

12

Unlock Your Exclusive Benefits   389

Index   393

Other Books You May Enjoy   404

Preface

TypeScript has rapidly become one of the most popular languages for developing large-scale applications. Its combination of strong typing, modern JavaScript features, and seamless integration with popular frameworks has made it a go-to tool for developers aiming to write more reliable and maintainable code.

This book, *TypeScript 5 Design Patterns and Best Practices*, explores how developers can leverage TypeScript to build scalable applications by mastering design patterns, best practices, and advanced programming concepts. The goal is to empower developers to write cleaner, more efficient code while embracing TypeScript's powerful type system.

Based on the success of the first edition, in this edition, I incorporated valuable reader feedback to deliver an even more comprehensive and user-friendly learning experience. Here's a breakdown of the key improvements:

- **Enhanced clarity and organization**: This edition prioritizes clear and efficient learning. I've restructured the content based on reader feedback, ensuring a smoother flow and better alignment with your learning goals. Additionally, references to previous topics are now linked throughout the book, allowing you to easily revisit key concepts and navigate the material seamlessly.

- **Expanded coverage**: I've listened to your requests and expanded on valuable topics. The *Criticisms* section, after each explained pattern, now dives deeper into anti-patterns, providing real-world examples to help you understand how to avoid common pitfalls and write cleaner, more efficient code. Furthermore, the testing code is now integrated throughout relevant sections, allowing you to solidify your understanding of best practices by putting them into action.

- **Added content**: This edition is packed with new content to enhance your learning journey. I've included a comprehensive exploration of the popular **Model-View-Controller** (**MVC**) pattern (*Chapter 9*) to equip you with a foundational approach to web application development. Additionally, the chapter on functional programming section (*Chapter 7*) has been improved to provide a more focused and practical understanding of this paradigm. Finally, I've added a brand-new chapter (*Chapter 11*) that demonstrates the real-world usage of design patterns in two popular open source projects.

- **Content refinements**: I've meticulously reviewed and refined the content to provide you with the best possible learning experience. Typos and inconsistencies have been addressed to ensure all code examples function as expected. Complex figures have been simplified for better understanding, with a focus on the needs of TypeScript beginners.

This comprehensive list of updates ensures you receive the relevant and effective material for mastering TypeScript development.

Who this book is for

This book is ideal for TypeScript developers seeking to enhance their skills in building scalable and maintainable applications. It's also valuable for software engineers, architects, and development team leads who aim to improve code quality and development practices in TypeScript projects.

Readers should have a basic understanding of TypeScript fundamentals, including syntax, data types, and basic language features. Familiarity with software development concepts and best practices is beneficial but not required.

What this book covers

Chapter 1, Getting Started with TypeScript 5, introduces TypeScript 5, a powerful extension of JavaScript with type-checking capabilities. The chapter also covers how to set up TypeScript with VSCode and introduces UML diagrams as a tool for modeling design patterns.

Chapter 2, TypeScript Core Principles, discusses fundamental **object-oriented programming** (**OOP**) principles in TypeScript, such as encapsulation, inheritance, and polymorphism. You will learn how TypeScript bridges the gap between JavaScript and OOP and how to use TypeScript in both browser and server environments, and will receive an introduction to design patterns, which will be expanded upon in later chapters.

Chapter 3, Creational Design Patterns, explores patterns such as Singleton, Prototype, Builder, Factory Method, and Abstract Factory. Each pattern will be explained with practical examples and use cases in TypeScript to showcase how they simplify object creation and resource management.

Chapter 4, Structural Design Patterns, delves into patterns such as Decorator, Façade, Composite, Proxy, Bridge, and Flyweight, with practical applications in TypeScript, illustrating how these patterns can reduce complexity and improve flexibility in code.

Chapter 5, Behavioral Design Patterns for Object Communication, focuses on behavioral design patterns that handle communication between objects. Patterns such as Strategy, Chain of Responsibility, Command, Mediator, and Observer are explored in depth.

Chapter 6, Behavioral Design Patterns for Managing State and Behavior, explores those patterns that govern the control and management of an object's state or behavior over time, such as Iterator, Memento, State, Template Method, and Visitor. These patterns show how to manage object life cycles and data flow efficiently in TypeScript applications.

Chapter 7, Functional Programming with TypeScript, teaches you about key concepts such as immutability, recursion, function composition, and higher-order functions, alongside advanced functional programming techniques such as Monads, Functors, and Lenses, all aimed at improving code maintainability and reusability.

Chapter 8, Reactive and Asynchronous Programming, explains Promises, Futures, and Observables, as well as how to apply reactive programming principles to manage.

Chapter 9, Developing Modern and Robust TypeScript Applications, shifts toward best practices for building modern TypeScript applications. By combining design patterns with utility types, **domain-driven design** (**DDD**), and SOLID principles, you will be well equipped to design scalable and maintainable applications.

Chapter 10, Anti-Patterns and Workarounds, focuses on anti-patterns, which are common mistakes made in TypeScript development. This chapter identifies these pitfalls and offers practical workarounds to avoid them. Topics include class overuse, incorrect type handling, and common type inference mistakes.

Chapter 11, Exploring Design Patterns in Open Source Architectures, is the final chapter. It explores the application of design patterns in popular TypeScript frameworks such as tRPC and Apollo Client. By studying real-world examples, you'll gain insights into how design patterns enhance the architecture and maintainability of TypeScript applications.

To get the most out of this book

All code examples have been tested using TypeScript 5 with Node.js 18 on macOS. However, they should work with future version releases too.

Software/hardware covered in the book	Operating system requirements
Node.js 18 and above	Windows, macOS, or Linux
TypeScript 5.0 and above	
A browser such as Chrome or Firefox	

No additional setup is required beyond having a code editor (e.g., VSCode) and Node.js installed on your system to follow the examples in the book. The code examples can be executed in any environment that supports modern JavaScript and TypeScript.

If you are using the digital version of this book, we advise you to type the code yourself or access the code from the book's GitHub repository (a link is available in the next section). Doing so will help you avoid any potential errors related to the copying and pasting of code.

Download the example code files

You can download the example code files for this book from GitHub at `https://github.com/PacktPublishing/TypeScript-5-Design-Patterns-and-Best-Practices`. If there's an update to the code, it will be updated in the GitHub repository.

We also have other code bundles from our rich catalog of books and videos available at `https://github.com/PacktPublishing/`. Check them out!

Conventions used

There are a number of text conventions used throughout this book.

`Code in text`: Indicates code words in text, database table names, folder names, filenames, file extensions, pathnames, dummy URLs, user input, and Twitter handles. Here is an example: "The returned function, `createVariantButtonProps`, can access this variable even after `buttonProps` has returned."

A block of code is set as follows:

```
function add(a: number, b: number): number {
  return a + b
}
console.log(add(2, 3)) // 5
console.log(add(2, 3)) // 5
```

When we wish to draw your attention to a particular part of a code block, the relevant lines or items are set in bold:

```
function sortList(list: number[]): number[] {
  return list.sort((a, b) => a - b)
}
let originalList = [3, 1, 4, 1, 5, 9]
let sortedList = sortList(originalList)
console.log(sortedList) // [1, 1, 3, 4, 5, 9]
console.log(originalList) // [1, 1, 3, 4, 5, 9] - Original list is
mutated!
```

Any command-line input or output is written as follows:

```
$ npm run test  --chain-of-responsibility
```

Bold: Indicates a new term, an important word, or words that you see onscreen. For instance, words in menus or dialog boxes appear in **bold**. Here is an example: "It then defines multiple auth strategies in the **Providers** section for authenticating with GitHub, Facebook, Google, and other OAuth providers."

> **Tips or important notes**
> Appear like this.

Get in touch

Feedback from our readers is always welcome.

General feedback: If you have questions about any aspect of this book, email us at `customercare@packtpub.com` and mention the book title in the subject of your message.

Errata: Although we have taken every care to ensure the accuracy of our content, mistakes do happen. If you have found a mistake in this book, we would be grateful if you would report this to us. Please visit `www.packtpub.com/support/errata` and fill in the form.

Piracy: If you come across any illegal copies of our works in any form on the internet, we would be grateful if you would provide us with the location address or website name. Please contact us at `copyright@packt.com` with a link to the material.

If you are interested in becoming an author: If there is a topic that you have expertise in and you are interested in either writing or contributing to a book, please visit `authors.packtpub.com`.

Share Your Thoughts

Once you've read *TypeScript 5 Design Patterns and Best Practices*, we'd love to hear your thoughts! Scan the QR code below to go straight to the Amazon review page for this book and share your feedback.

`https://packt.link/r/1835883230`

Your review is important to us and the tech community and will help us make sure we're delivering excellent quality content.

Free Benefits with Your Book

This book comes with free benefits to support your learning. Activate them now for instant access (see the "*How to Unlock*" section for instructions).

Here's a quick overview of what you can instantly unlock with your purchase:

PDF and ePub Copies	Next-Gen Web-Based Reader
Free PDF and ePub versions	**Next-Gen Reader**
Access a DRM-free PDF copy of this book to read anywhere, on any device. Use a DRM-free ePub version with your favorite e-reader.	**Multi-device progress sync**: Pick up where you left off, on any device. **Highlighting and notetaking**: Capture ideas and turn reading into lasting knowledge. **Bookmarking**: Save and revisit key sections whenever you need them. **Dark mode**: Reduce eye strain by switching to dark or sepia themes

How to Unlock

UNLOCK NOW

Scan the QR code (or go to `packtpub.com/unlock`). Search for this book by name, confirm the edition, and then follow the steps on the page.

Note: Keep your invoice handly. Purchase made directly from packt don't require one.

Part 1: Introduction to TypeScript 5

In this section, we introduce TypeScript 5, the latest version of this powerful language that extends JavaScript by adding static types. We'll explore key concepts such as TypeScript's relationship with JavaScript, the latest features introduced in version 5, and the benefits of type-driven development. You'll also learn about development tools such as VSCode and diagramming tools such as UML, both of which are useful for modern TypeScript development. By the end of this section, you'll be equipped with the essential skills needed to confidently develop TypeScript applications.

This part has the following chapters:

- *Chapter 1, Getting Started with TypeScript 5*
- *Chapter 2, TypeScript Core Principles*

1

Getting Started with TypeScript 5

Welcome to the updated edition of *TypeScript 4 Design Patterns and Best Practices*! Building on the success of the first edition (first published in 2021), this book incorporates valuable reader feedback and a wealth of new content. Whether you're familiar with design patterns from the *Gang of Four (GoF)* book or entirely new to the concept, this book is your comprehensive guide to leveraging TypeScript 5 for building robust and scalable applications. Here's what you'll gain:

- **Master the art of design patterns in TypeScript**: We'll delve into both the theory and practical implementation of architectural design patterns specifically in the context of TypeScript

- **Harness the power of TypeScript 5**: Learn how to leverage the latest features of TypeScript 5 to create efficient and maintainable code structures for your design patterns

- **Modernized best practices**: Explore effective design principles and best practices suitable for the modern TypeScript development landscape

Studying patterns serves multiple important purposes. Firstly, it provides a modern and concrete language for understanding design patterns, with TypeScript serving as a powerful and extensively employed framework. Secondly, the emphasis lies on fresh implementations rather than relying on outdated or generic examples. Lastly, studying patterns equips individuals not only with the ability to apply these design principles but also to adapt and enhance them using modern best practices. This ensures that their code remains efficient and up-to-date. The book prioritizes practical applications that follow the latest features and capabilities of TypeScript, ensuring relevance and applicability in real-world scenarios.

The first two chapters provide a solid foundation in TypeScript 5. They'll equip you with the essential knowledge to effectively work with the code examples throughout the book. Following this foundational setup, we'll go on a deep dive into design patterns, exploring them and their practical implementation in TypeScript one by one. Following up on this, we will explore architectural design patterns and best practices that help you build robust, scalable, and maintainable applications in TypeScript.

In this chapter, we are going to cover the following main topics:

- Introducing TypeScript 5

- Exploring useful TypeScript 5 features

- Understanding TypeScript and JavaScript's relationship

- Setting up your development environment

- Using VSCode with TypeScript

- Introducing Unified Modeling Language (UML)

By understanding these powerful tools, you'll be able to structure your code efficiently, promote reusability, and ensure long-term project success.

Let's get started!

> **Note**
>
> The links to all the sources mentioned in this chapter, as well as any supplementary reading materials, are provided in the *Further reading* section, toward the end of this chapter.

> **Free Benefits with Your Book**
>
> Your purchase includes a free PDF copy of this book along with other exclusive benefits. Check the *Free Benefits with Your Book* section in the Preface to unlock them instantly and maximize your learning experience.

Technical requirements

The code bundle for this chapter is available on `https://github.com/PacktPublishing/TypeScript-5-Design-Patterns-and-Best-Practices/tree/main/chapters/chapter01_Getting_Started_With_Typescript_5`.

In the *Setting up your development environment* section, we will discuss how to install and use the code examples in this book. First, let's refresh our knowledge of TypeScript, especially its latest version.

Introducing TypeScript 5

TypeScript continues the language's long-standing history of type safety, bringing a plethora of improvements to the developer experience. While not a revolutionary release in terms of core functionality, TypeScript 5 focuses on refinement and optimization.

In this section, we'll look at a quick breakdown of some key TypeScript features introduced in versions 4 and 5. For TypeScript 4, we've explored some of those features in the previous edition of the book:

- **Template literal types**: Enhanced type safety for template literals, allowing for more precise control over string manipulation

- **Enhanced mapped types**: More powerful manipulation of object types using mapped types

- **Const type parameters**: Improved type safety for generic functions by allowing constant values for type parameters

- **override keyword**: Explicitly mark methods that override a base class method, improving code clarity and catching potential errors

- **Improved `BigInt` support**: Better handling of `BigInt` values, a new JavaScript primitive for large integers

As for TypeScript 5, we will explore the following features later in this chapter:

- **Simplified module resolution**: Streamlined module resolution process for a smoother development experience

- **Decorator support**: Better support for decorators, a powerful syntactic feature for adding metadata to code

- **`const` type parameters**: Improving the type inference for functions by preserving the literal types of objects passed as arguments

- **Improved enum handling**: All enums are now considered union enums by default, enhancing type safety and flexibility

While TypeScript offers a rich set of features, we'll prioritize concepts that directly contribute to understanding and implementing design patterns effectively. While using inference with `const` type parameters is nice, in practical terms, it only serves to improve type safety and not to design programs. For this reason, these features, while valuable for broader development, can add complexity when our primary goal is mastering design patterns.

Instead, the book utilizes self-contained examples designed for independent learning and reference. This allows you to grasp the core functionality of each design pattern in its simplest form. By focusing on practical implementation without extraneous language features, you'll gain a solid foundation in design patterns that can be readily applied in your TypeScript projects.

TypeScript fundamentals

A strong foundation in TypeScript fundamentals is crucial for effectively learning and applying design patterns. Here's why:

- **Enhanced code quality and maintainability**: TypeScript introduces **static typing**, enabling you to define the data types your variables and functions will hold. This helps catch errors early in the development process, preventing issues such as assigning a string value to a variable expecting a number. By understanding basic types and type annotations, you can leverage TypeScript's type system to create more robust and maintainable code, especially when working with complex design patterns.

- **Effective refactoring**: **Refactoring** is the process of restructuring existing code to improve its design, readability, and maintainability without changing its external behavior. Most tools and IDEs have built-in tasks that allow us to perform refactoring tasks. TypeScript's type system assists with refactoring code, which is often necessary when implementing design patterns. As you modify your code structure to implement design patterns, type safety helps ensure that changes remain consistent and don't introduce unintended side effects. This safeguards your code base and simplifies future modifications.

Now, we'll move on to understanding basic types in the next section.

Building blocks of TypeScript – basic types

TypeScript programs are built using **statements** or **expressions**. Examples of statements include variable declarations, control flow statements (such as `if` or `for` loops), and function calls. An expression, on the other hand, is a piece of code that evaluates to a value.

> **Note**
> Statements perform tasks such as assignments, printing output, or controlling flow (`if/else` and loops). They don't produce values directly. Expressions, in contrast, evaluate a result (calculations, variable references, and function calls) that statements can then use. Think of statements as giving orders, while expressions supply the data for those orders.

Statements or expressions typically operate on data, and that's where **basic types** come in. Basic types define the fundamental building blocks for representing data in your TypeScript code. They are like the basic data types found in JavaScript, but TypeScript adds the benefit of static type checking, which helps catch errors early in development.

Before we explore the basics of TypeScript it would be beneficial to introduce key symbols and terminology in the initial chapters of the book. Here's a quick introduction:

- **Pipe symbol** (|): Used to denote union types, allowing a variable to hold multiple types

- **Ampersand symbol** (&): Used to denote intersection types, combining multiple types into one

- **Question mark** (?): Indicates optional properties in types
- **Square brackets** ([]): Denotes array types

Now let's do a breakdown of some common basic types in TypeScript:

- **Primitive types**: These are the most fundamental data types representing basic values. Some examples include the following:

  - **number**: Represents numeric values (e.g., 10 or 3.14)

  - **string**: Represents textual data enclosed in quotes (e.g., "Hello, World!")

  - **Boolean**: Represents true or false values (e.g., `true` or `false`)

  - **void**: Represents the absence of a value (e.g., functions that don't return anything)

- **Other basic types**: TypeScript offers additional basic types beyond primitives:

  - **null**: Represents the intentional absence of an object value (e.g., `let value: null = null;`)

  - **undefined**: Represents a variable that has been declared but not yet assigned a value (e.g., `let value: string;`)

  - **unknown**: Represents a value that has an unknown type at compile time

  - **any**: This type essentially disables type checking since it represents anything that cannot be typed; we aim to reduce the usage of this type as much as possible

  - **never**: This is typically used for functions that don't return anything (void) or throw an error

TypeScript offers a powerful feature called **type safety**. This means that variables and other data have associated types that define the kind of values they can hold. It's like labeling a box to describe its contents. To leverage TypeScript's type safety, you can explicitly define the type of a variable when you declare it. Here's an example:

intro.ts

```
const one: string = "one"
const two: boolean = false
const three: number = 3
const four: null = null
const five: unknown = 5
const six: any = 6
const seven = Symbol("seven")
function neverReturningFunction(): never {
  throw new Error("This function never returns")
}
// let eight: never;
```

This code example showcases various basic types in TypeScript. We have primitive types such as `string`, `number`, and `Boolean` for common data. Additionally, there are special types such as `null` for the intentional absence of a value and `unknown` for variables with unknown types. While `any` allows assigning any value, it bypasses type checking, so use it sparingly. Symbols are unique identifiers and are typically used for functions that never return or throw an error (demonstrated in the `neverReturningFunction` function). It's worth noting that some types such as `never` cannot be directly assigned values.

- **Enums**: Enums define sets of named constants for improved code readability, maintainability, and type safety. By default, enums create constants with numerical values starting from 0 and incrementing by 1 for each subsequent member:

enum.ts

```
enum Direction {
  Up = 0,
  Down, // Implicitly assigned 1
  Left, // Implicitly assigned 2
  Right, // Implicitly assigned 3
}
let userDirection: Direction = Direction.Up
```

TypeScript 5 introduced **union enums**, a powerful feature that elevates type safety by creating a unique type for each member within an enum. The following example showcases their usage:

enum.ts

```
const prefix = '/data';
const enum Routes {
  Parts = `${prefix}/parts`, // "/data/parts"
  Invoices = `${prefix}/invoices`, // "/data/invoices"
}
```

Previously, enums were separate numeric and literal enum types, causing confusion. Now, enums are unions of their member types. Members can have values computed by expressions (constant or non-constant) and those with constant values (such as numbers or strings) get literal types for enhanced type safety. This improves code clarity and makes enums more powerful!

- **Arrays and tuples**: TypeScript offers two ways to represent collections of data: arrays and tuples. Let's understand these better:

  - *Arrays* represent a collection of items with the same type (e.g., `number []`). They can have a variable size, meaning you can add or remove elements after creation. An example would be `const numbers: number [] = [1, 2, 3];`.

- *Tuples* represent a fixed-length array where each element has a specific type. They offer type safety by enforcing the number of elements and their individual types. An example would be `const student: [string, number] = ["Alice", 25];`.

Choose arrays when you need a collection with a variable size or when the elements might change dynamically. On the other hand, use tuples when you know the exact structure and types of elements in your collection upfront. Tuples provide better type safety and prevent accidental mismatches.

- **Classes**: Classes in TypeScript represent blueprints for creating objects. They encapsulate data (*properties*) and functionality (*methods*) within a well-defined structure. TypeScript supports two kinds of classes:

  - **Concrete classes**: These are standard classes that can be directly instantiated to create objects. They define properties and methods that implement the desired behavior. Here's an example of a concrete class:

classes.ts

```ts
class User {
  constructor(private readonly name: string) {
    this.name = name
  }

  public getName(): string {
    return this.name
  }
}
const user = new User("Theo")
console.log(user.getName()) // Output: "Theo"
```

This code defines a concrete class named `User` in TypeScript. The class represents a `user` object with a private `name` property and a public `getName` method.

  - **Abstract classes**: These serve as templates for subclasses and cannot be directly instantiated. They define abstract methods (without implementation) that subclasses must implement to provide specific functionality. This enforces a common interface across derived classes. Here's an example of an abstract class:

classes.ts

```ts
abstract class Animal {
  abstract makeSound(): void;
}
class Dog extends Animal {
```

```
    makeSound(): void {
      console.log("Woof!");
    }
  }
  new Dog().makeSound();
```

This code defines an abstract class named `Animal` that serves as a blueprint for creating `Animal` types. It has one abstract method, `makeSound`, that must be implemented by any class inheriting from `Animal`. This enforces that subclasses must define how they handle this method.

- **Interfaces and types**: TypeScript provides two powerful tools for defining object structures: interfaces and types:

  - **Interfaces**: These are abstractions that let you define the shape of an object and its properties, but without specifying an implementation. For example, we can define a `Comparable` interface like this:

---

interfaces.ts

```
export interface Comparable<T> {
  compareTo(other: Comparable<T>): -1 | 0 | 1;
}
```

This interface defines that any object implementing `Comparable` must have a `compareTo` method. This method takes another object of the same type (`T`) and returns a number indicating the comparison result (`-1` for less than, `0` for equal, `1` for greater).

Interfaces play a crucial role in promoting code clarity and maintainability. They enforce a consistent structure across objects that implement them, making your code easier to understand and reason about. Additionally, interfaces enable loose coupling – classes can implement the interface without relying on the specific implementation details.

  - **Types**: Types provide another approach to defining object structures. They are like interfaces but offer more flexibility. Types can act as aliases for complex data types, improving code readability. Additionally, they allow you to combine existing types using **unions (OR)** and **intersections (AND)** for more specific type definitions:

    - **Union types (OR)**: Combine multiple types with the pipe (|) symbol. The resulting type can be any of the combined types. Here is an example:

---

types.ts

```
type A = 'A';
type B = 'B';
type C = A | B; // C can be either 'A' or 'B'
```

> **Warning: avoid using union types with incompatible types**
>
> When using union types, ensure that the types being combined are compatible. For example, if you were to combine types that have no logical relationship, it could lead to confusion and increased complexity in your code. Here's an example:
>
> ```
> type D = 'A' | 40; // D can be either 'A' or a number
> ```
>
> In this case, D can either be the character 'A' or a 'number', which may lead to extensive type checking and casting in your code. This choice can create confusion and make your code harder to maintain.

- **Intersection Types (AND)**: Combine multiple types with the ampersand (&) symbol. The resulting type must share all properties from both original types. Here's an example:

types.ts

```
type User = {
  name: string
}
type ExtendedUser = User & {
  age: number
}
let user: ExtendedUser = {
  name: "Theo",
  age: 20,
}
```

> **Interfaces versus types**
>
> When working with types in TypeScript, prioritize using interfaces to establish clear contracts for objects. Interfaces define their structure and properties, making code easier to understand and maintain. However, for on-the-fly type creation or combining existing types with more flexibility, TypeScript also offers types. This allows for dynamic control over data types when your needs go beyond what interfaces can provide.

- **Generics**: Generics allow us to define functions, classes, and interfaces that can work with any data type while maintaining type safety. This means we can write code that is adaptable to various types without removing the benefits of TypeScript's static typing.

The syntax for defining a generic type involves using angle brackets (< >) to specify a type parameter. Here's a basic structure:

types.ts

```
function callMe<T>(parameter: T): T {
    return parameter;
}
```

In this example, T is a placeholder for any type. When the function is called, T is replaced with the actual type passed as an argument.

Generics can also be used with interfaces to create reusable data structures:

types.ts

```
interface Box<T> {
    content: T;
}
const numberBox: Box<number> = { content: 10 };
```

In this example, the Box interface can hold a value of any type specified when creating an instance of the interface.

By understanding the distinct roles of generics, interfaces, and types, you can effectively design robust and maintainable object-oriented applications in TypeScript. Now, let's move on and learn what's new in TypeScript 5.

Exploring useful TypeScript 5 features

As promised earlier, we will now explore some of the most prominent features introduced in TypeScript 5.

> **Note**
>
> In this section, we mention the concept of compiler errors. If you are coming from a background in languages such as C++ or Java, it's important to understand a particular distinction. A **compiler** is a tool that translates source code written in a programming language into another form, typically machine code or bytecode. The **TypeScript compiler**, on the other hand, focuses on type checking and converting TypeScript to JavaScript, rather than generating machine code. Experienced developers may skip this section if they are already familiar with these concepts.

- **Decorator support**: Decorators are a powerful syntactic feature that allows you to add metadata to classes, properties, methods, and other parts of your code. TypeScript 5 introduces better support for decorators, enabling you to explore this functionality for potential use cases.

For example, the **memoize decorator** is a common pattern used for performance optimization. It caches the results of a function call based on its arguments, avoiding redundant computations if the same arguments are used multiple times.

Here's how you can define a log decorator in TypeScript 5:

Decorators.ts

```
function log(originalMethod: any, context:
  ClassMethodDecoratorContext) {
    function replacementMethod(this: any, ...args:
      any[]) {
    console.log(`Calling ${String(context.name)}`)
    return originalMethod.call(this, ...args)
  }
  return replacementMethod
}

class Calculator {
  @log
  add(x: number, y: number): number {
    return x + y
  }
}
new Calculator().add(2, 3)
```

In this example, the `@log` decorator is applied to the `add` method within the `Calculator` class. Whenever we call the `add` method, the log decorator will be called beforehand and log the context name in the console.

- **Improved enum handling**: By default, TypeScript 5 considers all enums to be union enums. This means each enum value is treated as a distinct type, enhancing type safety and flexibility. For example, think of an enum representing color options:

```
enum Color {
  Red,
  Green,
  Blue,
}
let myColor: Color = Color.Red
```

Now with TypeScript 5, a variable assignment to a different value is not allowed.

```
// myColor = 'orange';
```

If you go and comment out the variable assignment, then the compiler will flag this with the error demonstrated in *Figure 1.1*:

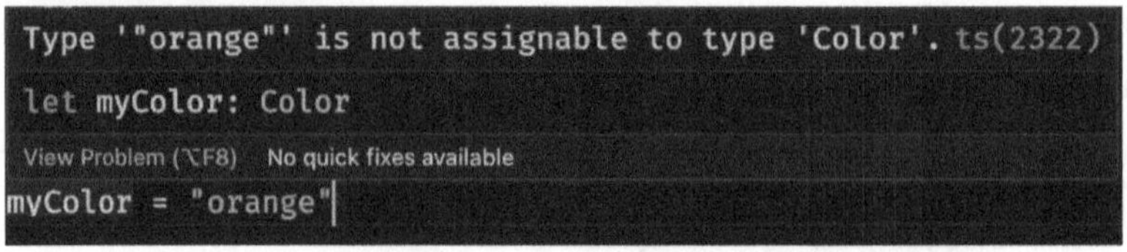

Figure 1.1 – Compiler error when assigning the wrong enum type

In this example, the `Color` enum is a union enum by default. You can't assign a value that's not explicitly defined in the enum, improving type safety. However, you can still assign enum values such as `Color.Red`.

- **New `NoInfer` utility type**: TypeScript 5.4 introduces the `NoInfer` utility type to improve type inference in generic functions. When calling generic functions, TypeScript might infer types that aren't ideal. For example, a function expecting a color from a list might allow an invalid color not to be present in the list. `NoInfer<T>` prevents TypeScript from considering the inner type `T` for further inference. This allows for stricter type-checking based on explicitly defined types.

Consider a simple example where you have a generic function that accepts a type `T`:

NoInfer.ts

```
class Animal {
  sleep() {}
}
class Cat extends Animal {
  miaw() {}
}
function petAnimal<T>(value: T,
  getDefault: () => T): T {
  // ... function logic ...
    return value || getDefault()
}
// This would compile without errors
petAnimal(new Cat(), () => new Animal())
```

In the example listed here, this `petAnimal` function takes two arguments: a value of type `T`, and `getDefault` as a function that should return the same type as value. By default, the last line will allow the widest type on the hierarchy to be inferred, so the actual type would be `petAnimal(animal, () => animal)`. Sometimes, however, you don't want the compiler to infer some types.

By using `NoInfer<T>` for the return type of `getDefault`, we prevent the compiler from inferring the type based on how `getDefault` is used within `petAnimal`. This ensures that `getDefault` must explicitly return a type compatible with `T`, maintaining type safety for the overall function.

In the next section, we'll delve into the relationship between TypeScript and JavaScript.

Understanding TypeScript and JavaScript's relationship

Having established a solid understanding of TypeScript's core concepts, you're likely keen to learn how to migrate existing JavaScript code. This is particularly valuable for those with strong JavaScript experience looking to transition projects to TypeScript. To effectively navigate this process, we need to grasp the fundamental differences between these languages.

In the next section, we'll perform a comparison of JavaScript and TypeScript, highlighting key distinctions that will guide your migration efforts.

How does JavaScript compare to TypeScript?

While both JavaScript and TypeScript share a similar syntax, key differences impact how you write and execute code. Here's a breakdown of some fundamental distinctions:

- **Typing versus no typing**: JavaScript is a *dynamically* typed language. This means the type of a variable is determined at runtime. TypeScript, on the other hand, is *statically* typed. You explicitly define the types of variables and functions before execution, leading to stricter type-checking and fewer runtime errors.

- **Implicit versus explicit types (with type inference)**: In JavaScript, types are often implicit. For example, `let x = 5;` implies that `x` is a number. TypeScript offers type inference, meaning it can often deduce the type based on the initial value assigned. So, `let x = 5` in TypeScript also infers `x` as a number. However, TypeScript allows you to explicitly override this inference and assign a different type when it is an equally allowed type.

- **Compilation versus interpretation**: JavaScript code is typically interpreted directly by the browser or server environment. TypeScript code goes through an additional compilation step that translates it into JavaScript while enforcing type checks. This compilation step can potentially reveal errors before your code even runs.

As a straightforward example, the following JavaScript program is also a valid TypeScript program by default when setting the noImplicitAny compiler flag to false, although no types are declared in the parameter name or the return type:

javascript-vs-typescript.ts

```
function calculateArea(length, width) {
    return length * width
}
```

This is a very simple function with two arguments, length and width, that multiplies them together. It does not provide any types. Instead, it assumes that the arguments can be multiplied by the mul (*) operator, which represents multiplication.

However, the pitfall here is that when the noImplicitAny flag is not enabled, the code will be considered less safe. Here is an example usage of this function passing valid arguments:

javascript-vs-typescript.ts

```
const area1 = calculateArea(5, 2); // Works fine
const area2 = calculateArea("5", "2"); // No error but riskier
```

In this example, the width and length parameters do not have an explicit type. As a result, TypeScript treats it as any, allowing both a number and a string to be passed as arguments. This could create issues if we were to pass a string that is not coerced as a number since the area calculation would result in returning **Not a Number (NaN)**.

> **Note**
>
> For the sake of the argument, you should enable the noImplicitAny flag by default. The noImplicitAny flag strengthens type safety in TypeScript. Without it, functions may default to the any type, bypassing type checks and potentially leading to errors. Enforcing explicit types for parameters and return values, as demonstrated in the preceding calculateArea function example, ensures the function operates on intended data types and prevents unexpected behavior during execution.

If you have a code base written in JavaScript, you may be asked to re-write it in TypeScript. The following section explains some techniques you can use to smoothen this effort.

Transitioning from JavaScript to TypeScript

A reasonable question you may have to answer when attempting to translate existing JavaScript code into TypeScript is this: *How can you do this efficiently and how can you write correct types?*

Here are some effective strategies:

- **Divide and conquer**: Break down large JavaScript projects into smaller, more manageable files and packages. This allows you to focus on specific areas and avoid feeling overwhelmed. For example, start by converting one module, such as `auth.js` or `utils.js`, to TypeScript. Create new files named `auth.ts` and `utils.ts` and add type annotations.

- **Embrace** `unknown` **and** `never` **types**: Consider using `unknown` instead of `any` to maintain flexibility while ensuring type safety. Similarly, use `never` to explicitly handle cases that should not occur, making your code more robust and maintainable. The `unknown` type specifically can represent any value. However, unlike `any`, the `unknown` type does not allow direct assignment to other types or access to properties without type checks. These types help you catch errors early and make your code more predictable.

- **Incremental file conversion**: Start by renaming your JavaScript files (`.js`) to TypeScript files (`.ts`). Depending on your `tsconfig` settings, you'll likely encounter compilation errors, which is expected. These errors typically signal missing type annotations.

Now, let's look at an example of addressing missing parameter types. Consider a JavaScript function that checks whether a parameter is an object:

isObject.js

```
export const isObject = (o) => {
  return o === Object(o) && !Array.isArray(o) &&
    typeof o !== "function"
}
```

Here is how to re-write it in TypeScript:

IsObject.ts

```
export const isObject = (value: unknown): value
  is object => {
  // Type guard using type assertion
  return typeof value === "object" && value !== null
    && !Array.isArray(value)
}
```

In this example, we've added the parameter value: unknown. However, we use a type guard with a type assertion (`value is object`) to narrow the type to `object` within the function body, ensuring a more accurate representation.

This only covers one function. Following an incremental approach can help you complete the whole task in pieces while reviewing the changes in a more controllable way.

Sometimes, you want to start using TypeScript right away and not wait for a complete re-factor. The following compiler setting allows you to adopt TypeScript incrementally.

Leveraging existing JavaScript code

While we recommend progressively converting JavaScript files to TypeScript, the `allowJs` compiler flag offers an optional approach. This flag allows you to import regular JavaScript files (`.js`) directly into your TypeScript project without compiler errors:

```
import { isObject } from "./utilities.js"; // Notice the .js extension
```

In this example, the code imports the `isObject` function from the `utilities.js` file (notice the `.js` extension). This allows you to utilize existing JavaScript code within your TypeScript project, with a simple line change.

> **Note**
>
> While `allowJs` provides flexibility, it bypasses type-checking for imported JavaScript code. This can potentially introduce type-related errors later. Consider converting these JavaScript files to TypeScript for a more robust and type-safe code base in the long run.

Addressing external libraries

When importing from libraries such as **Lodash** or **RxJS**, TypeScript might prompt you to download type definitions. These definitions provide type information for the library functions and objects. Typically, the compiler will suggest the appropriate installation command. For example, to install Lodash types, you would use the following:

```
$ npm install --save @types/lodash
```

Installing these type definitions enables type checking for the imported libraries, enhancing your code's overall type safety.

Following compiler guidance

In some cases, the compiler might offer suggestions or error messages that require further investigation. Carefully review these messages and leverage online resources or the TypeScript documentation located at `https://www.typescriptlang.org/docs/handbook/compiler-options.html` to understand how the different options change the behavior of the compiler.

Leveraging linting tools

Consider using tools such as **TSLint** or **ESLint** with TypeScript extensions to identify potential type-related issues and enforce coding conventions, improving code quality and maintainability. In the *Further reading* section of this chapter, we provide a link to the official ESLint TypeScript website that offers instructions on how to enable that in your project.

By following these tips and addressing external library types, you can streamline your JavaScript to TypeScript migration and establish a more robust and type-safe code base.

Design patterns in JavaScript

While you can implement design patterns in both JavaScript and TypeScript, TypeScript offers significant advantages in terms of clarity, maintainability, and type safety.

JavaScript's dynamic nature makes it less suitable for complex design patterns. Concepts such as interfaces are absent, forcing reliance on duck typing, property checks, and runtime assertions.

For example, while using interfaces as parameters, we can change the implementation logic at runtime, without changing the function signature. This is how the **Strategy design pattern** works, as will be explained in *Chapter 5*.

For example, let's look at duck typing versus structural typing. Consider a function that logs messages and sends emails:

---

triggerNotification.js

```
function triggerNotification(emailClient, logger) {
  if (logger && typeof logger.log === "function") {
    logger.log("Sending email")
  }
  if (emailClient && typeof emailClient
    .send === "function") {
      emailClient.send("Message Sent")
  }
}
```

The preceding example leverages duck typing. With duck typing, the function relies on objects having specific properties at runtime. This can lead to errors due to incorrect object shapes or argument order. So, long as the `log` and `send` properties exist in those objects and they are functions, this operation will succeed. There are many ways that this can go wrong, though. Look at the following call to this function:

```
triggerNotification({
    log: () => console.log("Logger call")
}, {
    send: (msg) => console.log(msg)
})
```

When you call the function this way, nothing happens. This is because the order of the parameters has changed (swapped) and `log` or `send` are not available as properties.

When you provide the right shape of objects, then the call succeeds:

```
triggerNotification({
    send: (msg) => console.log(msg)
}, {
    log: () => console.log("Logger call")
})
```

That would output the right outcome of this function when running it in the command line:

```
> Logger call
> Message Sent
```

With the correct arguments passed into the `triggerNotification` function, you will see the aforementioned output of the `console.log` command.

While TypeScript offers interfaces for clear contracts, its core strength lies in structural typing. This means that if an object has the required properties and methods, regardless of their declaration, it can be used in a specific context.

Here's the same function leveraging structural typing:

```
function triggerNotification(emailClient: {
    send(message: string): void
}, logger: {
    log(message: string): void
}) {
    logger.log('Sending email');
    emailClient.send("Message Sent");
}

triggerNotification({
    send: (msg) => console.log(msg)
}, {
    log: (msg) => console.log(msg)
});
```

In this example, we define the function's parameters using anonymous types that specify the required properties and methods (`send` and `log`). As long as the objects passed to the function have these properties with compatible functions, they can be used, even without formal interface declarations.

In conclusion, while both JavaScript and TypeScript can implement design patterns, TypeScript's static typing and features such as interfaces provide a more robust and type-safe foundation, especially for complex design patterns.

Having explored the fundamentals of design patterns and how TypeScript enhances their implementation, let's now turn our attention to setting up your development environment.

Setting up your development environment

The accompanying source code for this book is structured like a standard TypeScript project. All necessary libraries and configurations are included for you to run the examples directly from the command line or within Visual Studio Code. This section will equip you with the knowledge to do the following:

- Identify the libraries used and their purposes within the examples
- Understand the `tsconfig` parameters that govern the TypeScript compiler's behavior
- Execute and debug unit tests using Vitest

Let's get started!

Essential libraries and tools

The code utilizes various external libraries to showcase design patterns in practical contexts. Our aim is to help you review several of the design patterns within a specific use case. Here's a breakdown of their roles:

- **React**: This popular UI library promotes patterns such as composition, component factories, and higher-order components. We'll explain how to use TypeScript with React in *Chapter 2*.
- **Vitest**: This is a fast and feature-rich testing framework built specifically for TypeScript projects. It leverages the capabilities of Jest with additional functionalities such as built-in TypeScript support, improved test execution speed, and modern API.
- **Express.js**: Perfect for building Node.js web services with TypeScript, Express offers a minimal and stable framework, promoting modularity and performance. You will learn more about how to use TypeScript in the server in *Chapter 2*.
- **Immutable.js**: This library is responsible for working with data structures involving immutability. Immutability is a concept that we use quite frequently in functional programming, whereby we do not allow objects to be modified or altered once they have been created. We will learn more about immutability in *Chapter 7*.
- **fp-ts**: This library exposes functional programming abstractions such as Monads, Options, and Lens. We'll dive deeper into functional programming in *Chapter 7*.
- **RxJs**: This library offers reactive programming concepts such as Observables through a user-friendly API. Using Observables helps build scalable and resilient applications. You will learn more about Observables in *Chapter 8*.

Each chapter will explore how these tools empower you to implement design patterns with TypeScript effectively.

Understanding the tsconfig.json file

When working with TypeScript source code, the compiler needs guidance on locating and compiling your files with specific settings. This configuration is achieved through a `tsconfig.json` or `jsconfig.json` file. Typically, one file suffices for most projects. However, for this book, we'll leverage a more flexible approach:

- **Base** `tsconfig.json`: Defines common compiler flags applicable across all chapters

- **Chapter-specific** `tsconfig.json`: Each chapter will have its own configuration, inheriting from the base

Now, let's explore some key compiler flags:

- `module`: It defines how imports and exports work. We'll use CommonJS (Node.js format), generating `require` statements in the compiled code. Other options include `es2015`, `es2020`, `es2022`, and `esnext`, which target **ECMAScript Module** (**ESM**) versions. You can inspect the generated code in the `dist` folder to see this in action.

- `strict`: This flag is a combination of the `noImplicitAny`, `strictNullChecks`, `strictFunctionTypes`, and `strictBindCallApply` compiler flags.

- `baseUrl`: This specifies the base directory for resolving non-relative module names. This can simplify your import statements by providing a root path for your modules. For example, consider the following configuration:

```
"baseUrl": "./src"
```

Within the `src` folder, any component can import another component using this import declaration:

```
import { MyComponent } from 'components/MyComponent';
```

The import path will resolve this as `src/components/MyComponent`.

- `paths`: It specifies aliases for directories that should be used together with the `baseUrl` option. Here's an example:

```
"baseUrl": "./src",
"paths": {
  "@components/*": ["components/*"],
  "@utils/*": ["utils/*"]
}
```

With this setup, you can import modules using the defined aliases:

```
import { MyComponent } from '@components/MyComponent';
import { myUtility } from '@utils/myUtility';
```

- `target`: It specifies the target code generation version, such as ES6, ES2017, and so on. This flag ensures compatibility with your chosen environment (e.g., Node.js version or browser support). In this project, we'll use ES5 for broad browser compatibility.

- `noImplicitAny`: It disallows compiling when TypeScript infers a type as any. This often occurs with functions lacking parameter type specifications. Here's an example that errors out with this flag:

degToRad.ts

```
const degToRad = (degree): number =>
  (degree * Math.PI) / 180;
```

It declares the `degToRad` function without specifying the type of the `degree` parameter. With `noImplicitAny`, the compiler would throw an error, prompting you to define the expected number type for the parameter.

- `strictNullChecks`: It enforces stricter checks for undefined and null. The compiler will identify and raise errors for any code that might leave null unchecked. Here's an example:

maybeNumber.ts

```
// With strictNullChecks: error
let maybeNumber: number | null = null
let value = maybeNumber * 10
let value2
if (maybeNumber !== null) {
  value2 = maybeNumber * 10
} else {
  value2 = 0
}
let value3 = maybeNumber ?? 0
```

This code defines a `maybeNumber` variable that can be either a number or null type. The compiler would throw errors in the second line when attempting to assign the calculation to the `value` variable since it could potentially be null.

- `experimentalDecorators` and `emitDecoratorMetadata`: These are required flags for using decorators (especially with Inversify.js). Decorators are a powerful concept for enhancing class behavior.

- `sourceMap`: It enables source maps for debugging TypeScript code. This allows debuggers (such as VSCode or browser dev tools) to display the original TypeScript code when pausing at breakpoints.

- `lib`: It specifies a set of ambient declarations for external libraries. This can help the compiler understand common functions and objects used in your project without needing to install type definitions separately. For example, setting `lib: ["dom"]` provides declarations for browser DOM APIs.

- `noUnusedLocals`: It prevents compiling code with unused local variables. This helps identify and remove unnecessary variables, improving code clarity. Here's an example:

noUnusedLocals.ts

```
function greet() {
  const name = "Alice" // Used
  let message // Unused (errors with noUnusedLocals)
  message = "Hello, " + name + "!"
  return message
}
```

With this option enabled, the compiler would throw an error for the unused `message` variable. This flags potential issues where variables might have been accidentally declared but not utilized.

- `noUnusedParameters`: It prevents compiling code with unused function parameters. This helps identify and remove unnecessary parameters, promoting cleaner function definitions.

There are also many more compiler flags available that can tweak different aspects of the system. These options usually tweak more specific aspects of the compiler by customizing the restrictiveness of the type checks. Before enabling extra flags, reach a consensus with your colleagues to avoid confusion.

Of course, when writing software, having automated tests in place adds another layer of safety. Let's look at how to run the provided unit tests in this book.

Running the unit tests

As mentioned earlier, we'll utilize Vitest, a popular testing framework for JavaScript and TypeScript projects, to run unit tests. Vitest offers a user-friendly setup and integrates well with prominent frameworks. This book provides configurations to run tests directly within VSCode.

Here, we have provided configuration options for running the unit tests in the command line. To run the tests, you'll have to execute the following command in the console:

```
$ npm run test
```

For example, there is a file named `mul.ts` in *Chapter 1* that includes a function for multiplying two numbers:

---

mul.ts

```
function mul(a: number, b: number): number {
   return a * b
}
export default mul
```

Then, we also have the test file for this function, which has the same filename but with a `test.ts` extension:

---

mul.test.ts

```
import mul from "./mul"
import { test, expect } from "vitest"
test("multiplies 2 and 3 to give 6", () => {
   expect(mul(2, 3)).toBe(6)
})
```

When you execute these test cases, you will see the runner results:

```
$ npm run test
> typescript-5-design-patterns-and-best-practices@1.0.0 test
✓ |chapter-1_Getting_Started_With_Typescript_5| src/mul.test.ts (1)
   ✓ multiplies 2 and 3 to give 6
Test Files  1 passed (1)
     Tests  1 passed (1)
  Start at  12:46:37
  Duration  5ms
```

Leveraging the Vitest framework throughout this book, we'll validate key aspects of design patterns. This includes ensuring that the **Singleton pattern**, which we will explore in *Chapter 3*, for example, adheres to its single-instance principle, and that the **Factory pattern** reliably constructs objects of the correct type. As robust unit testing often precedes production deployments, consistently testing your code abstractions becomes paramount.

Using VSCode with TypeScript

Having explored the book's included libraries and how to run the examples, let's turn our attention to mastering your development environment. A good **Integrated Development Environment** (IDE) such as **VSCode** can significantly enhance your productivity when debugging, refactoring, and working with TypeScript code.

We used VSCode for developing this book's code base. You'll learn to leverage VSCode's inspection tools to visualize the inferred types of variables, gaining valuable insights into your code's behavior. Finally, we'll cover essential refactoring techniques to improve code readability and reusability.

By effectively utilizing VSCode, you'll gain a smoother development experience and a deeper understanding of TypeScript concepts as you work through the examples and explore the material further.

Using VSCode for this book's code

VSCode is a lightweight integrated editor that was released in 2015 by Microsoft. It offers an impressive array of features that aid us when writing code. It currently supports several major programming languages, including TypeScript, Java, Go, and Python. We can use VSCode's native TypeScript integration to write and debug code, inspect types, and automate common development tasks.

Let's get started:

1. To install it, visit the official Download page at `https://code.visualstudio.com/Download` (see *Figure 1.2*) and choose the right executable for your operating system. In this book, we are using **VSCode version 1.88.1**.

Figure 1.2 – VSCode Download Page (2024)

2. Once installed, you will want to open this book's projects folder by clicking on **File | Open | (Project)**. Since we are working on the first chapter, you can expand the Chapter 1 folder and inspect the code located there:

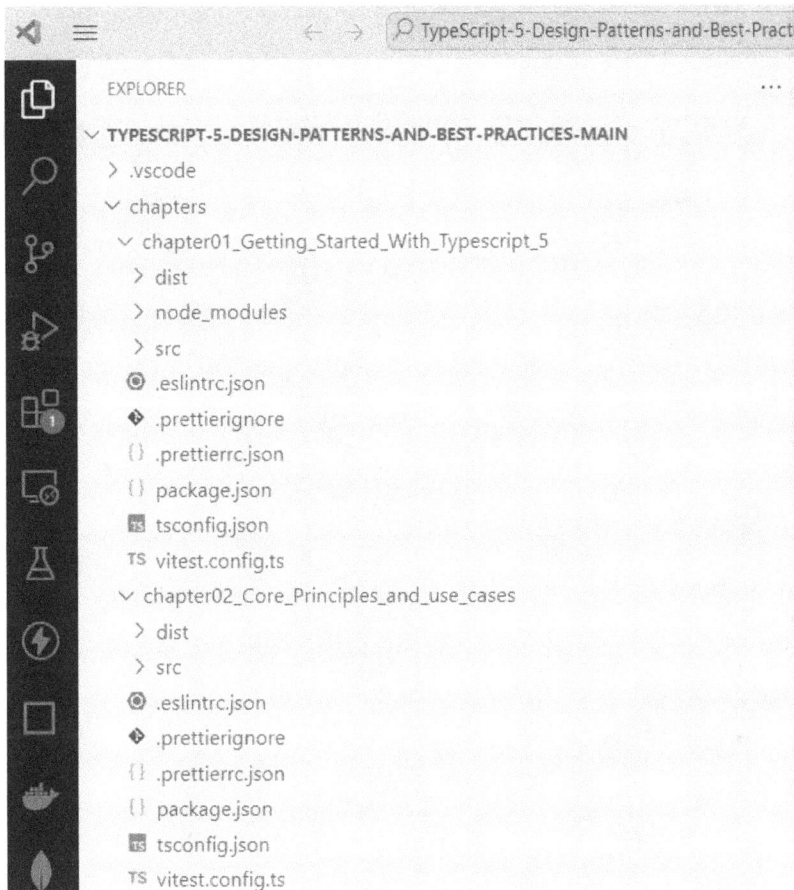

Figure 1.3 – Expanding project chapter code in VSCode

3. Next, you want to compile all the example code of each chapter using the following command from the root folder:

```
$ npm run build
```

We have configured the project to use npm workspaces, so the script will take care of running the build step in all related folders.

4. By the end, each chapter will contain the transpiled code in its respective dist folder as shown in *Figure 1.4* for *Chapter 1*:

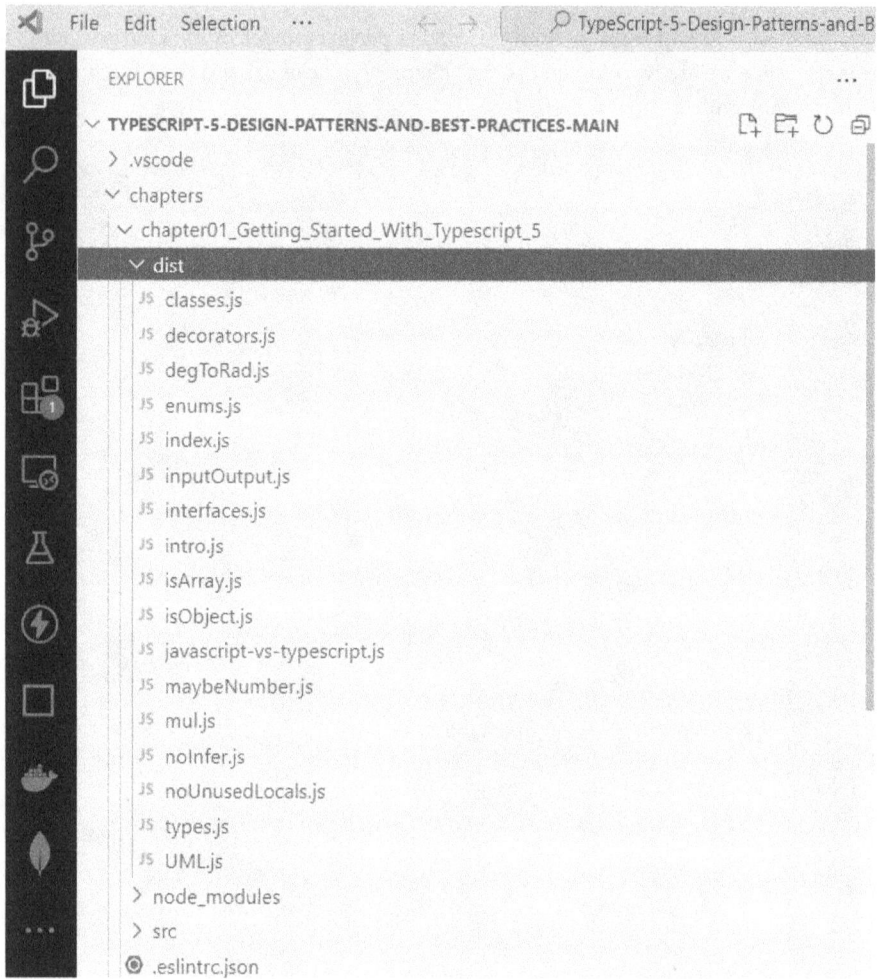

Figure 1.4 – Expanding the project chapter dist folder in VSCode

These are regular JavaScript files that you can run using Node.js with the following command structure:

```
$ node absolute-path-of-file/example.js
```

For example, here's how you would run the decorators.js file:

```
$ node chapters/chapter 1_Getting_Started_With_Typescript_5/
dist/decorators.js

Calculating 2 + 3
5
5
```

> **Note**
>
> Some examples may not produce any output in the console. Also, some examples contain commented-out code that will otherwise fail to compile if it's commented-out.

This section has explored the benefits of type safety and how to leverage VSCode's features to navigate the code examples included in the book. The following section, *Type inspection in action*, will equip you with the tools and techniques for effective type inspection within VSCode.

Type inspection in action

Now that you know how to run and debug programs using VSCode, you probably want to know how to inspect types and apply suggestions to improve consistency. VSCode helps you inspect types and improve code consistency as you write TypeScript. The built-in TypeScript language server provides suggestions and type information.

Inspecting types

Inspecting types allows you to verify the data types associated with variables, function parameters, and return values. This ensures your code adheres to type definitions and prevents potential runtime errors caused by mismatched data types. Here is how to inspect types using VSCode:

1. Open the `removeDuplicateChars.ts` file in the editor. This contains a function that accepts an input string and removes any duplicate characters. Feel free to run it and inspect how it works.

2. If you place the mouse cursor on top of the variables in the function body, you can inspect their types. Here is an example of this using the `result` variable:

```
          result.push(c)
 8      }
 9    }              const result: string[]
10    return result
11  }
12
```

Figure 1.5 – Inspecting the inferred return value

This is obvious as we declared its type. However, we can inspect types that have been inferred by the compiler and figure out when or why we need to add explicit types.

Using the correct types and relying on type inference whenever possible is very important when working with TypeScript. VSCode offers good inspection utilities to do this, but often, we need to help the compiler do this. You will learn how to work with types and understand type inference in *Chapter 2*, in the *Working with advanced types* section.

Refactoring with VSCode

Refactoring is a powerful technique for improving your code base. It involves restructuring existing code to enhance its readability, maintainability, and ability to adapt to future changes. More importantly, refactoring should not alter the code's core functionality.

Why do we refactor?

Refactoring helps you write cleaner, more maintainable code. Clean code is easier to understand for yourself and others, making it simpler to modify and extend in the future.

> **Note**
>
> When you perform refactoring, you want to have unit tests in place before changing any existing code. This is to ensure you did not introduce any breaking changes or fail to capture edge cases.

Extracting type aliases

As an example, we can consider extracting a function signature type into a type alias for better readability and reusability. However, before doing so, it's important to understand when to explicitly define types and when to rely on TypeScript's type inference.

Relying on type inference

In many cases, allowing TypeScript to infer types can lead to cleaner and more concise code. Here are some scenarios where type inference is preferable:

- For simple functions where the types are clear from the context, you can let TypeScript infer the types

- For local variables, especially within small scopes, type inference can be more readable than explicit type annotations

Using explicit types

On the other hand, there are situations where explicitly defining types is advantageous:

- For complex functions with multiple parameters or a complex return type, explicitly defining types can improve readability and clarify the function's purpose

- For public APIs, where we need types that will be used across different modules and explicit types to provide better documentation

Consider both approaches before beginning the refactoring process to ensure the final result leads to more maintainable code. Now, let's walk through the step-by-step process of refactoring a function.

Refactoring in action with VSCode

Using VSCode, we can refactor the code that we are working with using some refactoring helper actions. Let's see them in action with an example:

1. Open the `refactoring.ts` file in your *Chapter 1* source code on GitHub. It contains functions related to searching elements in an array:

refactoring.ts

```
function find<T>(arr: T[], predicate: (item: T) =>
  boolean) {
  for (let item of arr) {
    if (predicate(item)) {
      return item
    }
  }
  return undefined
}
```

2. We can improve the `find` function by creating a reusable type alias for the predicate parameter. This parameter defines a function that takes an item of type `T` and returns a `Boolean` type.

3. Highlight the entire function body of the predicate parameter: `(item: T) => boolean`.

4. Right-click and select **Refactor**, then choose **Extract to type alias** (see *Figure 1.6*).

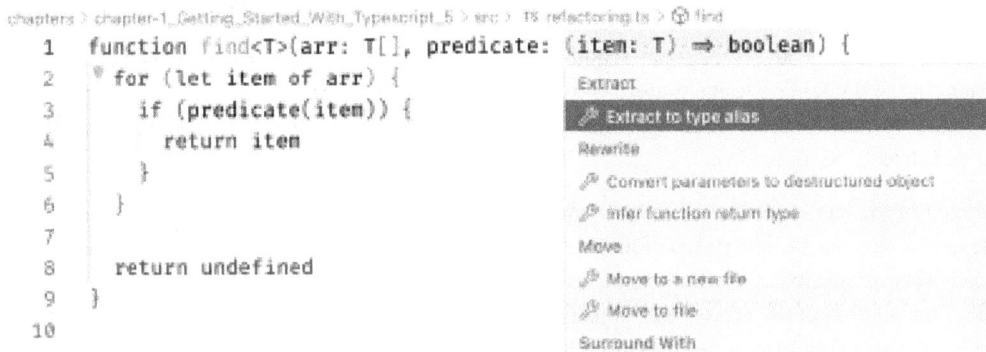

```
chapters > chapter-1_Getting_Started_With_Typescript_5 > src > TS refactoring.ts > find
1    function find<T>(arr: T[], predicate: (item: T) => boolean) {
2      for (let item of arr) {                    Extract
3        if (predicate(item)) {                    Extract to type alias
4          return item                             Rewrite
5        }                                         Convert parameters to destructured object
6      }                                           Infer function return type
7                                                  Move
8      return undefined                            Move to a new file
9    }                                             Move to file
10                                                 Surround With
```

Figure 1.6 – Extract to type alias refactoring

5. Name the type alias `Predicate`. This creates a reusable type of definition separate from the function:

```
type Predicate<T> = (item: T) => boolean;
```

6. Now, the refactored `indexOf` function can leverage the newly created `Predicate` type:

```
type Predicate<T> = (item: T) => boolean
function find<T>(arr: T[], predicate: Predicate<T>) {
  for (let item of arr) {
    if (predicate(item)) {
      return item
    }
  }
  return undefined
}
```

VSCode offers several other refactoring features that can save you time and effort:

- `Extract Method`: It isolates reusable blocks of code into dedicated functions
- `Extract Variable`: It creates variables to store frequently used expressions
- `Rename Symbols`: It renames variables consistently across your code base

These tools can significantly improve your development workflow by reducing the risk of errors during code modifications.

We'll now explore the world of **Unified Modeling Language** (**UML**) to explore how it visually represents software systems.

Introducing Unified Modelling Language (UML)

Effective software design and architecture requires a need to communicate complex ideas with clarity and precision. In the domain of design patterns – reusable solutions to common programming challenges – this clarity becomes crucial. UML is a visual language specifically crafted to depict software systems and their intricate relationships.

Developed in the late 1980s, UML has become a common communication tool for architects and developers to map out the blueprints of their creations. This chapter focuses on the essentials of UML, especially **class diagrams** as fundamental tools for describing design patterns. Class diagrams offer a visual representation of the classes and objects, as well as their interactions within a design pattern. As we learn more about them, we'll explore how UML empowers developers to not only leverage design patterns effectively but also document and share them in a readily comprehensible format.

What is UML?

As mentioned earlier, design patterns are pre-defined solutions to recurring software problems. Their effectiveness hinges on clear communication and understanding across development teams. This is where UML comes into place. UML, with its standardized notation and focus on visual representation, offers a language-agnostic way to depict design patterns. Through class diagrams, developers can model the core elements and interactions within a pattern, independent of any specific programming language. It's like a diagram that describes syntax.

> **Note**
>
> Although UML diagrams have a long history in software engineering, you should use them carefully. Generally, they should only be used to demonstrate a specific use case or sub-system, together with a short explanation of the architecture decisions. UML is not very suitable for capturing the dynamic requirements of very complex systems because, as a visual language, it is only suitable for representing high-level overviews.

Learning UML class diagrams

UML class diagrams provide a static snapshot of the classes and objects within a software system. TypeScript, with its support for classes, interfaces, and visibility modifiers (public, protected, and private) offers a perfect language to translate these concepts into code.

Let's examine the fundamental building blocks of class diagrams:

- **Classes**: Classes represent blueprints for creating objects. They define the structure (properties) and behavior (methods) that all objects of that class will share. Think of them as templates for creating similar entities. In TypeScript, a simple class definition might look like this:

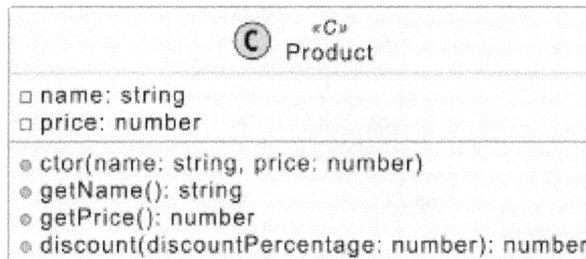

Figure 1.7 – Class diagram for the Product class

The `Product` class represents a product with a name and price. It provides methods to retrieve the name (`getName()`) and price (`getPrice()`), and to apply a discount (`discount(discountPercentage)`) based on a provided percentage.

- **Objects**: Objects are individual instances of a class. They hold specific values for the properties defined within the class. Imagine each object as a unique variation built from the class template, that contains both data and behavior related to that data.

- **Interfaces**: They define a set of functionalities (methods) that a class must implement. They specify the *what* (functionalities) without dictating the *how* (implementation details). This promotes loose coupling and easier code maintenance. Here's a sample interface that a class can implement:

```
interface Identifiable<T extends string | number> {
   id: T;
}
class Product implements Identifiable<string> {
   id: string;
   constructor(id: string) {
      this.id = id;
   }
}
```

This class corresponds to the diagram in *Figure 1.8*. *Notice the placement of the interface clause on top of the class name*:

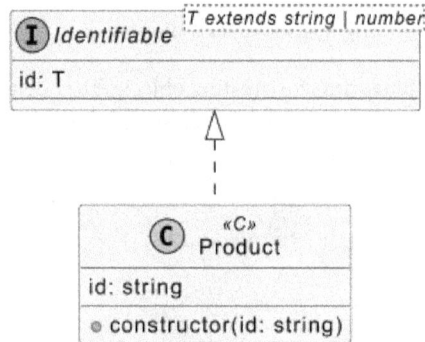

Figure 1.8 – Class diagram for Interfaces

`Identifiable` defines a generic type T that can be either a string or a number, representing the ID format. It enforces that any class implementing `Identifiable` must have an `id` property of type T. `Product` implements `Identifiable` with `string` as the specific type for its `id` property.

- **Abstract classes**: These classes act as blueprints that cannot be directly instantiated (meaning you can't create objects directly from them). They provide a foundation for building more specialized classes that inherit their properties and functionalities.

The following UML diagram (*Figure 1.9*) demonstrates how an abstract class can define common functionalities (protected constructor and abstract method) while allowing concrete subclasses (such as `Square`) to implement specific details and provide concrete implementations for abstract methods.

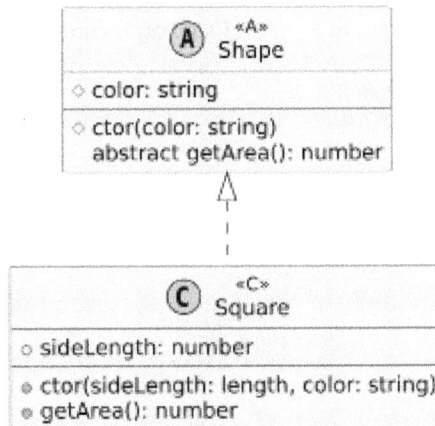

Figure 1.9 – Class diagram for abstract classes

The preceding diagram shows an abstract class, Shape, and a subclass, Square. Shape has a public color property and an abstract getArea() method that subclasses must implement. Square extends Shape, taking color in its constructor and adding a private sideLength property. It overrides the abstract getArea() method to calculate the area based on the side length.

- **Associations**: Associations are the building blocks for depicting relationships between classes, interfaces, or other elements within a UML diagram. Think of them as bridges connecting different parts of your system. These associations can be direct or indirect, offering flexibility in representing various interactions. A **direct association** occurs when a class holds a direct reference to another class as an object or property. An **indirect association** occurs when a class references another class through an identifier (such as an ID) but doesn't hold a direct object reference.

For example, we have the following models for Blog and Author:

associations.ts

```
class Author {
      constructor(private id: string, private name:
        string) {}
}
class Blog implements Identifiable<string> {
      constructor(private id: string, private
        author: Author) {}
}
```

This corresponds to the diagram in *Figure 1.10*. Blog is connected to Author with a *line*:

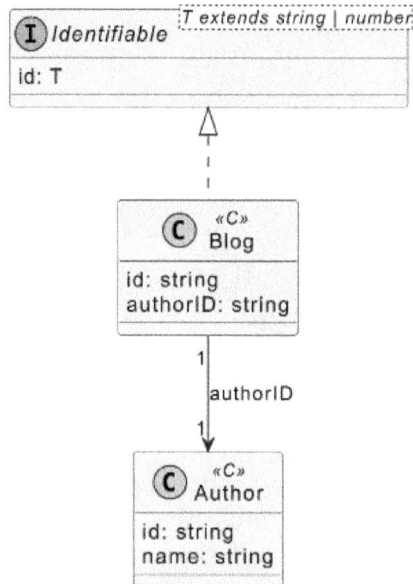

Figure 1.10 – Class diagram for associations

Notice that because the Author class is not being passed as a parameter here, it is referenced from the authorId parameter instead. The choice between direct and indirect associations depends on your specific design needs. Direct associations offer tighter coupling between classes, while indirect associations provide looser coupling and can be more flexible for certain scenarios.

- **Aggregations**: Aggregation, a specialized form of association in UML, depicts a *part-whole* relationship between classes. It signifies that one class (the whole) can exist independently, while the other class (the part) has a stronger dependency on the whole for its existence.

For example, let's say we have a SearchService class that accepts a QueryBuilder parameter and performs API requests on a different system:

aggregations.ts

```
class QueryBuilder {}
class EmptyQueryBuilder extends QueryBuilder {}
interface SearchParams {
  qb?: QueryBuilder;
  path: string;
}
class SearchService {
  queryBuilder?: QueryBuilder;
```

```
   path: string;
   constructor({ private qb = new EmptyQueryBuilder(),
      private path: string }: SearchParams) {
        this.queryBuilder = qb;
        this.path = path;
   }
}
```

This corresponds to the diagram in *Figure 1.11*. SearchService is connected to QueryBuilder with a *line* and a *white rhombus*:

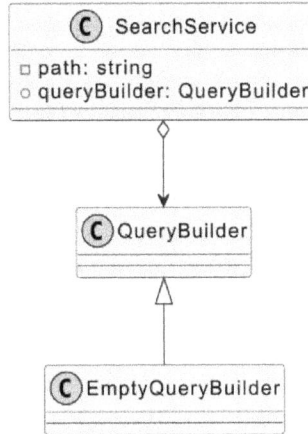

Figure 1.11 – Class diagram for aggregations

In this case, when we don't have a QueryBuilder class or the class itself has no queries to perform, then SearchService will still exist, although it will not actually perform any requests. QueryBuilder can also exist without SearchService.

*   **Compositions**: Composition, a powerful concept in UML, represents a stricter form of aggregation. It depicts a *has-a* relationship where the *parent class* (the *whole*) controls the lifetime of its *children* (the *parts*). This means that if the parent object is destroyed, all its child objects are also destroyed.

Here is an example with the House and Room classes:

compositions.ts

```
class Room {
   constructor(private name: string) {}
   getName(): string {
      return this.name;
   }
}
```

```
class House {
  constructor(private rooms?: Room[]) {
    this.rooms = rooms || [];
  }
  addRoom(room: Room): void {
    this.rooms.push(room);
  }
  removeRoom(room: Room): void {  }
  getRooms(): Room[] {
    return this.rooms;
  }
}
```

This corresponds to the diagram in *Figure 1.12*. House is connected to Room with a *line* and a *black* or *filled rhombus*:

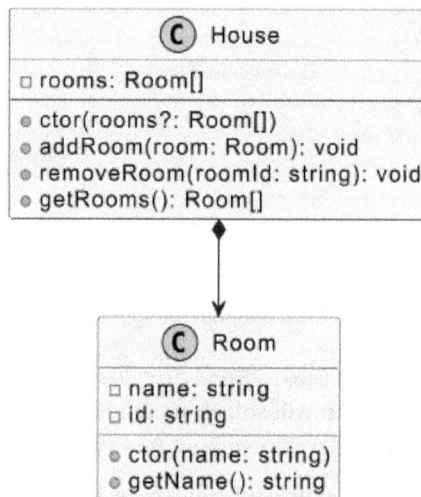

Figure 1.12 – Class diagram for compositions

The class diagram depicts two classes: Room and House. A Room class has a name and methods to access and set it. A House class has a private array of Room objects and methods to manage them, including adding room objects and retrieving the entire list. The composition relationship signifies that a House class can contain multiple room objects, and room objects can exist independently.

- **Inheritance**: Inheritance, a fundamental concept in object-oriented programming, allows classes to inherit properties and functionalities from other classes. It establishes a hierarchical relationship where a *subclass* (*child class*) inherits from a *base class* (*parent class*). This promotes code reusability and reduces redundancy. Let's revisit the example of `BaseClient` and `UsersApiClient` to illustrate inheritance:

inheritance.ts

```typescript
class BaseClient {
  constructor(protected baseUrl: string) {
    this.baseUrl = baseUrl;
  }
  protected getBaseUrl(): string {
    return this.baseUrl;
  }
}
class UsersApiClient extends BaseClient {
  constructor(baseUrl: string) {
    super(baseUrl);
  }
  getUsers(): void {
    console.log(`Fetching users from
      ${this.getBaseUrl()}/users`);
  }
}
```

This corresponds to the diagram in *Figure 1.13*. `UsersApiClient` is connected to `BaseClient` with a *line* and a *white pointed arrow*:

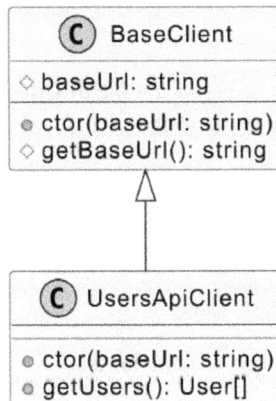

Figure 1.13 – Class diagram for inheritance

- **Visibility**: Visibility plays an important role in object-oriented design by controlling access to a class's internal elements (attributes and methods). In UML diagrams, specific symbols represent the visibility levels, ensuring clear communication within your team:

  - `Public` (+): Elements marked with a plus (+) are accessible from anywhere within the system.

  - `Private` (-): Elements marked with a minus (-) are only accessible within the class itself.

  - `Protected` (#): Elements marked with a hash (#) are accessible from the class itself and its subclasses.

  - `Package` (~): Elements marked with a tilde (~) are accessible within the same package. This visibility level is less commonly used in modern object-oriented design.

For example, we have an `SSHUser` class that accepts a private key and a public key:

visibility.ts

```
class SSHUser {
  constructor(
    private privateKey: string,
    public publicKey: string,
  ) {
    this.privateKey = privateKey
    this.publicKey = publicKey
  }

  public getBase64(): string {
    return Buffer.from(this.publicKey)
      .toString("base64")
  }
}
```

This corresponds to the diagram in *Figure 1.14*. `SSHUser` contains two properties and one method. We use a minus (-) for private visibility and a plus (+) for public visibility:

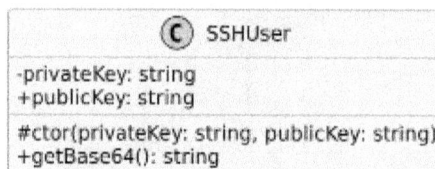

Figure 1.14 – Class diagram for visibility modifiers

Here, we can see that the methods are separated by a horizontal bar for visibility.

While drawing class diagrams on paper might seem straightforward, the true challenge lies in accurately modeling the underlying concepts and relationships within your problem domain. This process is often iterative, requiring collaboration with domain experts or knowledgeable stakeholders. *Chapter 9*, focusing on developing modern and robust TypeScript applications, will delve into how **Domain-Driven Design (DDD)** can be a valuable tool for effectively translating business rules into a well-structured UML representation.

Summary

That concludes our first introductory chapter. This chapter served as your starting point into the world of TypeScript. We began by unveiling the core types and language features that define TypeScript, along with its connection to JavaScript. We then walked through the process of converting a simple JavaScript program to its TypeScript counterpart.

Next, we explored the essential libraries you'll encounter throughout this book, highlighting their role in building scalable applications. We explored the `tsconfig` file and its various options, allowing you to customize your TypeScript development experience.

Moving on, we equipped you with the skills to effectively run, debug, and refine your code using the powerful VSCode editor. We explored its built-in capabilities for refactoring, allowing you to further improve the structure and maintainability of your code base.

Finally, we introduced UML and class diagrams, which serve as a traditional method for visualizing design patterns and abstractions. Understanding UML equips you with a standardized approach to documenting software systems and their models.

By combining the knowledge gained in this chapter, you're well-positioned to embark on creating basic TypeScript projects. This practical experience will solidify your understanding of the language. Additionally, learning to leverage VSCode tasks and launch configurations can significantly enhance your development workflow and productivity.

In the next chapter, we'll consider the intricacies of the TypeScript type system, exploring its more advanced features.

Q&A

Feel free to review the following questions and their corresponding answers to address any concerns or gain additional insights:

1. Beyond runtime errors, are there any other advantages to TypeScript's type safety?

    Answer: Yes, static type checking in TypeScript offers several benefits:

    *   **Improved code clarity**: Explicit types enhance code readability and maintainability for you and other developers

- **Early error detection**: Type errors are caught during development, preventing unexpected runtime bugs

- **Better IDE support**: Type information allows IDEs to offer features such as code completion and refactoring that are more accurate and helpful.

2. Can TypeScript be used with existing JavaScript code bases?

   Answer: Yes! TypeScript integrates seamlessly with JavaScript. You can gradually migrate existing JavaScript code to TypeScript piece by piece, ensuring a smooth transition.

3. When might refactoring with TypeScript be more challenging?

   Answer: While TypeScript generally simplifies refactoring, there can be situations where it presents more challenges. For instance, extensive code bases without existing type annotations might require more effort to refactor effectively. Missing compiler flags such as `noImplicitAny`, or `strict` mode, can reduce type safety. Additionally, even with TypeScript, highly complex code logic might still require testing during refactoring to ensure the changes don't introduce unintended consequences.

4. Are there any limitations to using UML diagrams?

   Answer: While UML diagrams are a valuable tool for visualizing software design, they have some limitations. As systems become larger and more complex, UML diagrams can become cumbersome and difficult to maintain. Additionally, UML diagrams primarily focus on the static structure of a system, representing the relationships between classes and components. They might not capture the dynamic aspects of a system's behavior, such as how objects interact and how data flows through the system.

Further reading

- For a good introduction to TypeScript, read *Learning TypeScript, Remo H. Jansen, Packt Publishing*. It's available at `https://www.packtpub.com/product/learning-typescript-2x-second-edition/9781788391474`.

- You can configure TypeScript with ESLint by following the *Getting Started* guide available at `https://typescript-eslint.io/getting-started`.

- Refactoring is explained in detail in *Refactoring: Improving the Design of Existing Code, 2nd Edition, Martin Fowler*. It's available at `https://martinfowler.com/books/refactoring.html`.

- UML, as explained by its creators, is detailed in *The Unified Modeling Language User Guide, Booch and James Rumbaugh.* It's available at `https://www.researchgate.net/publication/234785986_Unified_Modeling_Language_User_Guide_The_2nd_Edition_Addison-Wesley_Object_Technology_Series`.

- For comprehensive information about *npm (Node Package Manager)*, visit the official npm documentation at `https://docs.npmjs.com/`.

- To learn more about *React*, including its features and how to get started, check out the official React website at `https://react.dev/`.

- For detailed information on *Express.js*, including guides and API documentation, visit the official Express.js website at `https://expressjs.com/`.

- To understand the *V8 JavaScript engine*, which powers Node.js and Chrome, you can visit the official V8 project page at `https://v8.dev/`.

2

TypeScript Core Principles

Until now, we've discussed the basic programming constructs of TypeScript, for example, interfaces, classes, objects, and enums. In this chapter, we'll examine more details about TypeScript. We'll explore advanced types that provide the compiler with a more precise understanding of your code, leading to cleaner, more concise, and readable programs.

This chapter will not only equip you with advanced TypeScript features but also introduce the concept of design patterns. We'll explore their origins, their connection (and sometimes separation) from Object-Oriented Programming (OOP) and their role in overcoming limitations in your code. In the following chapters, we'll analyze them one by one for their practical considerations.

In this chapter, we will cover the following topics:

- Working with advanced types
- Developing in the browser
- Developing in the server
- Introducing design patterns in TypeScript

By the end of this chapter, you'll be empowered to write complex TypeScript programs, leverage OOP to represent real-world concepts through objects, and confidently work with TypeScript in both the browser and server environments.

> **Note**
> The links to all the sources mentioned in this chapter, as well as any supplementary reading materials, are provided in the *Further reading* section toward the end of this chapter.

Technical requirements

The code bundle for this chapter is available on GitHub here: `https://github.com/PacktPublishing/TypeScript-5-Design-Patterns-and-Best-Practices/tree/main/chapters/chapter02_Core_Principles_and_use_cases`.

Working with advanced types

Our journey with TypeScript doesn't stop at fundamental types. It offers a rich set of **advanced type** constructs that you'll frequently encounter in real-world code. By understanding these constructs and how they work together, you can create more precise and robust type representations. In the subsequent sections, let's review some commonly used utility types that are available out of the box.

Utility types

When you configure the TypeScript compilation target (e.g., ES5, ES6), the compiler automatically includes a corresponding global definition file (such as `lib.es5.d.ts` or `lib.es6.d.ts`). These files provide a wealth of pre-defined utility types for your projects.

As a quick reminder, **ES5** (or **ECMAScript 5**), is a JavaScript standard that introduced several key improvements to JavaScript, such as strict mode, new array methods for simplified manipulation, native JSON support, and additional object methods. **ES6** (or **ECMAScript 2015**) introduced arrow functions, classes for object-oriented programming, import modules for better code organization, promises, and template literals for string interpolation. We provide links to the standard documents in the *Further reading* section of this chapter.

Let's explore some key utilities and see them in practice:

- `Record`: The `Record<K, T>` utility helps define object types where property keys come from one type (`K`) and property values from another (`T`). This is particularly useful for creating configuration objects. The `Record` utility type is structurally similar to **index signatures** in TypeScript. Both allow you to define an object type where the keys are of a specific type, and the values can be of another type. We provide an example of an index signature in the next example.

  Imagine you're managing object pools in your application. You might want a function to retrieve usage statistics (`free`, `used`, `size`) for each pool and return them as a structured object. Here's how `Record` and other types can be used effectively:

Records.ts

```
type UsageStats = Record<'free' | 'used' | 'size',
  number>;
// type UsageStats = { free: number; used: number; size: number
}
type Metric = { name: string; totalFree: number;
```

```
    totalUsed: number; totalSize: number }
function stats<T extends Metric[]>(data: T):
  Record<string, UsageStats> {
  return data.forEach((item) => {
    const name = item.name
    stats[name] = { free: item.totalFree,
      used: item.totalUsed, size: item.totalSize }
  })
}
```

This code snippet calculates and returns usage statistics (free, used, size) for various entities (represented by objects) in a system. It achieves this by leveraging the Record type. The second type in the commented highlighted section shows how to write an index signature type, which is basically an object type with a specific key-value structure.

Record<string, UsageStats> defines the structure of the returned object: keys are strings, and values are objects of type UsageStats. The UsageStats type itself ensures each value object has properties such as free, used, and size. The function iterates through an array of objects (assumed to hold entity data) and builds the final statistics object by returning a Record type.

- Partial: The Partial<T> helps us create flexible object structures in our code. It allows us to define a type where all properties of another type become optional. This is particularly useful in scenarios such as handling user input or dealing with objects with potentially missing data.

Here is an example demonstrating the usage of Partial in TypeScript:

partial.ts

```
interface Product {
  name: string
  price: number
  stock?: number // Optional property with default value
  imageUrl?: string // Optional property
}
function createPartialProduct(initialData:
  Partial<Product>): Product {
  const defaultProduct: Product = {
    name: "Unnamed Product",
    price: 0.0,
    stock: 10,
  }
  return { ...defaultProduct, ...initialData }
}
const partialProduct = createPartialProduct({
```

```
    name: "Cool NFT Item",
    price: 29.99,
    imageUrl: https://example.com/cool.png,
})
console.log(partialProduct)
const minimalProduct = createPartialProduct({
    name: "Mystery Item", price: 9.99 })
console.log(minimalProduct) // { name: "Mystery Item", price:
9.99, stock: 10 }
```

The `createPartialProduct` function takes advantage of `Partial<Product>`. This means it expects an object where any `Product` property is missing. It then creates two product instances: `partialProduct` with all properties provided and `minimalProduct` with just the name and price. In both cases, the function guarantees a complete product object by filling in missing values with the defaults.

- `Required`: `Required<T>` takes an existing type `T` and creates a new type where all properties of `T` become mandatory. This helps enforce data integrity and prevents unexpected runtime errors due to missing data.

For example, let's consider a scenario where you are building a user profile management system in your TypeScript application. You define an interface, `UserProfile`, to represent the user data:

required.ts

```
interface UserProfile {
    name: string;
    email: string;
    // Optional properties
    bio?: string; // Optional user biography
    location?: string; // Optional user location
}
```

While the interface reflects the overall user profile structure, there might be situations where you need to ensure a complete profile type exists before performing certain actions. So, you create a new type based on `UserProfile` where all properties become mandatory:

required.ts

```
type RequiredUserProfile = Required<Pick<UserProfile,
  'name' | 'email'> >
function displayPublicProfile(profile:
  RequiredUserProfile): void {
  console.log(`Name: ${profile.name},
    Email: ${profile.email}`)
}
```

```
const incompleteProfile = { name: "John Doe" }
// Compilation error: email is missing
const completeProfile: RequiredUserProfile =
  { name: "Jane Doe", email: "jane.doe@example.com" }
displayPublicProfile(completeProfile)
```

Here, RequiredUserProfile is created by applying Required to a Pick utility type of UserProfile. The Pick utility type selects the name and email properties from UserProfile, and then Required makes them mandatory. The displayPublicProfile function leverages this type to guarantee it receives a profile with both a name and email for public display.

- Pick: Pick<K, T> allows you to create a new type by selecting a specific set of properties (K) from an existing type (T). This promotes code clarity and reduces the risk of working with irrelevant data within your components.

Consider a scenario where you're building a React component for a button. The underlying HTML button element has various attributes, but for this specific button, you only care about handling user interactions (click or submit events) and styling (className, focus). Here's how Pick can be used:

pick.ts

```
type ButtonAttributes = Pick<
    Partial<HTMLElement>, // Use Partial to make all attributes
optional
    'onclick' | 'className' | 'onfocus'>;

function createLoggingButton({ onclick, className,
  onfocus }: ButtonAttributes): HTMLButtonElement {
    const button = document.createElement('button');
    ...
    return button;
}
```

In the previous example, Pick was used to create a type, ButtonAttributes, that extracts only the relevant properties (onClick, className, and onFocus) from the HTMLElement of an HTMLButtonElement interface. This ensures that the developer doesn't have to type those properties manually as well.

- Omit: If you need to exclude certain properties, instead use the Omit<T, K> type. It's the opposite of Pick, and it helps you create a new type by removing specified properties (K) from an existing type (T). This is particularly useful when you want to modify a type's structure or create optional variations.

Imagine you're building a user registration form in your TypeScript application. You define a comprehensive user interface capturing all potential user data:

Omit.ts

```
interface User {
  name: string
  email: string
  password: string
  confirmPassword: string
  bio?: string // Optional user bio
  location?: string // Optional user location
}
```

However, when processing the submitted form data, you might not need certain properties such as confirmPassword (used for validation but not stored) or potentially missing optional fields such as bio and location. Omit can be used to create a new type that excludes these unnecessary properties, ensuring you work with a cleaner data structure for further processing:

omit.ts

```
// Expected form data
type UserInput = Pick<User, "name" | "email" |
  "password" | "confirmPassword">
// Excludes unnecessary properties
type ProcessedUserData = Omit<User,
  "confirmPassword" | "bio" | "location">
```

Here, Omit takes the existing user interface and removes the listed properties (confirmPassword, bio, and location). This results in a new ProcessedUserData type that excludes these properties.

> **Note**
>
> Both the Partial and Required types only work on the first level of the type property list. This means that they will not recurse into deeply nested properties of objects and so on. If you know that an object contains multiple nested objects, then you will have to explicitly mark them as Partial or Required as well.

Here is a summary table of the preceding utility types discussed so far:

Utility Type	Description	Example Usage
`Partial`	Creates a type with all properties of the given type set to optional.	`type User = Partial<{ name: string; age: number; }>`
`Required`	Creates a type with all properties of the given type set to required.	`type User = Required<{ name?: string; age?: number; }>`
`Pick`	Creates a type by picking the set of properties K from type T.	`type User = Pick<{ name: string; age: number; }, 'name'>`
`Omit`	Creates a type by omitting the set of properties K from type T.	`type User = Omit<{ name: string; age: number; }, 'age'>`

Figure 2.1 – Overview of the most common utility types in TypeScript

By recognizing when and why to use utility types in your programs, you can improve the readability and correctness of your data types. We'll continue learning about advanced type checks and transformations in subsequent sections.

Using advanced types and assertions

This section focuses beyond the foundational utility types you've encountered so far. As you work on larger projects, you might find the need to create custom utility types specific to your application's requirements. Additionally, there might be situations where you want to enforce stricter type checks based on conditional logic.

To name a few, in many applications, certain business rules dictate how data should be structured or validated. Stricter type checks enable you to enforce these rules at the type level, ensuring that only valid data can be processed. Furthermore, when interacting with external APIs, the structure of the data returned can vary. With stricter checks in place, you can ensure that your application correctly handles different API responses based on the context.

Here, we'll explore how to use the full potential of TypeScript's type system to achieve these goals.

The power of TypeScript's type system extends beyond pre-defined utility types. You'll discover techniques for generating entirely new and unique types tailored to your specific needs. This section will delve into concepts such as branded types and unique symbol properties, equipping you with the tools to create custom and distinct types within your TypeScript applications.

By exploring these advanced type manipulation techniques, you'll gain the ability to perform more granular type checks, leading to a more robust and maintainable code base.

The keyof operator

Imagine you're building a form in your TypeScript application. You define an interface, `SignupFormState`, to represent the structure of your signup form data:

keyof.ts

```ts
interface SignupFormState {
  email: string;
  name: string;
}
```

Now, you need to define an interface for the payload of an action that updates the signup form state. This action payload should have two properties:

- `key`: To identify which form field needs updating (e.g., `email` or `name`)

- `value`: The new value for the specified form field

Here's where the `keyof` operator comes in handy:

keyof.ts

```ts
interface ActionPayload<T> {
  key: keyof T; // Capture all keys of type T using keyof
  value: string;
}
// Usage with SignupFormState
type SignupFormAction = ActionPayload<SignupFormState>;
const updateEmailAction: SignupFormAction = {
  key: 'email', // Autocomplete suggests all keys from SignupFormState
  value: 'new_email@example.com'
};
const updateNameAction: SignupFormAction = {
  key: 'name',
  value: 'John Doe'
};
// Example of an invalid action
const updateInvalidAction: SignupFormAction = {
    key: 'username', // Error: Type '"username"' is not assignable to
type 'keyof SignupFormState'
    value: 'invalid_user'
};
```

By using `keyof`, you can create a generic interface, `ActionPayload<T>`, that captures all the keys of any type T. In our example, when we use `ActionPayload<SignupFormState>`, it creates a union type (`"email"` | `"name"`) representing all possible key names (email or name) within the signup form state.

During action creation, you can use the autocompletion list provided by your IDE. When setting the key property of an action object (e.g., `updateEmailAction`), the IDE will suggest all valid keys from `SignupFormState` as shown in *Figure 2.2*:

```
18   const updateNameAction: SignupFormAction = {
19     key: "name",
20     value: "John Doe",
21   }
22
23   updateEmailAction.|
                          ⊘ key           (property) ActionPayload<SignupF...
                          ⊘ value
```

Figure 2.2 – Autocomplete on keyof shows available properties

By effectively using `keyof`, you can create reusable and type-safe components that are flexible and customizable. Next, let's see how to enforce strictness in the typing system using branded types.

Unique branded types

In the realm of programming languages, type systems play a crucial role in ensuring code reliability and maintainability. Two primary approaches to type systems exist: **structural** and **nominal**. Once you understand their difference, then the concept of branded types will become relevant as we explain later in the section.

Nominal type systems place the highest importance on the specific name or identity of a type. If two types share an identical structure, a nominal system considers them distinct entities.

Structural type systems, on the other hand, prioritize the structure of a type, focusing on the names and data types of its properties. Compatibility between types relies solely on this structure. Remember that *TypeScript uses structural typing*. This means that when comparing types, it focuses on the structure (property names and types) rather than the name of the type itself.

Imagine you have two types: Point3d with x, y, and z properties, and Color with red, green, and blue properties. Then we define another type with a similar type structure as the Point3d type:

branded.ts

```
// Assume Point3d is defined in a library package (not exported)
type Point3d = { x: number; y: number; z: number }; // Defined in
Library Package 1
type Color = { red: number; green: number; blue: number };
type Dot = { x: number; y: number; z: number }; // Defined in Consumer
Package
const data: Dot = { x: 1, y: 2, z: 3 }
const red: Color = { red: 255, y: 0, z: 0 }
```

In this example, the Point3d type is defined in a library package (say it is Library Package 1), but it is not exported for use in other packages. The Dot type is defined in a consumer package where you are using the library.

Even though data was not explicitly assigned a type of Point3d, it structurally matches the requirements of Point3d. In structural typing, as long as the properties and their types align, the objects are considered compatible. So, the following usage of function calls is valid TypeScript:

branded.ts

```
function accept(p: Point3d) {}
// valid
accept(data)
// not valid
accept(red)
```

The function call accept(data) is allowed. TypeScript sees that data has the necessary properties (x, y, and z) with the correct types (numbers) to fulfill the requirements of the Point3d parameter in the accept function. However, the accept(red) call is not allowed since the object passed as an argument has different properties.

However, there might be situations where you desire a stricter type system, akin to nominal typing found in languages such as Java or Go. This is where **branded types** come in! Here's the core concept:

branded.ts

```
type NominalTyped<Type, Brand> = Type & { __type: Brand };
```

In the preceding code, we define a generic type, `NominalTyped<Type, Brand>`. This allows us to *brand* any type with a custom brand (`Brand`), which acts like a unique identifier. Now, let's plug it into our function parameter so it will accept only true `Point3d` types:

branded.ts

```
type EuclideanPoint = NominalTyped<{ x: number;
  y: number; z: number }, 'Point3d'>;
function accept2(point: EuclideanPoint) {
    console.log(`Point coordinates: (${point.x},
      ${point.y}, ${point.z})`);
}
```

We define a branded type, `EuclideanPoint`, by extending `Point3d` with a unique symbol brand. This brand acts as a flag, signifying that this specific point is intended for distance calculations. The `accept2` function now only accepts arguments of type `EuclideanPoint`, ensuring the calculation works with points specifically designed for this purpose. Any attempt to pass a regular `Point3d` object would result in a type error, preventing potential issues.

Using unique symbols as brands is crucial to enforce stronger type distinctions, even when the underlying structures are identical. This enhances type safety and prevents accidental assignment between similarly structured types.

The following example demonstrates the importance of using unique symbols for branding types to prevent accidental assignment between similarly structured types:

branded.ts

```
const Brand1 = Symbol("Brand1");
const Brand2 = Symbol("Brand2");
type TypeA = NominalTyped<number, typeof Brand1>;
type TypeB = NominalTyped<number, typeof Brand2>;
const a: TypeA = 10 as TypeA;
const b: TypeB = 10 as TypeB;
// This should cause a TypeScript error:
const c: TypeA = b; // Error: Type 'TypeB' is not assignable to type
'TypeA'
```

In this example, `TypeA` and `TypeB` are branded with unique symbols. Even though they are both branded number types, TypeScript considers them distinct due to the unique symbol brands. Attempting to assign a `TypeB` to a `TypeA` variable will result in a type error.

By incorporating branded types, you have another tool in your toolbox for enhancing the type safety and clarity of your TypeScript code, mimicking some of the advantages of nominal type systems.

Conditional types

TypeScript offers a powerful feature called **conditional types**, allowing you to define types based on conditional logic. This expands the capabilities of the type system beyond simple structural comparisons.

Here's how it works. The general syntax for a conditional type is A extends B ? C : D. Here, A, B, C, and D represent type parameters that can hold any type. The condition A extends B checks if type A is structurally compatible with type B. If the condition is true, type C is returned. Otherwise, type D is returned.

Say you want to create a type that detects if the generic type parameter is an array. You would write it like this:

conditional.ts

```
type IsArray<T> = T extends any[] ? true : false;
type Test1 = IsArray<number>; // false
type Test2 = IsArray<string[]>; // true
type Test3 = IsArray<boolean[]>; // true
```

The IsArray type uses a conditional check. If the provided type T could potentially be any array (T extends any[]), the resulting type is true, indicating it's indeed an array. Otherwise, the type is false. This allows you to capture the type information in a variable.

You can also use conditional types to create a type that conditionally removes null or undefined from a union type. Here's how to do it:

conditional.ts

```
type NonNullable<T> = T extends null | undefined ?
  never : T;
type Example = NonNullable<string | number | null>; // string | number
```

In this example, the NonNullable<T> type checks if T is null or undefined. If it is, it returns never, effectively removing it from the union. The Example type evaluates to string | number, as null is removed from the union.

Conditional types are utilized collectively with the infer keyword. You can give a name to a type or generic parameter so that you can subsequently perform conditional checks.

Imagine you're working with a program that uses boxes to store different types of data. These boxes have a single property called value that holds the actual data. But how do you know what kind of data is inside a box without opening it?

This is where conditional types with the `infer` keyword come in. They allow you to define a type that checks the structure of another type. In this example, we create a type called Box<T> to represent a box that can hold any type T:

infer.ts

```
// Define a box type that can hold any type of value
interface Box<T> {
  value: T
}
// Define a type to unpack a box and reveal its value type
type UnpackBox<A> = A extends Box<infer E> ? E : A
// Example usage:
type intStash = UnpackBox<{ value: 10 }> // type is number
type stringStash = UnpackBox<{ value: "123" }> // type is string
type booleanStash = UnpackBox<true> // type is boolean
```

This code defines a Box<T> interface representing a container that can hold any type of value. Then, it introduces a conditional type, UnpackBox<A>, which extracts the type of the value held within a Box. If A matches the structure of Box<infer E>, it returns E, the type of the value; otherwise, it returns A. The code provides examples demonstrating the usage of UnpackBox, showing that it correctly deduces the type of the value within the Box interface for various scenarios: a number, a string, and a Boolean.

Now, let's expand the example to include more complex conditional types, such as recursively unpacking nested boxes or conditional type inference based on multiple conditions. This is how you do it:

infer.ts

```
// Define a type to recursively unpack nested boxes
type DeepUnpack<T> = T extends Box<infer U>
  ? DeepUnpack<U> : T;
type nestedBox = Box<Box<number>>; // Box containing another Box
type unpackedNested = DeepUnpack<nestedBox>; // type is number
type deeplyNestedBox = Box<Box<Box<string>>>; // Box containing a Box
containing another Box
type unpackedDeeplyNested = DeepUnpack<deeplyNestedBox>;
// type is string
```

Here, the DeepUnpack<T> type recursively checks if T is a Box. If it is, it unpacks the value type U and applies DeepUnpack again. This continues until it reaches a type that is not a Box interface. In the example usage, nestedBox is a box containing another box with a number and deeplyNestedBox is a box containing a box containing another box with a string.

By practicing these advanced concepts, you generate sophisticated types that more accurately model the domain objects you want to use. Ultimately, you produce types to leverage the compilation process against mistakes, such as wrong assignments or invalid operations.

Mapped types

Mapped types in TypeScript allow you to take an existing type and transform it into a new one, applying a specific rule to each property within the original type. This lets you create variations of existing types that suit your needs.

Here are some examples to showcase their power:

---

mapped.ts

```
interface User {
  name: string
  avatar?: string // Optional avatar
}
type OptionalAvatarUser = {
  // Keyof gets all user properties
  [P in keyof User]?: User[P]
}
const user1: OptionalAvatarUser = { name: "Alice" }
const user2: OptionalAvatarUser = { name: "Bob",
  avatar: "avatar.png" }
```

Here, the `OptionalAvatarUser` type uses a mapped type syntax. It iterates over all the properties (P) of the user interface using the `keyof` operator. Within the square brackets, the type of each property (`User[P]`) is made optional by adding a question mark (`?`). This creates a new type where the name remains a string but the avatar can be either `string` or `undefined`. The two variables `user1` and `user2` are both valid using this mapping.

Mapped types can also be used to create a key remapping using the `as` keyword. Let's say you have a product object with properties such as `id` (number) and `price` (number). You might want to create a new type that displays both properties but with human-readable labels. A mapped type can achieve this:

---

mapped.ts

```
interface Product {
  id: number;
  price: number;
}
type ProductDetails = {
  [P in keyof Product as `product ${P}`]: string;
```

```
  // Transform property names
};
const product1: ProductDetails = {
  "product id": "123",
  "product price": "100", // Converted to string
};
```

This example defines a `ProductDetails` type. It uses a mapped type again, iterating over `Product` properties. However, this time, we use a template literal (as `` `product ${P}` ``) to transform the property names by prepending `product` interface before each one. Additionally, the type remains `string` for all properties, allowing you to store formatted product details.

These are just a few examples of how mapped types can be used in TypeScript. They offer a powerful and flexible way to manipulate and transform existing types, leading to cleaner and more expressive code.

Now, let's continue our exploration of TypeScript with how to develop applications with TypeScript in the browser environment.

Developing in the browser

TypeScript's power as a superset of JavaScript is well suited to the browser environment. It empowers you to write cleaner, more maintainable JavaScript code while ensuring type safety for a more reliable development experience. However, the browser presents its own set of considerations.

So, understanding the **Document Object Model (DOM)** is crucial. By mastering the DOM API, you can effectively interact with these elements, manipulating them and responding to user events such as clicks and scrolls. TypeScript's type safety helps avoid common errors in this process, but browser compatibility still needs consideration.

Tools such as **Webpack** and **Vite** simplify development. These bundlers automate tasks such as compilation and minification, optimizing your code for production. They manage dependencies, create bundles containing your code and libraries, and improve loading times. UI frameworks such as **React** take it a step further. They provide a component-based architecture for building complex and interactive web applications efficiently, often leveraging TypeScript for type safety within your components.

Figure 2.3 briefly summarizes the differences between Node.js versus frontend JavaScript:

Feature	Node.js (Backend)	Frontend JavaScript (Browser)
File Structure	Each file is treated as an individual module.	Multiple files are combined into a single file using bundlers and then loaded into the DOM as a `<script>` tag.
Module Management	Uses CommonJS or ES modules for importing/exporting.	Uses JavaScript ES modules and **Immediately Invoked Function Expressions (IIFEs)**
Execution Context	Runs on the server, allowing access to the file system and network.	Runs in the browser, interacting with the DOM.
Environment	Built for server-side applications, handling requests and responses.	Built for client-side applications, focusing on user interactions and the UI.
APIs	Provides built-in modules for the file system, HTTP, and more.	Access to DOM APIs for manipulating HTML/CSS and handling events.
Performance	Optimized for handling multiple requests simultaneously.	Performance can be affected by browser rendering and event handling. Mainly single-threaded but can be offloaded using Web Workers.

Figure 2.3 – Differences between Node.js and Browser environments

By combining your understanding of the browser environment, the DOM, and event handling with the strengths of TypeScript and efficient tools, you can construct scalable and dynamic web applications. TypeScript ensures type safety, leading to more robust and reliable web experiences.

First, you want to understand how to work with the DOM and TypeScript, so we'll provide a couple more practical examples next.

> **Note**
> Some of the examples cannot work when using Node.js as they depend on the global window object, so you will need to use a modern browser such as Chrome or Firefox.

Understanding the DOM

When you load an HTML page, the browser converts the code into a structured tree known as the **Document Object Model (DOM)**. This tree represents the visual elements on the page, with each node corresponding to an element such as `<div>` or `<p>`.

While we'll explore design patterns in later chapters, it's worth noting that the DOM utilizes these patterns for efficient creation and manipulation. For example, the *Factory Method*, explored in *Chapter 3*, ensures appropriate node elements are created based on tags (e.g., div, p), while the *Visitor pattern*, explored in *Chapter 6*, enables efficient traversal of the DOM structure.

To give you a quick demonstration, let's consider a simple HTML document and its corresponding DOM tree:

DOM/index.html

```
<!doctype html>
<html lang="en">
  <head>
    <title>Document</title>
  </head>
  <body>
    <div id="section-1">
      <span>Typescript 5 Design Patterns</span>
    </div>
    <p class="paragraph"></p>
    <button type="submit">Submit</button>
    <script src="dist/index.js"></script>
  </body>
</html>
```

In the preceding code, the top-level element is <html>, with two children: <head> and <body>. The <body> contains further children elements (<div>, <p>, <button>, <script>) that may also have their own nested elements.

The preceding tree is visualized in *Figure 2.4* as follows:

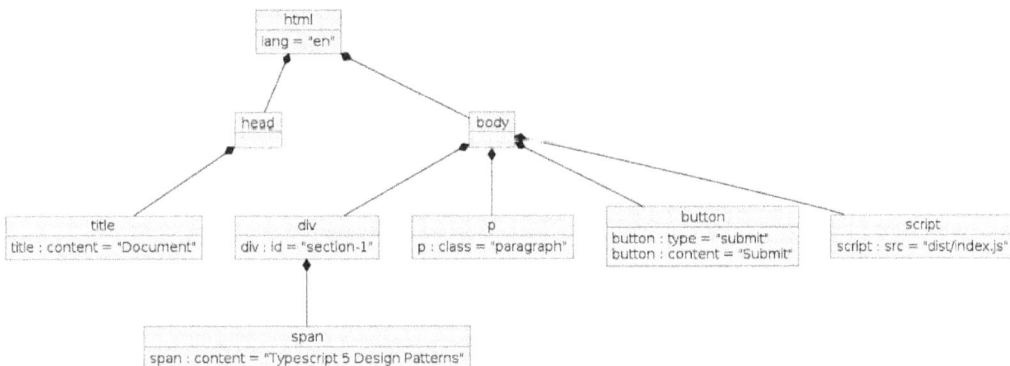

Figure 2.4 – DOM tree of the provided HTML example

The preceding tree can be manipulated or traversed using the DOM API, which is a set of functions and methods provided by the browser environment that allows complete control of its contents.

To set up a new project with DOM access in TypeScript, you can include the `lib.dom.d.ts` type definitions in your `tsconfig.json` file:

```
{
  "compilerOptions": {
    "lib": ["DOM"],
    "outDir": "./"
  }
}
```

These type definitions provide essential types for DOM elements, such as `Element`, `HTMLElement`, and `ShadowRoot`. The full scope of the DOM API is extensive, and detailed documentation can be found at `https://html.spec.whatwg.org/`.

You will need an HTML document to reference the compiled TypeScript. You can use the previous HTML document and `index.ts` as an example:

DOM/index.ts

```
const p = document.querySelector<HTMLParagraphElement>
  (".paragraph");
const spanArea = document.createElement("span");
spanArea.textContent = "This is a text we added dynamically";
p?.appendChild(spanArea);
const actionButton = document
  .querySelector<HTMLButtonElement>("button");
actionButton?.addEventListener("click", () => {
    window.alert("You Clicked the Submit Button");
});
```

Using the DOM API, we can perform a list of operations to query, create, and modify node objects. Let's look at each one of those operations in the following bullet points:

1. **Creating a new element**: Creating a new element of the span type:

   ```
   const spanArea = document.createElement("span");
   ```

This code creates a new HTML element of type span. The spanArea variable is inferred to be of type HTMLSpanElement, which inherits from the more general HTMLElement type. This provides type safety and code completion suggestions for available properties and methods specific to span elements.

2. **Finding existing elements**: Querying for elements by class name or ID property:

```
const p = document
  .getElementsByClassName< HTMLParagraphElement>
  ("paragraph")[0];
const div = document
  .getElementById <HTMLDivElement>("section-1");
```

The getElementsByClassName method takes a class name as an argument and returns an HTMLCollectionOf<Element> Interface. This collection might contain multiple elements with the specified class. In this example, we access the first element ([0]) assuming there's only one paragraph with that class. The getElementById method takes an element ID as an argument and returns a single HTMLElement interface if found. The ID attribute should be unique within the document to ensure you target the correct element.

3. **Attaching event handlers**: Adding an event listener on a button click event:

```
actionButton?.addEventListener("click", () => {
  window.alert("You Clicked the Submit Button");
});
```

This code snippet demonstrates attaching a click event listener to a button element. The addEventListener method takes two arguments: the event type ("click" in this case) and a callback function that executes when the event occurs. Here, we use the optional chaining operator (?.) to safely access the addEventListener method. It checks if the actionButton element exists before attempting to call the method, preventing potential errors.

You can check the preceding code by compiling index.ts to index.js and starting a static HTTP server to view the index.html document.

Follow these steps to set up a basic website that utilizes the previous scripts:

1. Start by installing a simple node static server by using this package:

```
$ npm -g install node-static
```

2. To compile the TypeScript file, you just need to run the following task: **Build Chapter 2 HTML DOM Example**. Run this from the VSCode task list via **Terminal | Run Task...**:

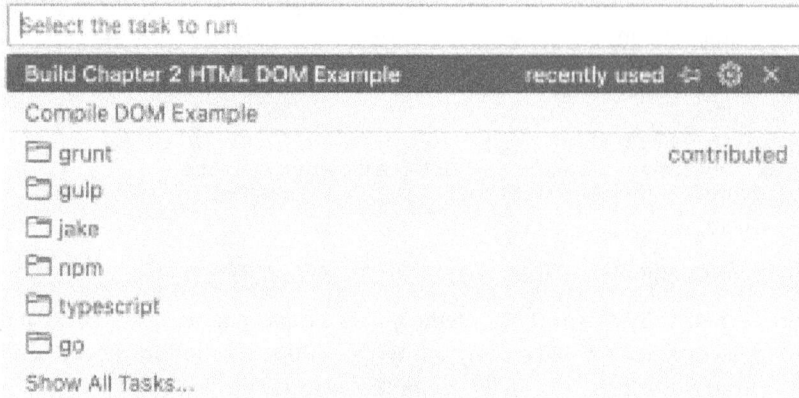

Figure 2.5 – Build Chapter 2 task

3. This task will compile index.ts into index.js and place them in the dist folder. Then, with the help of a static server, you can inspect the page:

```
$ cd chapters/chapter-2_Core_Principles_and_use_cases/src/DOM
$ static
```

4. Open a browser and navigate to http://localhost:8080. You will see the following page in *Figure 2.6*:

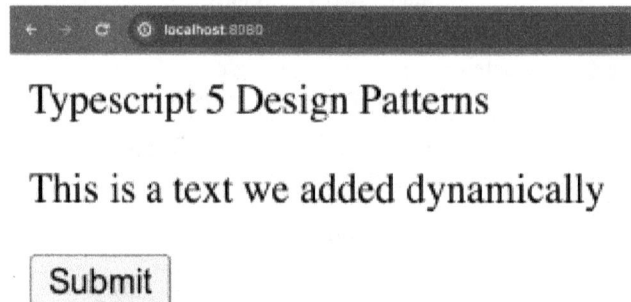

Figure 2.6 – Browser view of DOM example

With VSCode and some build tasks, we can quickly ramp up a simple project with ease and not many additional tools are needed. However, in larger programs with additional team members, it's useful to have a module bundler such as Webpack or Vite. Let's see how you can achieve that next.

Using TypeScript with Vite

Vite and TypeScript make a powerful duo for streamlined React and TypeScript development. This is a tool that scaffolds the project's configuration, automates production builds, creates a development server with auto-reloading, and, in essence, makes development more friendly.

Here's a concise guide to get you started in three easy steps:

1. **Create a new Vite project**: Use the following command in your preferred terminal, which creates a new Vite project with the vanilla typescript template specified:

   ```
   $ npx create-vite@latest my-app --template vanilla-ts
   ```

   Replace my-app with your preferred library name. The --template flag specifies the template to use.

2. **Build the project**: Once the project is created, change to the directory of the new application folder name and build the code:

   ```
   $ cd my-app
   $ npm run build
   vite v5.2.11 building for production...
   ✓ 7 modules transformed.
   dist/index.html                    0.46 kB | gzip: 0.29 kB
   dist/assets/index-Cz4zGhbH.css     1.21 kB | gzip: 0.63 kB
   dist/assets/index-Bd-pKGJy.js      3.05 kB | gzip: 1.62 kB
   ✓ built in 55ms
   ```

   A successful compilation will create those assets based on the vite.config.ts configuration file.

3. **Run the application**: To test the application, run the following command:

   ```
   $ npm run preview
   ```

   This will start the preview server of the compiled dist folder, typically accessible at http://localhost:4173/.

Speaking of using TypeScript in the browser, let's explore how to use TypeScript with React next and how to create type-safe components.

Using React

React, a popular UI library developed by Facebook, empowers you to create scalable and user-friendly interfaces. By learning React with TypeScript, you'll gain experience with design patterns such as composition, immutability, and statelessness.

A lot of frameworks like Next.js have built-in support with React and TypeScript but some of the typing definitions need some time to get used to.

To get started, we have included a sample project using TypeScript, React, and Vite that renders a simple component on the web page. This is located in the `react` folder inside this chapter's source code at `https://github.com/PacktPublishing/TypeScript-5-Design-Patterns-and-Best-Practices/tree/main/chapters/chapter02_Core_Principles_and_use_cases/src/react/src`.

You have to note some differences in the config though:

- We added a `"jsx": "react-jsx"` compiler option to enable JSX and TSX factories. This enables us to write idiomatic code that resembles HTML inside the source code. The compiler will create the necessary constructors for the React DOM library.

- The `lib` compiler option includes DOM and `DOM.Iterable`, which are libraries that support functionalities related to the DOM in JavaScript.

Here's a breakdown of three common ways to declare React functional components with props and children:

- **Using the** `React.FC<Props>` **type annotation**: This approach explicitly defines the type of props the component expects using a type interface or object. Here's an example:

---

components/Greeting.tsx

```
import React from "react"
interface GreetingProps {
  name: string
}
const Greeting: React.FC<GreetingProps> = ({
  name = "World" }) => {
  return <h1>Hello, {name}!</h1>
}
export default Greeting
```

This code snippet uses a React **functional component** (**FC**) with type safety using TypeScript. It defines a type interface named `GreetingProps` that specifies the expected type for the name prop (`string`). The component, `Greeting`, is declared as an FC using `React.FC<GreetingProps>`, indicating it accepts props of that type. It returns JSX that displays a heading element with the greeting message personalized by the `name` prop. The FC type includes some extra fields specific to React, such as `defaultProps` and `displayName`.

- **Using a function signature with the** `props` **argument**: A simpler way is to just declare a `props` argument that specifies the type of the component properties it can accept without any additional React-specific fields:

components/Greeting2.tsx

```
import React from "react"
interface GreetingProps {
  name: string
}
const Greeting2 = (props: GreetingProps) => {
  const { name = "World" } = props
  return <h1>Hello, {name}!</h1>
}
export default Greeting2
```

Here, it's a function that directly accepts an argument named `props` of type `GreetingProps` with only one property called name.

- **Using** `React.PropsWithChildren` **for children support**: A third way is useful if you want to include a `children` property for rendering the component children tree. Here's an example:

components/Button.tsx

```
import { PropsWithChildren } from "react"
export type ButtonProps = {
  onClick: (e: React
    .MouseEvent<HTMLButtonElement>) => void
}
const Button: React
  .FC<PropsWithChildren<ButtonProps>> =
    ({ children, onClick }) => {
  return <button onClick={onClick}>
    {children}</button>
}
export default Button
```

Here, the `PropsWithChildren` type from React handles components that can have child elements. The `Button` component itself is declared as an FC that wraps this type, enhancing their final types.

Now, if you want to compile and view this React project, showcasing the components, you just need to navigate to the project folder, run the following command line, and visit `http://localhost:5173/`:

```
$ npm run dev
```

The screenshot in *Figure 2.7* shows what you should expect to see:

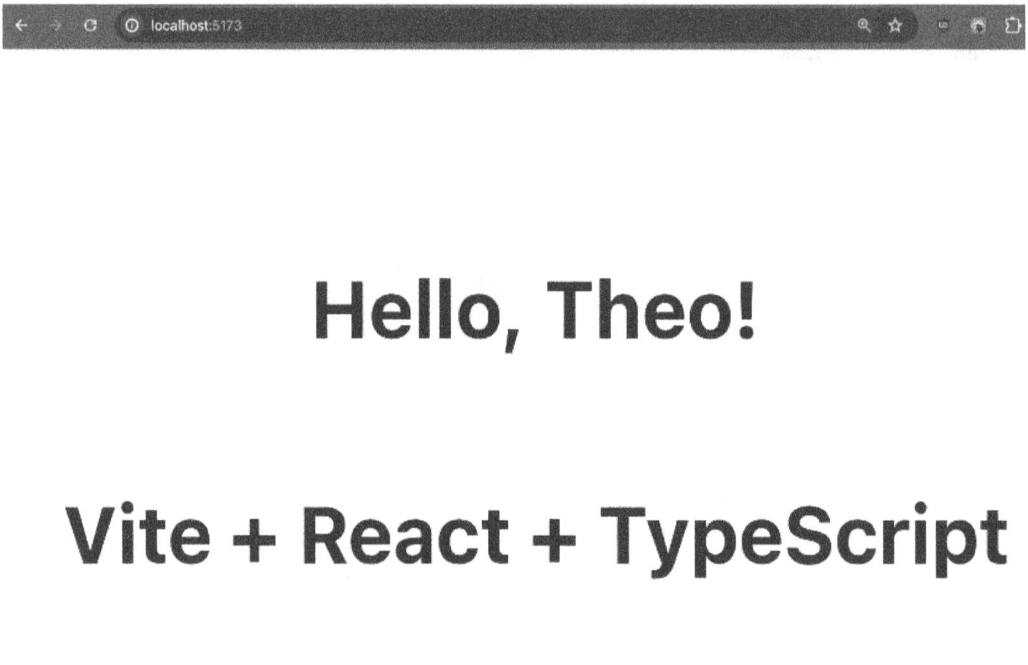

Hello, Theo!

Vite + React + TypeScript

Figure 2.7 – React with TypeScript example in the browser

As with other examples, using React and TypeScript is a good combination as we can leverage the best-of-breed patterns for UI development. By best-of-breed patterns, we mean that we can use composition, functional programming, and type safety to create scalable web applications.

Now that you have understood the basics of developing those applications with TypeScript in the browser, we'll explore the basics of developing in the server environment.

Developing in the server

Now that you know the basics of application development in the browser, you can expand your knowledge to the server side.

Here, the focus shifts since we gain access to much more computational power compared to user-installed browser applications. Client-side solutions might not translate directly to the server, and security becomes paramount. Server applications often interact with databases that store sensitive data, requiring robust security measures to protect this information.

This section lays down the foundations for exploring the nuances of server-side development, equipping you with the skills to craft secure and efficient applications that power the behind-the-scenes magic of the web.

Understanding the server environment

When working on the server side, your code handles requests sent over a network port (typically TCP/IP) by clients such as web browsers or mobile apps. Servers can handle various tasks, including serving web pages (HTTP servers), internal microservices that communicate within your application, or specialized tools such as daemons (long-lived processes running in the background).

We'll explore some important considerations when it comes to working in a server environment with TypeScript starting with *choosing the runtime environment* in the next section.

Runtime choices — Node.js versus Deno versus Bun.js

Traditionally, Node.js has been the dominant runtime environment for server-side JavaScript development. However, a couple of new frameworks have emerged as a secure alternative that can natively evaluate TypeScript code.

As an example, we'll demonstrate a simple HTTP server built with both Deno and Bun.js. We provide links to their home pages for installation instructions in the *Further reading* section of this chapter.

The following snippet of code demonstrates how to set up a simple Deno HTTP server using TypeScript. Note that you don't have to compile the code since Deno understands TypeScript natively:

src/deno/server.ts

```
const port = 8080;
const handler = async (req: Request) => {
  const body = "Hello, World!";
  return new Response(body, { status: 200 });
};
Deno.serve({ port }, handler);
console.log(`HTTP server listening on port ${port}`);
```

This code implements a basic HTTP server using Deno. It defines a port (8080) and a request handler (handler) that creates a response and a status code of 200 (OK). The Deno.serve function starts the server on the specified port and the handler function is used to process incoming requests.

You can run this server with the following command:

```
$ deno run --allow-net server.ts
Listening on http://localhost:8080/
HTTP server listening on port 8080
```

The --allow-net flag tells the server to allow network connections from external domains.

Then you can navigate to `http://localhost:8000` and view the message, as shown in *Figure 2.8*:

Figure 2.8 – Deno server browser view

Here's a similar example of a Bun server responding with `"Hello World!"`:

src/bun/server.ts

```
const server = Bun.serve({
  port: 3000,
  fetch(request) {
    return new Response("Hello World!")
  },
})
console.log(`HTTP server listening on port:${server.port}`)
```

This code snippet utilizes the `Bun.serve` function instead to create the server and configure its port. The `fetch` function handles incoming requests in a similar minimalistic manner.

The key takeaway here is that both approaches achieve the same goal: establishing a server that listens for incoming connections and responds to client requests over the network.

It's important to note that while we've used TypeScript for code definition, the actual runtime code will likely be transpiled to JavaScript based on the chosen environment's internal implementation. This means the runtime code itself might be more dynamic in nature, with less emphasis on type safety compared to the TypeScript source code.

Now let's talk about another characteristic of server applications, regarding their lifetime living as processes.

Long-living processes

Server applications are designed to operate for extended periods, making it crucial to ensure their resilience against errors and unexpected shutdowns. This section explores strategies for building resilient server processes in TypeScript.

How to secure processes from disruptions

One crucial aspect is resource management. Server processes can be resource-intensive, consuming significant memory, CPU, or storage. Implementing monitoring and resource management techniques is essential to prevent resource exhaustion and maintain overall system stability.

Another layer of protection comes from process managers. Tools such as PM2 or nodemon can act as guardians for your server processes. In the unfortunate event of a crash, these tools can automatically restart the process, potentially restoring service and minimizing downtime for your users.

Using process managers or monitors will make your applications more resilient and able to provide better chances of maintaining the availability of your services.

While TypeScript can protect against type errors at compile time, there are many classes of errors that happen at runtime. In such cases, you want to be able to catch those errors and respond accordingly. The following section explores this option.

Graceful shutdowns and having clean state

While process managers can handle unexpected crashes, there might be situations where you need to initiate a controlled shutdown. This could be due to critical errors requiring application termination or for maintenance purposes.

Here's an example using Node.js's process global variable, which is responsible for interfacing with the current application process:

src/shutdown/server.ts

```
import * as http from "http"
const shutdownHandler = () => {
  console.log("Received shutdown signal, gracefully exiting...")
  // Perform additional cleaning work here
  process.exit(0) // Indicate successful termination
}

//create a server object:
http
  .createServer((req: http.IncomingMessage,
    res: http.ServerResponse) => {
    res.write("Hello World!") //write a response to the client
    res.end() //end the response
  })
  .listen(8080) //the server object listens on port 8080
// Register shutdown signal listeners (SIGINT, SIGTERM)
process.on("SIGINT", shutdownHandler)
process.on("SIGTERM", shutdownHandler)
```

The provided code registers shutdown handlers for two signals: SIGINT and SIGTERM. Send the SIGINT signal using the kill command followed by PID (Mac or Linux):

```
$ kill -INT <PID>
```

For example, here are the commands I used to figure out the PID number and kill the process:

```
$ lsof -i 8080
COMMAND     PID            USER    FD    TYPE              DEVICE SIZE/OFF
NODE NAME
node    10416 theo.despoudis    22u   IPv6
0xc21ccc733b9504cf        0t0   TCP *:http-alt (LISTEN)
$ kill -INT 10416
(on the tab that started the server.ts example)
Received shutdown signal, gracefully exiting...
```

This code identifies and terminates a Node.js server process running on port 8080. The lsof command with the -i flag finds the process ID (PID) based on the port number. It then uses the kill command, providing the PID number, which will trigger the shutdown handler in our program. This demonstrates how the OS interacts with our application and what happens after.

> **Important note**
>
> Sending SIGINT (*Ctrl + C*) is typically used for a softer termination, allowing the process to perform cleanup tasks. SIGTERM is a more forceful termination signal, and processes might not have a chance to perform cleanup.

Ideally, you should carefully craft your services with statelessness in mind. That means you may and should be able to restart those processes at any time with no loss of information. By adhering to good engineering practices such as avoiding global states or mutable structures that retain data forever, it allows you to scale servers up or down without side effects.

Frameworks with TypeScript support

Once you explore the fundamentals of server-side scripting with TypeScript, frameworks can significantly accelerate your development process. These **frameworks** provide pre-built components, routing mechanisms, middleware support, and other functionalities to streamline building robust server-side applications. We'll take a brief look at a few of the most prominent ones.

Popular frameworks with TypeScript

Server-side development with TypeScript offers a variety of frameworks to streamline the process. Two prominent options include the following:

- **Express.js**: This well-established and lightweight Node.js framework provides a flexible foundation for constructing web applications and APIs. Its minimalist approach allows for a high degree of customization, making it suitable for various project requirements.

- **Nest.js**: Built on top of Express.js and inspired by Angular, Nest.js is a progressive server-side framework for Node.js. It leverages TypeScript to enforce type safety and promotes a structured development approach. Key features of Nest.js include dependency injection for managing object dependencies and modularity for organizing your application into well-defined components.

This section provides you with a short example of each, giving you a high-level view of what it entails to build a simple web application in TypeScript. Let's start with Express.js first and we'll follow up with Nest.js.

Express.js example with TypeScript

Express.js is a popular, minimalist web framework for Node.js that simplifies building web applications and APIs. It provides a foundation for handling incoming HTTP requests, defining routes, managing middleware, and structuring your application logic. By leveraging TypeScript in conjunction with Express.js, you gain the benefits of type safety, improved maintainability, and better tooling support.

Here's a simple version demonstrating routing and middleware:

src/express/server.ts

```
import express from "express"
import { json } from "body-parser"
const app = express()
const port = process.env.PORT || 3000
app.use(json())
app.get("/health", (req, res) => {
  res.send(«OK!»)
})
app.listen(port, () =>
  console.log(`Server listening on port ${port}`))
```

This code snippet showcases the creation of a simple server application using Express.js and TypeScript. The `app.use(json())` line integrates the JSON middleware function with the Express application. This ensures that any incoming request with a JSON body is automatically parsed, making the data accessible in the `req.body` property of the request object.

The code then defines a route handler for the `/health` endpoint using `app.get()`. This means the server will respond whenever it receives a GET request to the `/health` path. The route handler function simply sends a text response, `"OK!"`, back to the client.

To run this example, you can use the following command after you run `npm run build`:

```
$ npm run build
$ node chapters/chapter-2_Core_Principles_and_use_cases/dist/express/
server.js
```

Then, you can navigate to the `http://localhost300/health` endpoint to see the **OK!** message, as shown in *Figure 2.9*:

OK!

Figure 2.9 – Express.js server health check page

Let's look at how Next.js performs with the same functionality.

Nest.js example with TypeScript

Nest.js offers a more structured approach to building server-side applications. Here's a basic example demonstrating a controller and route. The example is split between three files, which is almost the minimal viable product for a simple web application written in this framework:

src/nest/app.module.ts

```
import { Module } from '@nestjs/common';
import { AppController } from './app.controller';
@Module({
  imports: [],
  controllers: [AppController],
})
export class AppModule {}
```

src/nest/app.controller.ts

```
import { Controller, Get } from '@nestjs/common';
@Controller()
export class AppController {
  @Get('/health')
  getHealth() {
    return 'OK!';
  }
}
```

src/nest/main.ts

```
import { ValidationPipe } from "@nestjs/common"
import { NestFactory } from "@nestjs/core"
import { AppModule } from "./app.module"
```

```
async function bootstrap() {
  const app = await NestFactory.create(AppModule)
  app.useGlobalPipes(new ValidationPipe())

  await app.listen(3000)
  console.log(`Application is running on:
    ${await app.getUrl()}`)
}
bootstrap()
```

Let's explore how the Nest.js example works and highlight the key differences in structure compared to Express.js:

- **Modules**: Nest.js revolves around the concept of modules. These modules encapsulate functionality and provide a way to organize your application logic. You need to declare any module dependencies using the `imports` field and any controllers using the `controllers` field.

- **Controllers**: Controllers are predefined pieces of code that accept inbound requests and perform some sort of logic about them. This is similar to function callbacks attached to a particular route. When the user visits a particular path, the controller gets activated. When you decorate a class with the `@Controller` annotation, it marks it as a valid class to use in the `controllers` fields when you declare a module.

- **Bootstrapping**: This refers to the process of initializing and starting a Nest.js application. It involves creating an application instance, configuring settings, and registering necessary components.

While both frameworks handle server-side development, Nest.js provides a more structured and opinionated approach, with built-in features such as dependency injection and modularity. Express.js offers a more flexible approach, allowing for greater customization. The choice between them depends on your project requirements and preferences.

Error handling

Error handling is the process of implementing policies and logic instructions when an application encounters faults or invalid arguments. Since server environments are very sensitive and critical, it's crucial to handle unexpected errors in the most graceful manner.

We'll explore various techniques for handling errors in TypeScript, considering different runtime environments such as Node.js, Deno, and Bun.js.

Custom error classes

TypeScript allows us to create custom error classes that extend the built-in `Error` class. This approach helps in creating more specific and meaningful error types that provide a specialized message for debugging or introspection purposes:

Errors.ts

```
class DatabaseConnectionError extends Error {
  constructor(message: string) {
    super(message)
    this.name = "DatabaseConnectionError"
  }
}
try {
  throw new DatabaseConnectionError("Unable to connect
    to the database.")
} catch (error) {
  if (error instanceof DatabaseConnectionError) {
    console.error(error.message) // Output: Unable to connect to the
database.
  }
}
```

Here, `DatabaseConnectionError` extends the `Error` class and sets a unique `name` property for it. The main idea of this is that if you throw an instance of this class then, later on, you will be able to check their instance type (using the `instanceof` operator) and perform additional cleanup checks based on that type of error.

Using union types for error handling

Of course, if you detest using classes, you can alternatively leverage union types to create error types. The main idea is to encode the success and failure cases as types and then utilize the type system to verify each use case when performing checks:

errors.ts

```
type SuccessResponse = { success: true; value: number }
type ErrorResponse = { success: false; error: string }
function divide(dividend: number, divisor: number):
  SuccessResponse | ErrorResponse {
  if (divisor === 0) {
    return { success: false, error: "Cannot divide by zero." }
  }
```

```
  return { success: true, value: dividend / divisor }
}
const result = divide(10, 0)
if (result.success) {
  console.log("Division result:", result.value)
} else {
  console.error("Division error:", result.error) // Output: Division
error: Cannot divide by zero.
}
```

It defines two types: `SuccessResponse` for successful calculations and `ErrorResponse` for errors. The `divide` function takes two numbers and returns one of these response types. It checks if the divisor is zero, returning an error response if true, or a success response with the division result otherwise. The function's return type uses a union of these responses, leveraging TypeScript's discriminated unions.

Of course, this approach, while it provides type safety and explicit error management, requires manual checking of error states at each step, leading to a more procedural programming style. Unlike exceptions that automatically propagate up the call stack, errors in this system must be explicitly passed through function calls. This approach forces developers to consciously handle potential errors, improving reliability but potentially making the code more verbose as a side effect.

Centralized error handling

For larger applications, especially those utilizing frameworks, **centralizing error handling** can improve maintainability and ensure consistent error responses across your application. The main idea is to have a God class or a function that handles a common set of errors for the whole application:

```
export function errorHandler(err, req, res, next) {
  res.status(500).json({ error: err.message });
}
import { globalErrorHandler } from "./error-handler";
app.use(globalErrorHandler);
```

Here, this global error handling middleware (via the `errorHandler` object) provides a centralized way to manage errors in an Express.js/Bun.js application, ensuring consistent error responses across the entire app.

However, it's also quite coarse-grained, meaning that it is only useful for handling the general use case of errors (**500** error codes, for example). If you want to handle specific types of errors or provide detailed error information, which could be crucial for debugging, then you would need to include `try/catch` statements inside the API handlers instead.

Now that you know how to work with TypeScript and have explored its ecosystem, you will start learning more about design patterns to understand their practicality.

Introducing design patterns in TypeScript

Design patterns are battle-tested solutions that offer reusable approaches to common software development challenges.

While design patterns have been around since 1994 (the *Gang of Four* book!), their core principles remain relevant. They shouldn't be seen as outdated relics, but rather as valuable tools to be evaluated through the lens of modern programming languages and best practices. Those patterns are an outcome of experience while working on large systems and future developers should invest their time in understanding their origins and their raison d'etre.

Why do design patterns exist?

Software development is like a vast landscape with many roads to follow. There are often multiple ways to reach a solution, and some approaches are demonstrably better than others. **Design patterns** provide a structured and repeatable way to tackle recurring issues. They help us avoid pitfalls such as tight coupling, weak cohesion, and inefficient resource management. They help us find the optimal route to achieve our goals while minimizing code complexity.

Object-oriented programming (**OOP**) and functional programming offer solid foundations for building large-scale systems. But sometimes, experience and pragmatism are needed to shape existing code into more elegant and adaptable structures. Design patterns provide a basic framework for achieving this by teaching us how to design systems that avoid common problems.

Are design patterns relevant now?

At the time of writing this book, design patterns remain relevant, but their application has evolved alongside advancements in languages such as TypeScript. Here's why:

- **Adaptability to modern languages**: While some patterns might need adjustments for TypeScript's features, the core concepts are still applicable. Modern interpretations of design patterns leverage these features to create cleaner, more type-safe solutions.

  For example, the way that we instantiate objects in TypeScript has changed. Depending on how we want those objects to behave, we have flexibility in creating them. However, we can still abstract the whole object creation using the **Factory pattern** and still get the same benefits.

- **Common terminology**: Design patterns provide a common language for developers. Understanding these patterns allows you to communicate design ideas effectively with your team and comprehend code written using these patterns in other projects. For example, developers often need to ensure that only one instance of an object exists in the system at any given time, so it makes sense to use the term **Singleton** to describe this requirement.

- **Foundational knowledge:** Learning design patterns strengthens your problem-solving skills and understanding of software design principles. This knowledge serves as a foundational step for exploring more advanced architectural concepts and design considerations in modern software development. This understanding is crucial for grasping concepts such as **reactive programming** (covered in *Chapter 8*). While Reactive programming might seem complex at first, a strong foundation in design patterns will equip you to connect the dots. You'll see how these patterns play a role in building reactive systems that efficiently handle data streams and asynchronous operations.

By leveraging type safety, clear communication, and a strong foundation for advanced concepts, design patterns empower you to build robust, maintainable, and scalable applications. TypeScript is an excellent language to start practicing those principles and we explain how to do it in the following chapters.

Design patterns in TypeScript

This brings us to the main effort of this book on how to apply classic design patterns to TypeScript as a natural first step. TypeScript's modern and expressive type system helps overcome limitations found in older languages such as C++ and Java, enabling cleaner and more optimized code.

Throughout this book, we'll explore both classic and modern approaches to design patterns. We'll examine whether a specific pattern retains its value in the context of a more expressive language such as TypeScript. Our goal is to equip you with the knowledge to evaluate when and how to apply design patterns effectively.

We'll follow a structured approach for each pattern: first, clearly defining the problem it solves. Then, we'll get into the proposed solution, explaining how it addresses the issue and its key benefits. To enhance understanding, Unified Modeling Language (UML) diagrams visualize the pattern's structure. Code examples will showcase practical implementations, followed by discussions on modern alternatives or variations you might consider. We'll solidify your knowledge by exploring concrete use cases where each pattern is valuable. Finally, to provide a well-rounded perspective, we'll acknowledge any potential drawbacks or criticisms associated with each design pattern.

As a useful note, it's important to remember that design patterns aren't a silver bullet. They should be thoughtfully applied based on the specific context of your project and its needs. This book will guide you through evaluating when and how to leverage design patterns effectively in your TypeScript projects.

Summary

This chapter explored advanced language primitives in TypeScript that empower you to define precise types within your abstractions. Utility types such as `Pick`, `Record`, and `Partial` are built-in types that let you provide accurate types; you will improve the safety of your code.

We further highlighted TypeScript's versatility as a multi-paradigm language. We provided examples of how TypeScript can be configured to run in both server and browser environments using bundlers or runtimes that provide native TypeScript support.

Frameworks such as Next.js and Express.js provide excellent support for TypeScript, unlocking type safety throughout the application code base.

Design patterns – established and reliable solutions to common software problems – were introduced. These patterns, created by software experts, offer valuable tools for managing complexity in large-scale projects, regardless of your chosen programming style (OOP or others).

The next chapter delves into design patterns, starting with the creational patterns. You'll gain a comprehensive understanding of these essential tools to enhance your software development skills.

Q&A

Feel free to review the following questions and their corresponding answers to address any concerns or gain additional insights:

1. When might you use `Pick<T, K>` or `Omit<T, K>`?

    Answer: `Pick<T, K>` creates a new type that includes only a specific set of properties (`K`) from the original type `T`. `Omit<T, K>` creates a new type that excludes a specific set of properties (`K`) from the original type `T`. These utility types are useful for selecting specific data from objects or removing unwanted properties.

2. How does the target option in `tsconfig.json` affect browser versus server-side compilation?

    Answer: The target option specifies the ECMAScript version your compiled JavaScript code should target. For browser environments, you might choose a lower target to ensure compatibility with older browsers. For server-side environments with Node.js, you can use a more modern target version.

3. How does TypeScript control browser compatibility when building for production?

    Answer: TypeScript code needs to be compiled into JavaScript before browsers can understand it. Bundlers such as Webpack and Vite can help combine and transpile your TypeScript code, along with other dependencies, into a single JavaScript file that works across browsers with the appropriate level of support.

Further reading

- *ECMAScript 5 specification* is at `https://262.ecma-international.org/5.1/`
- *ECMAScript 2015 (ES6) specification* is at `https://262.ecma-international.org/6.0/`

- For a more advanced guide to TypeScript, read *Mastering TypeScript 4th Edition, Nathan Rozentals, Packt Publishing*. It is available at `https://www.packtpub.com/product/mastering-typescript-fourth-edition/9781800564732`

- See the classic design patterns book, *Design Patterns: Elements of Reusable Object-Oriented Software, Erich Gamma, Richard Helm, Ralph Johnson, and John Vlissides, Addison-Wesley*. It is available at `https://www.amazon.co.uk/Design-patterns-elements-reusable-object-oriented/dp/0201633612`

- To learn more about *Nest.js*, see the *official documentation* at `https://docs.nestjs.com/`

- To learn more about *Bun.js*, see the *official documentation* at `https://bun.sh/`

Get This Book's PDF Version and Exclusive Extras

UNLOCK NOW

Scan the QR code (or go to `packtpub.com/unlock`). Search for this book by name, confirm the edition, and then follow the steps on the page.

Note: Keep your invoice handly. Purchase made directly from packt don't require one.

Part 2: TypeScript Core Design Patterns

In this section, we will explore core design patterns, diving into their structure, benefits, and practical implementation in TypeScript. Design patterns provide established solutions to common challenges that arise when developing large and complex systems. We will cover creational, structural, and behavioral design patterns. Creational patterns help with object creation mechanisms, ensuring objects are created in a controlled, efficient manner. Structural patterns focus on optimizing the relationships between objects and improving code organization and scalability. Lastly, behavioral patterns handle object communication and the management of object state over time.

This part has the following chapters:

- *Chapter 3, Creational Design Patterns*
- *Chapter 4, Structural Design Patterns*
- *Chapter 5, Behavioral Design Patterns for Object Communication*
- *Chapter 6, Behavioral Design Patterns for Managing State and Behavior*

3

Creational Design Patterns

When developing applications, you frequently design and manage objects. You create them dynamically or assign them to variables for later use. If left unchecked, this can lead to brittle code due to numerous alternative ways of object creation or improper management of their lifetime, resulting in memory leaks.

The first and most fundamental category of patterns we'll explore in this book is **creational design patterns**.

You'll start by learning how the Singleton pattern ensures that only one instance of an object is maintained throughout a program's lifetime. Then, we'll cover the Prototype pattern, which will teach you how to copy existing objects without recreating them from scratch.

Using the Builder pattern, you'll understand how to streamline the construction of complex objects by breaking down the construction flow into a more readable representation.

Next, you'll learn how the Factory Method pattern helps determine the appropriate time to instantiate objects of a specific type at runtime. Finally, the Abstract Factory pattern will show you how to use interfaces to model the creation of related objects while leaving the implementation details to concrete factories at runtime.

In this chapter, we'll cover the following main topics:

- Creational design patterns
- The Singleton pattern
- The Prototype pattern
- The Builder pattern
- The Factory Method pattern
- The Abstract Factory pattern

By the end of this chapter, you'll have a deep understanding of each of the main creational patterns and will be able to apply them practically in your applications. You'll also gain the necessary insights into using these patterns only when appropriate, avoiding premature optimization and unsuitable solutions.

> **Note**
>
> The links to all the sources mentioned in the chapter, as well as supplementary reading materials, are provided in the *Further reading* section toward the end of this chapter.

Technical requirements

The code bundle for this chapter is available on GitHub: `https://github.com/PacktPublishing/TypeScript-5-Design-Patterns-and-Best-Practices/tree/main/chapters/chapter03_Creational_Design_Patterns`.

Creational design patterns

When you declare interfaces and classes in TypeScript, the compiler utilizes this information for type checks and assertions. At runtime, the browser or server evaluates the code and manages these objects throughout the application's life cycle. Sometimes, objects are created at the start of the application. For example, in the previous chapter, you saw the creation of an `Express.js` application object:

```
const app = express();
```

Other times, objects are created dynamically using an object descriptor. For instance, in *Chapter 2*, you learned how to create HTML span elements:

```
const span = document.createElement("span");
```

Both approaches address object creation, focusing on how to instantiate a type of object and store it. Reflecting on this reveals two distinct phases:

- **Creating an object of a specific type or for a specific purpose**: You want to create an object during the application's runtime while maintaining a consistent and user-friendly way of instantiating these objects. Often, you need to control the parameters that are used, the category of objects to create, or how to clone objects based on existing ones.

- **Managing the object life cycle**: You need to control the number of object instances and their storage. Additionally, it's crucial to safely destroy instances when they're no longer required.

By learning about **creational design patterns**, you'll acquire the skills necessary to flexibly create and manage objects of any kind. Further, by separating the object creation process from its concrete implementation, you can achieve a decoupled system. Using interfaces with analogous methods that describe the types of objects you create, rather than how to create them, allows you to supply different implementations at runtime without altering the overall algorithm or conditional logic. Managing object references at runtime can become problematic if micromanaged or allowed to drift, so having a simple abstraction to lease objects on demand is beneficial.

Figure 3.1 shows a simple diagram that illustrates the concept of object creation and object management phases, as well as how creational design patterns fit into this flow:

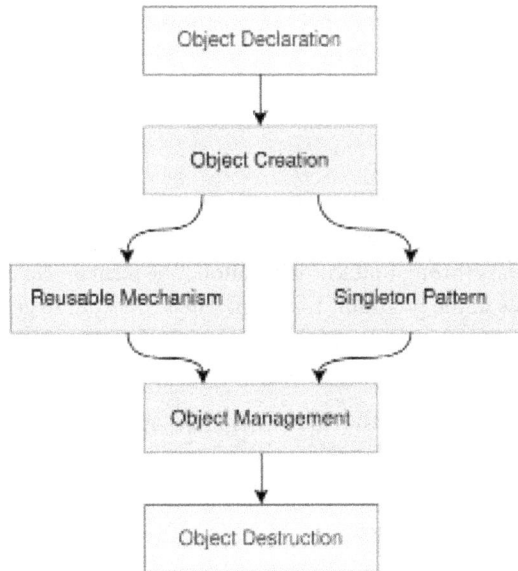

Figure 3.1 – A diagram illustrating the phases of object creation and management, emphasizing the role of creational design patterns in TypeScript applications

The preceding diagram illustrates the key concepts that will be discussed in this chapter:

- **Object declaration (types and interfaces)**: This phase involves defining the structure and behavior of objects through types or interfaces in TypeScript.

- **Object creation**: Once the object's structure has been declared, it's created during runtime as needed. This phase represents the instantiation of objects.

- **Reusable mechanisms**: Creational design patterns provide reusable mechanisms for object creation. These patterns offer standardized approaches for creating objects, enhancing code maintainability and flexibility.

- **The Singleton pattern**: One of the creational patterns that will be discussed in this chapter is the Singleton pattern. It ensures that only one instance of an object exists throughout the application's life cycle.

- **Object management**: After creation, objects need to be managed effectively. This includes tasks such as tracking instances, controlling their life cycle, and ensuring proper destruction when they're no longer needed.

- **Object destruction**: The final phase involves safely disposing of objects when they're no longer required. This helps prevent memory leaks and optimizes resource usage.

Object creation and management are crucial for certain types of applications, so it's important to utilize the right patterns for each use case.

In the subsequent sections, we'll learn more about creational design patterns, starting with the Singleton pattern.

The Singleton pattern

The **Singleton pattern** is a creational design pattern that ensures a class has only one instance and provides a global point of access to it. This pattern intends to control object creation and provide a single, shared instance of a class throughout the application. The term *Singleton* describes something that has only a single presence in the program. You use it when you want to get hold of a single object instead of many different ones for several reasons. Examples of this could be database connection objects or logging services that require a single point of access for all components in an application.

For example, you may want to keep only one instance of a particular class if it's either expensive to create or if it doesn't make sense to keep more than one for the lifetime of the program. Common use cases for the Singleton pattern include managing a database connection pool, managing a logging service, or managing a configuration object.

> **Note**
>
> When we mention a program, we refer to the current runtime environment, which in most cases consists of a single process that has access to all program memory. Due to the **operating system (OS)** and other considerations, when you spawn another process, it will create its own Singleton instances.

Key characteristics

Here are the key characteristics of the Singleton pattern:

- **Global access point**: When you have a Singleton, you essentially have one – and only one – access point to its instance. That's why a Singleton is often referred to as a global instance.

- **Instance caching**: The instance of the Singleton object is cached somewhere so that you can retrieve it on demand. Typically, it's stored within the class instance itself as a static variable, but it can also be stored inside an **Inversion of Control (IoC)** container.

- **Lazy initialization**: The instance isn't created at the time of declaration. Instead, it's created lazily, on the first demand, avoiding expensive initializations when starting applications.

- **Unique instance per class**: The instance is unique per class, meaning different classes have their own Singletons.

The key characteristic of this pattern is that it can be used in a variety of scenarios. Next, we'll explain the common practical uses of the Singleton pattern.

When to use the Singleton pattern

The Singleton pattern is commonly used to manage resources that must be shared across multiple parts of an application while ensuring that only a single instance of that resource exists. It's particularly useful in the following scenarios:

- **Managing global state or configuration**: When you have a configuration object or a state that needs to be accessed globally throughout the application, the Singleton pattern can provide a single point of access and ensure consistency.

- **Controlling access to shared resources**: The Singleton pattern is often used to control access to external resources such as database connections, filesystems, or API endpoints. It helps prevent race conditions, resource leaks, and integrity issues that could arise from multiple uncoordinated objects accessing the same resource.

- **Providing a caching layer**: Singletons can be used to implement a caching mechanism, where a single instance manages the caching logic and provides a centralized access point for cached data.

- **Logging and error handling**: A Singleton instance can be used to manage a global logging or error handling system, ensuring that log entries or error messages are written to a single location or handled by a single component consistently.

- **Thread pools or object pools**: When dealing with resource-intensive objects, a Singleton can be used to create and manage a pool of reusable objects, improving performance and reducing memory overhead.

However, it's important to note that the Singleton pattern should be used judiciously and only when necessary. Overuse or misuse of the pattern can lead to tight coupling, difficulty in testing, and potential thread-safety issues, especially in multi-threaded environments.

In situations where a single instance isn't truly required or loose coupling is preferred, modern alternatives such as dependency injection and IoC containers should be considered instead of the Singleton pattern.

> **Note**
>
> **Loose coupling** is a concept in software design that refers to the practice of keeping components or modules as independent and decoupled from each other as possible. In a loosely coupled system, components have minimal knowledge about the implementation details of other components they interact with. Instead, they rely on well-defined interfaces or abstractions to communicate and interact with each other.

The Singleton pattern is one of the first patterns you can encounter almost anywhere. It's simple and it's prevalent. Let's briefly look at its class diagram before we see some code examples.

UML class diagram

The **UML class diagram for the Singleton pattern** is straightforward. It communicates that a class is a Singleton when it contains at least the following elements:

- A private static variable (for example, `instance`) to hold the single instance of the class

- A private constructor to prevent direct instantiation from outside the class

- A public static method (for example, `getInstance()`) that returns the single instance of the class

Figure 3.2 displays the UML class diagram for the Singleton pattern:

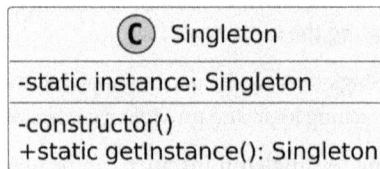

Figure 3.2 – Singleton class diagram

The private static instance variable is used to cache the single instance of the Singleton class. The private constructor ensures that instances can't be created directly from outside the class, enforcing the single instance rule. The public static `getInstance()` method is responsible for creating or returning the cached instance.

While the class diagram shows the component structure of a Singleton, you might need to inspect the implementation part to better understand what needs to be done to use this pattern.

In the next section, we'll explore the implementation details of the Singleton pattern and explain the importance of these elements.

Classic implementation

The classic implementation of the Singleton pattern follows some general steps, as derived from the key observations. We start with a base class declaration:

```
class Singleton {}
```

Then, you need to implement the following steps:

1. **Private constructor**: First, you must prevent new instances from being constructed by making the constructor private:

```
class Singleton {
    // Prevents creation of new instances
    private constructor() {}
}
```

Making the constructor private ensures that the Singleton class can't be instantiated from outside the class, preventing multiple instances from being created accidentally.

2. **Cached instance**: Next, you want to cache the global instance of the Singleton. You can use a static variable for this since the runtime will ensure only one instance per class is reserved:

```
class Singleton {
    // Stores the singleton instance
    private static instance: Singleton;
    // Prevents creation of new instances
    private constructor() {}
}
```

The cached instance is reserved for only one class and is private to prevent it from being retrieved or modified outside the class.

3. **Single access point**: Lastly, you want a single access point to retrieve the cached instance of the Singleton from this class. You can use a static method for this:

singleton.ts

```
class Singleton {
    // Stores the singleton instance
    private static instance: Singleton;
    // Prevents creation of new instances
    private constructor() {}
    // Method to retrieve instance
    static getInstance(): Singleton {
        if (!Singleton.instance) {
            Singleton.instance = new Singleton();
        }
        return Singleton.instance;
    }
}
```

Notice that we create the instance lazily, and not when the class is discovered at runtime. While lazy instantiation helps us avoid unnecessary memory usage and side effects during startup, it can delay the availability of critical resources until they're first requested. This may lead to performance bottlenecks if the initialization process is resource-intensive or if the resource is needed immediately at application startup.

Here's an example of a Singleton class with an actual method:

singleton.ts

```ts
class UserService {
  private static instance: UserService
  private constructor() {}
  static getInstance(): UserService {
    if (!UserService.instance) {
      UserService.instance = new UserService()
    }
    return UserService.instance
  }
  getUsers(): string[] {
    return ["Alex", "John", "Sarah"]
  }
}
// Usage
const userService = UserService.getInstance()
const users = userService.getUsers()
console.log(users) // Output: ['Alex', 'John', 'Sarah']
```

In this example, the `UserService` class is a Singleton that provides a `getUsers` method to retrieve a list of users. The `getInstance` method ensures that only one instance of `UserService` exists throughout the application and that the `getUsers` method can be accessed through this single instance.

While the classic implementation of the Singleton pattern is straightforward, it can be cumbersome to copy-paste the boilerplate code for every class that you want to apply this pattern to. Ideally, you should resort to utilizing the Singleton pattern only when you need to control a single instance of an object per application.

At the end of this section, we'll explain more shortcomings of this pattern and discuss modern alternatives, especially regarding the TypeScript language's features. For now, let's explore some alternative modern variations of this pattern that are more suitable to TypeScript idioms.

Modern implementations

The classical implementation of the Singleton design pattern follows a specific set of steps. however, this is not the only way you can create objects in TypeScript. Additionally, you can leverage some language and environment features to get Singleton behavior for free. Let's explore some alternative implementations and variations together.

Using module resolution Singletons

Instead of creating your own Singleton implementation and having the class cache this instance, you can leverage the module system loading mechanism. Node.js caches modules after they are first loaded, meaning that subsequent calls to `require()` for the same module will return the cached instance rather than re-executing the module code. This caching behavior is managed through the `require.cache` object, which stores references to loaded modules based on their resolved filenames.

In this example, you simply create a class:

```
class ApiServiceSingleton {}
```

Then, you export a default instance variable:

```
export default new ApiServiceSingleton();
```

This leverages the Node.js module system to export a default variable that points to an instance of `ApiServiceSingleton`. This pattern is used often as it's simple to implement. With this default export in place, whenever you import the default object, it will point to the same instance:

```
import apiService from "./ApiServiceSingleton";
// apiService instance here is the same as exported
```

Essentially, this approach delegates the control of the Singleton to the module system. You won't have the opportunity to change this instance unless you mock the whole module.

Additionally, you have to understand the caveats of the Node.js module system as it caches the modules based on the absolute required path of this module. If we import this file and it resolves to the same absolute path, then the module system will use the same cached instance. This might not be the case if your code resides in `node_modules` as a dependency with a conflicting version:

```
// Importing with the first absolute path
import apiService1 from
   "/users/theo/projects/typescript-4-design-patterns
   /chapters/chapter-3/ModuleSingleton.ts";
console.log(apiService1.getData()); // Output: API data
// Importing with a second absolute path (different node_modules)
import apiService2 from
   "/users/theo/projects/typescript-4-design-patterns
```

```
    /node_modules/SomeLibrary/node_modules/singleton
    /ModuleSingleton.ts";
console.log(apiService2.getData()); // Output: API data
```

In this example, both imports point to a different instance since the paths resolve a different location. This distinction underscores the importance of understanding the Node.js module system's caching behavior and how it influences Singleton implementations.

Using decorators for Singleton implementation

TypeScript decorators offer a powerful way to modify the behavior of classes and their members. We can use a decorator to enforce the Singleton pattern. Here's an example:

---

decorator-singleton.ts

```typescript
function Singleton<T extends { new (...args: any[]):
  {} }>(constructor: T) {
  return class extends constructor {
    private static _instance: T | null = null;
    constructor(...args: any[]) {
      super(...args)
      if (!(<any>this.constructor)._instance) {
        ;(<any>this.constructor)._instance = this
      }
      return (<any>this.constructor)._instance
    }
  } as unknown as T & { _instance: T }
}

@Singleton
class DecoratedSingleton {
  constructor() {
    console.log("DecoratedSingleton instance created")
  }}
```

In this case, the Singleton decorator function accepts a constructor function (T) as its parameter. It returns a new class that extends the original constructor (T). Within this extended class, a private static property called _instance is defined to hold the single instance of the class or null initially.

When an instance of the decorated class is instantiated with new DecoratedSingleton(), the overridden constructor checks whether _instance is null. If it is, the constructor assigns the current instance (this) to _instance, ensuring subsequent calls to new DecoratedSingleton() return the same instance. The usage of decorators makes assigning this behavior to objects easier and more trivial, so you should give it a try.

Parametric Singleton

One limitation of the classical Singleton pattern is that you can't pass initialization parameters when you first instantiate the object. This is because allowing different parameters would create different objects, contradicting the Singleton principle.

A solution to this is the **parametric Singleton pattern**, where instead of keeping a single instance, you keep multiple ones cached by a key. You generate a unique key based on the parameters supplied in the getInstance method. When passing two different parameters, it should return a different object; passing the same one will result in the same object being returned:

parametric-singleton.ts

```typescript
export class ParametricSingleton {
  private static instances: Map<string,
    ParametricSingleton> = new Map()
  private constructor(private param: string) {
    this.param = param;
  }
  public getParam(): string {
    return this.param;
  }
  static getInstance(param: string): ParametricSingleton {
    if (!ParametricSingleton.instances.has(param)) {
      ParametricSingleton.instances.set(param,
        new ParametricSingleton(param))
    }
    return ParametricSingleton.instances.get(param)
      as ParametricSingleton
  }
}
const singletonA = ParametricSingleton
  .getInstance('/v1/users');
console.log(singletonA.getParam()); // Output: /v1/users
const singletonB = ParametricSingleton
  .getInstance('/v2/users');
console.log(singletonB.getParam()); // Output: /v2/users
```

In this example, `singletonA` and `singletonB` are different instances of the `ParametricSingleton` class because they were created by calling the `getInstance()` method with different parameter values.

The previous solution works effectively with a few basic parameters, but you'll have to create your own scheme to create unique keys that correspond to each Singleton object. What's important is to keep it simple and have a consistent way of defining Singletons to permit this flexible approach.

Next, we'll explore how to test Singleton objects.

Testing

When you write an implementation of the Singleton pattern, you need to make sure it behaves as intended. You want to write unit tests that capture the expected behavior and are executed every time you run the test suite. This way, you can ensure that if you change the implementation in the future, the tests will verify that nothing has changed unexpectedly.

In the case of the classic Singleton implementation, verifying assumptions is relatively simple. You want to check whether two invocations of the `getInstance` method return the same object instance. Here's an example test that uses Vite:

> **Important note**
> This example uses **Vitest**, a modern testing framework that's designed to work seamlessly with Vite projects. Vite is a fast modern frontend build tool that's an improvement over the `create-react-app` package and offers better customization and performance.

singleton.test.ts

```
import { Singleton } from './singleton.js';
import { test, expect, describe } from 'vitest'
describe('Singleton', () => {
  test('getInstance returns the same instance', () => {
    const instance1 = Singleton.getInstance();
    const instance2 = Singleton.getInstance();
    expect(instance1).toBe(instance2);
  });
});
```

In this test, we import the Singleton class and use Vite's `test` function to define a test case. We call the `getInstance` method twice and store the returned instances in `instance1` and `instance2`. Then, we use Vite's `expect` function to assert that both instances are strictly equal (`===`).

To execute the test cases for the Singleton pattern, you can run the following npm script in the console:

```
$ npm run test -- Singleton
```

This command will run all test cases that include the word `Singleton` in their description or filename. In most cases, having the initial test, which verifies that the same instance is being returned, is the minimum requirement. However, as your implementation becomes more complex, you may need to write additional tests to cover edge cases, state management, and other functionality provided by your Singleton class.

Let's continue this section by considering some of the criticisms of this pattern.

Criticisms

In this section, we'll discuss the criticisms of the Singleton pattern, which often highlight its potential to become an antipattern when misused. Let's explain them briefly:

- **Global instance pollution**: Much criticism is made because Singletons are used as global variables, and many developers dismiss them for good reason. They are problematic to test or mock, and using global variables means ignoring any flexibility you can get from interfaces or other abstractions. This is altogether valid, so if you decide to use Singletons, they need to be treated as global static objects that perform some very specific and tightly interrelated work. Here's an example:

```
// Import singleton from a packageimport
  { Singleton } from './Singleton';
const instance1 = Singleton.getInstance();
instance1.addData('item1');
const instance2 = Singleton.getInstance();
console.log(instance2.data); // Output: ['item1']
```

In this example, the Singleton class acts as a global instance, making it difficult to mock or test in isolation. Any changes to the `data` property or `addData` method will affect the entire application, leading to unexpected behaviors. In the highlighted section, we can see that `instance2` only sees the modified data when its contents may change unexpectedly.

- **Not properly testable**: Other than testing the Singleton principles, if you want to test the behavior of an object, you'll need to overcome some restrictions. For example, let's say you want to mock some side effects such as API calls; you might perform actual API calls when testing, which isn't recommended. This is quite risky unless you adopt an advanced mocking framework such as Jest or Vitest.

- **Hard to get right**: The Singleton pattern is hard to implement, especially if you plan for testability and lazy initialization, and want to use it as a global variable. You need to make sure that the implementation part doesn't cause any more coupling than what's present already. If it manages a state, then this state needs to be properly guarded against concurrent modifications. If multiple parts of the program call an identical method of the Singleton, then they should always work as expected.

Given these points, it's recommended to keep Singletons isolated, usually in the global part of the application, with a set of rules for testing, and utilize them appropriately.

To wrap up our exploration of the Singleton pattern, let's delve into some real-world examples of this pattern in notable libraries and frameworks.

Real-world examples

We'll conclude our exploration of Singletons with some real-world examples. Singletons are widely used in popular open source TypeScript projects and libraries, including the following:

- **TypeScript compiler API**: The TypeScript compiler API, which is used by various tools and IDEs to integrate TypeScript support, utilizes the Singleton pattern for the `CompilerHost` and `CompilerOptions` objects. These objects represent the host environment and compiler options, respectively, and are designed as Singletons to ensure consistent behavior across the application.

- **Angular services**: In Angular, certain services, such as `Router` and `HttpClient`, are implemented as Singletons. This means that there's only one instance of these services throughout the application, ensuring consistent state management and preventing duplication of resources.

- **RxJS schedulers**: RxJS, the popular reactive programming library for JavaScript and TypeScript, uses the Singleton pattern for its schedulers. **Schedulers** are responsible for controlling the execution of observable sequences, and having a single instance of each scheduler type ensures consistent scheduling behavior across the application.

- **Nest.js modules**: In the Nest.js framework for building server-side applications with TypeScript, certain classes, such as the `Module` class, are implemented as Singletons. This ensures consistent behavior and prevents resources from being duplicated across the application.

You'll likely encounter more real-world examples of the Singleton pattern, often implemented with slight variations from what we've explored. However, the fundamental concepts remain consistent. These examples demonstrate the use of the Singleton pattern in popular TypeScript projects and libraries, covering areas such as compilers, frameworks, reactive programming, logging, databases, and server-side development.

While we've touched on some real-world examples here, we'll explore a more comprehensive analysis of design pattern usage in open source projects in the final chapter of this book.

Next, we'll explore the next most important pattern: the Prototype pattern.

The Prototype pattern

The next creational design pattern we'll study is the **Prototype pattern**. This pattern helps abstract the object creation process. Let's elaborate on what we mean.

A *prototype* is a kind of object that takes its initial state and properties from an existing object. The main idea is to avoid having to *manually create an object and assign properties to it from another object.*

Using the Prototype pattern, you can create objects that implement the Prototype interface. Instead of creating a new object by calling the new operator, you follow a different path. You construct objects that adhere to the Prototype interface, which has a single method, clone(). When called, it will create a copy (or clone) of the existing instance of the object and its internal properties. This way, you can avoid duplicating the logic of creating a new object and assigning common functionality.

When to use the Prototype pattern

You should consider using the Prototype pattern when you observe the following criteria:

- **You have a bunch of objects and want to clone them at runtime**: You have already created some objects and hold references to them at runtime, and you want to quickly get identical copies without going back to the factory method and assigning properties again.

- **You want to avoid using the new operator directly**: In this case, you want to call the clone method to get a copy. You want to avoid using the new operator as it may incur additional overhead. Instead, you have a different way to create an object and build it from the ground up at runtime.

- **You want to create objects with complex or hierarchical structures**: The Prototype pattern can be useful when you need to create objects with complex or hierarchical structures as it allows you to clone the entire structure, including nested objects, without manually recreating it.

Let's review the UML class diagram of this pattern to understand its structure. Then, we'll review the most common implementations of it in TypeScript.

UML class diagram

To demonstrate the Prototype pattern in UML, we'll start with the Prototype interface. This interface contains a single method called clone that returns the same interface type:

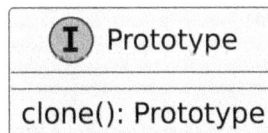

Figure 3.3 – Prototype interface

Then, we need to create concrete classes that implement this interface. This is necessary so that we can call the `clone` method on demand:

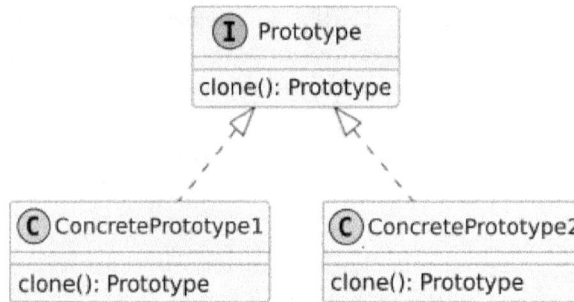

Figure 3.4 – Prototype instances

Now, clients will only use and see the Prototype interfaces instead of the actual objects. This will allow them to call the `clone` method so that they can return a copy of those objects:

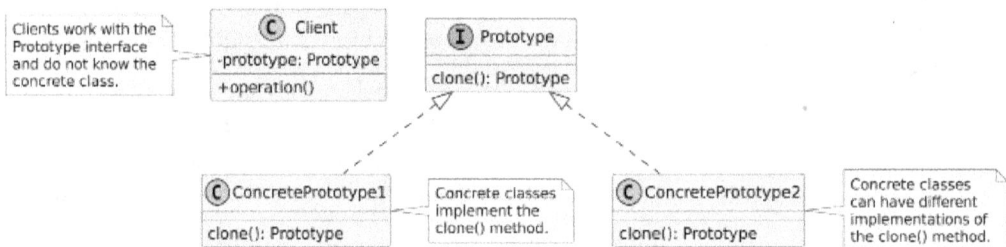

Figure 3.5 – Using Prototype

In the preceding diagram, the `Client` class has a reference to a `Prototype` object, which could be an instance of either `ConcretePrototype1` or `ConcretePrototype2`. The `Client` class can call the `clone` method on the `Prototype` object to create a new instance of the same type.

Next, let's use these diagrams as a reference for implementing the Prototype pattern in TypeScript.

Classic implementation

Following the UML diagram from the previous section, let's implement the Prototype pattern with a different example.

Imagine you're building a game where you need to create different types of animals. You can use the Prototype pattern to clone existing animal objects and create new instances with similar properties.

First, let's define the AnimalPrototype interface:

prototype.ts

```
interface AnimalPrototype {
  clone(): AnimalPrototype
}
```

Next, we'll implement two concrete classes that represent different types of animals, Dog and Cat, that implement the AnimalPrototype interface:

prototype.ts

```
function deepClone<T>(obj: T): T {
  return JSON.parse(JSON.stringify(obj));
}

class Dog implements AnimalPrototype {
  constructor(
    private breed: string,
    private age: number,
  ) {}

  clone(): Dog {
    return deepClone(this);
  }
}
class Cat implements AnimalPrototype {
  constructor(
    private furColor: string,
    private weight: number,
  ) {}

  clone(): Cat {
    return deepClone(this);
  }
}
```

I've highlighted the sections where the clone methods are unique to each type. In this example, the clone methods in each concrete class create a new instance of the same class using Object.create. This allows us to create shallow copies of the objects, preserving their initial state and properties.

When you want to clone these objects at runtime, you can use the AnimalPrototype interface and call the clone method:

prototype.ts

```
let dog: AnimalPrototype = new Dog("Boxer", 3);
let clonedDog: Dog = dog.clone() as Dog;
console.log(clonedDog); // Output: Dog { breed: 'Boxer', age: 3 }
let cat: AnimalPrototype = new Cat("Scott", 4.5);
let clonedCat: Cat = cat.clone() as Cat;
console.log(clonedCat); // Output: Cat { furColor: 'Scott', weight:
4.5 }
```

In this example, we created instances of Dog and Cat and then cloned them using the clone method. The cloned instances have the same properties as the original objects, but they're separate instances in memory.

Sometimes, you may want to ignore certain properties or perform additional operations when cloning objects. In such cases, you can modify the clone method's implementation so that it can handle those specific requirements.

Alternative implementation

A more streamlined implementation of this pattern involves you utilizing external tools such as **Lodash** to deep-clone an object instead of having to use your own deepClone method. This way, you can avoid issues such as circular dependency errors, which you may encounter when you use JSON. stringify(obj).

When you clone a Dog object, you get a completely independent copy with all its nested data structures properly duplicated – meaning changes to the clone won't affect the original object:

prototype.ts

```
import * as clonedeep from 'lodash.clonedeep';

export class Dog implements AnimalPrototype {
// ...
  clone(): Dog {
    return _.cloneDeep(this);
  }
}
```

The lodash.cloneDeep approach is more robust than the JSON.parse(JSON.stringify()) method. While both create deep copies of objects, the JSON method has several limitations: it can't handle circular references or special objects such as Date, RegExp, Map, and Set.

We'll continue by learning how to write unit tests for the Prototype pattern.

Testing

When testing the Prototype pattern, you want to verify that calling the `clone` method returns an object with the correct state and instance type. You'll typically write test cases to ensure that the cloned objects have the expected properties and values and that they are separate instances from the original objects.

Here are the key aspects we'll test:

- Creation of a cloned object from a prototype
- Verification that cloned objects have different references
- Confirmation that cloned objects can be modified independently

We've provided test cases in the `prototype.test.ts` file located in this chapter's source code (see the *Technical requirements* section) for you to review.

To run the test cases, you need to execute the following command:

```
$ npm run test --prototype
```

You should be able to review the test results in the console. By covering these various aspects, the test cases ensure that the Prototype pattern's implementation adheres to the expected behavior, creating separate instances with the correct properties, and allowing cloned objects to be modified independently so that the originals aren't affected.

Now, let's talk about the nuances of using this pattern in practice.

Criticisms

The Prototype pattern can be used to create new objects from already created instances by calling their `clone` method. However, this approach suffers from a few disadvantages:

- **Type casting**: When you rely solely on the `Prototype` interface, you may have to cast the cloned object to the correct instance type as you won't have access to any other fields or methods. This can be cumbersome and error-prone, especially in larger code bases:

prototype-issues.ts

```
interface Prototype {
  clone(): Prototype;
}
class Person implements Prototype {
```

```
  constructor(public name: string,
    public age: number) {}
  clone(): Person {
    const cloned = Object.create(this);
    return cloned;
  }
}
// Usage
const person: Prototype = new Person('John', 30);
const clonedPerson = person.clone();
// Type casting is required to access properties of Person
const clonedPersonName = (clonedPerson as Person)
  .name;
console.log(clonedPersonName); // Output: 'John'
```

In the preceding example, we need to cast `clonedPerson` to the `Person` type to access the name property, which can be error-prone and cumbersome, especially in larger code bases.

- **Repetitive clone method**: Creating a `clone` method for every object that implements the Prototype interface can be repetitive and cumbersome. If you decide to provide a base clone method and then use inheritance for all the subclasses, you contradict the purpose of the Prototype pattern, which is to avoid using inheritance when creating new objects:

prototype-issues.ts

```
class BasePrototype implements Prototype {
  clone(): BasePrototype {
    const cloned = Object.create(this)
    return cloned
  }
}
class Person2 extends BasePrototype {
  constructor(
    public name: string,
    public age: number,
  ) {
    super()
  }
}
class Employee extends BasePrototype {
  constructor(
    public name: string,
    public salary: number,
  ) {
```

```
    super()
  }
}
```

In the preceding example, we introduced a `BasePrototype` class that implements the `clone` method. However, to reuse this implementation, we need to inherit from `BasePrototype` for both the `Person` and `Employee` classes, which contradicts the purpose of the Prototype pattern. Extra work means extra maintenance, which leads to more technical debt.

- **Coupling and inheritance**: Judging from the previous issues, you need to ensure that you evaluate this pattern for specific use cases and certain objects that you want to construct from existing ones. This way, you can minimize any coupling introduced by inheritance or the need for type casting. Pay attention to how you expect those objects to evolve so that you don't introduce extra complexity.

With that out of the way, let's examine how this pattern is used in real projects.

Real-world examples

There are some real-world examples of prototype-like patterns in the wild that follow similar mechanics of the classical implementation.

The most obvious one is the JavaScript prototypical inheritance mode. Both JavaScript and TypeScript use prototypical inheritance under the hood, which is a similar concept to the Prototype pattern. It uses prototypes to inherit features from one object to another.

When you create an object, you have several options. One simple way is through literal object creation:

```
let x = {};
```

This creates a new object, `x`, that inherits from the `Object` prototype. This means it will contain all the properties and methods of the `Object` prototype. Eventually, you will reach the end of the prototype chain:

```
let o = Object.getPrototypeOf(x); // o is Object.prototype
Object.getPrototypeOf(o); // null
```

This prototypical inheritance model allows objects to inherit properties and methods from their prototypes, enabling code reuse and extensibility. It's a fundamental concept in JavaScript and TypeScript that shares similarities with the Prototype pattern in classical object-oriented programming.

It's important to note that while prototypical inheritance and the Prototype pattern share some conceptual similarities, they aren't the same. The Prototype pattern is a design pattern that's used in classical object-oriented programming languages, while prototypical inheritance is a language feature inherent to JavaScript and TypeScript.

In the context of the Prototype pattern, the focus is on creating new objects by cloning existing ones, rather than using class-based inheritance. It provides us with a way to create objects based on a *prototypical instance* and then customize them as needed.

Another way to create an object is by using the `Object.create` method. This technique allows you to specify which prototype object to inherit properties from:

```
let User = {
  type: 'Unauthenticated',
  name: 'Theo'
};


let u = Object.create(User, {name: {value: 'Alex'}});
console.log(u.name); // 'Alex'
console.log(u.type); // 'Unauthenticated'
```

With `Object.create`, you can create objects based on different hierarchies at runtime without using the new operator each time.

Another example is React's `cloneElement` function, which allows you to clone an existing React element and pass new props to it. It follows a more procedural way of cloning objects instead of calling their own clone method.

This function is useful when you need to create new elements based on existing ones while modifying some of their properties:

```
const baseElement = <button className="btn">Click Me
  </button>;
// Use cloneElement to create a new element with additional props
const clonedElement = React.cloneElement(baseElement,
  { className: 'btn btn-primary', onClick: () =>
    alert('Button clicked!') });
```

Here, React's `cloneElement` function clones an existing button element and adds new properties to it, such as a new CSS class and an `onClick` handler. The original `baseElement` is preserved, and a new `clonedElement` function is created with the added properties.

So far, we've learned that the Prototype pattern is a powerful tool in TypeScript, especially for scenarios where creating new instances of a class can be costly in terms of performance. By cloning existing instances, you can produce new objects with the same properties efficiently, thus saving resources and time.

As we move on to the next pattern, where we'll discover the Builder pattern, we'll explore how to construct complex objects step by step. The Builder pattern gives us a way to manage the construction process of objects, providing a flexible and readable approach to object creation.

The Builder pattern

The third design pattern we'll explore is the **Builder pattern**. This pattern simplifies the process of creating complex objects. We'll begin by understanding the Builder pattern and its purpose. Then, we'll provide a typical implementation in TypeScript, along with some modern variants. By the end of this section, you'll have the necessary skills to apply this pattern in real-world applications.

The Builder pattern is a creational design pattern that facilitates the step-by-step construction of objects that can have multiple representations. Often, you create objects that require more than two or three parameters, many of which aren't known in advance but are essential for initializing the object with the correct state.

Complex objects can arise for various reasons. For instance, the business domain might necessitate attaching several attributes to objects for easier access. Alternatively, you might want to develop a conceptual class model, such as `User`, `SearchQuery`, or `HTTPRequest`. Initially, you might have a single implementation of a class, but as the need to create more variations arises, you end up duplicating code.

When to use the Builder pattern

Here are the key criteria for using the Builder pattern:

- **A common set of steps to create an object**: You want to provide an interface with common steps to create an object that isn't tied to any implementation. These steps should be independent and should always return a usable object when requested.

- **Multiple representations**: You can have multiple representations of an object, perhaps as variants or as a subclass type. If you don't anticipate or require multiple representations in the future, this pattern might seem over-engineered and unnecessary.

Considering these criteria, the Builder pattern is advantageous because it allows you to have an interface with common steps for creating complex objects and the flexibility to provide multiple targets on demand.

In applying this pattern, evaluate the key criteria listed here. Additionally, examine the object you're building: does it have more than three parameters? Are many of these parameters optional, with defaults available if none are provided? Are all the steps to create it independent? If the answer to any of these questions is no, you might not need the Builder pattern yet. Assess how additional requirements affect the model fields over time and reconsider whether refactoring using this pattern is necessary. By making informed decisions, you can maximize the benefits of the Builder pattern.

Next, you'll learn how to translate this pattern from UML class diagrams into TypeScript implementations.

UML class diagram

Let's describe the Builder pattern using a UML class diagram while considering the example of building a car:

1. First, we have a `Car` class that represents the product being built. It has several properties representing different configurations:

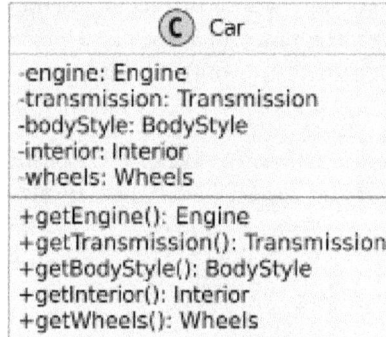

Figure 3.6 – Car product

The `Car` class can have its own getter methods to access the different configurations, but it's important to note that it may contain multiple optional parameters.

2. Next, we need an interface that breaks down the steps of creating the `Car` class into a reusable format:

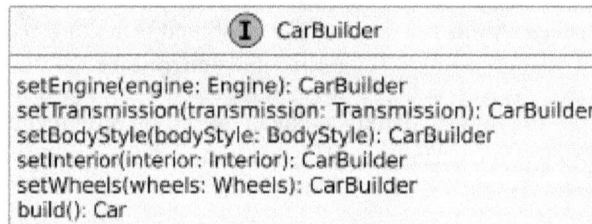

Figure 3.7 – CarBuilder interface

These interface methods describe, in an abstract way, how to create a `Car` product, and should be the same for any type of `Car` configuration.

3. Once we have these two pieces, we'll need a concrete `CarBuilder` implementation to create a specific representation of the `Car` class. *Figure 3.8* depicts all the components of this pattern pieced together:

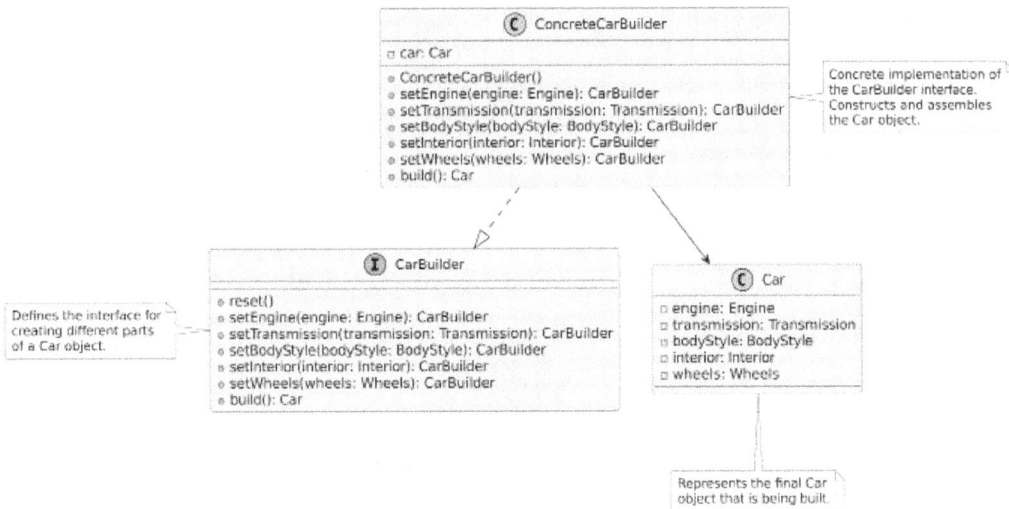

Figure 3.8 – The Builder pattern

The preceding diagram shows the `CarBuilder` interface, the `ConcreteCarBuilder` class that implements this interface, and the `Car` class that's being built using the Builder pattern. Additionally, it includes the `Engine`, `Transmission`, `BodyStyle`, `Interior`, and `Wheels` classes, which are components of the `Car` class.

The `ConcreteCarBuilder` class has a `build()` method to create a new instance of the `Car` class and methods to set the various components of the `Car` object (`setEngine()`, `setTransmission()`, `setBodyStyle()`, `setInterior()`, and `setWheels()`). These methods return the `CarBuilder` interface, allowing for method chaining.

4. The classic *Gang of Four* design patterns book also includes the `Director` object when describing this pattern. You can think of this object as an abstraction on top of the `CarBuilder` interface that acts as a simple interface behind a complex system; it consolidates those steps to produce certain products while utilizing one method instead of chaining multiple ones. You can accept the `CarBuilder` interface as a parameter or as a private variable. We won't show this diagram for now since it's simple to conceptualize.

Now that you've seen the class diagram and looked at an example of building a car using the Builder pattern, let's learn how to implement it in TypeScript.

Classic implementation

The classic implementation of the Builder pattern in TypeScript is straightforward after studying the UML class diagram provided in the previous section. First, we have the `Product` type, which consists of the `Car` class and the individual components of a car:

builder.ts

```
class Engine {}
class Transmission {}class Wheels {}
class Car {
  constructor(
    public engine?: Engine,
    public transmission?: Transmission,
    public bodyStyle?: BodyStyle,

    public wheels?: Wheels,
  ) {}
}
```

Next, we define the `CarBuilder` interface, which specifies the methods for setting different components of `Car` and the build method for creating the final `Car` object:

builder.ts

```
interface CarBuilder {
    setEngine(engine: Engine): CarBuilder;
    setTransmission(transmission: Transmission):
      CarBuilder;
    setBodyStyle(bodyStyle: BodyStyle): CarBuilder;
      setWheels(wheels: Wheels): CarBuilder;
    build(): Car;
}
```

Then, we create a concrete builder class that implements the `CarBuilder` interface. In this example, we have a `ConcreteCarBuilder` class that allows us to build a `Car` object with a specific configuration. I'll only show a couple of the methods of the `ConcreteCarBuilder` class as you can easily infer the rest:

builder.ts

```
class ConcreteCarBuilder implements CarBuilder {
  private car: Car
  constructor() {
```

```
      this.reset()
  }
  reset() {
    this.car = new Car()
  } // rest of setter methods here
}
```

The `ConcreteCarBuilder` class uses a chainable API, which means that each setter method returns the builder instance itself. This allows for method chaining when configuring the `Car` object. Here's an example of how to use the `ConcreteCarBuilder` class:

builder.ts

```
const carBuilder = new ConcreteCarBuilder();
const car = carBuilder
    .setEngine(new Engine())
    .setTransmission(new Transmission())
      .setInterior(new Interior())
    .setWheels(new Wheels())
    .build();
```

In this implementation, the `Car` class represents the final product; the `CarBuilder` interface defines the steps for building the product; and the `ConcreteCarBuilder` class provides a specific implementation of the builder interface.

The main ideas are as follows:

- The `Car` class represents the final product being built

- The `CarBuilder` interface defines the methods for setting different components of `Car` and the build method for creating the final `Car` object

- The `ConcreteCarBuilder` class is a concrete implementation of the `CarBuilder` interface, providing a specific way to build a `Car` object

- The `ConcreteCarBuilder` class uses a chainable API, where each setter method returns the builder instance itself, allowing for method chaining when configuring the `Car` object

- The build method in the `ConcreteCarBuilder` class returns the fully configured `Car` object, resetting the builder to its initial state for future use

This example demonstrates how the Builder pattern can be applied to create complex objects step by step while separating the construction logic from the object itself.

Next, we'll consider some testing strategies for this pattern.

Modern implementations

While the classic implementation of the Builder pattern provides a solid foundation, some modern approaches in TypeScript aim to offer a more reusable and flexible implementation by using language features such as ES6 Proxy objects and `Object.assign`. However, these approaches may introduce additional complexity and trade-offs.

One alternative implementation leverages TypeScript's generics and method chaining to provide a more intuitive and flexible builder implementation. Here's an example:

builder.ts

```typescript
interface Builder<T> {
  build(): T;
}
class GenericBuilder<T> implements Builder<T> {
  private obj: Partial<T> = {};
  public set<K extends keyof T>(key: K, value: T[K]):
    GenericBuilder<T> {
      this.obj[key] = value;
      return this;
    }
  public build(): T {
    return this.obj as T;
  }
}
```

In this implementation, we define a generic `Builder` interface and a `GenericBuilder` class that implements it. The `GenericBuilder` class has a `set` method, which allows you to set the properties of the object being built. The `build` method returns the fully constructed object.

While this modern implementation offers advantages in terms of flexibility and intuitive usage, it's important to consider potential trade-offs and limitations. For example, more complex object construction logic or advanced operations, such as adding or removing items from a list, may not be easily achievable with this approach. As with any design pattern implementation, it's crucial to evaluate the specific requirements of your project and choose the most appropriate approach accordingly.

Now, let's review some of the criticisms of this pattern.

Testing

When testing the Builder pattern, it's essential to do the following:

- Verify that the concrete builders create the desired objects correctly by checking the properties of the built objects.

- Ensure that there are no side effects when interleaving the construction steps and that the order of the steps doesn't create an unintended object.

- Provide specialized test cases for each concrete builder since they may produce unique object representations

We've provided test cases in the `builder.test.ts` file, located in this chapter's source code (see the *Technical requirements* section) for you to review.

To run the test cases, you need to execute the following command:

```
$ npm run test --builder
```

You should be able to review the test results in the console. Now, let's see some of the criticisms of this pattern.

Criticisms

While the Builder pattern provides a flexible approach to constructing complex objects step by step, it also has some potential drawbacks and criticisms that should be considered:

- **Increased complexity**: The Builder pattern introduces additional complexity by separating the construction logic from the actual object being built. This can lead to increased code size and a steeper learning curve, especially for simpler objects or projects with fewer object creation requirements.

- **Proliferation of classes**: To create different representations or configurations of an object, separate concrete Builder classes are required for each variation. This can result in a large number of Builder classes, leading to code duplication and increased maintenance overhead, especially if the variations are minor.

- **Unnecessary overhead**: In some cases, the Builder pattern may introduce unnecessary overhead and indirection for creating relatively simple objects. Depending on the specific use case, alternative approaches, such as constructors with optional parameters or object literals, might be more straightforward and efficient.

- **Lack of flexibility**: While the Builder pattern allows for step-by-step construction, it may lack flexibility in certain scenarios where the construction order or steps need to be dynamic or dependent on runtime conditions. In such cases, alternative patterns such as the Abstract Factory or Prototype patterns might be more suitable.

- **Violation of the Open-Closed Principle**: If new construction steps or object variations are required, the Builder pattern may violate the Open-Closed Principle (this principle will be explained in detail in *Chapter 9*) as existing Builder classes need to be modified or new ones created. This can lead to increased maintenance efforts and potential code fragility.

- **Potential for side effects**: As mentioned previously, it's essential to avoid side effects when creating objects using the Builder pattern. All method calls should perform mutable or immutable changes atomically to ensure consistent and predictable object construction.

- **Overengineering**: In some cases, the Builder pattern may be overengineered for simple use cases, leading to unnecessary complexity and reduced code readability. It's important to assess the trade-offs between the pattern's benefits and the added complexity it introduces.

To overcome these issues, consider the following suggestions:

- **Adopt the use of generics**: Use TypeScript generics to create reusable builder base classes so that you can alleviate the issues of having to write redundant builder code for each class

- **Adopt composition over inheritance**: By creating a single flexible builder and using configuration objects to define building behavior, you can minimize the number of builder classes

- **Include validation steps**: Add validation hooks before and after each building step so that you minimize side effects

While the Builder pattern can be a powerful tool for constructing complex objects flexibly and maintainably, it's crucial to carefully consider these potential criticisms and weigh them against the specific requirements of your project. In some cases, simpler approaches or alternative design patterns may be more appropriate, depending on the complexity of the object.

Real-world examples

To better understand the practical applications of the Builder pattern, let's explore a real-world example from the popular JavaScript utility library, Lodash.

Lodash provides a chainable API that allows you to perform a series of operations on arrays, objects, and other data structures. This chainable API follows the principles of the Builder pattern by allowing you to construct complex data transformations step by step.

One of the key features of Lodash's chainable API is the `chain` method. This method returns a wrapped value that can be used to chain multiple operations together. Here's an example:

```
const users = [
  { 'user': 'alex', 'age': 20 },
  { 'user': 'theo', 'age': 40 },
  { 'user': 'mike', 'age': 15 }
];
const youngestUser = _.chain(users)
  .sortBy('age')
  .head()
  .value();
// Output: { 'user': 'mike', 'age': 15 }
```

In this example, we start by calling `_.chain` with an array of user objects. Then, we chain multiple operations:

- `sortBy('age')`: Sorts the array of user objects by their age property in ascending order.

- `head()`: Retrieves the first element of the sorted array, which will be the youngest user.

- `value()`: Unwraps the wrapped value and returns the final result. This is like the `build` method of the classical implementation.

The chain method acts as a builder, allowing you to construct complex data transformations by chaining multiple operations together. Each operation returns a new wrapped value, representing the current state of the transformation, until the final `value()` method is called to retrieve the result.

Now that we've explored the most applicable and practical concepts of the Builder pattern, let's examine the next important pattern: the Factory Method pattern.

The Factory Method pattern

The **Factory Method pattern** is a creational design pattern that provides an interface for creating objects in a super-class while allowing sub-classes to alter the type of objects that will be created. It promotes loose coupling by eliminating the need to bind application-specific code to the concrete classes of objects it requires.

The Factory Method pattern consists of several components:

- **Product interface**: It defines the interface of objects that the Factory Method pattern will create.

- **Concrete products**: They implement the Product interface.

- **Factory interface**: This declares the method(s) for creating products.

- **Concrete factories**: They implement the Factory interface and create specific concrete products.

By using the Factory Method pattern, you can create objects without specifying their concrete classes, allowing the system to be more flexible and easier to extend. The decision of which specific object to create is deferred to the Factory, which promotes loose coupling and better code organization.

When to use the Factory Method pattern

The Factory Method pattern is particularly useful in the following scenarios:

- **Object creation logic is complex**: When the process of creating an object involves several steps or requires complex logic, encapsulating this logic in a Factory can improve code organization and maintainability.

- **A class can't anticipate the types of objects it needs to create**: If a class needs to create objects of different types, but the specific types aren't known until runtime, a Factory can handle the object creation process based on the current context.

- **You want to decouple object creation from object usage**: By separating the object creation logic from the code that uses the objects, the Factory Method pattern promotes loose coupling, making the code more flexible and easier to maintain.

- **You need to manage the life cycle of objects**: Factories can be used to manage the creation, initialization, and destruction of objects, providing a centralized control point for object life cycle management.

Next, we'll learn how to depict this pattern using a UML class diagram.

UML class diagram

Representing the Factory Method pattern as a class diagram is simple:

1. To begin with, we have the `Vehicle` interface, which describes the public methods of the concrete product:

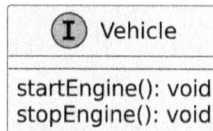

Figure 3.9 – Factory Product interface

In this example, the `Vehicle` interface represents the Product interface, which defines the `startEngine()` and `stopEngine()` methods that all vehicle implementations should have.

2. Next, we have one or more concrete implementations of the Product interface that we want to specialize:

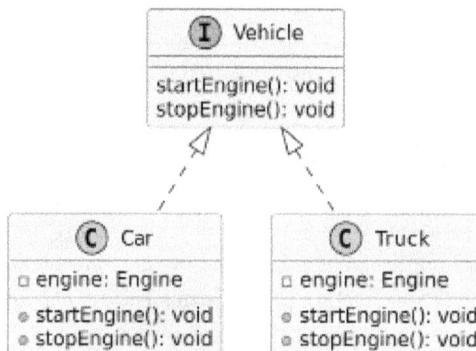

Figure 3.10 – Factory Product implementations

Here, the `Car` and `Truck` classes are concrete implementations of the `Vehicle` interface and represent different types of vehicles.

3. On the other side, we have a pair of Factory interfaces and concrete factory objects that represent the creation of new Product instances:

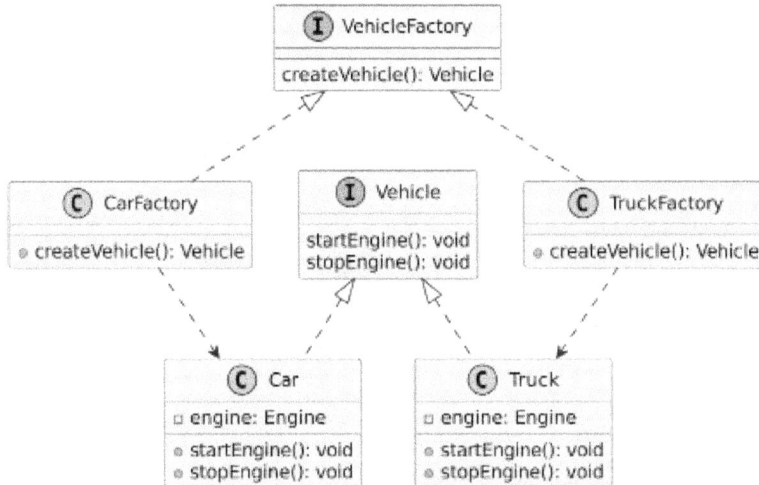

Figure 3.11 – The Factory Method pattern

Let's take a closer look at what's going on:

- The `VehicleFactory` interface declares the `createVehicle()` method for creating vehicles

- The `CarFactory` and `TruckFactory` classes implement the `VehicleFactory` interface and create instances of `Car` and `Truck`, respectively

By following this structure, you can create objects of different types (`Car` and `Truck`) without specifying their concrete classes directly. Instead, you rely on the concrete factory classes (`CarFactory` and `TruckFactory`) to handle the object creation process based on the specific requirements, promoting loose coupling and flexibility.

Next, let's learn how to implement this diagram using TypeScript.

Classic implementation

It's relatively easy to implement the Factory Method pattern in TypeScript. Let's see a reference implementation that uses the `Vehicle` example from the class diagram. First, you have the interface for the product:

factory-method.ts

```
interface Vehicle {
  startEngine(): void
  stopEngine(): void
}
```

You want to have two kinds of `Vehicle`: `Car` and `Truck`. Let's implement a class for each:

factory-method.ts

```
class Car implements Vehicle {
  startEngine(): void {
    console.log("Starting car engine...")
  }
  stopEngine(): void {
    console.log("Stopping car engine...")
  }
}
class Truck implements Vehicle {
  startEngine(): void {
    console.log("Starting truck engine...")
  }
  stopEngine(): void {
    console.log("Stopping truck engine...")
  }
}
```

This is what you usually describe as the models or products of an application. With this pattern, you want to try to avoid creating them using the `new` operator directly. Instead, you should define a factory for each of the vehicles:

factory-method.ts

```
interface VehicleFactory {
  createVehicle(): Vehicle;
}
class CarFactory implements VehicleFactory {
```

```
  createVehicle(): Vehicle {
    return new Car();
  }
}
class TruckFactory implements VehicleFactory {
  createVehicle(): Vehicle {
    return new Truck();
  }
}
```

When using the Factory Method pattern, you'll only instantiate the factories once in the lifetime of the program, after which you can pass them on every time you require a `VehicleFactory` interface. This way, you keep the logic of object creation in the same place without changing it.

The Factory Method pattern is particularly well-suited for integration with **dependency injection (DI)** frameworks such as Inversify.js and Nest.js. In these frameworks, factories can be registered as services, enabling the DI container to manage their life cycle and dependencies. For instance, when a Factory is injected into a class, it can create instances of various objects without the class needing to know how those objects are constructed:

factory-method.ts

```
const carFactory = new CarFactory();
const truckFactory = new TruckFactory();
const factories: VehicleFactory[] = [carFactory,
  truckFactory, carFactory];
factories.forEach((factory: VehicleFactory) => {
  const vehicle = factory.createVehicle();
  vehicle.startEngine();
  vehicle.stopEngine();
});
// Output:
// Starting car engine...
// Starting truck engine...
// Starting car engine...
```

Here, we created instances of `CarFactory` and `TruckFactory`. Then, we created an array of `VehicleFactory` instances, which allowed us to create different types of vehicles using the same factory interface. We iterated over the factories, created vehicles using the `createVehicle` method, and performed operations on them (`startEngine` and `stopEngine`).

The client code works with the `Vehicle` interface and the `VehicleFactory` interface, promoting loose coupling and allowing for easy extension by introducing new vehicle types or factories.

Let's see what alternative implementations of this pattern exist.

Alternative implementation

Instead of creating separate factories for each product, you can use a type parameter and a `switch` statement or a map to determine which object to instantiate.

Here's an example implementation that uses a `switch` statement:

---

factory-method.ts

```
enum VehicleType {
  CAR,
  TRUCK,
}
class VehicleCreator {
  create(vehicleType: VehicleType): Vehicle {
    switch (vehicleType) {
      case VehicleType.CAR:
        return new Car()
      case VehicleType.TRUCK:
        return new Truck()
      default:
        throw new Error("Invalid vehicle type")
    }
  }
}
```

This implementation may work well during development, but it can become a burden as you add more object types as you'll have to constantly update the `VehicleType` enum and the switch cases.

When your application grows, it's recommended to refactor this code and implement the Factory Method pattern using separate factory interfaces and classes.

Let's see what kinds of tests you can perform in the Factory Method pattern.

Testing

When testing factories, you want to verify that the `create` method produces the correct product types. You can use the `toBeInstanceOf` test method in Vitest to compare the runtime instance of the object with the expected instance type.

We've provided test cases in the `factory-method.test.ts` file located in this chapter's source code (see the *Technical requirements* section) for you to review.

To run the test cases, you need to execute the following command:

```
$ npm run test --factory-method
```

You should be able to review the test results in the console.

Next, we'll consider some of the criticisms of the Factory Method pattern.

Criticisms

While the Factory Method pattern is widely used, it's still not invulnerable to some key criticisms:

- **More boilerplate code**: Using the Factory Method pattern can lead to boilerplate code. You'll find yourself writing repetitive code to implement the pattern, which can detract from the overall readability and maintainability of the system.

- **Misuse**: The tendency to apply the Factory Method pattern indiscriminately, even in situations where it may not be necessary, can lead to over-engineering and a code base that's harder to navigate and maintain.

- **Increased complexity**: The Factory Method pattern can introduce additional complexity into the code base. You'll often need to create separate factory classes or methods for each type of object, which can lead to a larger and more complicated code structure.

To overcome these limitations, please consider the following suggestions:

- **Adopt decorator syntax**: Use TypeScript decorators to automate factory registration. That way, you can reduce the boilerplate code for the factory by using a base class that handles common operations.

- **Consider alternative patterns, such as the Builder pattern**: Use simpler alternatives such as the Builder pattern, or do direct construction for basic objects. Sometimes, this will make the code simpler and easier to understand without the need to introduce additional abstractions.

Next, we'll consider some real-world use cases of the Factory Method pattern.

Real-world examples

The Factory Method pattern is widely used in various libraries, frameworks, and applications. Here are some real-world examples:

- **Document Object Model (DOM) API**: As mentioned previously in this book, the DOM API is a great example of the Factory Method pattern. It provides methods such as `createElement`, `createTextNode`, and `createEvent` for creating different types of DOM elements and objects.

- **JavaScript UI libraries**: Many JavaScript UI libraries, such as React and Vue, use the Factory Method pattern to create instances of components. For example, React's `createElement` function is a factory method that creates component instances based on the provided component type and props. Similarly, Angular employs a component factory that allows for the dynamic creation of components at runtime. The Angular framework provides the `ComponentFactory` interface, which enables developers to instantiate components based on their metadata.

- **Game development**: In game development, the Factory Method pattern is commonly used to create different types of game objects, such as enemies, power-ups, or level elements. This allows for easy extensibility and customization of game objects without the need to modify the core game logic.

Overall, the Factory Method pattern is a valuable tool in any software developer's toolkit, enabling the creation of flexible and extensible object-oriented systems.

Next, we'll examine the final creation pattern: the Abstract Factory pattern.

The Abstract Factory pattern

The **Abstract Factory pattern** is a creational design pattern that provides an interface for creating families of related or dependent objects without the need to specify their concrete classes. It acts as a *factory of factories*, allowing you to create a common abstraction for creating objects from different factories.

The main idea behind the Abstract Factory pattern is to decouple the client code from the specific implementation details of the objects it needs to create. Instead of creating objects directly, the client code interacts with abstract factories, which are responsible for creating and returning instances of the desired objects.

Using this pattern, you retain the flexibility to define multiple concrete implementations of factories without the need to alter the process of using them. The client code remains agnostic to the specific factories it's working with as it interacts with the abstract factory interface. This makes it easier to change or introduce new factories at runtime, promoting extensibility and maintainability.

Let's consider the reasons to use this pattern in practice.

When to use the Abstract Factory pattern

The Abstract Factory pattern is particularly useful in scenarios where you need to create families of related or dependent objects, and you want to decouple the creation process from the client code. Here are the key criteria and observations that can help you determine when to apply this pattern:

- **A need for families of related objects**: You have a requirement to create multiple objects that are related or dependent on each other. These objects may be part of a larger composition or represent different aspects of a complex system. For example, in a user interface toolkit, you may need to create families of related UI components such as buttons, menus, and scrollbars, where each family has a different representation or implementation based on the target platform or style.

- **Clients interact with factories, not concrete classes**: The clients that need to create objects should interact with abstract factories, rather than directly instantiating concrete classes. This promotes loose coupling and allows you to change the concrete factories that are used at runtime without the need to modify the client code.

- **Abstraction over the object creation process**: The Abstract Factory pattern provides an abstraction over the object creation process. Clients interact with the Abstract Factory interface, which declares methods for creating different types of objects. The clients don't need to know the details of how these objects are created or the specific concrete factories involved.

- **Runtime factory interchange**: You want to enable the client to interchange different concrete factories at runtime, producing different representations or hierarchies of objects. This flexibility is particularly useful when you need to adapt to changing requirements, support multiple configurations, or provide extensibility for introducing new object families.

- **Consistent object families**: The created objects should be part of a consistent family, meaning they should work together and be compatible with each other. The Abstract Factory pattern ensures that objects created by the same concrete Factory are compatible and can be used together coherently.

The fundamental reason to use the Abstract Factory pattern is when you need a runtime client that can interchange different Factory objects at runtime, thus producing different representations or hierarchies of objects. The client only needs to know the operations available from the Abstract Factory interface; once the objects are constructed, they can be passed along to other services that know how to handle them accordingly.

Let's see how this pattern translates to UML.

UML class diagram

Let's start by describing the Abstract Factory pattern by going through a UML class diagram step by step.

First, you'll want to describe the interface of the Factory that creates the hierarchy of objects:

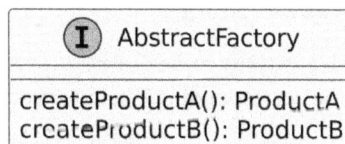

Figure 3.12 – The AbstractFactory interface

This part defines the `AbstractFactory` interface, which declares the methods for creating different types of products (`ProductA` and `ProductB`).

Each method will create a different product type but ideally, both product types should have some sort of relationship or hierarchical commonality. The products must also conform to an interface declaration:

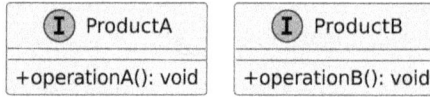

Figure 3.13 – The Product interface

This covers the abstraction part of this pattern. Now, if you want to provide concrete implementations for AbstractFactory, you'll need to implement all of those interfaces. Here's how they will look:

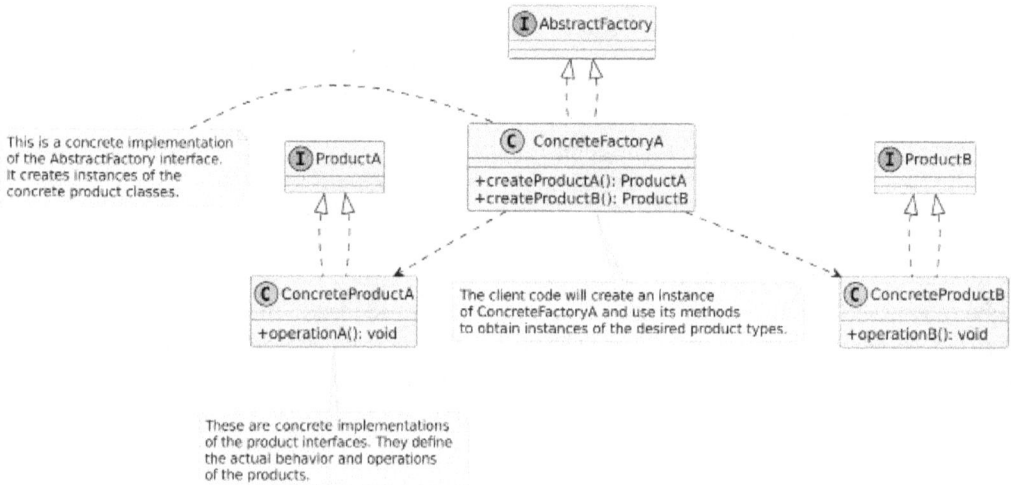

Figure 3.14 – AbstractFactory implementation

This part shows a concrete implementation of the AbstractFactory interface called ConcreteFactoryA. It also includes concrete implementations of the product interfaces (ConcreteProductA and ConcreteProductB).

The ConcreteFactoryA class implements the createProductA() and createProductB() methods, which return instances of the corresponding concrete product classes.

The client code will create an instance of ConcreteFactoryA and use its methods to obtain instances of the desired product types.

Next, we'll learn how to implement this pattern in TypeScript.

Classic implementation

You can implement the Abstract Factory pattern based on the UML class representation of this pattern that was shown in the previous section.

Let's consider an example where we're creating different types of vehicles, such as cars and motorcycles, for different manufacturing companies. First, we must define an interface for the Abstract Factory pattern that declares the methods for creating different types of vehicles:

abstract-factory-ts

```
interface VehicleFactory {
   createCar(): Car
   createMotorcycle(): Motorcycle
}
```

Next, we define interfaces for the vehicle products:

abstract-factory.ts

```
interface Car {
   drive(): void
}
interface Motorcycle {
   ride(): void
}
```

Then, we implement concrete factories for each manufacturing company, along with their respective concrete vehicle implementations. The following code shows how to define `CompanyAFactory`, `CompanyACar`, and `CompanyAMotorcycle`:

abstract-factory.ts

```
class CompanyAFactory implements VehicleFactory {
   createCar(): Car {
     return new CompanyACar()
   }
   createMotorcycle(): Motorcycle {
     return new CompanyAMotorcycle()
   }
}
class CompanyACar implements Car {
   drive(): void {
     console.log("Driving a Company A car")
```

```
    }
  }
  class CompanyAMotorcycle implements Motorcycle {
    ride(): void {
      console.log("Riding a Company A motorcycle")
    }
  }
  // rest of Abstract Factory implementations here.
```

Each company has its own Factory class (`CompanyAFactory` and `CompanyBFactory`) that implements the `VehicleFactory` interface. These factories are responsible for creating specific types of vehicles (cars and motorcycles) for their respective companies. The concrete product classes (`CompanyACar`, `CompanyAMotorcycle`, `CompanyBCar`, and `CompanyBMotorcycle`) implement the `Car` and `Motorcycle` interfaces, providing company-specific implementations of the `drive()` and `ride()` methods.

The client code can then use the Abstract Factory pattern to create instances of the desired vehicles without having to be coupled to their specific implementations:

abstract-factory.ts

```typescript
function produceVehicles(factory: VehicleFactory) {
  const car = factory.createCar()
  const motorcycle = factory.createMotorcycle()
  car.drive()
  motorcycle.ride()
}
produceVehicles(new CompanyAFactory())
// Output:
// Driving a Company A car
// Riding a Company A motorcycle
produceVehicles(new CompanyBFactory())
// Output:
// Driving a Company B car
// Riding a Company B motorcycle
```

In this implementation, the `VehicleFactory` interface defines the methods for creating `Car` and `Motorcycle` objects. The concrete factories, `CompanyAFactory` and `CompanyBFactory`, implement these methods and create instances of their respective concrete vehicle classes (`CompanyACar`, `CompanyAMotorcycle`, `CompanyBCar`, and `CompanyBMotorcycle`).

The client code interacts with the Abstract Factory interface (`VehicleFactory`) and can create instances of the desired vehicles by passing the appropriate concrete factory to the `produceVehicles` function. This allows for easy extension as we can introduce new concrete factories for different manufacturing companies without having to modify the client code.

Let's move on to testing.

Testing

When you want to test the Abstract Factory pattern, you need to verify that the concrete implementations of the Abstract Factory pattern produce objects of the correct types.

We've provided test cases in the `abstract-factory.test.ts` file located in this chapter's source code (see the *Technical requirements* section) for you to review.

To run the test cases, you need to execute the following command:

```
$ npm run test --abstract-factory
```

You should be able to review the test results in the console. Now, let's consider some of the criticisms of this pattern.

Criticisms

While the Abstract Factory pattern provides flexibility and extensibility in creating families of related objects, it also has some potential drawbacks and criticisms:

- **Increased complexity and upfront work**: Employing this pattern, as with similar design patterns, may result in unnecessary complexity and extra work when writing the code initially. The introduction of additional interfaces, abstract classes, and concrete implementations can make the code base more difficult to understand, especially for smaller projects or systems with fewer object families.

- **Premature abstraction**: It's not always obvious when you should start defining objects as part of a hierarchy and try to make an Abstract Factory over it without undergoing several iterations. There's a risk of introducing premature abstraction, which can lead to unnecessary complexity and make the code harder to understand and maintain.

- **Refactoring overhead**: Most likely, you will refactor your code so that it adheres to the Abstract Factory pattern at a later stage of the development process, rather than starting with it from the beginning. This refactoring process can be time-consuming and error-prone, especially in larger code bases with existing dependencies.

It's important to carefully evaluate the trade-offs and ensure that the benefits of using the Abstract Factory pattern outweigh the potential drawbacks in your specific context. In some cases, simpler approaches such as Factory methods or constructors may be more appropriate, especially for smaller projects or systems with fewer object families.

Additionally, proper documentation, code organization, and adherence to best practices can help mitigate some of the criticisms and make the Abstract Factory pattern more maintainable and easier to work with in larger code bases.

Real-world examples

In terms of real-world examples, there are some specific frameworks and libraries that utilize this pattern:

- **Nest.js Adapters**: **Nest.js**, a progressive Node.js framework, uses the Abstract Factory pattern in its Adapters module. Don't be confused by the name *Adapter* since the actual implementation creates different types of products. Here, `AbstractWsAdapter` serves as the Abstract Factory, providing methods to create different types of WebSocket adapters (for example, **IoAdapter** and **SocketIoAdapter**) based on the selected WebSocket library.

- **Inversify.js**: **Inversify** is a powerful and lightweight IoC container for JavaScript and TypeScript applications. Inversify.js uses the Abstract Factory pattern to manage dependencies and create instances of services. The following snippet showcases the usage of this pattern:

```
import 'reflect-metadata';
import { container } from './inversify.config';
import { Warrior } from './interfaces';
const warrior = container.get<Warrior>('Warrior');
console.log(warrior.fight()); // Outputs: Ninja fight!
console.log(warrior.sneak()); // Outputs: Ninja sneak!
```

By defining interfaces for services (for example, `Warrior`) and providing concrete implementations (for example, `Ninja`), Inversify.js leverages decorators such as `@injectable` to mark classes as injectable. The `container` class is then configured to bind interfaces to their implementations using the `bind` method, which allows for dependency injection.

These examples demonstrate how the Abstract Factory pattern is used in various TypeScript projects to create families of related objects, promoting flexibility, extensibility, and loose coupling between the client code and the concrete object implementations.

That concludes our extensive exploration of creational design patterns. Let's wrap this up before we continue explaining various structural design patterns.

Summary

In this chapter, we started by discovering the details of the Singleton pattern and how it aids us in controlling unique instances of objects. Next, we learned how the Prototype pattern allows us to specify what kinds of objects we want to create and clone them using those kinds as a base. Then, we learned how the Builder pattern allows us to construct complex objects. Lastly, we learned that by using the Factory and Abstract Factory patterns, we can separate the creation process of objects from their representation and can also describe factories of factories.

In the next chapter, you'll continue learning more about structural design patterns, which are patterns that ease the process of design by identifying a simple way to realize relationships between entities.

Q&A

Feel free to review the following questions and their corresponding answers to address any concerns or gain additional insights.

1. What's the primary purpose of the Singleton pattern, and when should it be used?

    Answer: The Singleton pattern is used when you want to have a single instance of a class for the whole program only. It ensures that whenever a client uses a Singleton, it will be the same instance as every other reference in the program.

2. Explain the difference between the Factory Method pattern and the Abstract Factory pattern.

    Answer: The Factory Method pattern deals with creating objects of a single type, while the Abstract Factory pattern deals with creating families of related objects. Thus, the Factory Method pattern is a specialization of the Abstract Factory pattern.

3. When would you use the Builder pattern, and what are its advantages?

    Answer: You should use the Builder pattern when you need to create complex objects that have many optional parameters or when the construction process involves multiple steps. Its advantages include better code readability, flexibility in constructing objects, and the ability to reuse the same construction code for different representations of the object.

4. Explain the intent and use case of the Prototype pattern.

    Answer: The Prototype pattern should be used when creating an instance of a class is expensive or complicated, and you want to clone an existing instance instead of creating a new one from scratch. It's useful when you need to create multiple instances of an object with a similar state, or when the object creation process is complex and time-consuming.

5. How does the Abstract Factory pattern help in creating families of related objects?

    Answer: The Abstract Factory pattern provides an interface for creating families of related or dependent objects without the need to specify their concrete classes. It helps in creating a system of objects that follow a specific theme or pattern, making it easier to swap entire families of objects with others.

6. What are the advantages of using the Factory Method pattern over direct object instantiation?

    Answer: Using the Factory Method pattern over direct object instantiation provides better code organization, encapsulation, and flexibility. It allows for easier object creation and extension, and it also allows us to introduce new object types without the need to modify existing code.

Further reading

The Builder pattern, as well as all creational patterns, are described in the classic *Gang of Four* book *Design Patterns: Elements of Reusable Object-Oriented Software*, by Gamma Erich, Helm Richard, Johnson Ralph, Vlissides John, and Addison-Wesley, from Professional Publishing. It's available at https://archive.org/details/designpatternsel00gamm/page/96/mode/2up.

4

Structural Design Patterns

Structural design patterns are powerful tools in a developer's arsenal that offer elegant solutions for organizing objects and classes in larger, more complex systems. These patterns focus on how objects are composed to form larger structures while keeping these structures flexible and efficient. In TypeScript 5, with its enhanced type system and language features, implementing these patterns becomes even more robust and type-safe.

This chapter delves deep into structural design patterns, exploring how they can be leveraged to create more maintainable, scalable, and adaptable TypeScript applications. We'll examine each pattern in detail, providing both theoretical insights and practical, TypeScript-specific implementations.

In this chapter, we'll cover the following main topics:

- The core principles of structural design patterns
- The Adapter pattern
- The Decorator pattern
- The Façade pattern
- The Composite pattern
- The Proxy pattern
- The Bridge pattern
- The Flyweight pattern

By the end of this chapter, you'll have a comprehensive understanding of structural design patterns and the skills to apply them effectively in your TypeScript projects. You'll also be able to identify scenarios where these patterns can solve common design problems, leading to more elegant and maintainable code.

Technical requirements

The code bundle for this chapter is available on GitHub at: `https://github.com/PacktPublishing/TypeScript-5-Design-Patterns-and-Best-Practices/tree/main/chapters/chapter04_Structural_Design_Patterns`.

Understanding structural design patterns

Structural design patterns offer a distinct approach compared to creational patterns. They focus on organizing objects and classes into larger structures while maintaining flexibility and extensibility. These patterns are particularly valuable in TypeScript 5 projects, where strong typing and advanced language features can enhance their implementation.

Understanding structural design patterns is important in team development because they provide a shared framework for organizing code. For instance, consider a logging system where different developers implement logging in inconsistent ways – some might log to the console, while others might write to files or databases. This inconsistency can lead to a messy, unscalable code base that's difficult to manage and debug.

By employing structural design patterns, such as the Adapter or Composite patterns, teams can standardize how logging is handled across the application. For example, using a common `Logger` class that adheres to a specific interface allows developers to swap out implementations (such as logging to different outputs) without having to change the core logic of the application.

Key characteristics and use cases

Structural patterns excel in several key scenarios. First, they're invaluable when you're composing objects into larger structures. This becomes crucial when you need to add new functionality to existing objects without significantly altering their core structure. Such situations often arise when adapting to changing requirements or improving code organization. These patterns allow for easy extension of objects while minimizing code duplication and overhead, a critical factor in maintaining clean and efficient code bases.

Another significant use case for structural patterns is in simplifying complex object relationships. These patterns excel at managing relationships between different objects efficiently. In object-oriented design, we primarily encounter two types of object relationships. The first is the **has-a relationship**, where one object contains a reference to another. The second is the **is-a relationship**, which involves inheritance or type-based relationships. Structural patterns aim to make these relationships more manageable, extensible, and replaceable, which is essential for creating flexible and maintainable software systems.

Furthermore, structural patterns play a crucial role in enhancing code flexibility and maintainability. They facilitate easier management of dependencies between components, which is particularly important in large-scale applications. By promoting loose coupling, these patterns make systems more adaptable to change. This adaptability is crucial in today's fast-paced development environments, where requirements can shift rapidly. Additionally, well-implemented structural patterns improve code readability, making it easier for developers to understand and maintain the code base over time.

For all these cases, you'll want to consider applying structural design patterns to overcome specific issues related to the structure and relationship type of your entities to accommodate future changes.

Now that you understand the basics of structural patterns, we can start exploring these patterns in detail one by one, starting with the Adapter pattern.

The Adapter pattern

The **Adapter pattern** is a powerful structural design pattern that allows us to integrate incompatible interfaces without altering their core implementation. This pattern is particularly useful in TypeScript 5 projects, where type safety and interface consistency are paramount.

> **Note**
>
> When using the Adapter pattern, it's essential to be cautious with the use of the unknown and any types in TypeScript when adapting objects or services. Enabling TypeScript's strict mode helps mitigate these risks by enforcing stricter type checks and ensuring that type casting is done correctly.

Understanding the Adapter pattern

At its core, the Adapter pattern acts as a bridge between two incompatible interfaces. It wraps an existing object within a new structure or interface, allowing it to be used by clients that expect a different interface. This wrapping mechanism expands the usability of objects across diverse interfaces, promoting code reuse and flexibility.

Think of the Adapter pattern as a universal power adapter you might use when traveling. Just as this device allows you to plug your electronics into different types of sockets worldwide, the Adapter pattern allows your code to work with diverse, seemingly incompatible interfaces.

When to use the Adapter pattern

The Adapter pattern proves invaluable in several scenarios:

- **Interface mismatch resolution**: When you have a client expecting an interface of type A, but you possess an object implementing type B, the Adapter pattern comes to the rescue. It's especially useful when you can't or don't want to modify the existing object to implement interface A directly.

- **Legacy code integration**: In scenarios where you're working with legacy systems or third-party libraries, the Adapter pattern allows you to integrate these components with your modern code base without extensive modifications.

- **Enhancing interoperability**: The pattern works well at making incompatible classes work together seamlessly. It's particularly useful when you want to use two classes together through their interfaces, but they're inherently incompatible.

- **Maintaining type safety**: In TypeScript 5, where type safety is crucial, the Adapter pattern allows you to maintain strong typing while bridging incompatible interfaces.

By using this pattern, you get many benefits as you can make incompatible things work together by using wrappers without breaking existing functionality. Sooner or later, you'll find this pattern handy in plenty of scenarios. We'll continue by showcasing the UML class diagram of this pattern.

UML class diagram

The Adapter pattern is a powerful tool for resolving interface incompatibilities without the need to modify existing code. It's particularly useful in TypeScript projects where you need to integrate components with different interfaces.

Let's consider a scenario where we have a `Client` class that expects to work with an `ApiServiceV1` interface, but we want to use a new `ApiClientV2` class that has a different interface. Here's a UML diagram illustrating this situation:

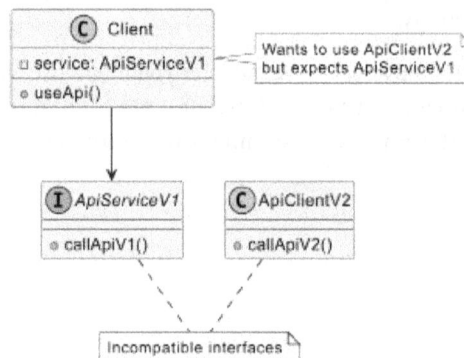

Figure 4.1 – Adapter interface incompatibility

In this diagram, the `Client` class uses the `ApiServiceV1` interface, which has a `callApiV1()` method. The `ApiClientV2` class has a `callApiV2()` method, which is incompatible with `ApiServiceV1`. However, we want the `Client` class to use `ApiClientV2` without changing its expected interface.

To solve this incompatibility, we'll introduce an adapter. Here's the UML diagram showing the Adapter pattern in action:

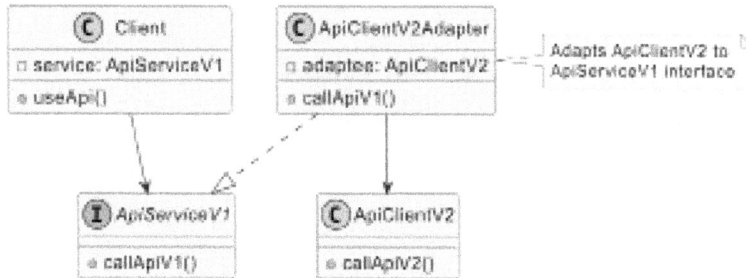

Figure 4.2 – Adapter for ApiClientV2

The key component here is `ApiClientV2Adapter`, which implements `ApiServiceV1` and contains a reference to `ApiClientV2`. The adapter's `callApiV1()` method will call the `ApiClientV2` class's `callApiV2()` method internally.

The `ApiClientV2Adapter` class solves this issue by aligning the interfaces so that the `Client` class can use a method from `ApiClientV2` without changing its interface reference. For example, the client wouldn't need to add another service object with an `ApiServiceV2` type.

A sample implementation is provided in the following section.

Classic implementation

Let's consider a simple scenario where we have a legacy system that works with meters, but we need to integrate it with a new system that uses feet. We'll use the Adapter pattern to bridge this gap.

First, let's define our interfaces and classes:

adapter.ts

```
interface MetricCalculator {
    getDistanceInMeters(): number;
}
class MetricSystem implements MetricCalculator {
    private distanceInMeters: number;
    constructor(distanceInMeters: number) {
```

```
        this.distanceInMeters = distanceInMeters;
    }
    getDistanceInMeters(): number {
        return this.distanceInMeters;
    }
}
class ImperialSystem {
    private distanceInFeet: number;
    constructor(distanceInFeet: number) {
        this.distanceInFeet = distanceInFeet;
    }
    getDistanceInFeet(): number {
        return this.distanceInFeet;
    }
}
```

The MetricCalculator interface specifies a method called getDistanceInMeters(), which is expected to return a distance in meters. The MetricSystem class implements this interface, storing a distance in meters and providing the getDistanceInMeters() method to return this value. The ImperialSystem class, on the other hand, handles distances measured in feet, storing a distance in feet and providing a method called getDistanceInFeet() to return this value.

> **Note**
>
> It's important to note that TypeScript interfaces are structurally typed. This means that an object doesn't need to explicitly implement an interface, so long as it conforms to the expected structure. This characteristic can lead to subtle differences in how the Adapter pattern behaves in TypeScript compared to other languages that use nominal typing, where explicit declarations are required for type compatibility. Additionally, if properties such as distanceInMeters and distanceInFeet aren't expected to change after initialization, leveraging TypeScript's read-only property feature in MetricSystem and ImperialSystem can reinforce immutability.

Now, we'll create an adapter to make ImperialSystem compatible with the MetricCalculator interface:

---

adapter.ts

```
class ImperialToMetricAdapter implements MetricCalculator {
    private imperialSystem: ImperialSystem;
    constructor(imperialSystem: ImperialSystem) {
        this.imperialSystem = imperialSystem;
    }
    getDistanceInMeters(): number {
```

```
        const feet = this.imperialSystem
          .getDistanceInFeet()

        if (typeof feet !== "number" || isNaN(feet)) {
          throw new Error("Invalid distance in feet provided")
    }
    return feet * 0.3048 // Convert feet to meters
  }
}
```

The preceding code defines an adapter class called `ImperialToMetricAdapter` that allows an `ImperialSystem` object to be used where `MetricCalculator` is expected. The `ImperialToMetricAdapter` class implements the `MetricCalculator` interface, ensuring it has the `getDistanceInMeters()` method. The `getDistanceInMeters()` method retrieves the distance in feet from the `ImperialSystem` instance using `getDistanceInFeet()`, converts this distance into meters, and returns the converted value. This allows the client code to work seamlessly with `ImperialSystem` while still expecting distances in meters.

Here's how a client might use these classes:

adapter.ts

```
class Reporter {
    static reportDistance(calculator: MetricCalculator) {
        console.log(`The distance is ${calculator
          .getDistanceInMeters()} meters.`);
    }
}
const metricDistance = new MetricSystem(5);
Reporter.reportDistance(metricDistance);
const imperialDistance = new ImperialSystem(10);
const adapter = new
  ImperialToMetricAdapter(imperialDistance);
Reporter.reportDistance(adapter);
```

When you run this code, you'll see an output similar to the following:

```
theo.despoudis ~/workspace/TypeScript-5-Design-Patterns-and-Best-Practices
● % node chapters/chapter-4_Structural_Design_Patterns/dist/adapter.js
                                                                    (main)

The distance is 5 meters.
The distance is 3.048 meters.
theo.despoudis ~/workspace/TypeScript-5-Design-Patterns-and-Best-Practices
○ % ▊                                                               (main)
```

Figure 4.3 – Output of the Adapter pattern example

This example demonstrates how the Adapter pattern allows you to use incompatible interfaces together. The `ImperialToMetricAdapter` class makes `ImperialSystem` appear as if it implements the `MetricCalculator` interface, allowing it to be used in places where `MetricCalculator` is expected.

Next, we'll learn how to test this pattern.

Testing

When implementing the Adapter pattern, it's crucial to verify that the adapter works as expected. We expect the adapter to accurately convert feet into meters, to properly implement the `MetricCalculator` interface, and to have the `getDistanceInMeters` method.

We've provided test cases in the `adaptor.test.ts` file located in this chapter's source code (see the *Technical requirements* section) for you to review.

To run the test cases, you need to execute the following command:

```
$ npm run test --adaptor
```

You should be able to review the test results in the console.

Criticisms

While the Adapter pattern is a powerful tool for integrating incompatible interfaces, it's important to consider its potential drawbacks and alternatives carefully before implementing it.

The primary criticism of the Adapter pattern is that it introduces additional layers of abstraction and code. The following points are valid issues when using this pattern:

- **Maintenance burden**: Each adapter adds another class to your code base that needs to be maintained and updated. Consider the use of **partial** or **mapped types** in TypeScript, which can help reduce boilerplate when you're building adapters. This can minimize the maintenance burden by dynamically creating types instead of hardcoding them.

- **Debugging challenges**: When issues arise, developers need to trace through the adapter, which can complicate debugging processes.

- **Potential performance overhead**: Though usually minimal, the extra layer can introduce slight performance costs, especially if the adapter performs complex transformations.

- **Behavioral inconsistencies**: Adapters might not perfectly mimic the behavior of the original interface, leading to subtle bugs.

- **Version mismatches**: As the adapted class evolves, the adapter might not keep pace, leading to outdated or incorrect functionality.

By carefully considering these caveats, you can make informed decisions about when and how to use the Adapter pattern, balancing its benefits against potential drawbacks to create more maintainable and efficient code.

Real-world use cases

The Adapter pattern is widely used in many popular libraries and frameworks. Let's consider an example use case in Sequelize.

Sequelize, a popular ORM for Node.js, uses the Adapter pattern to support multiple database systems. Sequelize provides different dialect adapters for MySQL, PostgreSQL, SQLite, and other databases. For example, while the core Sequelize API remains consistent, the adapters handle the specifics of each database system.

The following code snippet showcases how we can use this library to adapt two different database providers – MySQL and PostgreSQL:

```
import { Sequelize } from 'sequelize';
// MySQL adapter
const mysqlDB = new Sequelize('database', 'username',
  'password', {
    dialect: 'mysql'
  });
// PostgreSQL adapter
const postgresDB = new Sequelize('database', 'username',
  'password', {
    dialect: 'postgres'
  });
```

In the preceding code, the `Sequelize` class acts as an adapter that abstracts the underlying database details, allowing the application to interact with both MySQL and PostgreSQL databases using the same methods and properties. By configuring the Sequelize instance with different dialect options (`'mysql'` for MySQL and `'postgres'` for PostgreSQL), the code enables easy switching between database systems without the need to change the application logic, illustrating the flexibility and reusability provided by the adapter pattern.

Now that we've explored the most applicable and practical concepts of the Adapter pattern, let's examine the next pattern: the Decorator pattern.

The Decorator pattern

The **Decorator pattern** is a structural design pattern that enhances the functionality of an existing class without us having to modify the existing implementation. It's a flexible alternative to subclassing for extending functionality.

> **Note**
>
> In TypeScript 5, decorators have become part of the ECMAScript standard, allowing developers to decorate properties, methods, or entire classes. This differs from traditional **object-oriented programming** (**OOP**) implementations of the pattern, where decorators are often limited to class-level enhancements. In TypeScript, decorators can be applied to various elements, enabling more granular control over how functionality is extended.

Imagine that you have a plain room (our base object). Instead of permanently altering the room's structure (subclassing), you can add decorations such as flowers, paintings, or furniture (decorators) to enhance its appearance and functionality. These decorations can be added or removed easily without having to change the room itself. This is the essence of the Decorator pattern in OOP.

Key characteristics

The Decorator pattern has the following characteristics:

- **Runtime behavior extension**: Decorators allow you to modify an object's behavior at runtime
- **Composition over inheritance**: They use object composition to achieve flexible designs instead of relying on inheritance
- **Recursive wrapping**: They can be stacked, allowing multiple behaviors to be combined
- **Interface consistency**: Decorators typically implement the same interface as the decorated object, ensuring seamless integration

Now, let's look at scenarios where the Decorator pattern can be used.

When to use the Decorator pattern

You'll want to use the Decorator pattern once you've identified that you have the following problems:

- **Dynamic responsibility addition**: When you need to add responsibilities to objects dynamically and transparently, without affecting other objects
- **You're avoiding class explosion**: In situations where using subclassing would lead to creating many classes that degrade the maintainability of the code base
- **Extension without modification**: When you want to extend a class's behavior without modifying its existing code (adhering to the Open-Closed Principle)
- **Cross-cutting concerns**: For implementing cross-cutting concerns such as logging, transaction management, or caching, which apply to multiple classes
- **Conditional behavior**: When you need to add behavior that can be controlled or configured at runtime

When using this pattern, you get many benefits as you can just implement a new decorator for an object and attach it to the object dynamically at runtime. We'll continue by showcasing the class diagram for this pattern.

UML class diagram

The class diagram for this pattern follows the definition that we described previously. First, you have the object to which you want to attach the new behavior at runtime. If it doesn't have an interface, you can define one for it before creating the decorator:

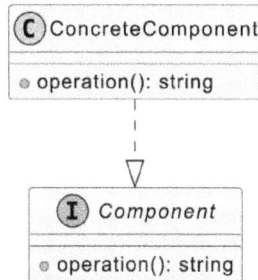

Figure 4.4 – Object to decorate

Here, `Component` is the base interface for all composite components. Note that `ConcreteComponent` implements the `Component` interface and provides an implementation of the functionality we want to expose.

To provide the `Decorator` class, you want to implement the same interface that the object implements and wrap the same method call:

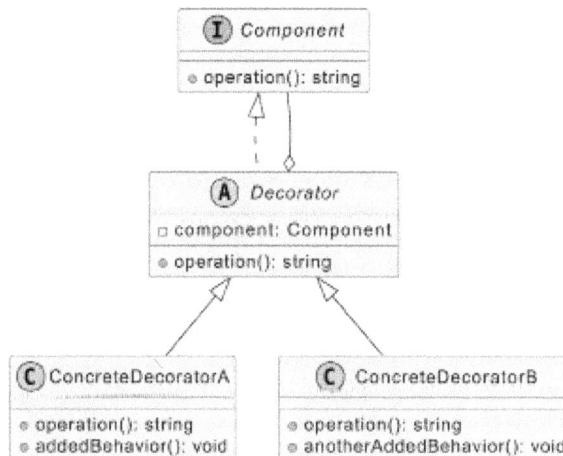

Figure 4.5 – The Decorator class

Next, we have ConcreteDecoratorA and ConcreteDecoratorB, which are specific decorator implementations. They extend the Decorator class and add their own behaviors. The composition relationship between Decorator and Component allows decorators to wrap around any component or other decorator, allowing multiple decorators to be stacked.

Now, we'll consider an example implementation.

Classic implementation

Let's consider a file processing system where we have a basic file reader, but we want to add various functionalities such as encryption and compression without having to modify the original class.

First, we must define our base component interface and a concrete implementation:

decorator.ts

```ts
interface FileReader {
  read(filePath: string): string
}
class SimpleFileReader implements FileReader {
  read(filePath: string): string {
    console.log(`Reading file from: ${filePath}`)
    return `Content of ${filePath}`
  }
}
```

Now, let's create decorators that add encryption and compression capabilities:

decorator.ts

```ts
abstract class FileReaderDecorator implements FileReader {
  constructor(protected readonly reader: FileReader) {}
  abstract read(filePath: string): string;
}
class EncryptionDecorator extends FileReaderDecorator {
// implement FireReaderDecorator methods
}
class CompressionDecorator extends FileReaderDecorator {
// implement FireReaderDecorator methods
}
```

The two concrete decorators, EncryptionDecorator and CompressionDecorator, extend FileReaderDecorator to add encryption and compression functionalities, respectively. Both override the read method to process the file's content by calling the base class's read method and then applying their specific operations (encrypt or compress) to the content and returning the modified content.

Utilizing an abstract class such as FileReaderDecorator helps us avoid code duplication across multiple decorators. By providing a base class with shared logic, such as the constructor and any common methods, you can streamline the implementation of various decorators.

Here's how we can use these decorators to create a file reader with combined functionalities:

decorator.ts

```ts
let reader: FileReader = new SimpleFileReader();
reader = new CompressionDecorator(reader);
reader = new EncryptionDecorator(reader);
const content = reader.read("example.txt");
console.log("Final content:", content);
```

The output might look something like this:

```
theo.despoudis ~/workspace/TypeScript-5-Design-Patterns-and-Best-Practices
% node chapters/chapter-4_Structural_Design_Patterns/dist/decorator.js
Reading file from: example.txt
Compressing content
Encrypting content
Final content: Encrypted(Compressed(Content of example.txt))
theo.despoudis ~/workspace/TypeScript-5-Design-Patterns-and-Best-Practices
%                                                                    (main)
```

Figure 4.6 – Output of running the decorator example

This implementation allows us to add or remove functionalities dynamically at runtime.

Next, we'll look at some modern variants of the Decorator pattern.

Modern variants of the Decorator pattern

The classic implementation of the Decorator pattern is suitable for classes and by default, it looks extraneous since you must create a class that exposes one method that decorates an object.

Luckily for us, TypeScript 5 offers some language features that make it easier to change existing behavior with the use of ECMAScript decorators. Instead of defining a class, we can define a special function that we use to decorate classes, methods, properties, or parameters.

Consider the following example:

decorator-variant.ts

```typescript
function Encrypt() {
  return function <T extends { new (...args: any[]):
    FileReader }>(constructor: T) {
    return class extends constructor {
      read(filePath: string): string {
        const content = super.read(filePath)
        console.log("Encrypting content")
        return `Encrypted(${content})`
      }
    }
  }
}
function Compress() {
  return function <T extends { new (...args: any[]):
    FileReader }>(constructor: T) {
    return class extends constructor {
      read(filePath: string): string {
        const content = super.read(filePath)
        console.log("Compressing content")
        return `Compressed(${content})`
      }
    }
  }
}
interface FileReader {
  read(filePath: string): string
}
@Compress()
@Encrypt()
class SimpleFileReader implements FileReader {
  read(filePath: string): string {
    console.log(`Reading file from: ${filePath}`)
    return `Content of ${filePath}`
  }
}
const reader = new SimpleFileReader()
const content = reader.read("example.txt")
console.log("Final content:", content)
```

The preceding code defines two TypeScript decorator functions, `Encrypt` and `Compress`, which add encryption and compression functionalities to a `FileReader` class, respectively. These decorators return a new class that extends the constructor that's passed to them, overriding the `read` method to first call the original `read` method, and then apply their specific transformation.

Because of this decorator syntax, you can attach common behavior in many places without instantiating new decorator classes every time, making the code more concise.

Next, we'll learn how to test decorators.

Testing

When testing decorators, there are several key aspects we need to focus on to ensure our implementation is working correctly:

- **Functionality preservation**: We need to verify that the original functionality of the decorated class or method is preserved. The decorator shouldn't interfere with the basic operation of the object it's decorating.

- **Decorator behavior**: We must test that the decorator is actually performing its intended functionality. This could be adding logging, modifying return values, or altering the behavior of the decorated object in some way.

- **Order of execution**: When multiple decorators are applied, we need to ensure they're executed in the correct order. This is particularly important when decorators modify the same aspects of an object's behavior.

- **Side effects**: We should verify any side effects the decorators might have, such as logging to the console or modifying the external state.

We've provided test cases in the `decorator.test.ts` file located in this chapter's source code (see the *Technical requirements* section) for you to review.

To run the test cases, you need to execute the following command:

```
$ npm run test --decorator
```

You should be able to review the test results in the console.

Now, we'll explain some of the criticisms of the Decorator pattern.

Criticisms

While the Decorator pattern is powerful and flexible, it's not without its drawbacks. Here are some expanded criticisms and considerations:

- **Interface dependency**: The Decorator pattern heavily relies on the interface of the object it's wrapping. If the interface of the wrapped object changes, all decorators must be updated to reflect these changes. Also, adding new methods to the interface requires updating all existing decorators, which can be time-consuming and error-prone.

- **Complexity and readability**: As more decorators are added, the code becomes harder to reason about their existence. For example, when multiple decorators are applied to a single object, debugging can become challenging.

- **Performance overhead**: Each decorator adds a level of indirection, which can introduce a small performance overhead. In most applications, this overhead is negligible; however, in performance-critical applications – such as real-time systems or data-intensive applications – this overhead can become significant. In such cases, it may be beneficial to profile the system to identify whether chains of decorators are introducing latency.

- **Ordering dependencies**: Decorator ordering is important in cases when a decorator introduces side effects that can alter the behavior of the system, leading to subtle bugs.

While these criticisms highlight important considerations, it's worth noting that the Decorator pattern remains a valuable tool in certain scenarios. The key is to carefully evaluate whether the benefits outweigh the drawbacks for your specific use case.

Real-world use cases

You may find many use cases of the Decorator pattern in popular libraries such as Nest.js. Here's an example of a `Controller` declaration:

```
import { Controller, Get } from '@nestjs/common';
@Controller('dogs')
export class DogsController {
  @Get()
  findAll() {
    return 'This action returns all dogs';
  }
}
```

The `@Controller('dogs')` decorator defines the base route for all methods within the controller. The `@Get()` decorator specifies that the `findAll` method should handle GET requests to the `/dogs` route.

This example demonstrates how the Decorator pattern can be used to add functionality to existing code without the need to modify its structure.

Now that we've explored the most applicable and practical concepts of the Decorator pattern, we'll examine the next pattern: the Façade pattern.

The Façade pattern

The **Façade pattern** is a structural design pattern that provides a simplified interface for a complex subsystem of classes, libraries, or frameworks. It encapsulates a group of interfaces in a higher-level interface, making the subsystem easier to use.

The Façade pattern acts as a *front-facing* interface that masks more complex underlying or structural code. Its primary purpose is to do the following:

- Simplify client interactions with a system

- Decouple the client from the subsystem's components

- Provide a simple abstraction on top of a complex system to make things easier to use

We can use a modern smart home system as an analogy for this pattern. Instead of interacting with individual components such as lights, thermostats, security systems, and entertainment devices separately, you use a single application on your smartphone. This application serves as a façade, providing a simple interface to control all these complex subsystems with just a few taps.

When implementing the Façade pattern, it's crucial to maintain simplicity while effectively hiding the complexity of the underlying systems. Failing to do that will nullify any practical benefits of using this pattern.

When to use the Façade pattern

The Façade pattern is particularly useful in the following scenarios:

- **Simplifying complex systems**: When you need to provide a simple interface for a complex subsystem

- **Creating subsystem abstractions**: To define an entry point to each subsystem level

- **Layering systems**: When you want to structure a system into layers

- **Reducing dependencies**: To decouple the client code from subsystem components

The Façade pattern acts as a front entity that hides the complexities of the subsystem from the client. Instead, it only exposes the minimal methods and parameters. This way, you can reform the internals of the system easily when needed in the future.

UML class diagram

The Façade pattern can be represented in a UML class diagram that clearly shows how it simplifies complex subsystems.

First, we have a complex subsystem consisting of `SubsystemA`, `SubsystemB`, and `SubsystemC`, where each subsystem has its own operations:

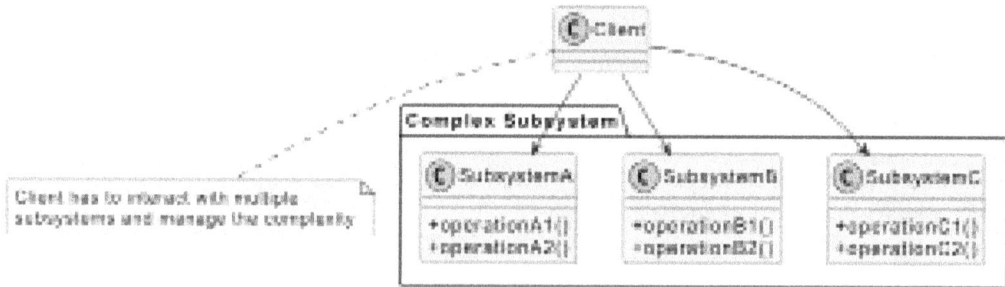

Figure 4.7 – Complex subsystems the client has to interact with

The `Client` class has to interact directly with all subsystems, managing the complexity itself. Now, let's see how the Façade pattern simplifies this:

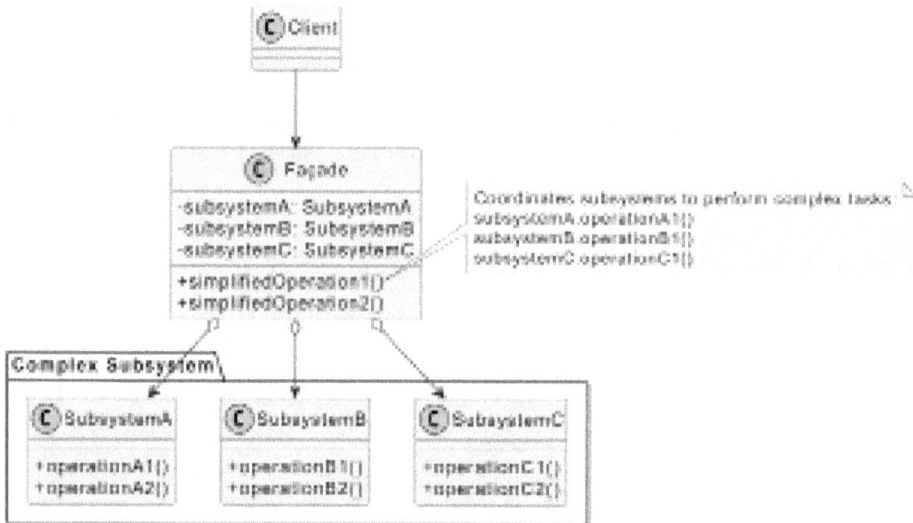

Figure 4.8 – The Façade object

Here, the `Facade` class is introduced, which composes (contains) instances of all subsystems. This `Facade` class provides simplified operations that manage the complexity of interacting with the subsystems internally.

Let's learn how to implement the Façade pattern in TypeScript.

Classic implementation

Based on the diagram shown in *Figure 4.8*, we can implement the Façade pattern as follows.

First, we must create the services that we want to use in the Façade pattern:

facade.ts

```typescript
interface SubsystemA {
  operationA1(): void
  operationA2(): void
}
interface SubsystemB {
  operationB1(): void
  operationB2(): void
}
class ConcreteSubsystemA implements SubsystemA {
  operationA1(): void {
    console.log("SubsystemA: Performing operation A1")
  }
  operationA2(): void {
    console.log("SubsystemA: Performing operation A2")
  }
}
class ConcreteSubsystemB implements SubsystemB {
  operationB1(): void {
    console.log("SubsystemB: Performing operation B1")
  }
  operationB2(): void {
    console.log("SubsystemB: Performing operation B2")
  }
}
```

Here, we defined the `SubsystemA` and `SubsystemB` interfaces, each with two operations. Then, we implemented these interfaces with the `ConcreteSubsystemA` and `ConcreteSubsystemB` classes.

Now, we must define the Facade class, which will use all of those services to perform complex actions:

facade.ts

```
class Facade {
  private subsystemA: SubsystemA
  private subsystemB: SubsystemB
  constructor(subsystemA: SubsystemA,
    subsystemB: SubsystemB) {
    this.subsystemA = subsystemA
    this.subsystemB = subsystemB
  }
  public simplifiedOperation1(): void {
    console.log("Facade: Coordinating operations
      in simplifiedOperation1")
    this.subsystemA.operationA1()
    this.subsystemB.operationB1()
  }
  public simplifiedOperation2(): void {
    console.log("Facade: Coordinating operations
      in simplifiedOperation2")
    this.subsystemA.operationA2()
    this.subsystemB.operationB2()
    this.subsystemA.operationA1()
  }
}
function clientCode(facade: Facade) {
  console.log("Client: Calling simplifiedOperation1")
  facade.simplifiedOperation1()

  console.log("\nClient: Calling simplifiedOperation2")
  facade.simplifiedOperation2()
}
const subsystemA = new ConcreteSubsystemA()
const subsystemB = new ConcreteSubsystemB()
const facade = new Facade(subsystemA, subsystemB)
clientCode(facade)
```

Here, the Facade class has been defined, which takes instances of SubsystemA and SubsystemB in its constructor. Then, we provided two simplified operations that coordinate actions on both subsystems.

The highlighted clientCode function demonstrates how a client would use the Facade class.

The output will be as follows:

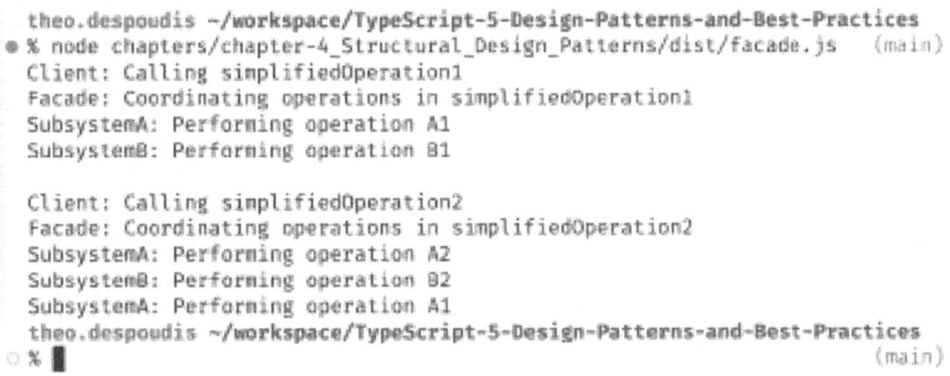

```
theo.despoudis ~/workspace/TypeScript-5-Design-Patterns-and-Best-Practices
% node chapters/chapter-4_Structural_Design_Patterns/dist/facade.js    (main)
Client: Calling simplifiedOperation1
Facade: Coordinating operations in simplifiedOperation1
SubsystemA: Performing operation A1
SubsystemB: Performing operation B1

Client: Calling simplifiedOperation2
Facade: Coordinating operations in simplifiedOperation2
SubsystemA: Performing operation A2
SubsystemB: Performing operation B2
SubsystemA: Performing operation A1
theo.despoudis ~/workspace/TypeScript-5-Design-Patterns-and-Best-Practices
%                                                                      (main)
```

Figure 4.9 – Output of the Facade class example

This output demonstrates how the `Facade` class coordinates different operations from both subsystems, providing a simplified interface to the client.

Next, you'll learn how we can test this pattern.

Testing

When testing the Façade pattern, the main goal is to verify the following aspects:

- The Façade pattern orchestrates calls to the subsystems correctly
- The Façade pattern handles any complex logic or conditions properly

We've provided test cases in the `facade.test.ts` file located in this chapter's source code (see the *Technical requirements* section) for you to review.

To run the test cases, you need to execute the following command:

```
$ npm run test --facade
```

You should be able to review the test results in the console.

Next, we'll review some of the major criticisms of this pattern.

Criticisms

While the Façade pattern is useful for simplifying complex systems, it can suffer from some drawbacks:

- **God object anti-pattern**: If a façade manages too many services and interfaces, it can become a *God object* – that is, a class that knows or does too much.

- **Scope creeping**: Over time, developers might be tempted to keep adding more and more functionality to the façade, making it increasingly complex.

- **Decreased flexibility**: While the Façade pattern simplifies the client interface, it might also limit the client's ability to use the subsystems in ways not anticipated by the façade.

- **Code rigidity**: If the underlying system evolves significantly, the Façade pattern may require frequent changes to adapt to new interfaces or system behavior. This can create a maintenance burden and may obscure access to features or configurations not exposed by the Façade pattern, further limiting the client's flexibility.

To mitigate these issues, you should aim to create multiple façades for different use cases rather than one large façade. Remember, the goal of the Façade pattern is to simplify usage and improve code readability. If it's not achieving these goals, it might be worth reconsidering its use or implementation.

Real-world use cases

Façades can be used in cases where you need to coordinate between the two services. For example, in authentication, we can have two subsystems – `AuthService` for handling authentication and `UserProfileService` for managing user profiles:

```
class UserManagementFacade {
  private authService: AuthService;
  private userProfileService: UserProfileService;
  constructor() {
    this.authService = new AuthService();
    this.userProfileService = new UserProfileService();
  }

  async login(username: string,
    password: string): Promise<object> {
    const token = await this.authService
      .login(username, password);
    const userProfile = await this.userProfileService
      .getUserProfile(username);
    return { token, userProfile };
  }
```

```
    // Other methods...
}
```

The façade coordinates between the two services. For example, the `login` method not only authenticates the user but also fetches their profile in a single operation.

The client code only interacts with the façade, without needing to know about the underlying services.

Now that we've explored the most applicable and practical concepts of the Façade pattern, let's examine the next pattern: the Composite pattern.

The Composite pattern

The **Composite pattern** is a structural design pattern that allows you to define trees of objects that belong to the same hierarchy.

The core idea is to create a common interface for both simple (leaf) objects and complex (composite) objects that may contain other objects. This unified interface allows us to handle both types consistently.

A common real-world analogy for the Composite pattern is a filesystem, where directories (composite objects) can contain both files (leaf objects) and other directories (composite objects). Both files and directories share a common interface, allowing clients to interact with them uniformly. For example, you can perform operations such as calculating the total size of a directory or listing its contents without needing to differentiate between files and subdirectories.

When to use the Composite pattern

Consider using the Composite pattern in the following instances:

- When you need to represent the hierarchical structures of objects
- When you want clients to ignore the difference between compositions of objects and individual objects
- When your structure can have any level of complexity, and you want operations to apply uniformly across all levels

Using the Composite pattern helps in breaking components up part by part if they're too big or combining them if they're too small. This operation doesn't alter how the container operates with those components, so it promotes modularity and extensibility.

Things will become clearer when we see the UML class diagram for this pattern.

UML class diagram

First, you must define an interface for the Composite hierarchy; all composite components should implement this. Then, you need to add a container composite component that acts as the main delegate. This is the component the client will use to perform operations on all child components.

Consider a scenario where we need to represent a filesystem hierarchy that consists of directories and files. Directories can contain both files and subdirectories. We want to perform operations on this hierarchy uniformly, whether it's a single file or a directory containing multiple files and subdirectories.

First, let's define an interface for FileSystemComponent. This component interface will define the common operations for both files and directories:

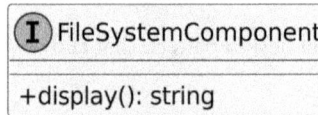

Figure 4.10 – Composite FileSystemComponent

Now, let's define the File and Directory components that implement this interface:

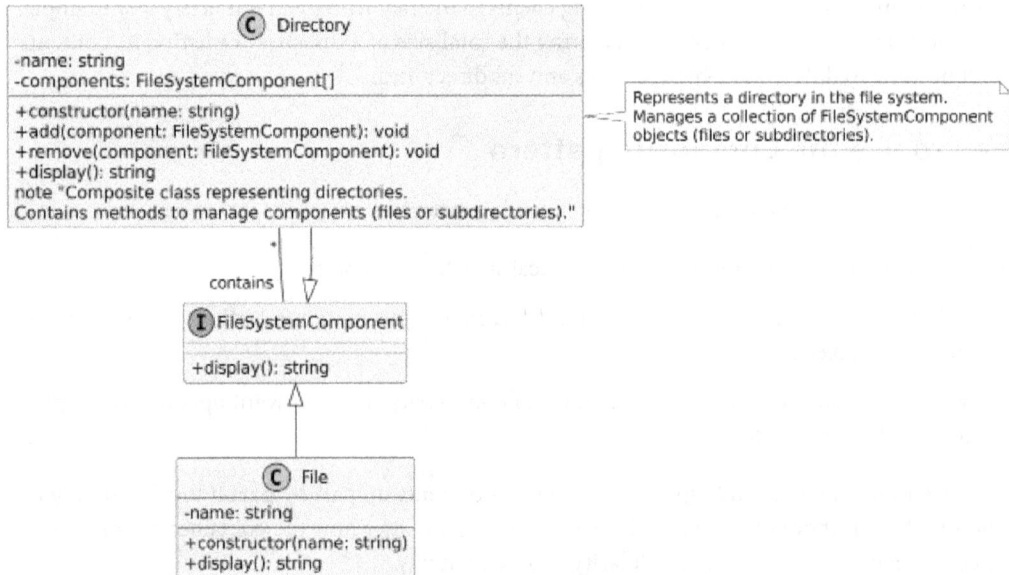

Figure 4.11 – The Composite pattern

Here, the composite part is the Directory class. It represents a directory in the filesystem that contains a list of FileSystemComponent objects (files and subdirectories). It implements methods to add and remove components, as well as the FileSystemComponent interface itself.

This pattern allows you to treat objects and compositions of objects as if they're part of the whole tree. It simplifies handling complex hierarchical structures by providing a unified interface and enabling recursive operations (via the `display()` method) across the hierarchy.

Now, let's learn how to implement this pattern.

Classic implementation

The classic implementation of the Composite pattern follows the class diagram depicted in *Figure 4.11*. It shows the definition of the base interface of the container and one leaf object:

composite.ts

```
interface FileSystemComponent {
    display(): string;
}
class File implements FileSystemComponent {
    private name: string;
    constructor(name: string) {
        this.name = name;
    }
    display(): string {
        return `File: ${this.name}`;
    }
}
class Directory implements FileSystemComponent {
    private name: string;
    private components: FileSystemComponent[];
    constructor(name: string) {
        this.name = name;
        this.components = [];
    }
    // Rest of methods to add and remove files or directories
}
```

To test this code, we must create a filesystem structure using `File` and `Directory` instances, adding files to directories and directories to other directories:

```
// Usage example
const root = new Directory("Root");
const file1 = new File("file1.txt");
const file2 = new File("file2.txt");
const subDir = new Directory("Subdirectory");
const file3 = new File("file3.txt");
```

```
subDir.add(file3);
root.add(file1);
root.add(file2);
root.add(subDir);
console.log(root.display());
```

In this series of instructions, we create one `Directory` object and one subdirectory as a child. Then, we add three files inside the root directory and one file inside the subdirectory.

Running the preceding code will produce an output similar to the following:

```
theo.despoudis ~/workspace/TypeScript-5-Design-Patterns-and-Best-Practices
 % node chapters/chapter-4_Structural_Design_Patterns/dist/composite.js
Directory: Root
 - File: file1.txt
 - File: file2.txt
 - Directory: Subdirectory
 - File: file3.txt
```

Figure 4.12 – The Composite pattern's output

You're free to define more child component types and add them to the container. The logic for displaying is encapsulated and shouldn't be of concern to the client. Each component in the composite knows how to render itself, so this greatly simplifies the client code.

Let's learn how to test this pattern.

Testing

To thoroughly test this code, we should create unit tests for the `File` and `Directory` classes and integration tests for the composite structure. They should assert that creating a `Directory` instance and adding more `File` class instances inside maintains the composite structure as expected.

We've provided test cases in the `composite.test.ts` file located in this chapter's source code (see the *Technical requirements* section) for you to review.

To run the test cases, you need to execute the following command:

```
$ npm run test --composite
```

You should be able to review the test results in the console.

Criticisms

You'll often face the following challenges when you try to apply this pattern in practice:

- **Balancing generality versus specificity**: Creating an interface that's generic enough to accommodate all components, yet specific enough to be meaningful, is challenging.

- **Method bloating**: Components may be forced to implement methods that don't fit into their intended functionality. For example, methods such as add(), remove(), and getChild() make sense for composite objects that can have children. But in the case of leaf components, it doesn't make sense to have them implemented, so we would just throw an error.

- **Potential performance issues**: Deep hierarchies can lead to performance issues, especially when traversing the entire tree structure.

- **Overhead**: Memory overhead can be significant if many small objects are created.

- **Component restriction**: It can be challenging to restrict certain components from being added to specific composites if the interface is too generic.

- **Cycles**: If not designed carefully, it's possible to create cycles in the component hierarchy, leading to infinite loops or stack overflow errors.

Sometimes, you can avoid these issues by maintaining a simple model for your composite tree and trying not to overgeneralize it. This will make this pattern easy to use and work with.

Real-world use cases

The DOM that's used by web browsers is a classic example of the Composite pattern. The DOM represents a tree-like structure for nodes that's used to represent an HTML document. Once we have a reference to the root component, we can traverse it using a simple for loop. The following code showcases this usage:

```
let body: HTMLBodyElement = document.createElement("body")
let div: HTMLDivElement = document.createElement("div")
let p: HTMLParagraphElement = document.createElement("p")
let text: Text = document.createTextNode("Hello, World!")
p.appendChild(text)
div.appendChild(p)
body.appendChild(div)
function traverse(node: Node, depth: number = 0): void {
  console.log(" ".repeat(depth) + node.nodeName)
  node.childNodes.forEach((child: Node) => {
    traverse(child, depth + 1)
  })
}
traverse(body)
```

Here, the body, ul, and li elements form a tree structure where each element can have child elements. This hierarchical structure allows each node to be treated uniformly, whether it's a composite node or a leaf node.

Then, we create body, ul, and li elements and compose them into a nested structure. The traverse function recursively traverses the DOM tree, printing each node's name and text content. This demonstrates how the Composite pattern allows for uniform treatment of individual and composite objects.

Now that we've explored the most applicable and practical concepts of the Composite pattern, let's examine the next pattern: the Proxy pattern.

The Proxy pattern

The **Proxy pattern** is a structural design pattern that gives us a way to call methods on an object via another object (sometimes called a surrogate object). This pattern is particularly useful for adding a layer of control over how and when an object is accessed.

The Proxy pattern can also be used to control access to objects in terms of security and performance optimizations. For instance, a proxy can be used to lazy load a resource-intensive object or restrict access to sensitive data.

One analogy of this pattern is a company secretary accepting calls on behalf of the company director. They can regulate the flow of calls and may or may not forward them to the director based on who's calling and why. This pattern works very similarly to the Decorator pattern that you learned about earlier. It also wraps an object and provides it with extra functionality.

With the Decorator pattern, you can wrap an object with the same interface and it will decorate some of the method calls. You can also add more than one decorator to the object. However, with the Proxy pattern, you usually allow only one proxy per object, and you use it to control its access and delegate its methods.

When to use the Proxy pattern

The Proxy pattern is versatile and can be applied in various scenarios. Here are more detailed reasons and situations where using a proxy can be beneficial:

- **Lazy initialization**: One of the primary use cases for the Proxy pattern is lazy initialization, which is often implemented as a virtual proxy. This approach is valuable when you're dealing with resource-intensive objects that aren't always necessary as it can significantly improve application startup time by deferring the creation of heavy objects until they're needed.

- **Access control**: Access control is another key application of the Proxy pattern that's typically implemented as a protection proxy. This method is instrumental in implementing role-based access control in applications, adding an extra layer of security to sensitive operations.

- **Logging and auditing**: Logging and auditing represent another significant use case for the Proxy pattern. By implementing a proxy, developers can add comprehensive logging without having to modify the core business logic. This is particularly useful for creating audit trails of all operations that are performed on an object and gathering metrics and performance data for system analysis.

- **Caching**: Caching is often implemented as a smart proxy. This approach can significantly improve system performance by implementing a caching layer for frequently accessed, but expensive to compute, data. In distributed systems, it can reduce network calls by caching remote object data locally, and in database applications, it can improve query performance by caching results.

- **Validation**: Validation and error handling allow input validation to be added before requests are passed to the real object, error handling to be centralized, and more user-friendly error messages to be provided. It can also be used to implement retry mechanisms for unreliable operations, improving system resilience.

By leveraging the Proxy pattern in these diverse scenarios, you can promote separation of concerns and allow cross-cutting concerns such as security, logging, and performance optimization to be integrated seamlessly.

Now, let's review the class diagram of the Proxy pattern.

UML class diagram

The class diagram for this pattern is similar to that of the Decorator pattern. You have an interface and an object that implements this interface with some methods. Let's start with a diagram that shows the basic structure with a `Store` interface and the `TextStore` class that implements it. This represents a class that stores a message:

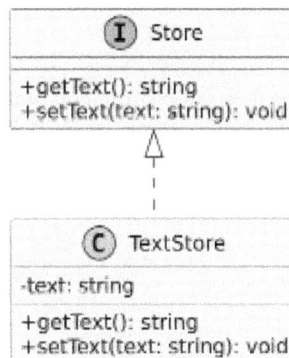

Figure 4.13 – Basic TextStore object

Now, let's add the proxy object to the diagram:

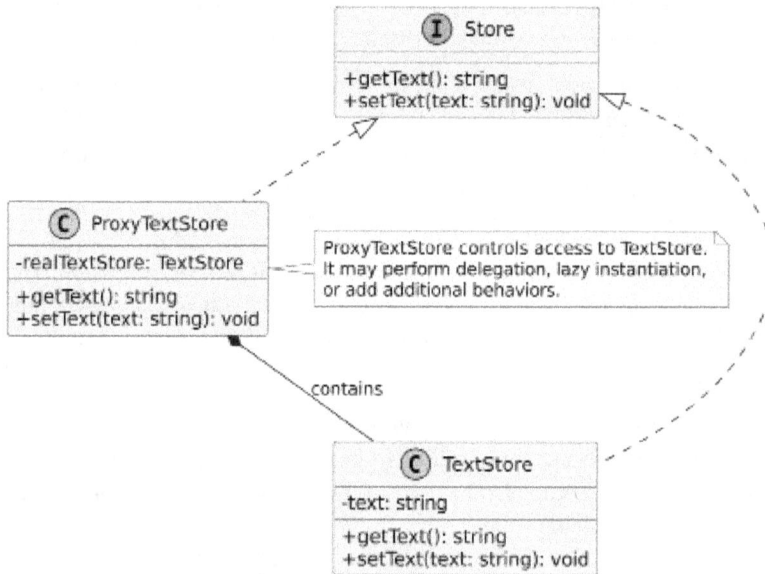

Figure 4.14 – Proxy object

This expanded diagram includes the ProxyTextStore class, which implements the Store interface and contains an instance of TextStore. The ProxyTextStore class acts as a surrogate for TextStore, controlling access to it and potentially adding extra behaviors.

The relationship between ProxyTextStore and TextStore is shown as a composition (filled diamond), indicating that the proxy contains and manages the life cycle of RealSubject. This relationship allows the proxy to control when and how RealSubject is created and accessed.

Next, we'll learn how to implement this pattern in TypeScript.

Classic implementation

Based on *Figure 4.14*, we can easily provide a sample implementation of this pattern. Here, we want to define the object we want by forwarding its method calls to the proxy object:

proxy.ts

```
export interface Store {
  save(data: string): void
}
export class TextStore implements Store {
  save(data: string): void {
```

```
      console.log(`Called 'save' from TextStore with
      data=${data}`)
    }
  }
```

The `Store` interface declares a method to save data. Here, `TextStore` is a concrete implementation of this interface and it's used to save data as text. The implementation part isn't defined here.

Then, we want to provide the `ProxyTextStore` class as well:

proxy.ts

```
export class ProxyTextStore implements Store {
  constructor(private textStore?: TextStore) {}
  save(data: string): void {
    console.log(`Called 'save' from ProxyTextStore with
    data=${data}`)
    if (!this.textStore) {
      console.log("Lazy init: textStore.")
      this.textStore = new TextStore()
    }
    this.textStore.save(data)
  }
}
```

We highlight the parts where the object is instantiated, such as a Singleton instance, and where the delegated method call happens. The proxy might perform more complex calls or other functions as well if needed.

Here's how the client would use this class:

proxy.ts

```
// Direct usage
const directStore = new TextStore();
directStore.save("Direct data");
// Proxy usage with lazy initialization
const proxyStore = new ProxyTextStore();
proxyStore.save("Proxy data 1");
proxyStore.save("Proxy data 2");
// Proxy with pre-initialized store
const preInitStore = new ProxyTextStore(new TextStore());
preInitStore.save("Pre-init data");
```

This client code demonstrates several scenarios. It uses `ProxyTextStore`, which will perform lazy initialization of `TextStore`. It uses the same `ProxyTextStore` class again, demonstrating that `TextStore` has already been initialized. Finally, it creates a new `ProxyTextStore` class with a pre-initialized `TextStore`. Let's test this pattern.

Testing

Just as with the Decorator pattern, you can test certain aspects of the Proxy pattern. First, you'll want to check that the Proxy pattern does lazy instantiation when needed. You'll want to provide an object that mocks either the save call or the constructor and is called only when the proxy method is called the first time. Additionally, you can check whether the call to the wrapped object is performed in the right order.

We've provided test cases in the `proxy.test.ts` file located in this chapter's source code (see the *Technical requirements* section) for you to review.

To run the test cases, you need to execute the following command:

```
$ npm run test --proxy
```

You should be able to review the test results in the console.

Now, let's talk about some of the criticisms of this pattern.

Criticisms

While the Proxy pattern offers numerous benefits, it's important to consider its potential drawbacks:

- **Performance overhead**: The additional layer introduced by the proxy can lead to performance degradation, especially in performance-critical applications. Each method call now goes through an extra object instead of accessing the object directly. This overhead can be particularly prohibitive in scenarios such as real-time systems or high-frequency trading platforms, where strict performance requirements demand minimal latency. In these contexts, even slight delays introduced by proxies can significantly affect overall system performance.

- **Complexity**: Proxies can make the system more complex, potentially making it harder to understand and maintain. This is especially true when multiple proxies are used or when proxies are deeply nested.

- **Lifetime management**: As mentioned previously, tying the proxy's lifetime to the wrapped object can lead to resource management issues. If not handled properly, this could result in memory leaks or premature object destruction.

- **Error handling**: When the proxy intercepts method calls, it needs to handle exceptions from both its own operations and the real object's methods. This can make error handling and debugging more complex.

- **Testing challenges**: Thoroughly testing proxies can be challenging, especially when they're used for things such as lazy loading or remote resource access. Mocking and simulating various scenarios becomes more complex.

To avoid these issues, it's crucial to carefully consider whether a proxy is truly necessary for your use case. When implementing proxies, focus on clear error handling, efficient resource management, and comprehensive testing, including edge cases and failure scenarios.

Real-world use cases

The Proxy pattern finds application in various real-world scenarios. We'll explore a handful of use cases here:

- **Vue.js reactivity system**: Vue.js uses a proxy-based system to track changes to data properties and trigger re-renders when necessary.

- **ORM libraries**: ORM libraries often use proxies to implement lazy loading of related database records.

- **Virtual proxy in image loading**: Many web applications use virtual proxies to lazily load images. A placeholder image is initially displayed, and the actual image is only loaded when it's about to enter the viewport.

- **MobX observed stores**: One popular open source library for state management is **MobX**. This library leverages the Proxy pattern to mark observable lists and sequences and intercepts any changes to them before calling any updates in the wrapped collection.

These real-world examples demonstrate how the Proxy pattern, despite its potential drawbacks, can be a powerful tool when used in appropriate scenarios.

Now that we've explored the most applicable and practical concepts of the Proxy pattern, let's examine the Bridge pattern.

The Bridge pattern

The **Bridge pattern** is a structural design pattern that splits an abstraction from its implementation and allows both entities to be extended individually without them being tightly coupled.

In large software systems, different components often need to interact with various underlying implementations. For example, consider a system that supports multiple **user interfaces** (**UIs**), such as desktop, web, and mobile. Each UI type may share a common abstraction (such as a user interface component) but requires distinct implementations tailored to their specific platforms. The Bridge pattern allows developers to manage these complexities by keeping the abstraction separate from the implementation.

One analogy that represents this pattern is a universal remote control system for various electronic devices. The remote control (abstraction) works with multiple types of devices, such as TVs, DVD players, or sound systems (implementations). New types of remotes or devices can be added without this affecting existing ones, so long as they adhere to the common interface.

Now, let's learn when to use the Bridge pattern.

When to use the Bridge pattern

You'll want to use the Bridge pattern for the following reasons:

- **Separation of concerns**: Use the Bridge pattern when you want to separate an abstraction's interface from its implementation. This allows you to change the implementation without affecting clients using the abstraction.

- **Extensibility**: This is when both the abstractions and implementations need to be extended independently. This pattern allows you to add new abstractions and implementations without the need to modify existing code.

- **Runtime flexibility**: Use the Bridge pattern when you need to be able to switch implementations at runtime. The abstraction can choose or change its implementation dynamically.

- **Shared implementation**: When multiple abstractions need to share an implementation, or vice versa. The Bridge pattern allows for this flexibility without creating a complex inheritance hierarchy.

This pattern might sound too complex, but it's comparatively simple. You construct two separate hierarchies of an object that are connected via an interface, and you provide different implementors.

Let's see how to depict this with UML.

UML class diagram

The Bridge pattern requires us to identify the abstractions and their respective implementations and restructure them so that they're extensible concerning each other. Let's break this process down into steps.

Step 1 – define the interfaces

We start by defining two interfaces – one for the abstraction and one for the implementation:

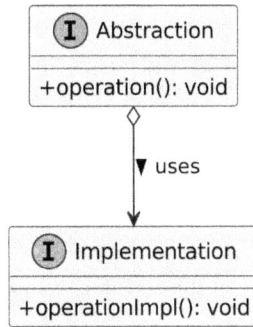

Figure 4.15 – Bridge interfaces

In the diagram shown in *Figure 4.15*, `Abstraction` defines the abstract interface, while `Implementation` defines the interface for implementation classes.

Step 2 – create concrete classes

Next, we create concrete classes that implement these interfaces:

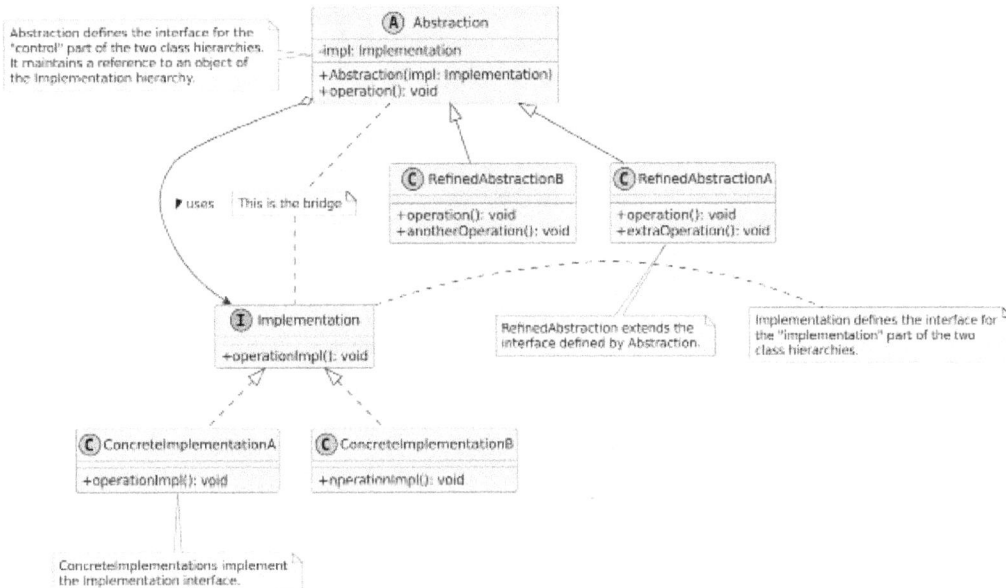

Figure 4.16 – Bridge implementations

In the final diagram shown in *Figure 4.16*, Abstraction is now an abstract class with a reference to Implementation and there's a solid line with an open arrow that represents composition. This shows that Abstraction contains an instance of Implementation. The crucial part is that Abstraction maintains a reference to an object of the Implementation type, forming the *bridge* between the two hierarchies.

This structure allows both the abstractions and implementations to be extended independently. You can add new abstractions or new implementations without affecting existing code, providing great flexibility and extensibility. Now, let's look at the code for this pattern.

Classic implementation

In this section, we'll showcase an example implementation of this pattern. Let's say we want to abstract a custom smart home system focusing on plant care.

We start by defining the interfaces and abstractions:

bridge.ts

```ts
interface WateringMechanism {
  water(amount: number): void
  checkWaterLevel(): number
  refill(amount: number): void
}
abstract class SmartPlantCare {
  protected mechanism: WateringMechanism
  protected moistureThreshold: number
  constructor(mechanism: WateringMechanism,
    moistureThreshold: number) {
    this.mechanism = mechanism
    this.moistureThreshold = moistureThreshold
  }
  abstract waterPlant(currentMoisture: number): void
  abstract adjustWatering(weatherForecast: string): void
}
```

The preceding code declares the WateringMechanism interface and the SmartPlantCare abstract class. Here, SmartPlantCare uses a WateringMechanism interface as part of its functionality. Since both types are abstractions, you need to provide concrete implementations for them.

We've provided these in the following code:

bridge.ts

```ts
class MistSprayer implements WateringMechanism {
  private waterReservoir: number = 500 // ml
  water(amount: number): void {
    this.waterReservoir -= amount
    console.log(`Misting ${amount}ml of water`)
  }
  checkWaterLevel(): number {
    return this.waterReservoir
  }
  refill(amount: number): void {
    this.waterReservoir += amount
    console.log(`Refilled misting system with
      ${amount}ml of water`)
  }
}
class TropicalPlantCare extends SmartPlantCare {
  constructor(mechanism: WateringMechanism) {
    super(mechanism, 60) // Tropical plants prefer moist soil
  }
  waterPlant(currentMoisture: number): void {
    if (currentMoisture < this.moistureThreshold) {
      this.mechanism.water(100)
    } else {
      console.log("Tropical plant doesn't need watering")
    }
  }
  adjustWatering(weatherForecast: string): void {
    if (weatherForecast.includes("humidity")) {
      this.moistureThreshold += 10
      console.log("Adjusted watering for humid weather")
    } else if (weatherForecast.includes("dry")) {
      this.moistureThreshold -= 10
      console.log("Adjusted watering for dry weather")
    }
  }
}
```

This abstraction of `SmartPlantCare` and `WateringMechanism` separates the logic for different plant types from the mechanism used for watering. The pattern allows us to swap mechanisms without affecting plant care strategies. It might be useful to include a discussion about the trade-off between using this pattern and creating a deep inheritance hierarchy, which might add complexity.

Adding a new mechanism such as `DripIrrigation` wouldn't affect the `SmartPlantCare` class, maintaining the flexibility of the system. This emphasizes the decoupling of abstraction and implementation that's central to the Bridge pattern.

Now, let's check out the test cases for this pattern.

Testing

In this section, we've provided unit tests for the smart plant care system that implements the Bridge pattern using Vitest. These tests will cover both the implementor logic (watering mechanisms) and the abstraction (smart plant care strategies). These tests demonstrate how to verify the behavior of the watering mechanism and the plant care strategies independently.

The test cases that have been provided can be found in the `bridge.test.ts` file in this chapter's source code (see the *Technical requirements* section) for you to review.

To run the test cases, you need to execute the following command :

```
$ npm run test --bridge
```

You should be able to review the test results in the console.

Next, we'll talk about some of the criticisms of the Bridge pattern.

Criticisms

While it offers flexibility and encourages loose coupling, the Bridge pattern isn't without its criticisms. Here are some additional valid criticisms of the Bridge pattern:

- **Increased complexity**: Implementing the Bridge pattern introduces additional layers of abstraction. This can make the code more complex and harder to understand, especially for developers who aren't familiar with the pattern. The added complexity may not be justified if the problem being solved is relatively simple. For instance, in a straightforward application where a single implementation suffices – such as a basic logging system that writes to a file – using the Bridge pattern might introduce unnecessary complexity. Instead of simply extending a logging class to add new functionality, implementing a separate abstraction and multiple implementations can lead to confusion and over-engineering.

- **Not suitable for a single implementation**: If your application only needs a single implementation of the abstraction, using the Bridge pattern can be overkill. In such cases, the benefits of the pattern aren't realized, making the pattern an unnecessary complication.

- **Over-engineering**: There is a risk of over-engineering when using the Bridge pattern. Developers might be tempted to use it preemptively, even if simpler design solutions would suffice. This can lead to unnecessarily complex designs that are harder to maintain and extend.

In summary, while the Bridge pattern offers several advantages, such as being able to decouple abstraction from implementation and promote flexibility, it also introduces complexity and may not be suitable for simpler scenarios or where only a single implementation is needed.

Real-world use cases

A good real-world use case of this pattern is the implementation of a logger. Here, the `Logger` class acts as the abstraction, and the `Appender` interface represents the implementation. This allows us to extend and change the logging mechanisms independently from the logger itself. Here's a quick implementation that provides this abstraction:

```
interface Appender {
    append(message: string): void;
}
abstract class Logger {
    protected appender: Appender;
    constructor(appender: Appender) {
        this.appender = appender;
    }
    abstract log(message: string): void;
}

class ConsoleAppender implements Appender {
    append(message: string): void {
        console.log(`Console: ${message}`);
    }
}

class DebugLogger extends Logger {
    log(message: string): void {
        this.appender.append(`Debug Log: ${message}`);
    }
}
```

We've only shown one implementation for each abstraction here, but you can easily add more. For example, you can have a `FileAppender` interface that appends to the file instead of the console or an `ErrorLogger` interface that uses an `Appender` interface and records specific error messages to the `Appender` interface. In either case, we can add new types of loggers or appenders without changing the existing code, promoting flexibility and scalability.

Now that we've explored the most applicable and practical concepts of the Bridge pattern, let's examine the last pattern that will be covered in this chapter: the Flyweight pattern.

The Flyweight pattern

The last structural design pattern you'll learn about in this chapter is the **Flyweight pattern**. The Flyweight pattern is a structural design pattern that optimizes memory usage of heavy objects – that is, objects that are very expensive to create and initialize. When we have to create lots of those objects, we might see lots of memory spikes, which could potentially affect parts of the system. In that case, we can use the Flyweight pattern to reduce the memory footprint by sharing or reusing functionality.

Environments such as game development, high-performance web applications, and large-scale data processing often require efficient memory management due to the frequent creation of numerous similar objects. In these contexts, the Flyweight pattern shines by allowing applications to share common data among many instances, significantly reducing memory consumption.

One analogy of this pattern is sharing a few traditional costumes among many dancers. Considering those costumes are very expensive to buy sometimes, some of the dancers may have to buy new ones but some may distribute them between performances. The manager, for example, takes the role of the flyweight and decides when they need to purchase new ones or share existing ones. Justifying why and how you should conserve memory resources depends mainly on the runtime platform – for example, with Node.js, the underlying engine of the V8 engine, and with Deno, which has its own engine, similar to V8, with a few differences but based on the same principles.

When to use the Flyweight pattern

Consider using the Flyweight pattern when you want to minimize the use of many objects in the application. In normal operations, this usually translates to common objects such as strings or state variables, though it can expand to other types of objects as well. If you find yourself having to create many objects with a duplicated shared state, then you may wish to consider using this pattern to avoid the extra costs.

Here are a few situations where you might want to use the Flyweight pattern:

- **When you want to use a large number of objects frequently**: The number of objects that are created on the fly is quite numerous and can result in many spikes in memory usage.

- **When you want to share some of the objects in memory or a cache**: You can share some of those most frequent objects with little modifications. You can use a fixed cache to store the most frequent ones.

- **When you have either limited memory or are trying to avoid overloading the garbage collection**: You want to keep the memory usage low and predictable. If you allow arbitrary object creation, then you'll reach limits soon and the application's performance might degrade.

For all the aforementioned reasons, this pattern is an ideal candidate for improving the overall performance of the system. Let's explain the UML class diagram for this pattern.

UML class diagram

When you're trying to implement this pattern, you'll want to structure your shared flyweight objects in a way that you have a separate shared state (*extrinsic*) with a unique parameter to make specializations (*intrinsic*). Then, you can provide different implementations on top of this interface.

The `Flyweight` interface declares the method that concrete flyweights must implement. These methods typically accept extrinsic (*unique*) states as parameters. This can be seen in the following diagram:

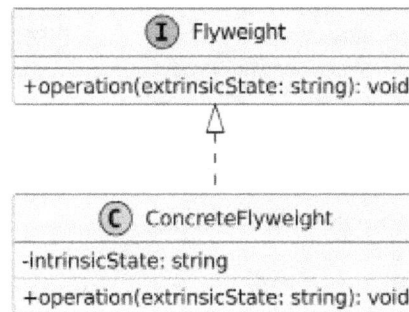

Figure 4.17 – The Flyweight interface

The `Flyweight` interface defines the operation method that all concrete flyweights must implement. Here, `ConcreteFlyweight` implements the `Flyweight` interface. The `intrinsicState` interface is the shared state among multiple objects and `extrinsicState` is the unique state that's passed by the client for each operation.

Next, we have `FlyweightFactory`, which manages flyweight objects and ensures they're shared properly:

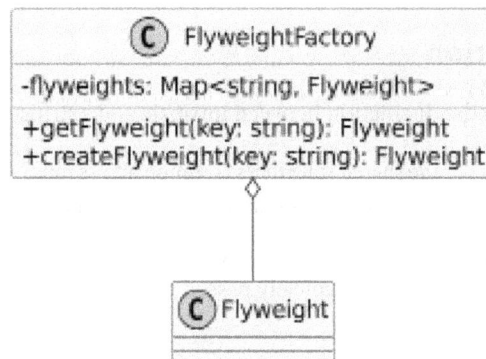

Figure 4.18 – FlyweightFactory

The `FlyweightFactory` method maintains a pool of flyweight objects. The `getFlyweight` method returns an existing flyweight or creates a new one if one doesn't exist, while the `createFlyweight` method creates a new flyweight object.

The following complete UML diagram shows all the components and their relationships:

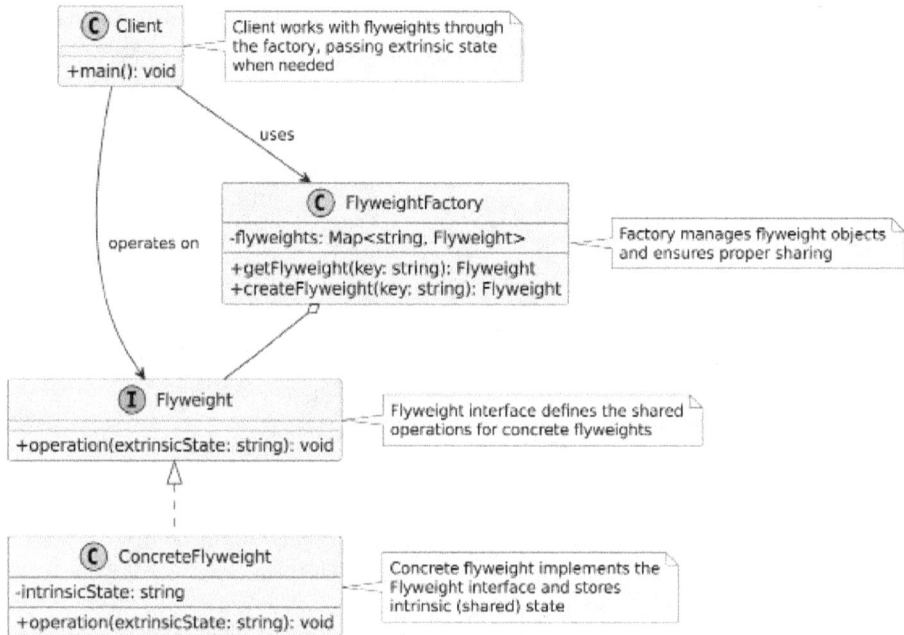

Figure 4.19 – The Flyweight pattern

The `Client` class will call the `FlyweightFactory` method instead of creating `FlyweightObjects` directly. This way, it can manage the creation of those objects in the most optimal way. Let's learn how to implement this pattern.

Classic implementation

A key aspect of this pattern is the distinction between intrinsic and extrinsic states:

- **Intrinsic state**: This refers to the shared state that's common across multiple instances of a flyweight. It typically includes properties that don't change and can be shared among different objects.

- **Extrinsic state**: This represents the unique state specific to each object instance. It can vary from one instance to another and is typically passed to methods when needed.

To implement this pattern, first, you must define the `Flyweight` interface and the `ConcreteFlyweight` object:

flyweight.ts

```typescript
export interface Flyweight {
  perform(customization: { id: string }): void
}
export class ConcreteFlyweight implements Flyweight {
  constructor(private sharedState: Object) {}
  public perform(customization: { id: string }): void {
    console.log(
      `ConcreteFlyweight: Shared (${JSON
      .stringify(this.sharedState)}) and
      unique (${customization.id}) state.`,
    )
  }
}
```

Then, you need to define `FlyweightFactory`. Depending on the type of resource savings you want to achieve, this can be done in many ways. This example shows how to use a cache to store instances of the flyweight objects based on their shared state parameter:

flyweight.ts

```typescript
import QuickLRU from 'quick-lru';
export class FlyweightFactory {
  private cache = new QuickLRU({maxSize: 1000});
  public getFlyweight(sharedState: Object): Flyweight {
    const key = JSON.stringify(sharedState)
    if (!this.cache.has(key)) {
      console.log("FlyweightFactory: Can't find
        a flyweight, creating new one.")
      this.cache.set(key, new
        ConcreteFlyweight(sharedState))
    } else {
      console.log("FlyweightFactory: Reusing
        existing flyweight.")
    }
    return this.cache.get(key)!
  }
  public listFlyweights(): void {
    const count = this.cache.size
```

```
        console.log(`\nFlyweightFactory: I have
          ${count} flyweights:`)
        this.cache.forEach((_, key) => {
            console.log(key);
        });
    }
}
```

This `FlyweightFactory` class uses a cache to share instances of flyweight objects at runtime. The `getFlyweight` method retrieves an already cached instance if available or does so by creating a new instance on the fly. In certain scenarios, it could save us the effort of having to create expensive objects from scratch.

Let's see how the client will use this pattern. The `addCar` function demonstrates how a client would use the Flyweight pattern. It separates the *intrinsic* state (brand, model, and color) from the *extrinsic* state (plates and owner). The intrinsic state is used to get or create a flyweight and the extrinsic state is passed to the `perform` method:

flyweight.ts

```
const factory = new FlyweightFactory()
function addCar(plates: string, owner: string,
    brand: string, model: string, color: string) {
    console.log("\nClient: Adding a car to database.")
    const flyweight = factory.getFlyweight({ brand,
        model, color })
    flyweight.perform({ id: `${plates}_${owner}` })
}
addCar("CL234IR", "James Doe", "Chevrolet",
    "Camaro2018", "pink")
addCar("CL234IR", "James Doe", "BMW", "M5", "red")
addCar("CL234IR", "James Doe", "BMW", "X1", "red")
factory.listFlyweights()
```

The highlighted code shows how the client will use this factory to retrieve objects. It provides the shared parameter that will always return the same object and passes on the customization part's `id` parameter, which is unique to this operation. This way, you can achieve some sort of storage or memory savings.

It's worth mentioning that the Flyweight pattern can often be combined with **object pooling** to optimize both memory and performance further. Object pooling involves managing a collection of reusable objects that can be borrowed and returned rather than created and destroyed repeatedly. This combination is particularly useful in memory-intensive applications such as games or large-scale data processing systems where resource management is critical.

Now, let's consider the test cases for this pattern.

Testing

When writing tests for this pattern, you want to check a few things. First, you'll want to make sure that `FlyweightFactory` creates memory-efficient flyweight objects. You can check that the shared object shares the same internal reference value. This will mean that the objects are shared. The other part of testing is that the flyweight objects themselves need to have the right state and customization based on the passed parameter.

The test cases provided can be found in the `flyweight.test.ts` file in this chapter's source code (see the *Technical requirements* section) for you to review.

To run the test cases, you need to execute the following command:

```
$ npm run test --flyweight
```

You should be able to review the test results in the console.

Now, let's have a look at some of the criticisms of the Flyweight pattern.

Criticisms

Overall, while this pattern is useful, it's still not without its flaws. Here are some of the valid criticisms of the Flyweight pattern:

- **Increased complexity**: Implementing the Flyweight pattern adds complexity to the code, which can make it harder to understand and maintain.

- **Performance overhead**: While it saves memory, the pattern can introduce a slight performance overhead due to the need to search for and retrieve flyweight objects from the cache.

- **Potential for premature optimization**: Implementing this pattern before it's clearly needed can lead to unnecessary complexity without significant benefits.

- **Difficulty in changing shared state**: Once flyweight objects are shared, changing their intrinsic state becomes challenging and can have wide-ranging effects. Imagine a game where multiple characters share a flyweight for their appearance (for example, skin color and outfit). If one character's appearance is modified (for example, their skin color has been changed), all characters sharing that flyweight will reflect this change. This could lead to unexpected results, such as characters appearing differently than intended. To mitigate this issue, consider using *immutable objects* for intrinsic state.

- **Limited applicability**: The pattern is most beneficial in specific scenarios with many similar objects but may not provide significant advantages in other cases.

These criticisms highlight that while the Flyweight pattern can be powerful for optimizing memory usage, it should be applied carefully and only when the benefits outweigh the added complexity and potential drawbacks.

Real-world use cases

A prime example of the Flyweight pattern in action is within text editors or word processing applications. Consider a document with thousands of characters, each potentially having different formatting (font, size, color, and so on). Without the Flyweight pattern, each character would be a separate object with its own formatting information, leading to significant memory usage.

The following code snippet provides a quick implementation of the Flyweight pattern for creating a shared pool of character instances:

```
interface CharacterFlyweight {
    render(position: { x: number, y: number }): void;
}
class CharacterFlyweightFactory {
  private characters = new Map<string,
    CharacterFlyweight>();

  getCharacter(char: string, font: string,
    size: number, color: string): CharacterFlyweight {
      const key = `${char}-${font}-${size}-${color}`;
      if (!this.characters.has(key)) {
        this.characters.set(key, new
          CharacterFlyweightImpl(char, font,
            size, color));
      }
      return this.characters.get(key)!;
    }
  }
}
```

In this example, `CharacterFlyweight` represents a character with its formatting, `CharacterFlyweightFactory` manages the creation and reuse of character flyweights, and `TextEditor` uses the flyweights to represent a document.

Instead of storing formatting information for each character instance, it's shared among similar characters. It's also easy to add new character styles without significantly increasing memory usage.

With this, we've finished exploring all the structural design patterns that matter. We covered quite a lot of content in this chapter, so feel free to take a break before the next one.

Summary

This chapter demonstrated all the fundamental aspects of structural design patterns and how to utilize them effectively in practice. These patterns focus on the internal and external composition of classes and how they share implementations.

We started by discovering the details of the Adapter pattern and how it helps make classes work with others by implementing a common interface. Then, we explored the Bridge pattern, which allows us to separate and abstract from its implementation. We also learned that after using the Decorator and Proxy patterns, you can enhance the functionality of objects at runtime without using inheritance.

Then, we explored how the Façade pattern uses a simpler interface to control complex workflows. By structuring a group of objects as composites, you can create a hierarchical system that shares a common interface. Lastly, using the Flyweight pattern, you learned how to use a shared state to minimize memory usage or space.

Using these patterns will help you structure your code in a nice, abstract way with scalability in mind. But we haven't finished yet. In the next chapter, you'll learn how to leverage behavioral patterns to increase the flexibility of the communication between entities.

Q&A

Feel free to review the following questions and their corresponding answers to address any concerns or gain additional insights:

1. How does the Façade pattern differ from the Proxy pattern?

   Answer: While both patterns can simplify complex systems, they serve different purposes. The Façade pattern provides a simplified interface to a complex subsystem without necessarily having the same interface as the subsystem components. Its primary goal is to reduce complexity for the client. The Proxy pattern, on the other hand, has the same interface as the object it represents. Its main purpose is to control access to an object, often adding functionality such as lazy loading, access control, or logging.

2. What distinguishes the Decorator pattern from the Proxy pattern?

   Answer: Both patterns involve wrapping one object with another, but their intents differ. The Decorator pattern is used to add new behaviors or responsibilities to objects dynamically. Clients can stack multiple decorators on a single object. The Proxy pattern controls access to an object and typically doesn't intend to add new behaviors. The client usually interacts with a single proxy that represents the underlying object.

3. What's the key difference between the Flyweight pattern and object pooling?

    Answer: Both techniques aim to improve resource utilization, but they operate differently. The Flyweight pattern shares a single instance of an object across multiple contexts, focusing on reducing memory usage by sharing an intrinsic state. On the other hand, object pooling maintains a pool of reusable objects so that we can focus on reducing the overhead of object creation and destruction, especially for objects that are expensive to instantiate.

Behavioral Design Patterns for Object Communication

Behavioral patterns address the challenge of assigning responsibilities to objects in a way that promotes decoupling and cohesion. These patterns aim to strike an optimal balance between these two important concepts, enabling client interfaces to interact with objects without needing to understand their internal relationships.

We have split all the behavioral patterns into two logical chapters for easier study.

In this chapter, we focus on patterns that facilitate communication and interaction between objects. In the following chapter, we will focus on the behavioral patterns that manage object state and behavior.

The patterns we provide the details of in this chapter aim to decouple the sender of a request from its receiver. By introducing intermediary objects or abstracting specific behaviors, these patterns ensure that objects can collaborate without needing detailed knowledge of each other's internal workings.

We will examine the following behavioral design patterns in this chapter:

- The Strategy pattern
- The Chain of Responsibility pattern
- The Command pattern
- The Mediator pattern
- The Observer pattern

Again, for each pattern, we will explain its core concept and purpose, benefits, and potential drawbacks, together with implementation details and best practices.

By the end of this chapter, you'll have a deep understanding of how to implement these patterns to decouple object communication, making your applications more flexible and easier to maintain.

Technical requirements

The code bundle for this chapter is available on GitHub here: `https://github.com/PacktPublishing/TypeScript-5-Design-Patterns-and-Best-Practices/tree/main/chapters/chapter05_Behavioral_Design_Patterns_Communication`.

Understanding behavioral design patterns

Behavioral design patterns, in general, focus on the communication between objects, defining abstractions that manage relationships and responsibilities. These patterns address how objects interact and distribute responsibilities by emphasizing efficient message passing and reference management.

One prominent example is the **Observer pattern**, which illustrates how certain patterns use native event systems to pass messages efficiently. This pattern is particularly relevant in JavaScript's event-handling model.

At the core of behavioral patterns are several key concepts:

- First, they establish communication protocols that dictate how and when objects exchange information. This ensures that object interactions are structured and predictable.

- Second, these patterns allow for flexibility in behavior, enabling objects to exhibit diverse behaviors without resorting to hardcoded logic or repetitive code.

- Lastly, behavioral patterns emphasize the encapsulation of functionality, often utilizing helper classes and interfaces to package object behaviors into reusable components.

Behavioral patterns are particularly adept at addressing common challenges in software design. They provide elegant solutions for accessing functionality without direct method calls, which can be beneficial when working with complex or evolving systems. These patterns also excel at managing complex object interactions, offering structured approaches to scenarios where multiple objects need to cooperate or communicate. Moreover, they provide alternatives to implementing varying behaviors without resorting to extensive conditional logic, leading to cleaner and more maintainable code.

I will explain what I mean in greater detail as we look at these patterns, starting with the Strategy pattern.

The Strategy pattern

The **Strategy pattern** is a behavioral design pattern that encapsulates a family of algorithms within a common interface, making them interchangeable at runtime. This powerful pattern allows a system to dynamically alter its behavior by switching between different implementations of a specific process or business logic.

At its heart, this abstraction is conceptually straightforward yet profoundly impactful, as it enables a system to adapt its behavior without modifying its core structure. To determine if this pattern is suitable for your use case, follow the next subsection considerations.

> **Note**
> While the Strategy pattern provides flexibility and maintainability, frequent switching between strategies can introduce performance overhead, especially when switching triggers side effects. Each time a strategy is changed, the system may need to instantiate a new strategy object, which can be costly in terms of performance, particularly if this occurs in a tight loop or high-frequency context.

When to use the Strategy pattern

The Strategy pattern is particularly useful in the following scenarios:

- **Algorithm variants**: When you have multiple variants of an algorithm and need to switch between them dynamically based on runtime conditions. For example, in a tax calculation system, different strategies might be applied based on an individual's marital status, income bracket, or disability status.

- **Behavior encapsulation**: When you want to isolate the implementation details of an algorithm from its usage. This separation allows clients to remain unaware of the specific algorithm being used, promoting loose coupling.

- **Avoiding conditional complexity**: Instead of using multiple conditional statements to determine behavior, the Strategy pattern leverages polymorphism to alter behavior, resulting in cleaner, more maintainable code.

- **Configurability**: When a system needs to be highly configurable, allowing users or administrators to change its behavior without modifying the source code.

- **Object communication**: In the Strategy pattern, communication between objects is facilitated through the context class that holds a reference to a strategy object (commonly prefixed as `Strategy`). This context class delegates specific tasks to the strategy object while remaining agnostic about which algorithm is being used.

While the Strategy pattern's concept is straightforward, its implementation requires careful consideration of how and when to switch between strategies. This often involves designing a mechanism to select the appropriate strategy based on the current context or configuration.

> **Comparing state versus Strategy pattern**
>
> Since we've only introduced the Strategy pattern, it's important to note that it is often compared with the state pattern, which will be introduced in the next chapter. Both patterns encapsulate behavior and allow for dynamic changes, but they serve different purposes. The Strategy pattern is used when you want to select an algorithm from a family of algorithms at runtime, such as a sorting algorithm based on user preference. In contrast, the state pattern is utilized when an object's behavior needs to change based on its internal state. For instance, a media player might behave differently when in *playing*, *paused*, or *stopped* states, with each state encapsulating its own behavior.

In the following sections, we'll explore a UML class diagram of the Strategy pattern and review practical examples to illustrate its implementation and benefits.

UML diagram

The Strategy pattern, at its core, consists of an interface with multiple implementors and a context object that manages the current strategy. Here's a basic UML representation:

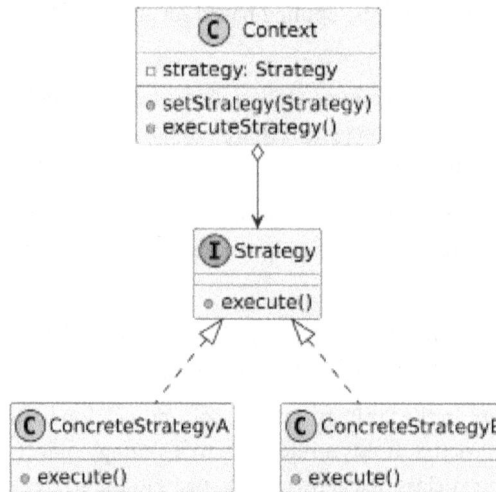

Figure 5.1 – The Strategy pattern

In the diagram shown in *Figure 5.1*, Strategy defines the common method for all concrete strategies. ConcreteStrategyA and ConcreteStrategyB are implementations of the Strategy interface, and Context is the class that manages the current strategy and provides a method to execute it.

This structure allows for flexible billing calculations. Context can switch between different strategies at runtime, providing the ability to alter the billing behavior dynamically based on various conditions or business rules.

We will now implement two different concrete strategies that implement this interface for flexibility.

Classic implementation

Let's implement the Strategy pattern using a simple example of sorting algorithms. This example will demonstrate how different sorting strategies can be used interchangeably. Here, we'll focus on the core structure of the Strategy pattern. If you want to see the full code listing, it will be in the current chapter source code (see the *Technical requirements* section).

Here is an example implementation of the Strategy pattern using sorting algorithms:

Strategy.ts

```
interface SortStrategy {
    sort(data: number[]): number[];
}
class BubbleSort implements SortStrategy {
    sort(data: number[]): number[] {
        // bubble sort implementation }
}
class QuickSort implements SortStrategy {
    sort(data: number[]): number[] {
        //quick sort implementation
        if (data.length <= 1) return data;
    }
}
class Sorter {
  constructor(private strategy: SortStrategy) {
    if (!strategy || typeof strategy.sort !== 'function')
    {
        throw new Error('Invalid strategy provided');
    }
    }


}
const data = [64, 34, 25, 12, 22, 11, 90];
const sorter = new Sorter(new BubbleSort());
sorter.setStrategy(new QuickSort());
```

The provided code defines a flexible sorting mechanism using the Strategy design pattern in TypeScript. It starts with a SortStrategy interface that mandates a sort method, which any sorting algorithm must implement. Two concrete implementations of this interface are provided: BubbleSort and QuickSort, each with its own sorting logic. The BubbleSort class implements the bubble sort algorithm, while the QuickSort class implements the quicksort algorithm.

The Strategy pattern allows for flexible and interchangeable algorithms, making it easy to add new sorting strategies or switch between them based on different requirements without changing the client code.

Now, we'll examine some of the testing strategies of this pattern.

Testing

The most fundamental test you can write for this pattern is to verify that each `Strategy` object performs as expected. For example, if you utilize two different strategies for calculating employee payments based on whether they have a bonus or not, you might check whether the calculation is correct without bonuses and with bonuses.

Use mocking to simulate the context class that uses the strategies. This allows you to test how the context interacts with different strategies without relying on their actual implementations.

Additionally, you may want to test the logic that determines which strategy is applied internally depending on the context. You may want to add test cases that trigger the `setStrategy` method and verify that the correct strategy is used.

We provide test cases in the `strategy.test.ts` file located in the current chapter source code (see the *Technical requirements* section), which you will be able to review.

To run the test cases, you need to execute the following command:

```
$ npm run test --strategy
```

You should be able to review the test results in the console. Now, let's discuss the criticisms of this pattern.

Criticisms

While the Strategy pattern offers significant benefits in terms of flexibility and maintainability, it's important to consider how appropriate it is for each specific use case. Here are some key points to consider:

- **Complexity versus benefit**: The Strategy pattern introduces additional classes and interfaces, which can increase the overall complexity of your code base. For simple scenarios with only two or three variations, a simple `if` statement or a lambda function might be more appropriate and easier to understand. The pattern becomes more valuable when you have multiple, complex algorithms that need to be interchanged.

- **Overuse in simple scenarios**: It's tempting to apply the Strategy pattern everywhere once you're familiar with it. However, for very simple variations or when you're unlikely to add more strategies in the future, this pattern might be overkill. Always consider the current and future complexity of your system.

- **Increased number of classes**: Each new strategy typically requires a new class, which can lead to a proliferation of classes in your project. This can make the code base harder to navigate, especially for developers unfamiliar with the pattern.

- **Context sharing**: If strategies need to share a state or context, you might need to pass additional parameters to the strategy methods or maintain a shared state in the context object. This can sometimes lead to tighter coupling between the context and the strategies.

In practice, the decision to use the Strategy pattern should be based on a careful analysis of your specific requirements, the complexity of your algorithms, and the likelihood of future changes or additions to these algorithms. Let's explore some real-life examples of this pattern next.

Real-life use cases

This pattern is very popular in auth frameworks where you want to define multiple strategies for authentication. For example, we can inspect the code base of the `nuxt-auth` module, which is a Vue.js framework for developing web applications. In the type definition of this module for the provider, we can see the `addAuthorize` function:

```
https://github.com/nuxt-community/auth-module/blob/5a3c3a8a53195618
923726b70f19b2ee8336b333/src/utils/provider.ts
```

The code accepts a `StrategyOptions` type, which can be several different types of auth strategies based on the OAuth framework. It then defines multiple auth strategies in the **Providers** section for authenticating with GitHub, Facebook, Google, and other OAuth providers:

```
https://github.com/nuxt-community/auth-module/tree/75c20e64cc2bb8d4
db7d7fc772432132a1d9e417/src/providers
```

Frameworks such as `Passport.js` work similarly. They define multiple authentication strategies for each provider.

OK, now we will examine in detail the basic concepts of the Chain of Responsibility pattern.

The Chain of Responsibility pattern

The **Chain of Responsibility pattern** is a behavioral design pattern that allows an object to be processed as a series of independent handlers along a chain. Each handler gets to process the current object reference and decide whether to pass it along to the next handler or process it before doing so.

Imagine a corporate hierarchy handling customer complaints:

1. The front desk employee tries to resolve the issue.

2. If unable, they escalate to their supervisor.

3. The supervisor attempts to address the problem.

4. If still unresolved, it's passed to the department manager.

5. Finally, if necessary, it reaches the CEO.

Each level in this hierarchy represents a handler in the chain of responsibility.

The pattern's strength lies in its ability to distribute responsibilities among multiple objects, avoiding the concentration of logic in a single function or class. This distribution enhances maintainability and allows for more flexible and scalable systems.

When to use the Chain of Responsibility pattern

The Chain of Responsibility pattern is particularly valuable in scenarios where you need to process a request through multiple handlers dynamically. Here are some key situations where this pattern is useful:

- **Multiple handler scenarios**: When you have multiple objects that can handle a request, and the handler isn't known *a priori*. The pattern allows you to chain these handlers and let the request be processed by the appropriate handler dynamically.

- **Decoupled request processing**: When you want to decouple the sender of a request from its receivers. This pattern allows you to build a chain of objects that will pass the request along until an object handles it.

- **Dynamic chain configuration**: When you need the ability to add, remove, or reorder handlers at runtime. This flexibility allows for easy configuration and customization of the processing pipeline without modifying existing code.

- **Hierarchical request handling**: In systems with a natural hierarchy (such as GUI event handling or logging systems), where requests should be passed up the hierarchy until handled.

Using this pattern provides several benefits with decoupling, as it provides a way of having the two objects connected to each other but without any hard dependencies. If you change one object, it will not affect the other and vice versa. You will see the UML class diagram of this pattern next.

Comparing Mediator versus Chain of Responsibility pattern

The Mediator pattern, which will be discussed later in this chapter, has similar responsibilities. Both patterns aim to decouple components and facilitate communication. The Chain of Responsibility pattern allows a request to be passed along a chain of potential handlers until one of them processes it. In contrast, the Mediator pattern centralizes communication between components, allowing them to interact indirectly through a mediator object, without them being aware of each other. For instance, in a chat application, users (colleagues) communicate through a chat room (mediator), which manages the flow of messages and ensures that users do not need to know about each other's implementations.

UML class diagram

The main class model of this pattern is the `Request` object. This is passed along the chain and gets transformed based on the handlers attached to that chain. Here is an example visualization:

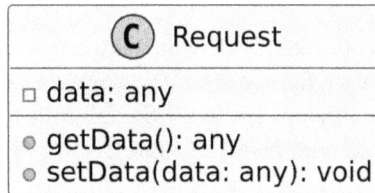

Figure 5.2 – The Request object

Then, you will need to attach the chain of handlers that will process this `Request` object. This is done by having an interface or a `RequestHandler` abstract class that each concrete handler will implement:

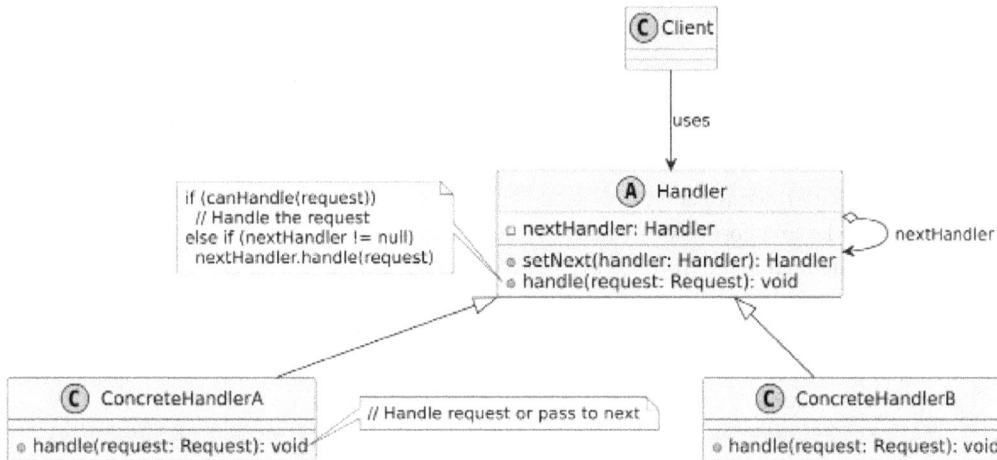

Figure 5.3 – Chain of Responsibility

In the preceding diagram, you can see that both the `ConcreteHandler` classes are chained together. `Handler` is an abstract class that defines the interface for handling requests and maintaining the chain. The `setNext` method allows for chaining handlers and `handle` is an abstract method that concrete handlers must implement. `ConcreteHandlerA` and `ConcreteHandlerB` are specific implementations of `Handler`.

Now that you have examined the class diagram, you will learn how to implement it in TypeScript.

Classic implementation

If you were to implement this pattern, you would need to figure out the details of the `Request` object. You want to design it in a way that makes it easy to access its fields to perform additional actions on top of it.

Here, we create a customer support ticket system, which is a common real-life application of this pattern. We define the `Request` object, for example, as a `SupportTicket` class. Here, we'll focus on the core structure of the pattern. If you want to see the full code listing it will be in the current chapter source code (see the *Technical requirements* section).

Here is an example implementation of a customer support ticket system using the `Request` object pattern:

```
constructor(
  private id: number,
  private customer: string,
  private issue: string,
  private priority: number,
) {}
 // Getter and Setter methods here
}
```

The `SupportTicket` interface and the `CustomerSupportTicket` class represent a customer support ticket with relevant information and include methods to get ticket details and set/get resolutions. The actual chain is defined in the `SupportHandler` class as follows:

Chain-of-responsibility.ts

```
    if (ticket.getPriority() <= 1) {
      ticket.setResolution("Resolved by Front Desk: General inquiry
handled")
      console.log(`Ticket ${ticket.getId()} handled by Front Desk`)
    } else if (this.nextHandler) {
      this.nextHandler.handle(ticket)
    }
  }
}
class TechnicalSupportHandler extends SupportHandler {
  handle(ticket: SupportTicket): void {
    if (ticket.getPriority() <= 3) {
      ticket.setResolution("Resolved by Technical Support: Technical
issue addressed")
      console.log(`Ticket ${ticket.getId()} handled by Technical
Support`)
```

```
      } else if (this.nextHandler) {
        this.nextHandler.handle(ticket)
      }
    }
  }
}
const frontDesk = new FrontDeskHandler();
const techSupport = new TechnicalSupportHandler();
frontDesk.setNext(techSupport);
const tickets: SupportTicket[] = [
    new CustomerSupportTicket(1, "John Doe",
      "General inquiry", 1),
    new CustomerSupportTicket(2, "Jane Smith",
      "Software bug", 2),
];
tickets.forEach(ticket => {
    console.log(`Processing ticket ${ticket.getId()} for ${ticket.
getCustomer()}`);
    frontDesk.handle(ticket);
    console.log(`Resolution: ${ticket.getResolution()}\n`);
});
```

The SupportHandler abstract class defines the structure for handlers in the chain and includes a setNext method for easy chaining of handlers. FrontDeskHandler handles low-priority tickets and TechnicalSupportHandler handles medium-priority tickets. We can also add another handler that handles high-priority tickets.

The usage example creates a chain of handlers (Front Desk | Technical Support) and processes various tickets through the chain. Each chain handler will be called based on the order that was attached to the list. Let's learn how to test this pattern next.

Testing

When writing test cases for this pattern, you want to check the core functionality of the Chain of Responsibility pattern, ensuring that tickets are processed correctly, the chain is traversed as expected, and the overall system behaves consistently. The key is to test not just individual components but also their interaction within the chain. Write tests for the expected behavior of each handler before implementing them.

Use mocking to ensure that when one handler cannot process a request, it correctly passes it to the next handler in the chain.

We provide test cases in the chain-of-responsibility.test.ts file located in the current chapter source code (see the *Technical requirements* section), which you will be able to review.

To run the test cases, you need to execute the following command:

```
$ npm run test --chain-of-responsibility
```

You should be able to review the test results in the console.

Criticisms

If you utilize this pattern, you will soon encounter the following issues:

- **Chain breakage**: The chain can break if a handler fails to pass the request to the next handler or throws an unhandled exception.

- **Performance overhead**: Long chains can lead to performance degradation, especially. Each request must traverse the chain until it finds a handler, which can introduce latency. Additionally, if many handlers are involved, the overhead of passing the request through multiple objects can accumulate.

- **Complexity and debugging**: As the chain grows, it can become difficult to debug and understand the flow of control. You need to be able to inject debugging handlers so that this process becomes easier.

- **Guarantee of handling**: There's no guarantee that a request will be handled if it reaches the end of the chain without being processed. You will have to include a default handler just in case this happens.

- **Potential for duplicate code**: Like the Decorator pattern, there might be code duplication across handlers, especially in the logic for passing to the next handler.

- **Difficult to visualize at runtime**: The dynamic nature of the chain can make it challenging to understand the current state of the system.

- **Potential for circular references**: If not carefully managed, it's possible to create circular chains, leading to infinite loops.

To successfully address some of the preceding issues, you need a thoughtful approach. Clear documentation of the chain structure and individual handler responsibilities is important. Handlers should be designed to be modular and independent, facilitating easy rearrangement and testing. A robust configuration system can manage chain composition, allowing for modifications without code changes. Comprehensive logging and monitoring are essential for tracking request flow and identifying issues. Regular reviews of the chain structure ensure it remains optimal and doesn't grow unnecessarily complex. Finally, performance profiling, especially in production-like environments, helps maintain efficiency.

With those caveats explained, we explore a real-life use case of this pattern.

Real-life use case

One good real-life use case of this pattern is in `Express.js` middleware handlers. Those are functions that have access to the request and response objects as part of the application's HTTP handling workflow.

You can see an example implementation of this pattern by inspecting the `handle` method here: `https://github.com/expressjs/express/blob/master/lib/application.js#L165`.

In this method, it retrieves the internal instance of the router and calls the route's `handle` method, which subsequently triggers the chain of handlers:

```
var router = this._router;
router.handle(req, res, done);
```

In this case, the router represents the `RequestHandler` object. Each handler is registered in the application by using the `app.use` method, which adds more handlers to the chain. Typically, you pre-register those handlers before starting the server to listen to requests, but this is not a limitation as you can do it dynamically as well.

These real-life examples demonstrate the versatility and wide applicability of the Chain of Responsibility pattern. It's particularly useful in scenarios where the exact sequence of processing is not known in advance or needs to be dynamically configurable.

As you've understood the basic principles of this pattern in practice, you will now learn about the next pattern on the list, which is the Command pattern.

The Command pattern

The **Command pattern** is a behavioral design pattern that uses an object to represent actions that work on behalf of the original caller. This pattern provides several benefits:

- **Separation of concerns**: It separates the caller of the operation from the actual implementor (aka the code that executes the operation)
- **Extensibility**: New commands can be added without changing existing code
- **Queueing and logging**: Commands can be queued, logged, or undone easily
- **Parameterization**: Objects can be parameterized with different requests

An analogy of this pattern is in a restaurant scenario: The customer (client) creates an order (command). The waiter (invoker) takes the order, and the chef (receiver) prepares the dish according to the order.

When to use the Command pattern

The Command pattern is particularly useful in several scenarios:

- **Decoupling sender and receiver**: When you need to distinguish the object that initiates an operation (sender) from the object that performs the operation (receiver). This separation allows for greater flexibility and extensibility in your system.

- **Parameterizing objects with actions**: When you want to configure objects with different requests or operations at runtime. This allows for dynamic behavior changes without modifying existing code.

- **Implementing undo/redo functionality**: The Command pattern is excellent for implementing undo and redo operations in applications, such as text editors or graphic design tools. Each command can store the state required to undo its effects.

- **Queueing operations**: When you need to queue requests and execute them at different times or in a specific order. This is particularly useful in multi-threaded applications or when dealing with transactional systems.

- **Creating composite commands**: When you need to implement complex operations that consist of simpler operations. The Command pattern allows you to create composite commands (macros) that execute multiple commands in sequence.

- **Supporting transactional behavior**: When you need to ensure that all operations in a transaction are completed, or none are. Commands can be designed to support rollbacks in case of failures.

The pattern also makes it easy to extend the system with new commands. As long as the commands are implemented with the same interface, you can support multiple types of actions.

> **Comparing Command versus Observer pattern**
>
> The Observer pattern, which will be discussed later, shares common functionality with the Command pattern as both patterns aim to decouple components from each other. The Command pattern encapsulates requests as objects, allowing you to parameterize actions and implement features, such as undo/redo functionality. In contrast, the Observer pattern allows an object (the subject) to notify multiple observers about changes in its state without them being tightly coupled. For instance, in a stock market application, multiple display components can observe stock price changes and update automatically when prices change.

Now, let's explore the class diagram of this pattern.

UML class diagram

The Command pattern involves several key components that work together to decouple the sender of a request from the object that performs the request. We depict this in the following class diagram:

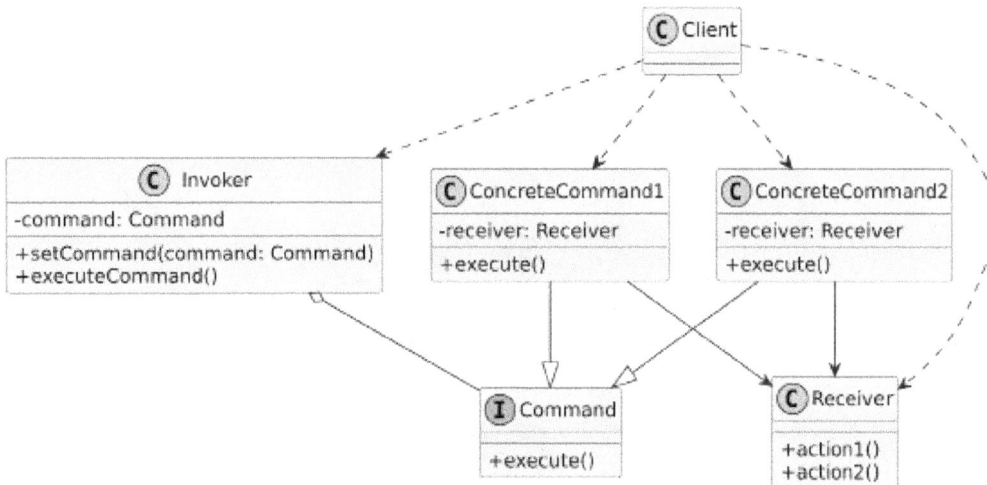

Figure 5.4 – The Command pattern

Let's break down the UML class diagram into its constituent parts and explain each component:

- Command: The Command interface declares the method for executing a command.
- **Concrete commands**: These are specific implementations of the Command interface. Each concrete command defines the binding between a Receiver class and an action.
- Receiver: The Receiver class knows how to execute the implementation part of the command.
- Invoker: The Invoker class knows when to send the command to the potential receivers.
- Client: The Client class creates a ConcreteCommand object and sets its receiver.

The relationships in the diagram show that Client creates and configures the concrete commands, Receiver, and Invoker. The concrete commands inherit from the Command interface. The concrete commands have a reference to Receiver, and finally, Invoker has a composition relationship with Command, meaning it contains a Command object.

This structure allows for new commands to be added without changing existing code and Commands can be swapped at runtime, allowing for dynamic behavior changes. We'll show how to implement this pattern next.

Classic implementation

Based on the previous class diagram, you can define the following classes that represent a simple smart home system using TypeScript:

Command.ts

```
  turnOff(): void {
    console.log("Light is turned off")
  }
}
class TurnOnLightCommand implements Command {
  constructor(private light: Light) {}
  execute(): void {
    this.light.turnOn()
  }
}
class TurnOffLightCommand implements Command {
  constructor(private light: Light) {}
  execute(): void {
    this.light.turnOff()
  }
}
```

In the preceding code, you define the `Command` interface, the `Light` class, and some concrete implementations. Each command calls a specific method of the `Receiver` object (`Light`).

Then, you want to define the controller object that will accept commands from the client:

Command.ts

```
    private commands: Command[] = [];
    addCommand(command: Command): void {
        this.commands.push(command);
    }
    executeCommands(): void {
        this.commands.forEach(command =>
            command.execute());
        this.commands = [];
    }
}
const light = new Light();
const controller = new SmartHomeController();
```

```
controller.addCommand(new TurnOnLightCommand(light));
controller.addCommand(new TurnOffLightCommand(light));
controller.executeCommands();
```

The pattern decouples the requester of an action (`controller`) from the object that performs the action (`light`). The main element here is the `SmartHomeController` class, which accepts `Command` objects.

The client creates `Light` and `SmartHomeController` objects, adds commands to the controller, and then executes them. This structure allows for an easy addition of new commands and devices without modifying existing code. Let's see how to test this pattern next.

Testing

To ensure our Command pattern implementation works correctly, we'll write unit tests for each component. These tests will verify that commands are executed properly and that `SmartHomeController` manages commands as expected. Use mocking receivers to ensure that commands execute correctly without needing to invoke real operations. This isolates tests and focuses on command behavior.

We provide test cases in the `command.test.ts` file located in the current chapter source code (see the *Technical requirements* section), which you will be able to review.

To run the test cases, you need to execute the following command:

```
$ npm run test --command
```

You should be able to review the test results in the console. Now, let's discuss some criticisms of the Command pattern.

Criticisms

While the Command pattern offers several benefits, it's important to consider its potential drawbacks and limitations. Understanding these can help developers make informed decisions about when and how to apply this pattern. Here are some valid points:

- **Increased complexity and abstraction**: The primary criticism of the Command pattern is that it introduces additional layers of abstraction, which can make the code base more complex and harder to navigate. The pattern creates a level of indirection between action creators and handlers. This can make it challenging to trace the flow of execution, especially for developers new to the code base.

- **Potential performance overhead**: The pattern introduces additional method calls (e.g., `execute()`), which, while usually negligible, could impact performance in extremely performance-sensitive applications.

- **Overengineering risk**: For simple applications or those with a limited set of operations, implementing the Command pattern might introduce unnecessary complexity without providing significant benefits. In systems where commands rarely change, the additional structure imposed by the pattern could create a maintenance burden without valued benefits.

- **Potential for misuse**: There's a risk of creating too many small, specific command classes, leading to a proliferation of classes in the system. Also, if not implemented carefully, commands can become tightly coupled to their receivers, reducing the flexibility that the pattern is meant to provide.

As always, the Command pattern, like any design pattern, is a tool that should be applied judiciously. While it can greatly enhance the flexibility and maintainability of a system, it's crucial to weigh its benefits against its potential drawbacks in the context of your specific project requirements, team expertise, and long-term maintenance considerations.

Real-life use case

One real-life use case of this pattern is with the **Redux library**, which is a state management tool for React. It is explained in more detail on their documentation site:

`https://redux.js.org/tutorials/essentials/part-1-overview-concepts`

In Redux, you use actions to encapsulate events that occur in the app based on user activities or triggers. Here is an example action:

```
const addTodoAction: Action = {
  type: 'todos/addTodo',
  payload: 'Buy groceries'
}
```

This code represents the command object and it entails all the information for the handler to perform updates. On the other side, the handler in Redux is called `Reducer` and it's a function that receives the current state and an action and reduces or produces a new state based on that action payload:

```
(state: TodoState, action: Action) => TodoState
```

The return type of this function is a new `TodoState` object after it has processed the action.

As you can examine, there are similar concepts involved here and it's a great way to see that pattern used in practice. Next, you will learn how to master the Mediator pattern.

The Mediator pattern

The **Mediator pattern** is a behavioral design pattern that reconciles the communication between multiple objects or components. It introduces a mediator object that acts as an intermediary, coordinating interactions between various elements of a system. Its key characteristics are as follows:

- **Centralized communication**: The mediator serves as a hub, managing and simplifying the communication between different parts of a system

- **Reduced dependencies**: By routing all interactions through the mediator, individual components don't need to have direct knowledge of each other, reducing dependencies

- **Simplified interfaces**: The mediator presents a unified interface for complex subsystems, hiding their intricacies from clients

- **Flexibility and maintainability**: Changes in the subsystem can be localized to the mediator, minimizing the impact on client code

As an analogy, consider the role of a solicitor in interactions with a government agency. You (the client) need to interact with a government agency (complex subsystem) in a different region. Instead of dealing directly with the agency, you hire a solicitor (mediator). The solicitor, with power of attorney, acts on your behalf, handling all communications and processes with the agency.

> **Note**
> It is crucial to maintain clear boundaries regarding the responsibilities of the mediator. Overloading the mediator with too many responsibilities can lead to a monolithic design, making it difficult to manage and maintain.

You will learn the main reasons why you should use this pattern next.

When to use the Mediator pattern

The Mediator pattern is beneficial when you want to do the following:

- **Reduce coupling and centralize communication**: Use a `Mediator` object to decouple communication between objects and to maintain a single point of communication. It will allow changes to one set of objects without affecting others.

- **Simplify complex interactions between systems**: Use this pattern to manage intricate relationships between objects. Ease modification of individual components without widespread impact. For example, to replace direct method calls between objects with `Mediator`-coordinated communication.

By employing the Mediator pattern, we can significantly reduce system complexity and improve overall design flexibility. Let's see what the class diagram looks like for this pattern.

UML class diagram

The Mediator pattern's structure is represented in a UML class diagram that illustrates the key components and their relationships. The diagram showcases the following elements (see *Figure 5.5*):

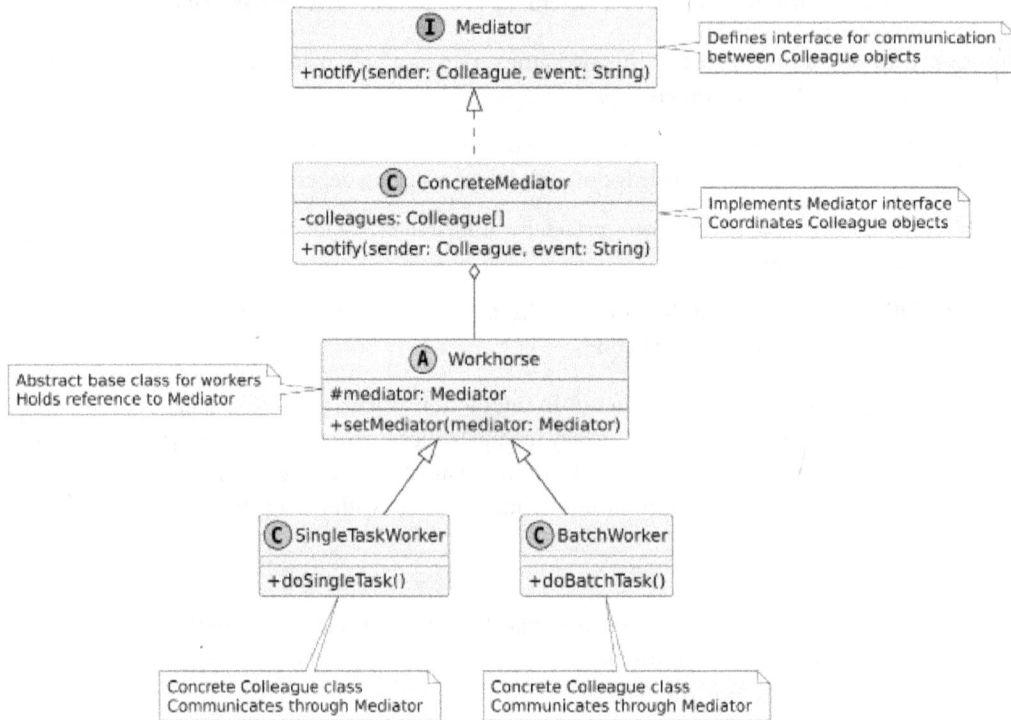

Figure 5.5 – The Mediator pattern

The diagram visually represents the relationships between the classes in the Mediator pattern. The `Mediator` interface is implemented by the `ConcreteMediator` class, which has a composition relationship with the `Workhorse` abstract class. `ConcreteMediator` aggregates all the objects it needs to coordinate. It acts as a central point of communication, triggering methods or events on `SingleTaskWorker` or `BatchWorker` as needed. Both `SingleTaskWorker` and `BatchWorker` inherit from `Workhorse`, allowing them to utilize `Mediator` for communication.

We'll explain what we mean by seeing an example implementation next.

Classic implementation

First, we define the basic interface for `Mediator` and its concrete implementation:

```
    if (message.startsWith("batch_job_completed")) {
      this.workerB.performWork()
    }
  }
}
```

Here, the `WorkerCenter` class implements the `WorkerMediator` interface. It manages the communication between the `BatchWorker` and `SingleTaskWorker` objects. The `triggerEvent` method contains the core logic for coordinating interactions between workers.

Next, we define the abstract base class for workers and the concrete worker classes:

mediator.ts

```
    this.mediator?.triggerEvent(this,
      "batch_job_completed")
  }
  public finalize(): void {
    console.log("Performing final work in BatchWorker")
    this.mediator?.triggerEvent(this,
      "final_job_completed")
  }
}
class SingleTaskWorker extends Workhorse {
  public performWork(): void {
    console.log("Performing work in SingleTaskWorker")
    this.mediator?.triggerEvent(this,
      "single_job_completed")
  }
}
```

Here, the `Workhorse` abstract class provides a common structure for all worker classes, including a reference to the mediator. The following two classes extend the `Workhorse` base class and implement their specific work methods.

Here's how a client would use this pattern:

mediator.ts

```
const workerA = new BatchWorker();
const workerB = new SingleTaskWorker();
```

```
const mediator = new WorkerCenter(workerA, workerB);
workerA.performWork();
```

The mediator is passed as a reference to each worker. The client interacts with the workers directly, but the mediator handles inter-object communications. `performWork` is the starting point of the whole chain of events. Thus, by implementing this pattern, you create a flexible system where objects can interact without direct knowledge of each other. Now, let's move on to learning how to test this pattern.

Testing

When testing this pattern, you want to verify that the mediator responds to the events from the objects it listens to and delegates their events in a specific order. For example, when it accepts a message from a particular sender, it should trigger a message to the relevant objects based on the business logic we defined. In our example, if you get a message from `SingleTaskWorker`, then you should expect another message to the `finalize()` method of `BatchWorker`.

On the other hand, you want to check whether the concrete components trigger a message to the mediator during their method calls. This ensures that the mediator receives events too.

Mock components that interact with the mediator to isolate their behavior during testing. This allows you to verify that messages are sent and received correctly.

We provide test cases in the `mediator.test.ts` file located in the current chapter source code (see the *Technical requirements* section), which you will be able to review.

To run the test cases, you need to execute the following command:

```
$ npm run test --mediator
```

You should be able to review the test results in the console. Now, let's discuss some criticisms of the Mediator pattern.

Criticisms

One significant issue of using this pattern is stack overflows. If one service calls another through `Mediator`, there is a chance of unintentionally triggering the same function again, leading to an infinite loop. For example, in our implementation, if the first call in the mediator were replaced with the following code, it would cause a stack overflow:

```
if (message.startsWith("single_job_completed")) {
    this.workerB.performWork(); // stack overflow error
}
```

Additionally, using the Mediator pattern can lead to complex interactions that are difficult to test and debug. Since the mediator acts as the single point of interaction for various components, it can become a bottleneck and a potential source of bugs. When the mediator's logic becomes intricate, identifying and resolving issues can be challenging. Testing also becomes more complicated because you need to account for the mediator's state and behavior along with the individual components.

Furthermore, the mediator can grow into a monolithic piece of code if not managed properly. As more components interact through the mediator, it might accumulate numerous responsibilities, violating the Single Responsibility Principle. This complexity can make the system harder to maintain and extend over time.

Real-life use cases

There are many good use cases where you can apply the Mediator pattern in practice. Here are some suggested options:

- **Chatroom application**: You are designing a chatroom application and you create entities for the chatroom, chat users, and inbox. You want to implement a feature to allow two users to communicate with each other via direct messages. You don't want to allow one user to directly receive a reference from another user to send a message. Preferably, you'd use a mediator to trigger message events so that whenever a message is posted, it will forward it to the right recipient.

- **UI elements interacting with each other**: You have some UI elements, such as an icon with a counter, and in some parts of the application, you have a button that, when you click on it, should update that counter after it has performed an operation. You may use this pattern to trigger an event when the button completes the operation so that the mediator will forward a new counter update for that icon.

As always, you should always think twice before applying this pattern as you will have to make sure it does not become too big or full of surprises when used in production. Hopefully, if you can apply reason, you will gain lots of benefits from this pattern. Next, we look at the last pattern of this chapter, the Observer pattern.

The Observer pattern

The **Observer pattern** is a behavioral design pattern that implements a system for objects to post events and other objects to subscribe to those events and act accordingly. This pattern is also known as the **publish-subscribe pattern**.

At its core, the Observer pattern consists of two main components:

- **Subject (publisher)**: An object that facilitates posting new events into the registered list of subscribers

- **Observer (subscriber)**: An object with a method that gets called when the Subject's state changes

As an analogy, think of a newspaper subscription service: The newspaper company (subject) maintains a list of subscribers (observers). When a new edition is published, all subscribers are automatically notified, and subscribers can join or leave the subscription list at any time.

The Observer pattern is particularly useful in scenarios where you want to avoid direct calls between subsystems that should not know each other's existence. It's a fundamental pattern in event-driven programming and is widely used in implementing distributed event-handling systems. Let's explain when to use this pattern next.

When to use the Observer pattern

The Observer pattern is useful when you want to establish a one-to-many relationship between a single sender and multiple receivers. Allowing multiple objects to be notified of changes promotes loose coupling. Here are the main use cases and benefits:

- **Create a one-to-many communication between objects**: This is when you have an object that publishes events to multiple objects in a decoupled way. The publisher does not know the details of the subscriber list and it can change its implementation details irrespectively. For example, say you have a `Counter` store object that counts clicks on a web page. You also have multiple widgets that show the count of the web page. When the `Counter` store gets updated, you want the widgets to reflect the current count as well.

- **Trigger events to different parts of an application without coupling dependencies**: The subscribers join the publisher object mainly because it needs to receive updates for specific cases. Then, it will perform its internal business logic or update its own state. This way, you can update different parts of the application without even passing references of objects as parameters.

This pattern is particularly powerful in event-driven and reactive programming paradigms, enabling a clean separation of concerns and dynamic object relationships. Now, we'll look at the UML class diagram of the Observer pattern.

> Comparing the Observer versus Chain of Responsibility pattern
>
> Both the Chain of Responsibility and Observer patterns have similar purposes. One can implement the Chain of Responsibility using Observables, but not vice versa. In my opinion, the Observer pattern covers a more general case since it allows for dynamic subscriptions and the composition of observable operators.

UML class diagram

The Observer pattern's structure is represented in a UML class diagram that illustrates the key components and their relationships. The diagram showcases the following elements:

- **Subject (publisher):** This is the core class that maintains the state and notifies observers of any changes

- **Observer (subscriber):** This is an interface or abstract class that defines the update method for observers

- **Concrete Observer:** These are the classes that implement the Observer interface and receive updates from the Subject.

Here's the UML diagram representing this structure:

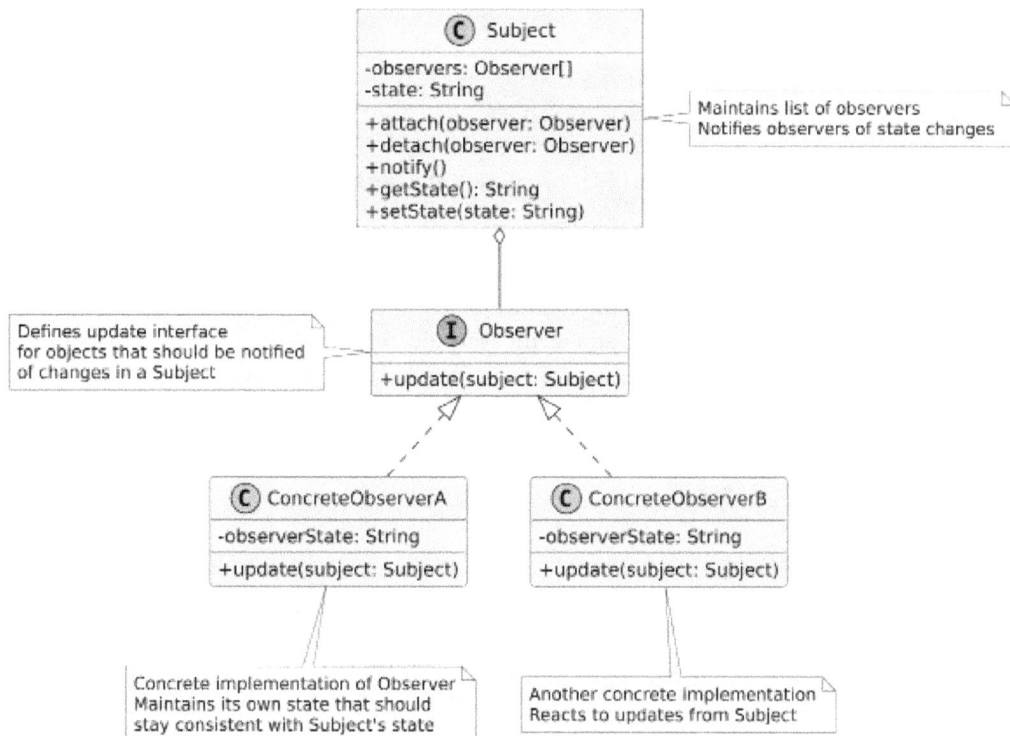

Figure 5.6 – The Observer pattern

In the preceding diagram, `Subject` represents the object that holds the state of the application and notifies the subscribers of any updates of this state. `Subscriber` represents the `Observer` object that listens to events from `Subject`. The shared state property is retrieved by the `Subscriber` object once it is notified by `Subject`.

The `Subject` object can also add or remove subscribers on the fly. This is to ensure the dynamic nature of the list and to ensure accurate message passing. In the next section, we will now show how to implement this pattern.

Classic implementation

This implementation follows the UML class diagram we discussed earlier. We'll create a `Subscriber` interface, a `Subject` abstract class, and concrete implementations for both:

Observer.ts

```
  }
  public notify(message?: any): void {
    console.log("Notifying all subscribers")
    this.subscribers.forEach((s) => s.notify(message))
  }
}
```

Here, the `Subscriber` interface defines the contract for all concrete subscribers and the `Subject` class manages the subscriber list and provides methods to add, remove, and notify subscribers.

Then, we provide the rest of the classes:

Observer.ts

```
    }
  }
class ConcreteSubscriber implements Subscriber {
    private state: any;

    constructor(private subject: ConcreteSubject) {}
    public notify(message: any): void {
        this.state = message;
        console.log(`ConcreteSubscriber: Received update with state:
${this.state}`);
    }
}
```

Here, ConcreteSubject extends Subject and manages the state. It notifies subscribers when the state changes. ConcreteSubscriber implements the Subscriber interface and defines how it reacts to notifications.

The following code demonstrates how the clients will use this pattern:

```
const subject = new ConcreteSubject();
const subscriberA = new ConcreteSubscriber(subject);
subject.addSubscriber(subscriberA);
const subscriberB = new ConcreteSubscriber(subject);
subject.addSubscriber(subscriberB);
subject.setState(19);
subject.removeSubscriber(subscriberB);
subject.setState(21);
```

The Subject class adds all subscriber lists at runtime. Then, it updates its state property and calls notify(). This will trigger all the associated subscribers who will receive the new state and perform their own updates. This way, the communication between the subject and the subscriber list is decoupled.

We'll describe some ideas for how to test this pattern next.

Testing

When testing this pattern, you want to establish the following test criteria. First, you need to have a solid Subject class implementation that does not hold references or introduce memory leaks when destroyed. It needs to clean up its resources properly. The methods for unsubscribe should also be consistent and remove the associated subscribers from the list for any subsequent messages. Then, for each observer, you will need to write test cases that perform correct business logic when they receive a message from Subject.

Use mocks for observers in your tests to verify that they receive updates from the subject without relying on their actual implementations.

We provide test cases in the observer.test.ts file located in the current chapter source code (see the *Technical requirements* section), which you will be able to review.

To run the test cases, you need to execute the following command:

```
$ npm run test --observer
```

You should be able to review the test results in the console. Now, let's discuss some criticisms of the Observer pattern.

Criticisms

While the Observer pattern is widely used and offers many benefits, it's important to be aware of its potential drawbacks and challenges. Here are the key criticisms and considerations:

- **Memory leaks**: One of the most significant risks is the potential for memory leaks. If subjects hold strong references to observers and are not properly removed, observers may be kept in memory even when they're no longer needed.

- **Performance concerns**: Calls can become a bottleneck, especially with many observers. Notifying observers typically happens in linear time ($O(n)$), which can cause noticeable delays with many observers. In single-threaded environments, long-running observer updates can block the entire application.

- **Unexpected updates**: Observers might receive updates at unexpected times, leading to complex and hard-to-debug behavior. The loose coupling that makes the pattern flexible can also make it harder to reason about the flow of updates. Cascading updates (where one update triggers another) can lead to subtle bugs.

- **Overhead in simple scenarios**: For simple relationships, the Observer pattern might introduce unnecessary complexity. Setting up the infrastructure for subjects and observers can be overkill for straightforward one-to-one relationships.

Despite these criticisms, the Observer pattern remains a valuable tool in software design when used appropriately. Proper implementation and awareness of these potential issues can help mitigate many of these drawbacks.

Real-life use cases

This pattern is used quite frequently in production systems because of its flexibility. You will examine the real-life use cases of this pattern in *Chapter 8*. For reference, we will explain the usage of **Observables**, which is a construct that builds upon the principles of reactive programming, functional programming, and the Observer pattern. You will learn how to use **RxJS**, which is a reactive programming library to create, operate, and combine Observables at scale.

Summary

This chapter explored five key behavioral design patterns for object-to-object communication, enabling flexible and decoupled interactions without unnecessary complexity.

The strategy pattern offers interchangeable algorithms swappable at runtime without affecting client code. Chain of Responsibility creates a modular operation flow through sequential request processing by multiple handlers. The Command pattern encapsulates requests into standalone objects, separating initiation from handling. Mediator centralizes object interactions, simplifying communication and preventing direct dependencies. Lastly, the Observer pattern implements a publish-subscribe model where objects react to state changes in another and promoting loose coupling.

Mastering these patterns equips you to design flexible, maintainable systems with clear and manageable object communication.

As we move forward, the next chapter will dig into behavioral design patterns for managing state and behavior, further enhancing your ability to create systems that effectively handle state management.

Q&A

Feel free to review the following questions and their corresponding answers to address any concerns or gain additional insights:

1. How is the Mediator pattern different from the Observer pattern?

    Answer: Both patterns facilitate communication between system components, but their goals and implementations differ. The Mediator pattern aims to eliminate direct communication between components, centralizing interaction logic within a mediator. In this setup, the mediator is aware of the dependent structures and handles calls based on received events. In contrast, the Observer pattern promotes a more loosely coupled design where the publisher is unaware of the specific subscribers. Subscribers independently decide whether to respond to or ignore the messages they receive.

2. How is the Chain of Responsibility pattern different from the Decorator pattern?

    Answer: The Decorator pattern focuses on extending the behavior of a single object by wrapping it with additional functionalities, without disrupting the flow of requests. On the other hand, the Chain of Responsibility pattern allows multiple objects to process a request sequentially, with the possibility of halting the request flow if a certain condition is met.

Get This Book's PDF Version and Exclusive Extras

UNLOCK NOW

Scan the QR code (or go to packtpub.com/unlock). Search for this book by name, confirm the edition, and then follow the steps on the page.

Note: Keep your invoice handly. Purchase made directly from packt don't require one.

Behavioral Design Patterns for Managing State and Behavior

In the previous chapter, we reviewed behavioral design patterns that facilitate communication and interactions between objects.

In this chapter, we will focus on behavioral design patterns that help manage the state and behavior of objects over time. These patterns provide options for controlling how objects change, behave, or execute based on different states or processes by decoupling an object's internal state from its behavior. They introduce ways to make object interactions more flexible by defining control structures for object behavior.

We will examine the following behavioral design patterns in this chapter:

- The Iterator pattern
- The Memento pattern
- The State pattern
- The Template Method pattern
- The Visitor pattern

Again, for each pattern, we will explain its core concept and purpose, benefits, and potential drawbacks, together with implementation details and best practices.

By the end of this chapter, you will have gained a comprehensive understanding of how to manage complex state transitions and object behaviors. You will be well-informed to implement these patterns in real-world scenarios where managing object states or organizing complex behavior is important.

Technical requirements

The code bundle for this chapter is available on GitHub at: `https://github.com/PacktPublishing/TypeScript-5-Design-Patterns-and-Best-Practices/tree/main/chapters/chapter06_Behavioral_Design_Patterns_State`.

The Iterator pattern

The **Iterator pattern** is a behavioral design pattern that provides a way to aggregate over a collection of objects without knowing what the objects internally consist of. This pattern is fundamental in many programming languages and is a core concept in designing efficient and flexible collection traversal mechanisms.

Some of its key concepts are as follows:

- **Abstraction of traversal**: The Iterator pattern abstracts the process of traversing a collection, separating the traversal algorithm from the collection's structure. This separation allows for different traversal methods without modifying the collection.

- **Uniform interface**: It provides a standard interface for traversing different types of collections, making it easier to write generic code that works with various data structures.

- **Encapsulation of collection details**: The pattern encapsulates the internal structure of the collection, allowing the developer to change the implementation part without changing the code that uses the pattern.

An analogy for this pattern is when you have a saved list of favorite shows on your hard drive. Each of these videos is saved in a different folder, but you can iterate over them one by one from your UI view without knowing the details of their location on the disk.

We will explain in detail when to use this pattern next.

When to use the Iterator pattern

You will want to consider using an Iterator for the following use cases:

- **Complex data structures**: When dealing with complex data structures such as trees, graphs, or custom collections where traversal logic can be complicated

- **Multiple traversal algorithms**: When you need to provide multiple ways to traverse a collection (e.g., in-order, pre-order, or post-order for a tree)

- **Decoupling clients from collections**: To allow client code to access collection elements without knowing the internal structure of the collection

- **Parallel iteration**: When you need to maintain multiple traversal positions in the same collection simultaneously

- **Lazy evaluation**: For implementing lazy loading or generating elements on-the-mean, where elements are computed only when requested

- **Providing a uniform interface**: When you want to provide a standard way to traverse different types of collections in your system

In these cases, you can use an `Iterator` object that will encapsulate the traversal operation of the underlying data structure or an aggregate object. The main benefit for the clients that will use this pattern is that they will be able to use it for loops without knowing how the objects are structured behind the scenes. We will now show you what the class diagram of this pattern looks like.

UML class diagram

The Iterator pattern's structure can be represented clearly using a UML class diagram. Let's examine each component of this pattern and how they interact:

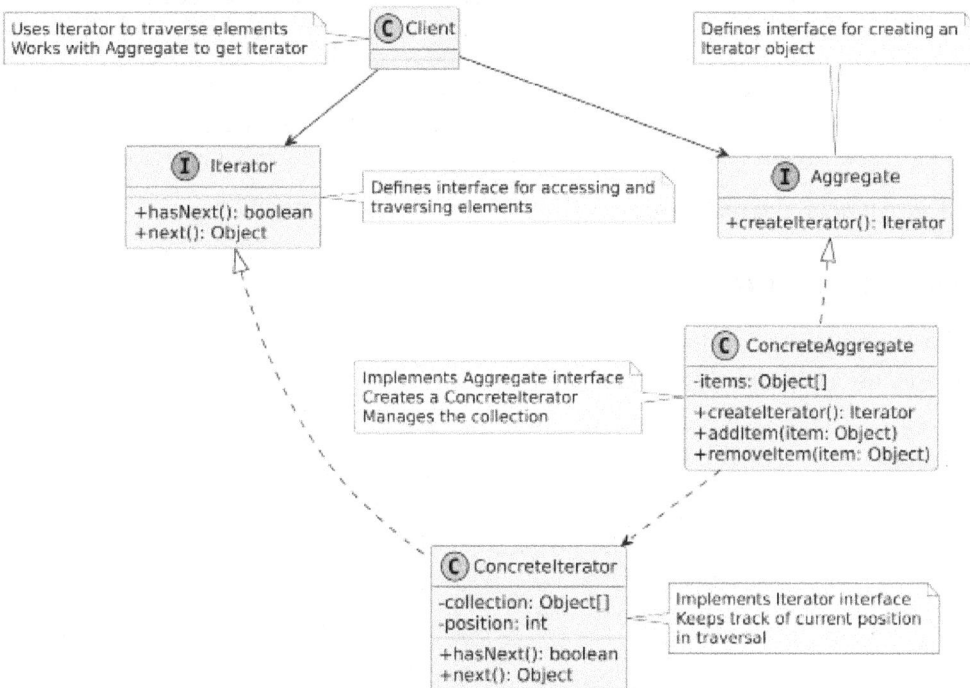

Figure 6.1 – The Iterator pattern

Let's break down each component of this UML diagram:

- `Iterator`: This interface declares the methods for accessing and traversing elements. It typically includes two primary methods: `hasNext()` to check whether there are more elements to iterate over, and `next()` to retrieve the next element in the sequence.

- `Aggregate`: This interface declares a method for creating an `Iterator` object. It's implemented by concrete collections that want to be iterable.

- `ConcreteIterator`: This class implements the `Iterator` interface. It stores the current position of the iteration and implements the logic for moving through the collection. The `ConcreteIterator` class has as a reference to the collection it's iterating over.

- `ConcreteAggregate`: This class implements the `Aggregate` interface. It represents the collection being traversed and implements the method to create a `ConcreteIterator` class for itself. It also typically includes methods to manage the collection, such as adding or removing items.

- `Client`: This represents the code that uses the `Iterator` interface. The `Client` class works with both the `Aggregate` interface to obtain an iterator and the `Iterator` interface to traverse the elements.

This structure allows for great flexibility. New types of collections can be added by implementing the `Aggregate` interface, and new ways of traversing can be added by implementing new `Iterator` classes. The `Client` code remains unchanged, working only with the abstract interfaces.

You will learn how to code this pattern next.

Classic implementation

You can start implementing the Iterator pattern based on the class diagram that you saw in the previous section. We'll use a music playlist as our example, which is an example use case for iterators:

iterator.ts

```ts
class Song {
  constructor(public title: string,
    public artist: string,
    public duration: number) {}
  toString(): string {
      return `${this.title} by ${this.artist}
        (${this.duration} seconds)`;
  }
}
interface Iterator<T> {
  hasNext(): boolean;
```

```
  next(): T | null;
}
interface Playlist {
  createIterator(): Iterator<Song>;
}
```

Here, the Song class represents a single song with properties such as title, artist, and duration. The Iterator interface defines the contract for iterators with two methods: hasNext() to check whether there are more elements, and next() to retrieve the next element. Then the Playlist interface is the Aggregate interface, declaring the createIterator() method that returns an Iterator<Song> interface.

Next, you want to implement the rest of the classes:

iterator.ts

```
class PlaylistIterator implements Iterator<Song> {
  private currentIndex: number = 0;
  constructor(private playlist: Song[]) {}
  hasNext(): boolean {
    return this.currentIndex < this.playlist.length;
  }
  next(): Song | null {
    if (this.hasNext()) {
      if (!this.playlist[this.currentIndex]) {
      // Lazy load more songs from an external source
        this.loadMoreSongs();
      }
      return this.playlist[this.currentIndex++] || null;
    }
    return null;
  }
  // Load more songs from an external source
  private loadMoreSongs(): void {//}
}
class MusicPlaylist implements Playlist {
  private songs: Song[] = [];
  addSong(song: Song): void {
    this.songs.push(song);
  }
  createIterator(): Iterator<Song> {
    return new PlaylistIterator(this.songs);
  }
}
```

```
const myPlaylist = new MusicPlaylist();
myPlaylist.addSong(new Song("Bohemian Rhapsody",
  "Queen", 354));
myPlaylist.addSong(new Song("Stairway to Heaven",
  "Led Zeppelin", 482));
myPlaylist.addSong(new Song("Imagine",
  "John Lennon", 183));
const iterator = myPlaylist.createIterator();
console.log("My Playlist:");
while (iterator.hasNext()) {
  const song = iterator.next();
  if (song) {
    console.log(song.toString());
  }
}
```

Here, the `PlaylistIterator` class serves as the concrete `Iterator`, responsible for tracking the current position in the playlist. It supports **lazy loading**, meaning it can dynamically fetch additional songs from an external source when needed, rather than loading all songs upfront. The `MusicPlaylist` class acts as our `Concrete Aggregate` class, managing a collection of songs. The client code in the end demonstrates how to use the Iterator pattern.

As a slightly more practical example of the Iterator pattern, consider the use of `async/await` in the `AsyncSongIterator` class. This implementation allows for asynchronous iteration over a collection of songs that may be fetched from an external source, such as an API:

iterator.ts

```
class AsyncSongIterator {
  private currentIndex: number = 0
  private songs: string[] = []
  constructor() {}
  // Simulate fetching songs from an API
  private async fetchSongs(): Promise<string[]> {
    await new Promise((resolve) => setTimeout(
      resolve, 1000))
    return ["Song 1", "Song 2", "Song 3"]
  }

  async next(): Promise<{ value: string | null;
    done: boolean }> {
    if (this.currentIndex === 0) {
      this.songs = await this.fetchSongs()
```

```
    }

    if (this.currentIndex < this.songs.length) {
      return { value: this.songs[this.currentIndex++],
        done: false }
    } else {
      return { value: null, done: true }
    }
  }
  [Symbol.asyncIterator]() {
    return this
  }
}
const songIterator = new AsyncSongIterator()
for await (const song of songIterator) {
    console.log(song)
}
```

The `AsyncSongIterator` class implements an asynchronous iterator that fetches a list of songs from an external source, simulating an API call. The class implements the `[Symbol.asyncIterator]` `()` method, allowing it to be used in a `for await...of` loop as shown in the code. This allows for a more elegant and concise use of Iterators in TypeScript projects.

This example showcases how the Iterator pattern can be used in a real-world scenario. Now let's provide a way to test this pattern.

Testing

Here is what to test in the Iterator pattern. You want to verify that the `Iterator` implementation is sound. What this means is that when calling `next()` and `hasNext()` over the collection. The methods will retrieve the next item in the collection and return `true` or `false`, respectively, if the next item exists. Then, in `Aggregate`, you want to check whether the call to the `createIterator()` method returns the correct `ConcreteIterator` instance.

We provide test cases in the `iterator.test.ts` file located in the current chapter source code (see the *Technical requirements* section), which you will be able to review.

To run the test cases, you need to execute the following command:

```
$ npm run test --iterator
```

You should be able to review the test results in the console.

Let's discuss some criticisms of the Iterator pattern.

Criticisms

While the Iterator pattern is widely used and offers several benefits, it's important to consider its potential drawbacks and situations where it might not be the best solution. Let's explore these aspects in more detail:

- **Complexity for simple collections**: The primary criticism of the Iterator pattern is that it can introduce unnecessary complexity for simple collections. In cases where you're dealing with basic lists or arrays, the additional abstractions of the Iterator pattern might be overkill.

- **Maintenance overhead**: Introducing the Iterator pattern means more classes and interfaces to maintain. This can increase the code base size and potentially make it harder for new developers to understand the system.

- **Overkill for read-only collections**: For collections that are only ever read and never modified, a simple method returning an array or list might be sufficient and more intuitive.

In the next section, we'll look at a use case involving the Iterator pattern.

Real-world use case

The Iterator pattern finds significant application in reactive programming libraries such as RxJS, which is widely used in TypeScript projects. RxJS leverages this pattern to handle asynchronous data streams efficiently.

Here is an example of usage in RxJS:

```
const observable = new Observable<number>(observer => {
  observer.next(1);
  observer.next(2);
  observer.next(3);
  observer.complete();
});

observable
  .map(x => x * 10)
  .filter(x => x > 10)
  .subscribe(value => console.log(value));
```

This example implementation demonstrates how the Iterator pattern can be extended beyond simple collection traversal. The `for` loop construction is possible because the `Observable` class uses ES6 iterators. These are special properties that you attach to classes or objects and can denote those objects as `Iterable` as part of a for loop. It also allows the Observable a way to use composable operations on data flows.

As you've understood the basic principles of this pattern in practice, you will now learn about the next pattern on the list, which is the Memento pattern.

The Memento pattern

The **Memento pattern** is a powerful design solution for managing an object's state throughout an application without compromising encapsulation. This pattern uses a mechanism to store an internal state, effectively creating a snapshot at a particular point in time. It then exposes operations that manipulate this state to perform certain tasks in a safe way.

At its core, the Memento pattern consists of three key components:

- **Originator:** This is the object whose state needs to be saved and restored. This is the object that contains the state we wish to manage.

- **Memento:** This is a simple object that stores the actual state of the Originator. It provides a straightforward interface for storing and retrieving data, acting as a snapshot of the Originator's state at a specific moment.

- **Caretaker:** Responsible for keeping track of multiple Memento objects, it maintains a history of states but never modifies the contents of a Memento.

The beauty of this pattern lies in its ability to externalize an object's internal state without violating encapsulation. The `Originator` and `Caretaker` classes interact with the Memento to save and restore states, but neither has direct access to the other's internal workings. This separation of concerns allows for flexible state management across different parts of an application.

When should you consider using the Memento pattern? Let's explore its practical applications and benefits.

When to use the Memento pattern

The Memento pattern is particularly valuable in scenarios that require fine-grained control over an object's state. Here are the key reasons to consider implementing this pattern:

- **Preserving and restoring object state**: The Memento pattern excels when you need to create snapshots of an object's state, including private properties, store these snapshots in a reproducible format, and restore the object to a previous state on demand

- **Maintaining encapsulation**: The pattern allows storing or retrieving the state object via an abstraction that is hidden from clients and provides a clean interface for state management operations

- **Simplifying complex state management**: The Memento pattern is particularly useful when dealing with objects that have complex internal states, needing to implement multi-level undo/redo functionality, and managing checkpoints in long-running processes or simulations

The Memento pattern's straightforward concept and implementation make it an excellent choice for these scenarios. Its ability to cleanly separate state management from business logic enhances code maintainability and flexibility.

In the next section, we'll explore how to represent the Memento pattern using UML class diagrams, providing a visual understanding of its structure and relationships.

UML class diagram

The following diagram shows the main components of the Memento pattern:

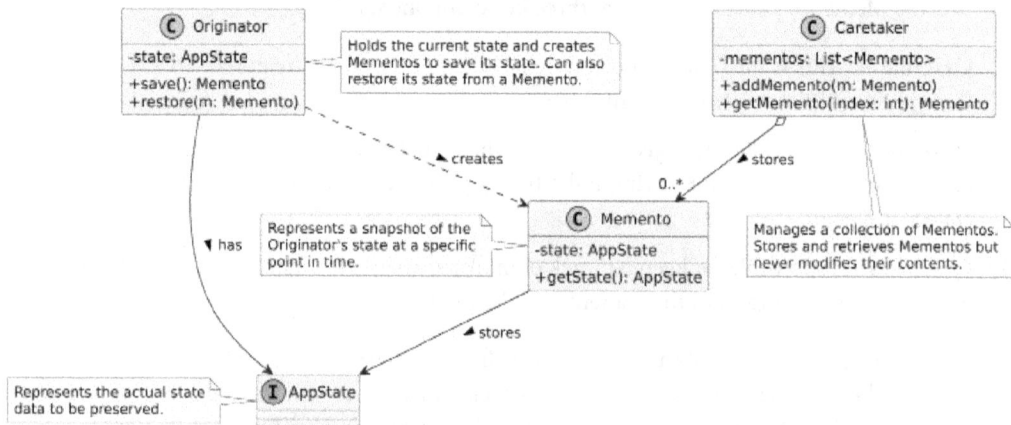

Figure 6.2 – The Memento pattern

In the preceding diagram, we have four main elements: the `AppState` (interface), `Originator`, `Memento`, and `Caretaker` classes. The `Originator` class creates `Memento` objects and the `Caretaker` class stores multiple `Memento` objects.

Both `Originator` and `Memento` have a relationship with the `AppState` interface, which represents the state object that you want to save or restore. The `Originator` class holds this state to perform work and updates it when required. Then, it will call the `save()` method, which will return a `Memento` object. Since this object is of no use to the `Originator` class, you need a `CareTaker` class that will aggregate all those memento objects.

When the user wants to restore a previous memento, they will use the `restore()` method, which will update the `CareTaker` state directly.

Let's see how to implement this pattern in practice next.

Classic implementation

We provide an example that demonstrates how the pattern can be used to implement an undo feature, which is a familiar and practical use case. Let's start with the Memento and AppState objects:

memento.ts

```
interface TextEditorState {
  content: string;
  cursorPosition: number;
}
class EditorMemento {
  constructor(private readonly state: TextEditorState) {}
    getState(): TextEditorState {
      return this.state;
    }
}
```

Here, TextEditorState represents the state of the text editor, including content and cursor position. EditorMemento encapsulates the TextEditorState class, providing a way to save and retrieve the editor's state. The rest of the code represents the Caretaker and Originator objects, which are located in the current chapter source code (see the *Technical requirements* section).

Here is how the client will use this pattern:

memento.ts

```
const editor = new TextEditor();
const caretaker = new EditorCaretaker(editor);
editor.type("Hello, ");
caretaker.save();
editor.type("world!");
caretaker.save();
console.log(editor.getContent()); // Output: Hello, world!
caretaker.undo();
console.log(editor.getContent()); // Output: Hello,
caretaker.redo();
console.log(editor.getContent()); // Output: Hello, world!
```

The example demonstrates how to use the Memento pattern to implement undo and redo functionality in a text editor. It shows how to add text and save states, move the cursor, insert text, and undo or redo actions.

Let's explore some of the testing strategies for this pattern.

Testing

When testing this pattern, you need to ensure the correctness of the Memento pattern implementation in the context of a text editor. They should cover all aspects mentioned in the original section (saving/restoring state, Originator operations, and `Caretaker` functionality) and include integration tests and edge cases.

We provide test cases in the `memento.test.ts` file located in the current chapter source code (see the *Technical requirements* section), which you will be able to review.

To run the test cases, you need to execute the following command:

```
$ npm run test --memento
```

You should be able to review the test results in the console. Now, let's discuss some criticisms of the Memento pattern.

Criticisms

While the Memento pattern offers powerful state management capabilities, it's essential to consider its implications carefully before implementation. Let's explore its potential drawbacks:

- **Complexity**: The pattern introduces additional classes and relationships, potentially increasing system complexity. For simple state management needs, this complexity might be unnecessary.

- **Memory concerns**: Storing multiple states can lead to significant memory usage, especially with large or numerous objects. This could be mitigated by implementing state compression techniques or limiting the number of stored states.

- **Performance impact**: Creating and restoring Mementos frequently may affect performance, particularly with complex states. Consider the frequency of state changes and restorations in your specific use case.

When using Memento, pay close attention to memory management and performance implications. In modern web development, consider leveraging established state management libraries that often provide similar functionality with additional benefits tailored to specific frameworks or architectures without building it from scratch.

We will now see a real-world use case of the Memento pattern next.

Real-world use case

Visual Studio Code, Microsoft's popular open source code editor, implements a sophisticated undo/redo system that leverages principles such as the Memento pattern.

Some of its key components are as follows:

- **ITextSnapshot (Memento)**: It represents an immutable snapshot of the editor's text at a specific point in time
- **TextModel (Originator)**: It manages the current state of the text and creates snapshots
- **EditStack (Caretaker)**: It maintains a stack of edits and provides undo/redo functionality

All the above abstractions can be found in the following model file, which you can review: `https://github.com/microsoft/vscode/blob/main/src/vs/editor/common/model.ts`

The VS Code's implementation demonstrates how the principles of the Memento pattern can be adapted and optimized for high-performance real-world applications. By storing edit operations instead of full-text snapshots, it achieves efficiency while maintaining the core benefits of this pattern.

Let's continue by learning more about the State pattern.

The State pattern

The **State pattern** is a behavioral design pattern that allows an object to alter its behavior when its internal state changes. This pattern is particularly useful in scenarios where an object's behavior must change dynamically based on its state, without resorting to manual statements.

Its key concepts are as follows:

- **Context**: The object that controls all the state instances and exposes methods to interface with those states
- **State**: An interface or abstract class defining the state-specific behaviors
- **Concrete states**: Implementations of the `State` interface, each encapsulating behavior associated with a particular state

Instead of the object managing its state-dependent behavior internally, the State pattern externalizes these behaviors into separate state objects. The context delegates state-specific work to these objects, switching between them as their state changes.

When to use the State pattern

You can use the State pattern in the following cases:

- **Complex state-dependent behavior**: When an object's behavior varies significantly based on its state, and you want to avoid large conditional statements
- **State transitions**: When state transitions are frequent or complex, and you want to manage them more cleanly

- **Reducing duplication**: When different states have similar behavior with slight variations, the State pattern can help eliminate code duplication

- **Runtime state changes**: When an object's state can change dynamically at runtime

- **Enhancing flexibility**: It allows changing parts of the behavior by including new object states without modifying the context class

The State pattern shines in scenarios with complex, state-dependent behaviors. It promotes cleaner, more maintainable code by encapsulating state-specific logic and facilitating easy state transitions. While it may introduce additional classes, the benefits of code organization and flexibility often outweigh this drawback in complex systems.

We show the UML class diagram of this pattern next.

UML class diagram

The State pattern organizes the behavior of an object based on its internal state. This pattern involves several key components working together to achieve flexible and maintainable state-dependent behavior. Let's examine the structure in detail:

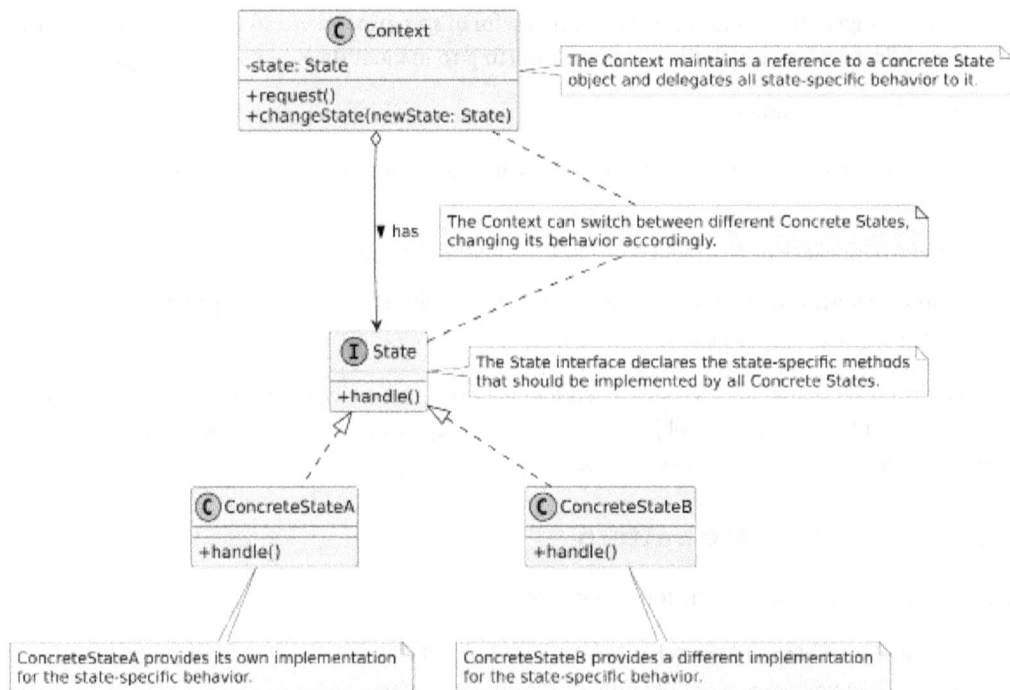

Figure 6.3 – The State pattern

In the preceding diagram, the `Context` class has a composition relationship with the `State`. This allows the `Context` class to work with any `Concrete` state that implements the `State` interface. The Concrete States inherit from the `State` interface, ensuring they provide implementations for all required state-specific behaviors. The `Context` class can change its current state by calling the `changeState()` method. This flexibility allows the Context's behavior to change dynamically.

Now, let's see how to implement the State pattern in TypeScript.

Classic implementation

The implementation of the State pattern follows the class diagram details. First, you need to define the `State` and `Context` objects with their parameters:

state.ts

```typescript
interface State {
  handle(): void
}
class Context {
  private state: State
  constructor(initialState: State) {
    this.state = initialState
  }
  public request(): void {
    this.state.handle()
  }
  public changeState(newState: State): void {
    if (this.state instanceof ConcreteStateA &&
      !(newState instanceof ConcreteStateB)) {
      throw new Error("Invalid state transition");
    }
    this.state = newState
  }
}
```

We define a `State` interface with a `handle()` method. The `Context` class maintains a reference to a `State` object and forwards any operations that require interfacing with the current state instance. It includes the `request()` and `changeState()` methods.

Now let's implement the concrete state classes and the client code:

state.ts

```
class ConcreteStateA implements State {
    public handle(): void {
        console.log("Handling request in ConcreteStateA");
    }
}
class ConcreteStateB implements State {
    public handle(): void {
        console.log("Handling request in ConcreteStateB");
    }
}
const context = new Context(new ConcreteStateA());
context.request();
// Output: Handling request in ConcreteStateA
context.changeState(new ConcreteStateB());
context.request();
// Output: Handling request in ConcreteStateB
```

Here, both `ConcreteStateA` and `ConcreteStateB` implement the `State` interface, providing their own implementations for the `handle()` method. The usage example demonstrates how the `Context` class can switch between different Concrete States, changing its behavior accordingly.

We will explore some testing strategies next.

Testing

When you write tests for this pattern, you want to verify a few cases. Each state type you define should capture the right state parameters and you should verify that the data they hold is correct. Then, you want to verify that the state transition logic is correct when you call the `changeState()` method. For example, when changing state, the object should behave accordingly based on its current state.

We provide test cases in the `state.test.ts` file located in the current chapter source code (see the *Technical requirements* section), which you will be able to review.

To run the test cases, you need to execute the following command:

```
$ npm run test --state
```

You should be able to review the test results in the console.

Let's discuss some criticisms of the State pattern.

Criticisms

Here is a list of some important criticisms and considerations of the State pattern:

- **Complexity versus benefit**: The primary criticism of the State pattern is that it can introduce unnecessary complexity for simple state management scenarios. If your system only has a few states with minimal variations, the overhead of implementing the full pattern might outweigh its benefits. In such cases, simpler solutions such as enums or `if-else` statements might be more appropriate.

- **Potential for over-engineering**: There's a risk of over-engineering when using this pattern. Developers might be tempted to create separate state classes for minor variations, leading to a proliferation of classes that don't provide significant value. This can make the code base harder to maintain and understand.

- **Difficulty in defining meaningful states**: It can be challenging to define states in a way that provides real value without introducing repetition. If the behavior differences between states are minimal, the pattern might lead to a lot of boilerplate code with little payoff.

- **Coverage of edge cases**: Ensuring comprehensive coverage of all possible state transitions and edge cases can be tricky. Missed cases might lead to unexpected behaviors or require the introduction of additional error states, further complicating the system.

While the State pattern is a powerful tool for managing complex state-dependent behavior, it's crucial to carefully evaluate whether its benefits outweigh its complexities for your specific use case or project.

Let's explore a real-world use case of this pattern.

Real-world use-case

One example I can think of is how the **React Router** works. The React Router uses a state-like pattern to manage different routing behaviors. Here is a quick demonstration of its implementation:

```
interface RouteState {
  match(path: string): boolean;
  render(component: React.ComponentType):
    React.ReactElement;
}
 class Route {
  private state: RouteState;
  constructor(path: string | RegExp) {
    // Initialize state based on path type
  }

  matches(path: string): boolean {
    return this.state.match(path);
```

```
    }
    // Other methods...
}
```

This approach allows the `Route` class to handle different types of path matching (exact `string` or `regex` pattern) without needing to change its core logic. The behavior is encapsulated in the state objects, making it easy to add new types of route matching in the future without modifying existing code.

This concludes all that you need to know about the State pattern. Next, we will look at the concepts of the Template Method pattern.

The Template Method pattern

The **Template Method pattern** is a behavioral design pattern that defines the basic template methods to perform a particular operation and exposes abstract methods for the subclasses to implement. This allows the subclasses to complete the algorithmic steps by overriding the base class methods. It's a fundamental technique for code reuse that leverages inheritance to customize parts of an algorithm.

Some of its key concepts are as follows:

- **Abstract base class**: It defines the Template Method and abstract operations
- **Template Method**: It is the algorithm's skeleton, calling both concrete and abstract operations
- **Concrete operations**: It is implemented directly in the abstract base class
- **Abstract operations**: These are placeholders for steps to be implemented by subclasses
- **Hook operations**: These are optional steps with default implementations that subclasses can override

Let's explain in detail when to use this pattern.

When to use the Template Method pattern

The Template Method pattern is particularly useful in scenarios where you need to define a skeleton of an algorithm while allowing specific steps to be implemented or customized by subclasses. Here are key situations where this pattern is beneficial:

- **Algorithmic variations with common structure**: You have an algorithm or process with a fixed structure, but certain steps need to vary. For example, a document processing system where different document types (PDF, Word, and HTML) share a common processing flow but require type-specific parsing or formatting.
- **Reducing code duplication**: When multiple classes have similar implementations with only slight variations, this pattern is useful. As an example, data validation processes can have different types of user input.

- **Framework development**: You're developing a framework where certain parts of an algorithm should be customizable by the framework users, such as a web application framework with customizable request handling.

You can think of this pattern as having an algorithm in a method, and in certain steps, it calls another method that is implemented in the subclasses to perform some specific logic. This method could either return a result or just return nothing. The subclasses can choose to implement these life cycle methods to return some specific results or ignore them if they are optional. This way, you can write code that has customized behavior but still does not introduce extra code duplication.

Let's see what this looks like as a UML class diagram.

UML class diagram

The Template Method pattern uses a base class as a template and allows its subclasses to override specific methods to complete their indented functionality. Let's examine this pattern using a simple document processing example.

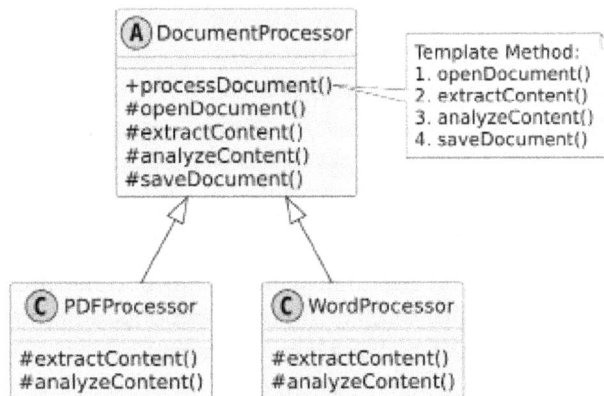

Figure 6.4 – The Template Method pattern

This is the core of the pattern, defining the document processing algorithm's structure. `processDocument()` is a Template Method that defines the skeleton of the algorithm. `openDocument()` and `saveDocument()` are concrete methods common to all document types. The last two, `extractContent()` and `analyzeContent()`, abstract methods to be implemented by subclasses.

Then we define the two concrete classes: `PDFProcessor` and `WordProcessor`. These classes inherit from `DocumentProcessor` and provide specific implementations for different document types.

Let's explore the implementation part of this pattern in detail.

Classic implementation

The classic implementation of this pattern follows the class diagram we explained earlier. Let's walk through a concrete implementation using our document processing example.

First, we define the abstract `DocumentProcessor` class that hosts the basic steps for the algorithm:

template-method.ts

```
abstract class DocumentProcessor {
  public processDocument(): void {
    this.openDocument()
    this.extractContent()
    this.analyzeContent()
    this.saveDocument()
  }
  protected openDocument(): void {
    console.log("Opening document")
  }
  protected abstract extractContent(): void
  protected abstract analyzeContent(): void
  protected saveDocument(): void {
    console.log("Saving processed document")
  }
}
```

This abstract class defines the steps of the algorithm in the `processDocument` method. Each step calls respective methods that can be either concrete (such as `openDocument` and `saveDocument`) or abstract (such as `extractContent` and `analyzeContent`).

Next, we implement the concrete subclasses that provide specific implementations for different document types. Here, we will provide an example of the first Template implementation and the rest can be reviewed in the current chapter source code (see the *Technical requirements* section):

template-method.ts

```
class PDFProcessor extends DocumentProcessor {
  protected extractContent(): void {
    console.log("Extracting content from PDF");
  }
  protected analyzeContent(): void {
    console.log("Analyzing PDF content");
  }
}
```

Here, each subclass implements the abstract `extractContent` and `analyzeContent` methods because they're required to satisfy the abstract class extension.

When the client uses these implementations at runtime, the correct methods are dispatched via polymorphism:

```
const pdfDoc: DocumentProcessor = new PDFProcessor();
const wordDoc: DocumentProcessor = new WordProcessor();
pdfDoc.processDocument();
wordDoc.processDocument();
```

The client assigns instances of `DocumentProcessor`, and it will dispatch the right template methods at runtime. This approach provides flexibility without having to reimplement the same steps each time.

Next, we will discuss some testing strategies.

Testing

When testing the Template Method pattern, we focus on verifying that the subclasses deliver the expected outcomes and that the algorithm steps are executed in the correct order. Since we can't instantiate the abstract class directly, our tests will focus on the concrete implementations.

We provide test cases in the `template-method.test.ts` file located in the current chapter source code (see the *Technical requirements* section), which you will be able to review.

To run the test cases, you need to execute the following command:

```
$ npm run test --template-method
```

You should be able to review the test results in the console.

Let's discuss some criticisms of the Template Method pattern.

Criticisms

While the Template Method pattern is widely employed in many established libraries, such as **React**, it has notable limitations:

- **Difficulty in deprecation**: If template steps need to be deprecated after the code has been distributed to clients, it can be challenging to remove or alter these steps without disrupting the clients' code that relies on them. This lack of flexibility can hinder the maintenance and evolution of the codebase.

- **Limited flexibility**: To maintain flexibility and avoid future issues, it's advisable to define fewer required or optional steps for customization. This approach allows for easier modifications to the base template, reducing the likelihood of needing to deprecate methods.

The next section will explore a popular use case of the Template Method pattern.

Real-world use cases

React popularized the idea of the Template Method, more specifically with the React Component class. These are React components defined as a class. They have some optional life cycle hook methods that are called at various stages, such as just before or after mounting in the DOM or before or after updating. Here is an example component:

```
class WelcomeHome extends React.Component<{
  name: string},{}> {
    componentDidMount() {
      console.log("Just loaded");
    }
    componentWillUnmount() {
      console.log("Goodbye!");
    }
    shouldComponentUpdate() {
      return false;
    }
    render() {
      return <h1>Hello, {this.props.name}</h1>;
    }
}
```

Out of all those methods, the `render` method is the required one and each React component needs to define one that returns another React component or null. However, there are also other optional life cycle methods, `componentDidMount`, `componentWillUnmount`, and `shouldComponentUpdate`, which are called by React at different times. You can define these methods and adhere to the reasoning behind them if you want to further customize the behavior of the `WelcomeHome` component.

Another prevalent example is in the Angular framework with the usage of life cycle hooks. This pattern allows you to define a skeleton of an algorithm in a base class while letting subclasses override specific steps without changing the overall structure.

Here is an example that uses the `onInit` hook:

```
import { Component, OnInit } from '@angular/core';

@Component({
    selector: 'app-user-profile',
    template: `<h1>User Profile</h1><div>{
      { userData }}</div>`,
})
export class UserProfileComponent implements OnInit {
```

```
    userData: string;

    // Template Method
    ngOnInit(): void {
        this.initialize();
        this.loadData();
    }
    private initialize(): void {
        console.log('Initializing User Profile');
    }
    private loadData(): void {
        // Simulate data loading
        this.userData = 'User data loaded from API';
    }
}
```

In this example, the `UserProfileComponent` class implements the `OnInit` life cycle interface and defines the `ngOnInit()` method as a Template Method. Angular will call this method shortly after it has initialized all of a component's data-bound properties. This typically occurs once the component is created and just before it is displayed to the user.

We'll now explore the last behavioral design pattern of this chapter, which is the Visitor pattern.

The Visitor pattern

The final pattern we will explore is the **Visitor pattern**. This pattern allows for the application of customized behavior to an existing collection of components that form a hierarchy, such as a tree or a linked list, without altering their structure or requiring them to implement an interface.

In practice, this involves adding a method to your components that accepts a reference to a Visitor object and passes its own instance as a parameter to this visitor. The Visitor object, in turn, gains access to each type of visited object's public methods, enabling it to aggregate the state of each object it visits into a different result.

Next, we will explore more on when and how to use this pattern in more detail.

When to use the Visitor pattern?

The Visitor pattern is particularly useful in several scenarios:

- **Abstracting functionality for collecting public state**: When you have a composite hierarchy of objects and need to traverse through them to collect certain parameters or state variables, this can be useful. Instead of calling each object's public methods directly, which can be cumbersome and type-checking intensive due to method existence only in specific subclasses, the Visitor pattern provides a cleaner solution.

- **Applying new operations to groups of objects with common interfaces**: When you have a group of objects that implement a common interface but have specific methods in their concrete subclasses that you want to utilize, this can also be used. By creating concrete visitors for these subclasses, you can leverage those specific methods to accumulate information or apply operations without altering the objects themselves.

The primary benefit of the Visitor pattern is its ability to add functions to existing classes without modifying their source code. If the necessary data is accessible via public instance methods, you can employ different Visitor implementations to perform logic on these objects without altering their internal structure.

Let's see how this pattern translates to a UML class diagram.

UML class diagram

The Visitor pattern allows you to separate algorithms from the objects on which they operate. This pattern is useful when you need to perform operations across a disparate set of objects. Let's examine the structure using a document processing system as an example:

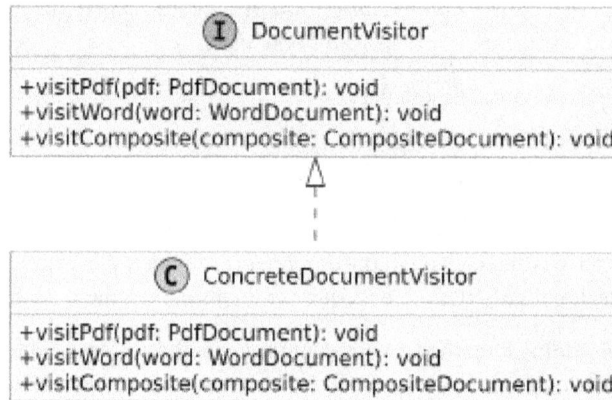

Figure 6.5 – The Visitor object

Here, the `DocumentVisitor` interface declares a visit operation for each concrete element class in the object structure and `ConcreteDocumentVisitor` implements the `DocumentVisitor` interface. The `ConcreteDocumentVisitor` class knows how to process specific types of documents (`PdfDocument`, `WordDocument`, and `CompositeDocument`) because it has separate methods for each.

Now let's provide the rest of the classes that represent the types of documents and the class that collects all the document types:

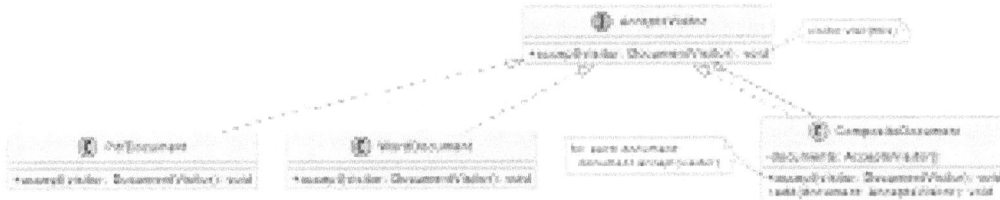

Figure 6.6 – The Visitor pattern

Here, the `AcceptsVisitor` interface declares the `accept` operation, which takes a visitor as an argument. The `DocumentVisitor` interface declares a `visit` operation for each concrete element class in the object structure. Then the concrete elements (`PdfDocument` and `WordDocument`) implement the `AcceptsVisitor` interface. Each concrete document type implements the `accept` method and passes its own instance to the appropriate `visit` method. Since each concrete visitor knows how to handle each type of `DocumentVisitor` interface based on the `visit` method it was called, the operation would be completed in the right order.

The `CompositeDocument` class has an `accept` method that iterates over its collection of `AcceptsVisitor` objects, calling `accept` on each one and passing the visitor. This structure allows for double dispatch, where the correct `visit` method is called based on both the type of visitor and the type of element being visited.

Let's get into the implementation details next.

Classic implementation

Let's implement the Visitor pattern using our document processing system example using TypeScript to demonstrate the classic object-oriented approach.

First, we define the core interfaces:

visitor.ts

```
export interface DocumentVisitor {
  visitPdfDocument(pdfDocument: PdfDocument): void
  visitWordDocument(wordDocument: WordDocument): void
  visitCompositeDocument(compositeDocument:
    CompositeDocument): void
}
export interface AcceptsVisitor {
  accept(visitor: DocumentVisitor): void
}
```

Here, the DocumentVisitor interface declares visit methods for each concrete document type. The AcceptsVisitor interface defines the accept method for objects that can be visited.

Next, we implement the concrete document classes:

---

visitor.ts

```
export class PdfDocument implements AcceptsVisitor {
  accept(visitor: DocumentVisitor): void {
    visitor.visitPdfDocument(this);
  }
  // PDF-specific methods...
}
export class WordDocument implements AcceptsVisitor {
  accept(visitor: DocumentVisitor): void {
    visitor.visitWordDocument(this);
  }
  // Word-specific methods...
}
```

Each concrete document implements the accept method, which calls the appropriate visit method on the visitor. The concrete implementations of the visitor can be found in the current chapter source code (see the *Technical requirements* section).

We show how to implement the composite structure and how the client uses it:

---

visitor.ts

```
export class CompositeDocument implements AcceptsVisitor
{
  private documents: AcceptsVisitor[] = []
  addDocument(document: AcceptsVisitor): void {
    this.documents.push(document)
  }
  accept(visitor: DocumentVisitor): void {
    for (let document of this.documents) {
      document.accept(visitor)
    }
    visitor.visitCompositeDocument(this)
  }
}
```

The `CompositeDocument` class can contain multiple documents and implements the `accept` method to visit all its children. Here's how a client might use this structure:

```
const composite = new CompositeDocument();
const visitor = new DocumentProcessingVisitor();
composite.addDocument(new PdfDocument());
composite.addDocument(new WordDocument());
composite.accept(visitor);
```

This will process all documents in the composite, calling the appropriate `visit` method for each document type. This implementation demonstrates how the Visitor pattern allows for flexible operations on a set of document types without modifying those types. Let's see how to test this pattern.

Testing

Testing the Visitor pattern involves verifying several key aspects of its implementation. Here are the main areas to focus on:

- The composite component forwards the visitor to each of its children
- Individual components call the correct visitor method
- Concrete visitor methods perform as expected for each component type

We provide test cases in the `visitor.test.ts` file located in the current chapter source code (see the *Technical requirements* section), which you will be able to review.

To run the test cases, you need to execute the following command:

```
$ npm run test --visitor
```

You should be able to review the test results in the console.

Let's discuss some criticisms of the Visitor pattern.

Criticisms

While the Visitor pattern offers powerful capabilities for separating algorithms from object structures, it's important to be aware of its limitations and potential drawbacks. Let's explore these in detail:

- **Tighter coupling**: The Visitor interface typically includes methods for each concrete element type, creating a tight coupling between the visitor and the element hierarchy. Adding new element types requires modifying all existing visitor implementations which makes future changes unwieldy.

- **Potential for error in method selection**: Developers must ensure they call the correct visitor method for each component type. This is prone to runtime errors if the wrong method is called and requires careful maintenance as the system evolves.

- **Limited access to internal state**: Visitors typically only have access to public methods and properties of the elements they visit. This creates inconveniences if internal data needs to be exposed for the visitor and it can result in less efficient operations if multiple method calls are needed to gather required data.

Again, it's important to carefully consider the criticisms and potential drawbacks before implementing this pattern. In some cases, simpler patterns or custom solutions might be more appropriate, especially for less complex object structures or when flexibility in adding new element types is a priority.

Real-world use cases

A very common use case for the Visitor pattern could be in a static code analysis tool. Here's an example:

```
interface ASTVisitor {
  visitFunctionDeclaration(node:
    FunctionDeclaration): void;
  visitVariableDeclaration(node:
    VariableDeclaration): void;
  // ... other visit methods
}
class ComplexityAnalyzer implements ASTVisitor {
  private complexity = 0;
  visitFunctionDeclaration(node:
    FunctionDeclaration): void {
      this.complexity += 1;
      // Analyze function body
  }
  // ... other visit methods
}
```

In this use case, the Visitor pattern allows you to separate different analysis concerns (such as complexity calculation and security checks) from the **Abstract Syntax Tree (AST)** structure. You can easily add new types of analysis by creating new visitor classes without modifying the AST nodes.

The TypeScript compiler itself uses the Visitor pattern extensively. You can find examples in the compiler directory of the TypeScript repository at `https://github.com/microsoft/TypeScript/tree/main/src/compiler`.

Another open source project that uses the Visitor pattern is **@typescript-eslint**. This is a tool that enables ESLint to work with TypeScript code by providing TypeScript-specific linting rules and a parser. It's widely used in the TypeScript ecosystem for static code analysis and maintaining code quality.

You can review the existing implementation of this pattern in the implementation of the Visitor at `https://github.com/typescript-eslint/typescript-eslint/blob/main/packages/scope-manager/src/referencer/VisitorBase.ts`. The pattern is extensively used across the codebase for implementing various linting rules, demonstrating how the Visitor pattern can be effectively applied in static analysis tools.

Summary

This chapter examined five behavioral design patterns for managing object state and behavior over time for efficient state changes.

We learned that the Iterator pattern enables collection traversal without exposing the underlying implementation. Memento allows objects to save and restore internal state, controlling operation reversal while maintaining encapsulation. The State pattern dynamically alters object behavior based on the current state, managing state transitions. Furthermore, we learned that the Template Method defines high-level algorithms while allowing subclasses to implement specific steps. The Visitor pattern adds new operations to class hierarchies without modifying original classes, as we learned in this chapter.

These patterns provide powerful tools for managing complex state transitions and organizing object behavior, enabling more dynamic and adaptable systems.

In the next chapter, we will take a closer look into the principles of functional programming, exploring how this paradigm emphasizes immutability, first-class functions, and higher-order functions to create more predictable and maintainable code.

Q&A

Feel free to review the following question and the corresponding answer to address any concerns or gain additional insights.

How is the Visitor pattern different from the Composite pattern?

Answer: The Visitor and Composite patterns often work together but address different concerns. The Visitor pattern is behavioral, aiming to separate algorithms from the object structures they operate on, allowing new operations to be added without modifying those structures. In contrast, the Composite pattern is structural, focusing on treating individual objects and compositions of objects uniformly, allowing clients to interact with single objects and compositions in the same way.

Get This Book's PDF Version and Exclusive Extras

UNLOCK NOW

Scan the QR code (or go to packtpub.com/unlock). Search for this book by name, confirm the edition, and then follow the steps on the page.

Note: Keep your invoice handly. Purchase made directly from packt don't require one.

Part 3: Advanced TypeScript Concepts and Best Practices

In this section, we will dive into advanced TypeScript concepts that extend beyond foundational design patterns and into more specialized programming paradigms and best practices. You will learn how TypeScript supports functional programming, reactive and asynchronous patterns, and the development of modern and robust applications by combining these techniques. In addition, we'll explore common pitfalls, anti-patterns, and real-world applications of design patterns in open source TypeScript architectures.

This part has the following chapters:

- *Chapter 7, Functional Programming with TypeScript*
- *Chapter 8, Reactive and Asynchronous Programming*
- *Chapter 9, Developing Modern and Robust TypeScript Applications*
- *Chapter 10, Anti-Patterns and Workarounds*
- *Chapter 11, Exploring Design Patterns in Open Source Architectures*

7

Functional Programming with TypeScript

In this chapter, we'll start exploring some programming paradigms available in the TypeScript language, beginning with **functional programming**. Unlike design patterns, which are reusable solutions to common problems, functional programming concepts serve as the fundamental building blocks that can be combined in various ways to create robust and flexible programming patterns.

Functional programming is already inherent in JavaScript, allowing developers to leverage concepts such as **Higher-Order Functions** (**HOFs**), closures, and recursion. TypeScript builds on these principles by adding static typing, which provides greater safety when building larger, more complex applications.

Functional programming is centered around key concepts such as expressions, function composition, recursion, immutability, purity, and referential transparency. By leveraging these concepts, particularly through HOFs, you can achieve greater flexibility and maintainability in your application design.

Throughout this chapter, you'll discover how these concepts come to life in TypeScript, allowing you to build advanced structures that enhance your ability to produce larger, more complex programs without compromising type safety.

In this chapter, we will cover the following topics:

- Understanding key concepts in functional programming
- Exploring practical functional structures
- Implementing functional lenses
- Understanding and utilizing monads

By the end of this chapter, you'll have acquired the skills and techniques necessary to write highly composable software using powerful functional programming concepts. You'll be equipped to leverage TypeScript's type system to ensure type safety while adopting the functional paradigm.

Technical requirements

The code bundle for this chapter is available on GitHub at: `https://github.com/PacktPublishing/TypeScript-5-Design-Patterns-and-Best-Practices/tree/main/chapters/chapter07_Functional_Programming_Concepts`.

Learning key concepts in functional programming

Functional programming is a paradigm that uses functions as the primary building blocks to construct larger programs. It's built on several core concepts that distinguish it from other paradigms.

We'll make a distinction now between what we have learned so far about design patterns and what we will learn now about **design concepts** as they have a different meaning.

Design concepts are the building blocks of any programming paradigm. For example, the basic concepts of **Object-Oriented Programming** (**OOP**) are *encapsulation, abstraction, inheritance*, and *polymorphism*. If you don't have encapsulation, then you can't protect access to private object members, making it difficult to apply certain design patterns.

Under the functional programming paradigm, there are key concepts you ought to use to gain the best benefits. We'll explain the essential concepts of functional programming one by one and then follow up by exploring some practical abstractions.

Let's explore these concepts with clear examples.

Declarative versus imperative programming

There are many programming paradigms that offer different approaches to structuring programs. In the context of functional programming, the preferred method is **declarative programming**, which emphasizes stating what the program should accomplish rather than detailing how to achieve it. This approach often leverages TypeScript's array methods, which are both functional and chainable, enhancing readability and maintainability.

Conversely, when you specify how to perform tasks step by step in a particular order, the program follows the **imperative programming** model.

Imperative programming

Imperative programming is a paradigm that focuses on describing how to perform tasks, specifying the exact steps the computer must take to accomplish a goal. With this approach, each step must be executed in a specific sequence. For example, consider the typical sum of even numbers expressed in imperative form:

paradigms.ts

```ts
let evenSum = 0;
for (let i = 1; i <= 10; i++) {
  if (i % 2 === 0) {
    evenSum += i;
  }
}
```

Here, there is a mutable evenSum variable that gets updated inside the for loop only when the if condition is satisfied. The whole process is order-sensitive. If you split the variable declaration and assignment into two parts and move the assignment inside the for loop, then the result would be different making this section more fragile if you move code pieces around. On the other hand, imperative programming is intuitive when it comes to manipulating state. Now let's contrast this example with declarative programming.

Declarative programming

Declarative programming is a paradigm that focuses on describing what the program should do without specifying how it should be done. This approach abstracts away the implementation details, allowing developers to declare the expected outcome in a more natural and intuitive flow. It emphasizes the desired results rather than the specific steps to achieve them.

For example, consider how we can express the sum of even numbers using a declarative programming model:

paradigms.ts

```ts
const numbers = Array.from({ length: 10 },
    (_, i) => i + 1);
const sum = numbers
    .filter(n => n % 2 === 0)
    .reduce((acc, n) => acc + n, 0);
console.log(sum); // Output: 30
```

The first line declares that we want to generate an array of numbers from 1 to 10. Then the second line creates a pipeline of functions: `filter` the even numbers from a list and then `reduce` them to a sum. The control flow and state management are abstracted away, making the code more readable and expressive. It focuses on what information is desired and what transformations are required. Then the program will follow the instructions and perform the job.

While both declarative and imperative programming have their uses and advantages, in terms of functional programming, the first option is preferred since it can make it easier to understand and maintain. With that in mind, we now explain the concept of purity in functional programming.

Pure functions

Pure functions are a cornerstone of functional programming. These are functions with two key characteristics:

- **Deterministic output**: They produce the same output with the same arguments. The function may or may not accept an input, but for the same arguments, it must return the same output. Here is an example of a pure function:

pure-functions.ts

```
function add(a: number, b: number): number {
  return a + b
}
console.log(add(2, 3)) // 5
console.log(add(2, 3)) // 5
```

This `add` function is pure because it always returns the same result for the same inputs and it doesn't modify any external state or produce side effects.

- **No side effects**: A function becomes *impure* when it performs actions that affect or depend on the outside world beyond just returning a result. These actions are known as side effects. A **side effect** is something that interfaces with the system and is not part of the program. For example, printing to the console and opening a file are both considered side effects because the screen or the file itself is not part of the program. Those interfaces are part of the system used to interact with the user or the filesystem. Here is an example of an impure function:

impure-functions.ts

```
let count = 0
function incrementAndLog(value: number): number {
  count++ // Modifies external state
  console.log(`Count is now ${count}`)
  // Side effect: logging
```

```
      return value + 1
    }
    console.log(incrementAndLog(5)) console.log(incrementAndLog(5))
```

This incrementAndLog function is impure because it modifies an external variable (count), logs into the console, and, for the same input, produces different outputs (the log message changes).

You can think of pure functions as mathematical functions because math functions relate input to an output. The input is the *domain* of the function and is the argument that you use in programming. The output is the *codomain* of the function and is the return type of the function. There is also the *range* of the function, which is the actual return value. Here's an example:

---

pure-functions.ts

```
function toZero(num: number): 0 {
  return 0
}
```

In the preceding code, the domain of this function is real numbers, for example, -1, $-\infty$, $+\infty$, 10, 5, and 55. The codomain is only the number 0. So whatever number we use in this function, it will always return zero.

Closures

A **closure** is a function that has access to its own scope as well as the scope of its outer functions. This means that a closure can use variables from its local definition list and from other enclosing functions.

While closures provide significant benefits, they also come with common pitfalls that developers should be aware of. For instance, unintended variable capturing can lead to bugs, especially when closures are used within loops. If not handled carefully, closures may capture variables that change over time, leading to unexpected behavior.

Since both TypeScript and JavaScript allow us to declare functions inside another function and call anonymous functions (or functions without a name), it allows those functions to access the scope of the parent function. Here is an example of a closure in action:

---

closure.ts

```
function makeFunc() {
  const name = "Alex"
  function displayName() {
    console.log(name)
  }
  return displayName
```

```
  }
const myFunc = makeFunc()
myFunc() // Alex
```

In this example, makeFunc returns displayName, which is a closure. Even though makeFunc has returned, displayName still has access to the name variable from the outer function's scope. This allows us to make cool things, like store states within functions, and reuse them later.

Consider the following code snippet with a function that utilizes closures to create and return another function:

closure.ts

```
let buttonProps = (borderRadius) => {
  const createVariantButtonProps = (variant, color) => {
    const newProps = {
      borderRadius,
      variant,
      color
    };
    return newProps;
  };
  return createVariantButtonProps;
};
let primaryButton = buttonProps("1rem");
const primaryButtonProps = primaryButton("primary", "red");
console.log(primaryButtonProps);
// Output: { borderRadius: "1rem", variant: "primary", color: "red" }
```

In this example, buttonProps returns a closure that captures the borderRadius variable. The returned createVariantButtonProps function can access this variable even after buttonProps has returned.

Now let's talk about side effects.

Handling side effects – IO actions

In real-world applications, side effects are often necessary because they interact with the outside world and produce visible or other sensory outcomes. Functional programming doesn't eliminate side effects but instead manages them carefully. One approach is to wrap side effects in **IO** (**Input-Output**) **actions**. Here is an example:

io-actions.ts

```
interface IO<A> {
    (): A;
}
const getCurrentTime: IO<string> = () =>
  new Date().toISOString();
const logMessage = (message: string): IO<void> =>
  () => console.log(message);
const time = getCurrentTime();
console.log(time);
logMessage("Hello, World!")();
```

So basically, IO acts as a wrapper for IO actions and IO denotes that it wraps a function that produces side effects. In this way, the developer is made aware of this situation.

By wrapping side effects in IO actions, we can do the following:

- Clearly indicate which functions interact with the outside world
- Compose and manipulate these actions without immediately executing the side effects

IO represents just one of many approaches to managing side effects in functional programming, but it effectively illustrates how we can handle impure operations without compromising the core principles of the paradigm.

The table in *Figure 7.1* provides comparisons of the IO action pattern with other approaches to managing side effects, such as dependency injection and the observer pattern:

Approach	Description	Strengths	Limitations
IO actions	Encapsulates side effects	Clear indication of side effects; composable	May introduce complexity in managing actions
Dependency injection	Inverts control of dependencies, allowing for easier testing	Decouples components, enhances testability	Can increase complexity; requires a DI framework

Approach	Description	Strengths	Limitations
Observer pattern	Allows objects to subscribe and react to events	Promotes loose coupling	Can lead to memory leaks if not managed properly; complex event chains can be hard to decipher

Figure 7.1 – Comparison of approaches to managing side effects

Let's continue with the next functional programming concept, which is **recursion**.

Recursion

Recursion is a fundamental concept in functional programming where we have a function call itself on the original body, often with various parameters. Instead of using imperative loops, recursive functions provide a more elegant and often more intuitive solution to many problems. Let's start with a classic example of recursion: calculating the factorial of a number:

---

recursion.ts

```
function factorial(n: number): number {
  if (n <= 1) return 1
  return n * factorial(n - 1)
}
console.log(factorial(5)) // Output: 120
```

We will explain the base cases of this calculation. This function demonstrates two key elements of recursion:

- A base case (n <= 1) that stops the recursion
- A recursive case that breaks the problem into a smaller subproblem

Look at the `if` statements that are used to return an actual value and to check whether the algorithm terminates. In this case, if the current call to the factorial returns with a number that is less or equal to 1, we return 1. Otherwise, we calculate the current number times the factorial of the number, minus one. We know that this algorithm terminates because, eventually, the number -1 will equal 1. In that case, we trigger the second `else` statement so it will return 1.

To better understand how recursion works, let's visualize the call stack for `factorial(5)`:

```
factorial(5) -> 5 * factorial(4)
             -> 5 * 4 * factorial(3)
             -> 5 * 4 * 3 * factorial(2)
             -> 5 * 4 * 3 * 2 * factorial(1)
```

```
            -> 5 * 4 * 3 * 2 * 1
            -> 120
```

In the preceding code, each call to this function will subsequently call the same function with different parameters. The parameters in this function converge into the base case check. In the end, the program will evaluate the factorial of n as n * n-1 * n-2 * ... 1 = n!. Since the last call to `factorial(1)` resolves to the base case of 1, it then evaluates the whole multiplication of all expanded values.

Now we will check out a slightly more complex example of how to use recursion.

Using tree recursion

Now let's see a more complicated example of recursion. Recursion shines when dealing with naturally recursive structures like trees. Here's an example of a binary tree traversal:

recursion.ts

```ts
interface TreeNode {
  value: number
  left?: TreeNode
  right?: TreeNode
}
function inOrder(node: TreeNode | undefined): number[] {
  if (!node) {
    return []
  }
  return [...inOrder(node.left), node.value,
    ...inOrder(node.right)]
}
const tree: TreeNode = {
  value: 1,
  left: { value: 2, left: { value: 4 },
    right: { value: 5 } },
  right: { value: 3, left: { value: 6 },
    right: { value: 7 } },
}
console.log(inOrder(tree))
```

This is a more complex example of recursion by performing an in-order traversal on a binary tree. It begins with defining a `TreeNode` interface, which includes a `value` number and optional `left` and `right` child nodes. The `inOrder` function implements the in-order traversal algorithm, which recursively visits the left subtree, processes the current node, and then visits the right subtree. If the node is `undefined`, it returns an empty array, effectively handling leaf nodes. This example shows how recursion can be used to iterate over a tree with an unknown number of levels in a seamless way.

Now we discuss another recursion technique called tail recursion.

Tail recursion and optimization

While powerful, recursion can lead to stack overflow errors for large inputs. The solution is to use a technique called **tail call optimization**, which happens whenever you change the recursive function to make sure the last call always returns a function instead of an expression.

Here's our factorial function rewritten to be tail-recursive:

recursion.ts

```
function factorialTail(n: number,
  accumulator: number = 1): number {
  if (n <= 1) return accumulator;
  return factorialTail(n - 1, n * accumulator);
}
console.log(factorialTail(5)) // Output: 120
```

The base case of the recursion is when n is less than or equal to 1. In this case, the function returns the `accumulator` number. This is where the recursion stops. For the recursive case, when n is greater than 1, the function calls itself with two arguments: `n - 1` (decreasing the input by 1) and `n * accumulator` (multiplying the current n number with the accumulator).

> **Important note**
>
> Note that although conceptually, the code presented is a correct way to form this call to support tail calls, TypeScript/JavaScript unfortunately does not support them in the low-level runtime execution. This means that for large numbers, this could still fail with stack overflow errors.

Let's continue with the next functional programming concept, which is functions as **first-class citizens**.

Functions as first-class citizens

The concept of first-class citizens in programming languages treats certain types of values or entities as native elements that can be used flexibly in various operations. In TypeScript, functions are treated as first-class citizens, which means they can be used in the ways explained in the subsequent sections.

Assigned to variables

Functions can be assigned to variables, allowing you to store and reuse them easily. Here's an example:

first-class-citizens.ts

```
const greet = function(name: string): string {
    return `Hello, ${name}!`;
};
console.log(greet("Alice")); // Output: Hello, Alice!
```

Here, the `greet` function is assigned to a variable, allowing it to be called as the assigned variable name. Subsequent calls will call the variable as a function passing the right arguments.

Passed as arguments to other functions

Functions can be given as inputs to other functions, allowing creation of flexible callback pattern combinations:

first-class-citizens.ts

```
function executeOperation(x: number, y: number,
  operation: (a: number, b: number) => number): number {
    return operation(x, y);
}
const add = (a: number, b: number) => a + b;
const multiply = (a: number, b: number) => a * b;
console.log(executeOperation(5, 3, add));        // Output: 8
console.log(executeOperation(5, 3, multiply)); // Output: 15
```

Here, the `operation` parameter is a function that we can call by name inside the `executeOperation` function implementation.

Returned as values from other functions

Functions can be returned from other functions, enabling the creation of function factories and closures:

first-class-citizens.ts

```
function createMultiplier(factor: number):
  (x: number) => number {
    return function(x: number): number {
        return x * factor;
    };
}
const double = createMultiplier(2);
const triple = createMultiplier(3);
console.log(double(5)); // Output: 10
console.log(triple(5)); // Output: 15
```

Here, the `createMultiplier` function accepts a parameter and returns a function. When you first call `createMultiplier`, you pass a parameter that gets saved inside the function closure. On the second call, which is when you call the returned function, the expression is evaluated using the saved parameter. This example demonstrates how to store these returned functions in two variables and then call them independently.

Stored in data structures

Functions can be stored in arrays, objects, or other data structures:

```
const mathOperations = {
    add: (a: number, b: number) => a + b,
    subtract: (a: number, b: number) => a - b,
    multiply: (a: number, b: number) => a * b,
    divide: (a: number, b: number) => a / b
};
console.log(mathOperations.add(10, 5));
console.log(mathOperations.multiply(3, 4));
```

This feature is an extension of storing functions in variables. We can store functions in data structures as properties for later use.

These capabilities make functions in TypeScript extremely versatile and powerful. They enable the creation of HOFs, which are functions that can either take other functions as arguments or return functions as their output. This flexibility is an important cornerstone of functional programming and allows for the creation of more modular, reusable, and composable code.

For instance, in a middleware setup, you can create a chain of functions that process data sequentially. Each function can modify the input or output, demonstrating how first-class and HOFs work together to create flexible and reusable code structures.

In the next section, we'll explore **function composition**, another important concept in functional programming that builds upon the idea of functions as first-class citizens.

Function composition

Function composition is a mathematical concept whereby you apply one function to the results of another. This is simply an extension of the knowledge we accumulated about functional programming. When we have two functions that take arguments and return a result, you can combine them if their types fit. Here is an example of function composition:

function-composition.ts

```
function double(x: number): number {
  return x * 2
}
function increment(x: number): number {
  return x + 1
}
const doubleAndIncrement = (x: number):
  number => increment(double(x))
console.log(doubleAndIncrement(3)) // Output: 7
// Explanation: (3 * 2) + 1 = 7
```

In this example, we compose double and increment to create a new function that doubles a number and then increments it.

> **Note on performance and type safety**
>
> When composing functions, there are some type inference limitations you need to be aware of. **Complex nested compositions** may require explicit type annotations to maintain type safety. Additionally, deeply nested function compositions can impact performance due to increased call stack depth and memory usage. This is especially true more often if you use recursion and don't impose a limit on the recursion steps. A good rule of thumb is to limit composition depth to 3-4 functions – beyond this, consider breaking the composition into smaller, more manageable chunks.

When composing functions, TypeScript can automatically infer the types of input and output parameters based on the provided functions. Here is an example:

Function-composition.ts

```
interface Person {
  name: string;
  age: number;
}
function getDisplayName(p: Person): string {
  return p.name.toLowerCase();
}
function getLength(s: string): number {
  return s.length;
}
const getDisplayNameLength =
  compose(getDisplayName, getLength);
```

In this example, TypeScript infers that getDisplayNameLength is a function that takes a Person object and returns a number.

> **Note**
> We used function overloading on the compose function to make this work, which we omitted showing here. The overloads allow TypeScript to correctly infer the types of the composed function based on the input functions that each have different types throughout the composition chain. The full listing is located in the function-composition.ts file.

The simplest case of composition is when you have two functions, f and g, which accept a single parameter and form the following expression:

```
f(g(x)) or f ∘ g
```

However, the simplest case is not always attainable because many functions take more than one parameter. This makes it unwieldy when trying to propagate the parameters to the right and you will have to either modify the functions to match the signature or not use function composition at all.

The following section explains how to deal with composing functions with multiple arguments.

Composing functions with multiple arguments

Composing functions with multiple arguments can be more challenging. Let's look at a more complex example:

function-composition.ts

```ts
function capitalizeFirstLetter(str: string): string {
    return str.charAt(0).toUpperCase() +
        str.slice(1).toLowerCase();
}
function removeSpaces(str: string): string {
    return str.replace(/\s+/g, '');
}
function truncate(str: string, length: number): string {
    return str.length > length ? str.slice(0,
        length) + '...' : str;
}
const formatUserInput = (input: string): string => {
    return truncate(removeSpaces
        (capitalizeFirstLetter(input)), 10);
};

console.log(formatUserInput("  john doe  ")); // Output: "Johndoe..."
console.log(formatUserInput("ALICE IN WONDERLAND"));
  // Output: "Aliceinwo..."
```

This example demonstrates composing functions with different arities (number of arguments) to create a more complex string formatting function. The `truncate` function accepts two arguments of different types so they must be called in that order. So, the caller of the function needs to be aware of this setup to avoid passing wrong arguments.

Ideally, you want to have functions that are easily composed to take only one argument at a time. We can achieve that composability by **currying** the functions. Currying means that we take a function that accepts more than one parameter and turn it into a function that accepts one parameter at a time.

We can greatly improve the readability and flexibility of calling by using the following `compose` function.

Using a composition utility

To make function composition more readable and flexible, we can create a simple `compose` utility.

function-composition.ts

```ts
function compose<T>(...fns: Array<(arg: T) => T>) {
  return (x: T) => fns.reduceRight((acc, fn) => fn(acc), x)
```

```
}
const formatName = compose(
    (s: string) => truncate(s, 10),
    removeSpaces,
    capitalizeFirstLetter
);
console.log(formatName("  john doe  ")); // Output: "Johndoe..."
console.log(formatName("ALICE IN WONDERLAND")); // Output:
"Aliceinwo..."
```

This `compose` function allows us to compose multiple functions in a more declarative way, reading from bottom to top. The output of a function will be fed to the input of the next function in the list in that order. This allows an easy way to plug in functions that form a pipeline of processing events.

Now we can see examples of currying in practice that utilize function composition.

Currying for better composition

Currying can make function composition more flexible, especially when dealing with functions that take multiple arguments. Here is a simple implementation of `curry`:

function-composition.ts

```
function curry<T, U, V>(fn: (a: T, b: U) => V):
   (a: T) => (b: U) => V {
   return (a: T) => (b: U) => fn(a, b)
}
const curriedTruncate = curry(truncate)
const formatAndTruncate = compose((s: string) =>
   curriedTruncate(s)(7), removeSpaces,
     capitalizeFirstLetter)
console.log(formatAndTruncate("  john doe  ")) // Output: "Johndoe..."
console.log(formatAndTruncate("ALICE IN WONDERLAND"))
// Output: "Alicein..."
```

The preceding example shows how to combine both `compose` and `curry` functions in practice. The `curry` function is defined with generics (`<T, U, V>`) to handle functions with different types of arguments. It takes a function fn that accepts two arguments of the T and U types and returns a value of the V type.

This essentially creates a new function that takes the first argument (a) and returns another function that takes the second argument. Then, it calls the original function (fn) with both arguments. It's worth noting that this implementation only works for functions with two arguments. For a more general `curry` function that works with any number of arguments, we'd need a more complex implementation using recursion or a loop.

The usage code shows how the `formatAndTruncate` function (composed of multiple functions with different arguments) can be used to apply transformations of a string using pure functions.

We'll continue with the next functional programming concept, which is **referential transparency**.

Referential transparency

Referential transparency is another name for consistency and determinism. This means that once you define some functions that accept parameters and call them, you can replace them with their value without changing the results. This means that you regard your functions as data and vice versa.

The benefits of referential transparency are significant, especially in debugging and testing. It simplifies reasoning about code, as developers can easily predict the behavior of functions based solely on their inputs. When a function is referentially transparent, any issues that arise can be isolated to that specific function. Let's examine examples that demonstrate both referential transparency and its absence:

referential.ts

```typescript
function sortList(list: number[]): number[] {
  return list.sort((a, b) => a - b)
}
let originalList = [3, 1, 4, 1, 5, 9]
let sortedList = sortList(originalList)
console.log(sortedList) // [1, 1, 3, 4, 5, 9]
console.log(originalList) // [1, 1, 3, 4, 5, 9] - Original list is
mutated!
```

This function lacks referential transparency because it mutates the input list. Using it multiple times with the same input might yield different results, depending on the list's current state. This is because we return the result of the array sort method which modifies the existing list.

Now let's see an example of an actual referential transparent function:

referential.ts

```typescript
function pureSort(list: number[]): number[] {
  return [...list].sort((a, b) => a - b)
}
let numbers = [3, 1, 4, 1, 5, 9]
let sorted1 = pureSort(numbers)
let sorted2 = pureSort(numbers)
console.log(sorted1) // [1, 1, 3, 4, 5, 9]
console.log(sorted2) // [1, 1, 3, 4, 5, 9]
console.log(numbers) // [3, 1, 4, 1, 5, 9] - Original list remains
unchanged
```

This function is referentially transparent. It always produces the same output for the same input without side effects. This time, we copy the existing list (using the *array spread* operation) before we call `sort` method.

When adhering to good functional programming principles, you aim to eliminate the sources of mutability and undesired side effects in your code. It helps if you think of your programs as a composition of many small functions together. Here is an example:

referential.ts

```
import * as R from "ramda"
export interface IO<A> {
  (): A
}
const log =
  (s: unknown): IO<void> =>
  () =>
    console.log(s)
function main(): IO<void> {
  return R.compose(log, sumList, getArgs)(11, 4)
}
function sumList(numbers: number[]): number {
  return numbers.reduce((prev, curr) => prev + curr, 0)
}
function getArgs(a: number, b: number): number[] {
  return [a, b]
}
console.log(main()()) // 15
```

We highlight the whole program as a list of composable functions that accept an input and calculate an output. We are using the IO type to denote that the `main` function represents an action that produces side effects and is the program's entry point. With referential transparency, we can replace any of those functions in the `compose` list with their value and still get the same result.

Here is an example of replacing the `sumList` function with the 15 value. Now that we have used the 15 value instead of the function, the output remains the same:

referential.ts

```
function main(): IO<(a, b) => void> {
  return R.compose(log, 15, getArgs)(11, 4);
}
console.log(main()()); // 15
```

The `main` function is defined to return an `IO` monad (see the *Understanding monads* section for a more extensive exploration) that wraps a function taking two parameters, a and b, and returning `void`. Inside `main`, we see a composition of functions using `R.compose`, which is a utility from a functional programming library called **Ramda.js**. However, you can also use the `compose` function we defined earlier as well.

By adhering to referential transparency, we create more predictable, testable, and maintainable code. It enables powerful optimizations and reasoning about program behavior.

We'll continue with the last functional programming concept, which is **immutability**.

Immutability

Immutability is the concept of not allowing a variable or an object to change once it's defined and initialized. This means that you cannot use the same variable to re-assign it to another object or modify the object itself so that it is no longer the same object.

TypeScript offers `readonly` arrays and tuples, which enforce immutability at the type level. This means that once an array or tuple is defined as `readonly`, its elements cannot be modified or reassigned.

In performance-critical applications, immutable data structures may introduce overhead due to the need to create new copies of data rather than modifying existing structures. This can lead to increased memory usage and slower performance if not managed carefully.

There are various ways in which we can enforce immutability in TypeScript. We take a closer look at those together with some examples.

Basic immutability with const

At the most basic level, you have `const` declarations that assign a value to a variable that cannot be changed later:

immutability.ts

```
const name = "Alice";
name = "Bob"; // Error: Cannot assign to 'name' because it is a
constant.
const numbers = [1, 2, 3];
numbers.push(4); // This is allowed and modifies the array
numbers = [5, 6, 7]; // Error: Cannot assign to 'numbers' because it
is a constant.
```

Here, `const` declarations bind the variable name to a constant so that it cannot change once assigned to this reference. If the reference holds a complex data structure such as arrays or objects, it only protects against a re-assignment; methods such as `sort` or `push` would still modify the array itself.

This only works for variable assignments though. If you want to enforce it in types, you can use the Readonly modifier.

Readonly types

TypeScript provides the Readonly utility type to create immutable versions of types:

immutability.ts

```
interface User {
    name: string;
    age: number;
}
const user: Readonly<User> = {
    name: "Alice",
    age: 30
};
user.age = 31; // Error: Cannot assign to 'age' because it is a read-
only property.
```

Marking a type as Readonly means that if we attempt to re-assign one of the properties of the constructed type, it will fail to compile.

As explained earlier, the main problem is that we can still modify an array using certain methods as long as we don't reassign it to a different list. One quick workaround to this issue is to create a new type that traverses deep into the object and marks it as read-only. We will explain this in the next section.

Deep immutability

Here is an example of the data structure that applies a Readonly modifier to all deeply nested properties or items of a complex data structure (such as objects and arrays):

immutability.ts

```
type DeepReadonly<T> =
    T extends (infer R)[] ?
    ReadonlyArray<DeepReadonly<R>> :
    T extends Function ? T :
    T extends object ? {readonly [K in keyof T]:
    DeepReadonly<T[K]>} : T;
interface Department {
    name: string;
    employees: {id: number, name: string}[];
}
const dept: DeepReadonly<Department> = {
```

```
        name: "Engineering",
        employees: [{id: 1, name: "Alice"}, {id: 2,
        name: "Bob"}]
};
dept.name = "Sales"; // Error
dept.employees.push({id: 3, name: "Charlie"}); // Error
dept.employees[0].name = "Alicia"; // Error
```

The highlighted parts of the code focus on the recursive application of the DeepReadonly type. This is one of the powerful features of TypeScript, allowing this to happen at the compiler level. The subsequent examples show that trying to modify this new value leads to type errors.

You have to be aware that you can still bypass this safeguard by typecasting:

```
(dept.name as string) = "Billing"; // works
```

The preceding line uses a type assertion to tell the TypeScript compiler to treat dept.name as a regular string, even if it was originally declared as Readonly. By doing this, the developer is essentially saying to the compiler, *"Trust me, I know what I'm doing."*

Now regarding immutability with classes, here is a way to tackle this issue:

immutability.ts

```
class ImmutablePerson {
    readonly #name: string;
    readonly #age: number;
    constructor(name: string, age: number) {
        this.#name = name;
        this.#age = age;
    }
    get name(): string {
        return this.#name;
    }
    get age(): number {
        return this.#age;
    }
    withAge(newAge: number): ImmutablePerson {
        return new ImmutablePerson(this.#name, newAge);
    }
}
const person1 = new ImmutablePerson("Alice", 30);
const person2 = person1.withAge(31);
console.log(person1.age); // 30
console.log(person2.age); // 31
```

Here, the withAge method takes a single newAge parameter of the number type and returns a new instance of the ImmutablePerson class with the new value as the age property. This would work well, of course, if you don't expect to create many modifications to happen, since creating multiple instances of a class might trigger excessive garbage collection events.

Maybe there is a better way to handle this? Let's look at what some third-party libraries have to offer.

Using Immutable.js

A further safety measure you can use is having truly immutable and purpose-built data structures that are specially defined data structures that do not allow modification.

With Immutable.js, for example, which is a library that provides many data structures, including list, stack, map set, and record, we can safely perform these operations without side effects at runtime:

immutability.ts

```
import { List, Map } from 'immutable';
const list1 = List([1, 2, 3]);
const list2 = list1.push(4);
console.log(list1.toArray()); // [1, 2, 3]
console.log(list2.toArray()); // [1, 2, 3, 4]
const map1 = Map({ a: 1, b: 2 });
const map2 = map1.set('b', 3);
console.log(map1.toObject()); // { a: 1, b: 2 }
console.log(map2.toObject()); // { a: 1, b: 3 }
(list1 as any).push(5);
console.log(list1.toArray()); // [ 1, 2, 3 ]
```

In the highlighted section, we disabled the type check of the list type. However, because it is backed by a truly immutable data structure at runtime, the contents of this list are not modified, and they will still hold the original values.

The immutable nature of variables in a functional programming language has the benefit of preserving the state throughout the execution of a program. Let's discover some advanced uses of functional programming, starting with **functional lenses**.

Understanding functional lenses

A **functional lens** is another name for an object's getter and setter methods paired together in a tuple. We call them that mainly because the idea is to have a functional way to compose getters and setters without modifying an existing object. So, you use a lens to create scopes over objects, and then you use those scopes if you want to interface with the objects in a composable way.

You can think of lenses as having an **Adapter pattern** where the *Target* is the object you want to adapt and the lenses are the *Adaptees*. You can create lenses that adapt over an object type and you can get or set their properties. The main benefit here is that the Lenses object is generic, and you can compose it in a functional way.

Figure 7.2 shows an example application of lenses on a User object that contains a nested Address field:

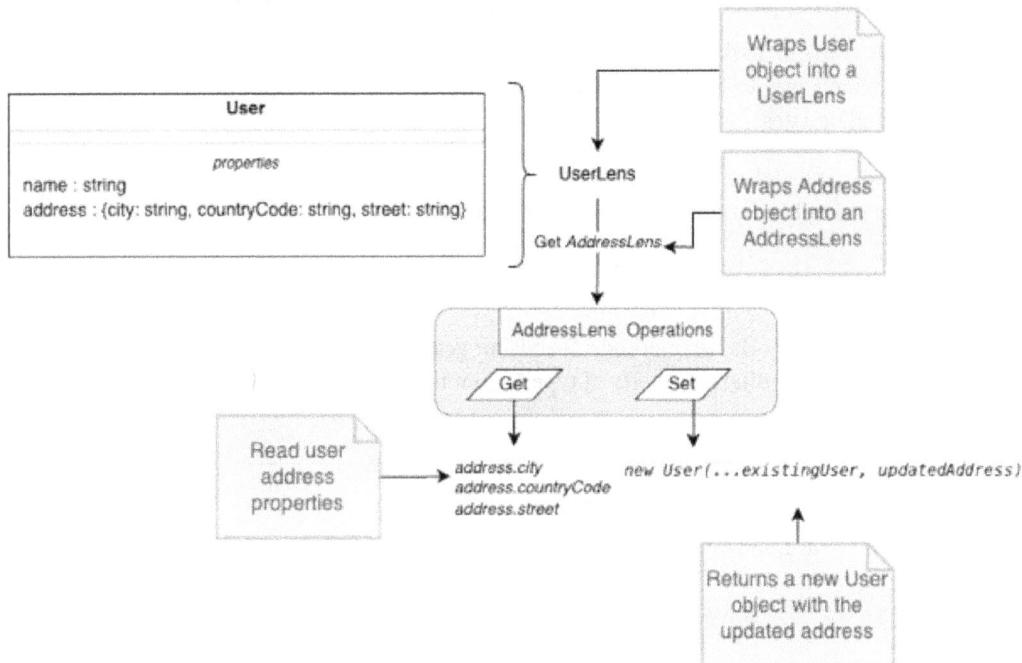

Figure 7.2 – Visualization of a Lens pattern focusing on nested user
address data through UserLens and AddressLens

This shows a User object containing basic properties such as name and a nested address object (with city, countryCode, and street). The UserLens function wraps this entire structure, while the AddressLens function specifically focuses on the address portion. Through lens operations (Get and Set), developers can safely read address properties and create new User objects with updated addresses, all while maintaining immutability.

Let's explain more about lenses next and how to implement them in TypeScript.

When to use functional lenses

Functional lenses are particularly useful in scenarios where you need to interact with or manipulate deeply nested or complex data structures in a clean and functional manner. Here's when to consider using them:

- **Modify complex data objects**: Use lenses when dealing with complex objects or data structures where accessing or updating nested properties can be cumbersome. Lenses allow you to compose functions that focus on specific parts of these structures without having to manually traverse them.

- **Maintain immutability**: Use lenses in scenarios where immutability is the preferred method of updating state. Lenses provide a functional approach to accessing and updating nested properties without modifying the original object, which aligns well with immutable data practices.

- **Better data transformations**: When transforming or aggregating data from nested structures, lenses provide a way to focus on specific parts of the data without manually handling the traversal and updates.

Lenses are quite powerful and can streamline the way you work with nested or complex data structures. Let's explore how to implement them in TypeScript next.

Implementation of lenses

A basic **lens interface** supports two methods: `Get` is for getting a property of type A from an object of type T, and `Set` is for setting a property of type A from the object of type T. Here is the interface of `Lens`:

lenses.ts

```
export interface Lens<T, A> {
  get: (obj: T) => A
  set: (obj: T) => (newValue: A) => T
}
```

This is an example of how you can use the `Lens` interface over an object of type T. We create a `Lens` interface for managing a specific property. Here is how we can define it:

lens.ts

```
function lensProp<T, K extends keyof T>(key: K):
  Lens<T, T[K]> {
  return {
    get: (obj: T): T[K] => obj[key],
    set:
```

```
      (obj: T) =>
      (value: T[K]): T => ({ ...obj, [key]: value }),
  }
}
```

The get method retrieves the object key if it's available. The set method performs an object assignment by copying all existing properties and updating the specific property with the passed key parameter. Here is how the client will use this function:

lens.ts

```
interface Person {
  name: string
  age: number
  email: string
}
const person: Person = {
  name: "John",
  age: 30,
  email: "john@example.com",
}
const ageLens = lensProp<Person, "age">("age")
const currentAge = ageLens.get(person);
console.log(currentAge); // Output: 30
const updatedPerson = ageLens.set(person)(35);
console.log(updatedPerson);
```

You have to note that the ageLens.set function cannot modify the object passed. Instead, it creates a new object with the assigned property. For this example, it will be a user object with the age 35 and all the other properties unmodified. This is why when you call ageLens.get(user) the second time, it will still point to the original user.

It's common to define some extra helper functions for viewing, setting, and mapping lenses. This is to make it easier to compose them with different lenses. This is how the functions are defined:

lens.ts

```
function view<T, A>(lens: Lens<T, A>, obj: T): A {
  return lens.get(obj)
}
function set<T, A>(lens: Lens<T, A>, obj: T, value: A): T {
  return lens.set(obj)(value)
}
function over<T, A, B>(lens: Lens<T, A>,
```

```
  f: (x: A) => A, obj: T) {
    return lens.set(obj)(f(lens.get(obj)))
  }
```

Here, the `view` function accepts a Lens structure and an object and calls the `get` method on this object. The set function performs the same operation for the `lens.set` method. The `over` function is a specialized form of mapping. It takes a function that transforms a value of type A into another value of the same type A. This function allows you to apply a transformation to the value retrieved from the object using the lens, and then it sets the transformed value back into the object. Essentially, over combines the operations of getting and setting in a convenient way.

Here's an example of prefixing the name with a title:

lens.ts

```
const increaseAge = over(ageLens, (val: number) =>
  val + 1, person)
console.log(view(ageLens, increaseAge)) // 31
```

The mapping function takes the `lens` object that we defined earlier, a function that increments the age of the `person` object. This returns a new object with that new property. Then, to evaluate the operation, you use the `view` function by passing the `ageLens` and `increaseAge` objects. This will evaluate as ageLens. `get(increaseAge)`, which, in turn, will evaluate as `person.age + 1`, which will be 31.

We'll showcase some real-world use cases of lenses next so you can understand their benefits better.

Use cases of lenses

One good use case of lenses is when you are managing state in UI applications, and you need to perform updates on it based on some incoming requests. For example, with Redux, you can find yourself doing a lot of object de-structuring to update a deeply nested variable.

We'll show an example with a to-do list model:

lens.ts

```
interface TodoItem {
  id: string
  title: string
  completed: boolean
}
interface TodoListState {
  allItemIds: string[]
```

```
    byItemId: { id: TodoItem }
}
```

We have a `TodoItem` interface that stores a task that we would like to do. Then, in our application, we store the list of to-dos in a `TodoListState` interface. When we want to update the application state, we issue an action that modifies the state. Here is an example updating the completed flag of `TodoItem`:

lens.ts

```
interface UpdateTodoItemCompletedAction {
  type: "UPDATE_TODO_ITEM_COMPLETED"
  id: string
  completed: boolean
}
const byItemIdLens = lensProp<TodoListState,
  'byItemId'>('byItemId');
function todoItemLens(id: string):
  Lens<{ [key: string]: TodoItem; }, TodoItem> {
  return lensProp<{ [key: string]: TodoItem },
    string | number>(id as keyof {
    [key: string]: TodoItem });
}
const completedLens = lensProp<TodoItem,
  'completed'>('completed');
function reduceState(currentState: TodoListState,
  action: UpdateTodoItemCompletedAction): TodoListState {
  switch (action.type) {
    case "UPDATE_TODO_ITEM_COMPLETED":
      const itemLens = todoItemLens(action.id);
      const currentTodoItem = view(itemLens,
        currentState.byItemId);
      const updatedTodoItem = over(completedLens,
        () => action.completed, currentTodoItem);
      const updatedByItemId = {
        ...currentState.byItemId,
        [action.id]: updatedTodoItem,
      };
      // Return the new state with updated byItemId
      return set(byItemIdLens, currentState,
        updatedByItemId);
  }
  return currentState;
}
```

The provided code defines actions for updating a to-do item's completion status. Lenses are used to access and modify specific parts of the state: the byItemId property in TodoListState, individual TodoItem objects, and their completed property. The reduceState function handles an action to update a TodoItem's interface completion status immutably by using lenses to view, update, and set new state values.

The following example concludes with a demonstration of how to apply this state update to an initial state and log the updated state to the console:

lens.ts

```
const initialState: TodoListState = {
  byItemId: {
    '1': { id: '1', title: 'Learn TypeScript',
      completed: false },
    '2': { id: '2', title: 'Build a project',
      completed: false },
  },
};
const action: UpdateTodoItemCompletedAction = {
  type: "UPDATE_TODO_ITEM_COMPLETED",
  id: '1',
  completed: true,
};
const newState = reduceState(initialState, action);
console.log(newState);
```

In this example, initialState is defined and an action is created to update the completed status of a to-do item. Then reduceState is called with the initial state and action, and the new state is logged into the console. It demonstrates the simple effectiveness of functional composition to produce deterministic transitions of state.

To grasp the concept of monads, it is essential to first understand several fundamental structures that serve as foundational elements in functional design. Familiarity with these concepts will enhance your understanding of monads and equip you with a comprehensive toolkit for functional programming in TypeScript.

We'll start by examining functors, applicatives, semigroups, monoids, and traversables. Understanding these concepts will lay the groundwork for a deeper exploration of monads, ensuring a smooth transition into this advanced topic. This revision provides a clearer and more gradual transition to the discussion of monads, ensuring that the reader is well-prepared for the upcoming content.

Exploring practical functional structures

This section takes a deeper look into some of the most practical and widely used functional structures: functors, applicatives, semigroups, monoids, and traversables. These structures provide elegant solutions to common problems and offer a nice way of thinking about code composition and data manipulation in a more principled way while adhering to functional programming principles. Let's start with **functors**.

Functors

Functors are a fundamental concept in functional programming that provide a way to apply functions to values wrapped inside a context. They use a mapping operation to apply a function to all values transforming the contents to a new instance of a functor without changing its own structure.

Let's start by defining a custom functor for a simple container of the Box type:

---

functional-structures.ts

```typescript
class Box<T> {
    constructor(private value: T) {}
    map<U>(f: (value: T) => U): Box<U> {
        return new Box(f(this.value));
    }
    toString(): string {
        return `Box(${this.value})`;
    }
}
const box = new Box(5);
const result = box.map(x => x * 2).map(x => x + 1);
console.log(result.toString()); // Box(11)
```

Here, we've created a Box class that acts as a functor. It wraps a single value and provides the key map method that applies a function to that value, returning a new Box class with the transformed value. We can chain multiple map operations, as shown in the example.

A key requirement for anything to be a functor is the ability to map or transform the value of the boxed variable without changing the structure of the functor. Since each call to map returns a functor, we can chain them together to perform compositions.

As a more practical example, consider the following basic functor operation using **fp-ts**, which is a library that provides utilities that are more ergonomic and type-safe for dealing with such patterns because they handle various type complexities internally:

functional-structures.ts

```typescript
import { pipe } from "fp-ts/function"
import * as A from 'fp-ts/Array'
const numbers = [1, 2, 3, 4]
const doubleArray = pipe(
  numbers,
  A.map(n => n * 2)
)
// Output: [2, 4, 6, 8]
```

This code starts with an array of numbers, `[1, 2, 3, 4]`, and uses fp-ts's `pipe` and `Array map` functions to transform each number. The mapping function doubles each number, resulting in `[2, 4, 6, 8]`, while the `pipe` function enables function composition.

Now we will explore the next practical functional structure, which is **applicatives**.

Applicatives

Applicatives are another powerful abstraction in functional programming that extends the concept of functors. While functors let us apply a function to a value inside a container (such as a `Box` class) functors, applicatives go a step further by allowing us to apply a function that is itself wrapped in a container to a value wrapped in a container. In other words, applicatives enable us to take a `Box` containing a function and apply it to a `Box` class containing a value, resulting in a new container with the result. Let's explore the concept of applicatives in TypeScript. We'll be starting with a simple implementation of `Maybe`, which represents a value that can be either `Existent` or `None`. This `Maybe` implementation also adheres to the applicative interface:

> **Note**
>
> A more detailed explanation of the `Maybe` monad will be provided in the *Introducing the Maybe monad* section later on.

functional-structures.ts

```typescript
interface Applicative<T> {
  map<U>(f: (value: T) => U): Applicative<U>
  ap<U>(f: Applicative<(value: T) => U>): Applicative<U>
}
```

```
class Maybe<T> implements Applicative<T> {
  private constructor(private value: T | null) {}

  static just<T>(value: T): Maybe<T> {
    return new Maybe(value)
  }
  static nothing<T>(): Maybe<T> {
    return new Maybe<T>(null)
  }
  map<U>(f: (value: T) => U): Maybe<U> {
    return this.value === null ? Maybe
      .nothing() : Maybe.just(f(this.value))
  }
  ap<U>(f: Maybe<(value: T) => U>): Maybe<U> {
    if (this.value === null || f.value === null) {
      return Maybe.nothing<U>()
    }
    return Maybe.just(f.value(this.value))
  }
  getOrElse(defaultValue: T): T {
    return this.value !== null ? this.value : defaultValue
  }
}
```

We highlight the key requirement of an applicative structure with the ap (or apply) method. It allows us to apply a function wrapped in a Maybe class to a value also wrapped in another Maybe class and return a new wrapped value.

Let's see how we can use this applicative in practice. However, you'll notice that it doesn't work as intended because it encounters a type error when you try to use it in an example. This issue arises due to the mismatch between the expected types, preventing the applicative from functioning correctly in this context:

---

functional-structures.ts

```
const add = (a: number) => (b: number) => a + b;
const maybeNumber1 = Maybe.just(5);
const maybeNumber2 = Maybe.just(10);
const maybeAdd = Maybe.just(add);
const result = maybeNumber1.ap(maybeAdd.ap(maybeNumber2));
```

In this example, we're trying to apply a function that takes two arguments (add) to two separate Maybe values and the structure allows us to chain these operations together.

However, as you can see, there is an error on top of the call to apply `maybeAdd.ap(maybeNumber2)`:

```
 96 |            Argument of type 'Maybe<number>' is not assignable to parameter of type
 97 |            'Maybe<(value: (a: number) ⇒ (b: number) ⇒ number) ⇒ (value: number)
 98 |            never>'.
 99 |              Type 'number' is not assignable to type '(value: (a: number) ⇒ (b:
100 |            number) ⇒ number) ⇒ (value: number) ⇒ never'. ts(2345)
101 |            const maybeNumber2: Maybe<number>
102 | const maybe
103 | const maybe const maybeNumber2 = Maybe.just(10)
104 | const maybe View Problem (^F8)  Quick Fix... ⌘. Fix using Copilot (⌘I)
105 | const result2 = maybeNumber1.ap(maybeAdd.ap(maybeNumber2))
106 |
```

Figure 7.3 – Error when calling ap from maybeAdd to maybeNumber2

The error you're seeing highlights some of the limitations of TypeScript when dealing with complex type inference, particularly in scenarios involving HOFs and applicative functors. There is no easy solution for it.

The compiler confuses the two different types of wrapped values that are available in the `Maybe<T>` applicative. TypeScript does not have built-in support for **Higher-Kinded Types (HKTs)**, which are types that operate on other types. This absence makes it challenging to implement certain functional programming abstractions (sych as applicative, monad, etc.) in a type-safe and ergonomic way.

To overcome this limitation, we can outsource the nitty gritty implementation details to a third-party tool such as fp-ts.

> **Additional resource**
>
> Feel free to explore more functional structures offered by fp-ts in their learning resources section at `https://gcanti.github.io/fp-ts/learning-resources/` since it provides a lot more beyond the scope of this book.

Here is how to do applicative operations using `fp-ts`:

functional-structures.ts

```typescript
import { pipe } from 'fp-ts/function';
import * as O from 'fp-ts/Option';
import { sequenceT } from 'fp-ts/Apply';
const add = (a: number) => (b: number) => a + b;
const maybeNumber1 = O.some(5);
const maybeNumber2 = O.some(10);
const maybeAdd = O.some(add);
const result2 = pipe(
  sequenceT(O.option)(maybeAdd, maybeNumber1,
    maybeNumber2),
  O.map(([fn, a, b]) => fn(a)(b))
);
console.log(O.getOrElse(() => 0)(result2)); // Should output 15
```

Here, the `sequenceT` function from `fp-ts/Apply` is used to combine `Optional` (another word for `Maybe`) values into a tuple, which is then passed through a pipe. The `pipe` function chains operations, and within it, `O.map` extracts the values from the tuple and applies the curried add function to the numbers.

Finally, `O.getOrElse` is used to extract the result, providing a default value of 0 in case any of the `Option` values were `None`. This essentially fixes the issue with the incorrect type inference.

With that resolved, we can explore the last practical functional structure, which is **semigroups**.

Semigroups

Semigroups are algebraic structures that consist of a set of values and an associative operation (typically concatenation). What it means is that a semigroup is any type that has a way to combine two values of that type into a single value of the same type, and this combination operation must be associative. In an associative operation, grouping the operation or changing its order does not change the result.

For example, the multiplication of three numbers a, b, and c is associative:

```
(a x b) x c = a x (b x c)
```

Let's implement this concept in TypeScript by looking at two implementations of semigroups for strings and numbers:

functional-structures.ts

```typescript
interface Semigroup<T> {
  concat(other: T): T
}
class Sum implements Semigroup<Sum> {
  constructor(public value: number) {}
  concat(other: Sum): Sum {
    return new Sum(this.value + other.value)
  }
}
class Str implements Semigroup<Str> {
  constructor(public value: string) {}
  concat(other: Str): Str {
    return new Str(this.value + other.value)
  }
}
// Generic function to combine a list of semigroups
function concatAll<T extends Semigroup<T>>(xs: T[]): T {
  return xs.reduce((acc, x) => acc.concat(x))
}
```

```
// Usage examples
const sums = [new Sum(1), new Sum(2), new Sum(3)]
console.log(concatAll(sums).value) // Output: 6
const strings = [new Str("Hello, "),
  new Str("functional "), new Str("programming!")]
console.log(concatAll(strings).value) // Output: "Hello, functional
programming!"
```

Here, we define a `Semigroup` interface with a single `concat` method. This method takes another value of the same type and returns a new value of that type. We implement two semigroups for `Sum`, representing string concatenations, and `Num`, representing numbers. The generic `concatAll` function works with any semigroup and takes an array of semigroup values and combines them all using the `concat` method.

In our usage examples, we create arrays of `Sum` and `Str` semigroups and use `concatAll` to combine them printing the result. The power of semigroups becomes apparent when we need to combine values in a consistent way, regardless of the specific type or operation. For example, having a `rules` system and then combining the `rules` list together to form a value:

```
const rules = [
new SecurityRule(context),
new ComplianceRule(context),
new BusinessRule(context)
];
console.log(concatAll(rules).value); // Output: false if a rule fails
```

Thus, semigroups provide a unified way to think about combining values, which can lead to more generic and reusable code. They are particularly useful in scenarios where you need to aggregate or combine values in a consistent way.

Here is an example usage of semigroups using fp-ts for reference:

functional-structures.ts

```
const numberSum = N.SemigroupSum
const result1 = numberSum.concat(1, 2)
const stringConcat = S.Semigroup
const result2 = stringConcat.concat('Hello ', 'World')
```

This code shows two different semigroups in action. The first uses a number semigroup that combines numbers through addition ($1 + 2 = 3$). The second uses a string semigroup that combines strings through concatenation (`'Hello ' + 'World' = 'Hello World'`).

Now let's continue by exploring the concept of **monoids**.

Monoids

Monoids are semigroups that include an identity rule. That includes a set of elements, an associative binary operation, and an identity element, which, when combined, returns the element unchanged.

For example, the multiplication semigroup has the number 1 as the identity element:

```
(a x 1) = a

(1 x a) = a
```

We can easily extend the `Semigroup` interface to implement the two monoids for `Sum`, representing string concatenations, and `Num`, representing numbers:

functional-structures.ts

```ts
interface Monoid<T> extends Semigroup<T> {
  identity(): T;
}
class Product implements Semigroup<Product>,
  Monoid<Product> {
  constructor(public value: number) {}
  concat(other: Product): Product {
      return new Product(this.value * other.value);
  }
  identity(): Product {
      return new Product(1); // 1 is the identity element for
multiplication
  }

}
// Example usage:
const a = new Product(2);
const b = new Product(3);
const c = new Product(4);
const result = a.concat(b).concat(c); // (2 * 3) * 4
console.log(result.value); // Output: 24
```

This example shows how to extend the basic semigroup functionality to include monoid features, using both the associative operation and the identity element.

The `Product` class implements both `Semigroup` and `Monoid` interfaces. The `Semigroup` interface requires a `concat` method that combines two instances of the class using multiplication. The `Monoid` interface extends this by including an `identity` method, which returns the identity element for the operation, in this case, 1 for multiplication.

Monoids are more flexible than semigroups because they introduce the concept of an identity element, which ensures that there is a neutral element in the set that doesn't alter other elements when combined with them.

Here is an example usage of monoids using fp-ts for reference:

---

functional-structures.ts

```
import { pipe } from "fp-ts/function"
import * as A from 'fp-ts/Array'
import * as N from 'fp-ts/number'
const numberMonoid = N.MonoidSum;
const numbers2 = [1, 2, 3, 4]
const sum = pipe(
   numbers2,
   A.foldMap(numberMonoid)(n => n)
)
```

This example demonstrates using a monoid to reduce an array to a single value. The `MonoidSum` object for numbers uses `0` as its identity element and addition as its combination operation. `foldMap` combines all the numbers in the array using this monoid, effectively summing them (`1 + 2 + 3 + 4 = 10`).

We now concentrate on the concept of **traversables**.

Traversables

A **traversable** is a functional structure that works by applying a function to each element and collecting the result in a data structure, such as a list. The concept of traversable basically works as an *accumulator*. This allows for applying a function to each element of the data structure and accumulating the results in a sequence.

The key method that any traversable implements is the `traverse` method:

---

functional-structures.ts

```
interface Traversable<T> {
    traverse<A>(fn: (item: T) => A[]): A[];
}
```

This `traverse` method takes a function `fn` as its argument and returns an array of results for each item. The implementor of this contract should apply this function to each element and flatten the resulting arrays into a single array.

Now let's implement a simple traversable backed by a list:

functional-structures.ts

```
class TraversableList<T> implements Traversable<T> {
  constructor(private items: T[]) {}

  // Traverse method applies the function to each element and collects
  the results in an array
  traverse<A>(fn: (item: T) => A[]): A[] {
    return this.items.flatMap(fn)
  }
}
// Example usage:
const list = new TraversableList<number>([1, 2, 3])
// Function to apply
const expand = (num: number): number[] => [num, num * 2]
// Applying the function using traverse
const result4 = list.traverse(expand)
console.log(result) // Output: [1, 2, 2, 4, 3, 6]
```

The TraversableList class implements this interface by managing a list of items and providing the traverse method to apply a given function to each item. The traverse method uses flatMap internally to apply the function to each item and merge the resulting arrays into one, thus combining all results into a single flattened array.

In the example usage, a TraversableList instance is created with the numbers [1, 2, 3] and a function that generates an array containing the number and its double. The result for an input number 4, for example, would be [4, 8]. The traverse method then combines these arrays into one flattened array showcasing the simplicity of this structure.

We also provide an example using **fp-ts** for reference:

functional-structures.ts

```
const maybeNumbers = [O.some(1), O.some(2),
  O.none, O.some(4)]
const traverseResult = pipe(
  maybeNumbers,
  A.traverse(O.Applicativo)((n) => n)
)
```

This code shows how traversables handle collections of an array of Option objects. In such case, the traverse operation attempts to sequence these Option objects. If all elements are Some, it would return Some of an array; if any element is None, it returns None. In this example, since there's a None object in the array, the result is None.

We now finalize our discovery of advanced functional programming structures by looking at **Monads**.

Understanding monads

A **monad** is a powerful abstract structure in functional programming that encapsulates computations and allows for their composition in a consistent way. Monads provide solutions to various programming challenges, including handling side effects, managing optional values, and sequencing operations.

You can think of the monad as an object that exposes a set of methods that make it easier to compose other monads of the same type together. Usually, an object called a monad needs to follow what we call monadic laws, which we will explain later in the *Understanding Monad laws* section.

In functional programming, monads are often used to handle operations that might fail or involve side effects without compromising the purity of functions. For instance, the `Maybe` monad is commonly used to represent optional values, allowing functions to return either a value or nothing (`null`) without throwing errors.

Figure 7.4 shows how the `Maybe` monad works in simple terms:

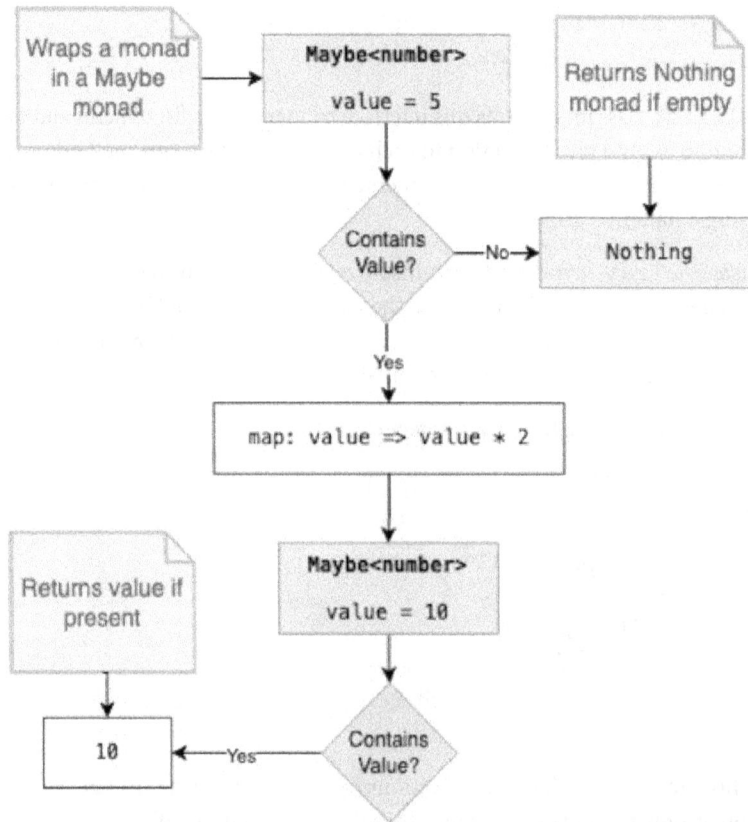

Figure 7.4 – Maybe monad workflow that shows how it handles optional values with safe transformations

This diagram shows how a `Maybe` monad safely handles optional values in functional programming. It starts with a `Maybe` monad containing the number 5, then applies a transformation (mapping the value to double itself). The diagram shows two decision points where the monad checks whether a value exists: first with the initial value of 5, which gets mapped to 10, and then with the resulting value. At each step, the monad could either contain a value or be empty (resulting in `Nothing`).

Let's start with a simple example and gradually build up to more complex scenarios.

Consider these basic functions that add and multiple two numbers by a fixed amount:

monads.ts

```
function add2(x: number): number {
    return x + 2;
}
function mul3(x: number): number {
    return x * 3;
}
```

The `add2` function takes a number `x` and returns the result of adding 2 to it. The `mul3` function takes a number `x` and returns the result of multiplying it by 3.

We can compose these functions easily:

monads.ts

```
console.log(mul3(add2(2))); // (2 + 2) * 3 = 12
console.log(add2(mul3(2))); // (2 * 3) + 2 = 8
```

The first way is to have `mul3` composed with `add2`, and the second way is the other way around.

This works well for simple, pure functions. However, what about more complex scenarios?

Let's introduce a scenario where our functions might not always produce a single value, rather they can return optional values. The `safeDivide` function takes two numbers, `x` and `y`, and returns their division result if `y` is not zero; otherwise, it returns `null` to avoid division by zero. The `safeSquareRoot` function computes the square root of a number `x`, returning the result if `x` is non-negative; if `x` is negative, it returns `null` to prevent the calculation of an undefined square root:

monads.ts

```
function safeDivide(x: number, y: number): number | null {
    return y !== 0 ? x / y : null;
}
  function safeSquareRoot(x: number): number | null {
```

```
        return x >= 0 ? Math.sqrt(x) : null;
    }
```

The `safeDivide` function takes two numbers, `x` and `y`, and returns their division result if `y` is not zero; otherwise, it returns `null` to avoid division by zero. The `safeSquareRoot` function computes the square root of a number `x`, returning the result if `x` is non-negative; if `x` is negative, it returns `null` to prevent the calculation of an undefined square root.

Now, composing these functions becomes tricky since we must cater for the `null` value:

monads.ts

```
const result = safeSquareRoot(safeDivide(16, 4) as number); // Type:
number | null
```

The result of the call to `safeDivide` is fed to the `safeSquareRoot` function, which itself propagates a potential `null` value as well.

This creates a constant need to handle potential `null` values at each step, which can lead to nested conditionals:

monads.ts

```
const result = safeDivide(16, 4);
if (result !== null) {
    const sqrtResult = safeSquareRoot(result);
    if (sqrtResult !== null) {
        console.log(sqrtResult);
    }
}
```

The first result of the `safeDivide` function can be `null` so we need to check before feeding it to the next function. As you can understand, this quickly becomes unwieldy and very verbose as we have to perform this check on each step.

This is where monads come in. Let's implement a simple `Maybe` monad in the next section.

Introducing the Maybe monad

In this section, we'll implement a `Maybe` monad that captures both a `null` type and an existing value and provides methods to extract the value in a safe way:

monads.ts

```
class Maybe<T> {
    private constructor(private value: T | null) {}
```

```
    static just<T>(value: T): Maybe<T> {
        return new Maybe(value);
    }
    static nothing<T>(): Maybe<T> {
        return new Maybe<T>(null);
    }
    map<U>(fn: (value: T) => U): Maybe<U> {
        return this.value === null ? Maybe
            .nothing() : Maybe.just(fn(this.value));
    }
    flatMap<U>(fn: (value: T) => Maybe<U>): Maybe<U> {
        return this.value === null ? Maybe
            .nothing() : fn(this.value);
    }
}
```

The `Maybe` monad encapsulates the state of having a value or not, eliminating the need for `null` checks. It allows for easy composition of functions that might fail or not produce a value using the map and `flatMap` static methods. The `flatMap` method is useful for preventing nested `Maybe` (`Maybe<Maybe<T>>`) generic types.

Now we can rewrite our functions to use the `Maybe` monad:

monads.ts

```
function safeDivide(x: number, y: number): Maybe<number> {
    return y !== 0 ? Maybe.just(x / y) : Maybe.nothing();
}
function safeSquareRoot(x: number): Maybe<number> {
    return x >= 0 ? Maybe.just(Math.sqrt(x)) :
        Maybe.nothing();
}
```

Notice that we return a `Maybe<number>` type instead of `number | null`. With this new structure, we can compose the existing examples more elegantly:

monads.ts

```
const result = safeDivide(16, 4).flatMap(safeSquareRoot);
console.log(result); // Maybe { value: 2 }
const invalidResult = safeDivide(16,
  0).flatMap(safeSquareRoot);
console.log(invalidResult); // Maybe { value: null }
```

In this example, `safeDivide` returns a `Maybe` object to handle the case of division by zero. The operations are chained safely, and if any step results in `Nothing`, the subsequent operations are skipped.

Those examples demonstrate one useful use case of Monads as functional structures that allow better composition of other functions but they are not the only ones. We discuss in what ways we tend to use monads next.

When to use monads

Monads are powerful abstractions in functional programming, but it's important to understand when they're most beneficial. In the following sections, we'll look at some key scenarios where monads can significantly improve your code.

Error handling

The `Either` monad (or `Result` type) is excellent for error handling without exceptions. It uses two type parameters to handle the success and error cases respectively:

monads.ts

```typescript
class Either<L, R> {
    private constructor(private left: L | null,
      private right: R | null) {}
    static left<L, R>(value: L): Either<L, R> {
      return new Either<L, R>(value, null);
    }
    static right<L, R>(value: R): Either<L, R> {
      return new Either<L, R>(null, value);
    }
    // more methods here
}
function divide(a: number, b: number):
  Either<string, number> {
    return b === 0
        ? Either.left("Division by zero")
        : Either.right(a / b);
}
function squareRoot(n: number): Either<string, number> {
    return n < 0
        ? Either.left("Cannot calculate square root of negative
number")
        : Either.right(Math.sqrt(n));
}
const result = divide(10, 2)
    .flatMap(squareRoot);
```

This implementation provides an `Either` monad that can create `Either` instances for error (`left`) and success (`right`) cases. The example usage shows how to compose functions (`divide` and `squareRoot`) that return `Either` instances together, leading to cleaner type safety.

Let's look at one more example of a Monad that controls the state.

State management

When you need to control state through a series of computations, the `State` monad can be very helpful. The `State` monad represents a function from some state to a tuple of a result and a new state: `S -> (A, S)`. It allows you to chain state-dependent computations where each operation can read the current state, produce a result, and potentially modify the state.

The following code shows how the `State` monad is implemented in TypeScript:

monads.ts

```typescript
class State<S, A> {
    constructor(public run: (s: S) => [A, S]) {}
    static of<S, A>(a: A): State<S, A> {
        return new State(s => [a, s]);
    }
    map<B>(f: (a: A) => B): State<S, B> {
        return new State(s => {
            const [a, s1] = this.run(s);
            return [f(a), s1];
        });
    }
    flatMap<B>(f: (a: A) => State<S, B>): State<S, B> {
        return new State(s => {
            const [a, s1] = this.run(s);
            return f(a).run(s1);
        });
    }
}
const increment = new State<number, void>(s =>
    [undefined, s + 1]);
const getCount = new State<number, number>(s => [s, s]);
const program = increment.flatMap(() => increment)
    .flatMap(() => getCount);
  const [count, finalState] = program.run(0);
console.log(count, finalState); // 2, 2
```

The `run` method executes the state computation with an initial state. The `of` method creates a `State` instance that just wraps a value without modifying the state. Finally, the `map` method transforms the result value without affecting the state and the `flatMap` method chains state computations, allowing each step to depend on the previous value.

This monad resembles the Chain of Responsibility pattern we explored in *Chapter 5*, where each state value is passed along the chain. However, the main difference here is that new updates return a new state instead of modifying the existing state leading to less side effects.

One final observation about monads is about their common functionality and how they can be formulated mathematically. For that, there is a concept of monad laws, which is explained next.

Understanding Monad laws

Monads are defined by a set of laws that ensure they behave consistently and can be composed reliably. These laws are fundamental to the concept of monads and help us reason about their behavior. Let's break down these laws in a more accessible way:

- **Functor law**: Every monad must be a functor, meaning it must provide a `map` function:

  ```
  map<U>(fn: (value: T) => U): M<U>
  ```

- **Unit law**: Also known as **pure**, for this, there must be a way to create a monad from a value:

  ```
  of<T>(value: T): M<T>
  ```

- **Flatten law**: There must be a way to flatten nested monads:

  ```
  flatMap<U>(fn: (value: T) => M<U>): M<U>
  ```

Given these components, a monad must adhere to the following laws:

- **Left identity**: Creating a monad from a value and then using flatten it (using the `flatMap` method) with a function is the same as applying the function directly to the value:

  ```
  M.of(a).flatMap(f) === f(a)
  ```

- **Right identity**: Using `flatMap` on a monad with the `of` function should return the original monad unchanged:

  ```
  m.flatMap(M.of) === m
  ```

- **Associativity**: The order of nested `flatMap` operations should not matter:

  ```
  m.flatMap(f).flatMap(g) === m.flatMap(x => f(x).flatMap(g))
  ```

Here is an example demonstrating these laws using the `Maybe` monad:

monads.ts

```
// Left Identity
const a = 5
const f = (x: number) => Maybe.just(x * 2)
console.log(Maybe.just(a).flatMap(f).equals(f(a))) // true
// Right Identity
const m = Maybe.just(3)
console.log(m.flatMap(Maybe.just).equals(m)) // true
// Associativity
const g = (x: number) => Maybe.just(x + 1)
const h = (x: number) => Maybe.just(x * 3)
const m1 = Maybe.just(2).flatMap(g).flatMap(h)
const m2 = Maybe.just(2).flatMap((x) => g(x).flatMap(h))
console.log(m1.equals(m2)) // true
```

The provided examples illustrate the three monadic laws—*left identity*, *right identity*, and *associativity*—using the `Maybe` monad in TypeScript.

These rules simply exist because we want to allow certain compositions between functions and monads of the same instance type. For example, the first rule means that if you chain an identity function from the left, you get the same function. The second deals with chaining on the right. The last rule is for associativity and means that it does not matter whether you chain from the left or from the right; you will get the same result.

There are more technical theories and applications of monads in the real world. What is more important is to grasp how the composition of functions is the glue to make those pieces fit together. Without composition and associated laws, there would be no use for those advanced structures to exist and be used in applications. Hopefully, this chapter has demystified some of those concepts and helped you see the benefits of composition in functional programming.

Summary

Within this chapter, we explored the fundamental concepts of functional programming and looked at some practical examples. Those concepts constitute the backbone of functional programming in general. We started by understanding the concepts of purity, function composition, and immutability. We noted practical examples of recursion and discovered the benefits of referential transparency. We made a distinction between declarative programming and imperative programming, highlighting their fundamental differences in approach.

We continued our exploration with practical functional programming constructs, starting with lenses, which form an abstraction over getters and setters. Finally, we looked at monads and their crucial helpfulness in constructing composable structures at scale.

Utilizing these concepts will support you in structuring your code in a pleasant, abstract way with scalability in mind. In the subsequent chapter, you will learn how reactive programming can help us deliver event-driven, scalable, responsive, and resilient systems.

Get This Book's PDF Version and Exclusive Extras

UNLOCK NOW

Scan the QR code (or go to `packtpub.com/unlock`). Search for this book by name, confirm the edition, and then follow the steps on the page.

Note: Keep your invoice handly. Purchase made directly from packt don't require one.

8

Reactive and Asynchronous Programming

Reactive programming is a powerful paradigm that focuses on the flow of data through a system and how that system responds to changes. By adopting this approach, you can simplify communication between components and enhance overall performance.

This paradigm is particularly useful in various scenarios, such as creating interactive **user interfaces** (**UIs**), real-time feeds, and communication tools. At its core, reactive programming emphasizes asynchronous communication between services, allowing systems to efficiently manage how and when they respond to changes in data.

When combined with functional programming principles, reactive programming enables the creation of composable operators that facilitate the development of scalable and maintainable systems. In this chapter, we will delve into fundamental concepts and techniques of reactive programming, equipping you with the knowledge to build responsive applications.

The following are the topics that will be discussed in this chapter:

- Learning reactive programming concepts
- Asynchronous propagation of changes
- Understanding Promises and Futures
- Exploring Observables

By the end of this chapter, you will have amassed the necessary skills and techniques to write highly scalable and decoupled software using useful reactive programming concepts.

Technical requirements

The code bundle for this chapter is available on GitHub at: `https://github.com/PacktPublishing/TypeScript-5-Design-Patterns-and-Best-Practices/tree/main/chapters/chapter08_Reactive_Programming_concepts`.

Learning reactive programming concepts

When we refer to *reactive* in computer programming, we typically discuss three key concepts:

- **Reactive programming**: Reactive programming is a computing paradigm that emphasizes the asynchronous propagation of information flow. In this model, when one service object queries another for data, the response does not occur simultaneously. Instead, the response may be accepted and evaluated later. Once the data is ready, it can be propagated to consumers through various predefined mechanisms, such as callbacks, Promises, or Futures. This approach allows systems to remain responsive and efficient, even when dealing with asynchronous operations.

- **Reactive systems**: A reactive system is a set of design principles and concepts aimed at building scalable and distributed applications that maintain asynchronous communication. These principles are derived from the *Reactive Manifesto* (see the *Further reading* section), a foundational document that outlines the core tenets of reactive programming. Reactive systems are designed to be responsive, resilient, elastic, and message-driven, enabling them to handle varying loads and failures gracefully.

- **Functional reactive programming (FRP)**: FRP combines the concepts of reactive programming with functional programming. This paradigm utilizes functional composition to manipulate streams of data while ensuring referential transparency. As discussed in *Chapter 7*, referential transparency allows us to replace a function with its value without altering the program's outcome. In this chapter, we will demonstrate the use of FRP with **Observables**, showcasing how these concepts can be applied in practice.

> **Reactive Manifesto concepts in brief**
>
> The **Reactive Manifesto** is a collective document that outlines the key principles of reactive programming. The key principles are divided into four distinct concepts. Reactive systems are **responsive**, meaning they respond in a timely manner. Reactive systems are **resilient**, meaning they are tolerant and responsive in mission-critical systems. Reactive systems are **elastic**, meaning they can adjust their scalability based on their available workloads. Finally, reactive systems are **message-driven**, meaning they have decoupled methods of communication that allow them to be loosely coupled and efficient. All of those principles unlock ways to create systems that are highly responsive, can handle failures gracefully, scale efficiently, and maintain clear communication between components.

Now, let's move on to understanding the advantages of using reactive programming.

Benefits of reactive programming

In terms of practical benefits, all the aforementioned reactive concepts offer several practical benefits, including the following:

- **Efficiency**: By enabling asynchronous communication and non-blocking operations, reactive programming optimizes resource utilization and improves overall system performance

- **Decoupled operations**: The communication patterns fostered by reactive programming promote loose coupling between components, making systems easier to maintain and extend

- **Simplified development**: Developers can leverage standardized, easy-to-use clients to perform asynchronous tasks or compose them abstractly without needing to manage the complexities of data propagation

The drawback of this style is that it introduces increased complexity. This complexity can manifest in both code structure and system architecture, as communication must adhere to specific rules of synchronicity. If the asynchronous, non-blocking nature of reactive programming is not maintained, it can lead to performance degradation and potential data loss.

When to use reactive programming?

Reactive programming is a powerful paradigm that can greatly enhance the development of certain types of applications. We will now explain, with the help of some practical examples, the use of reactive programming with TypeScript:

- **Asynchronous data flows**: If your application involves handling multiple asynchronous data flows, such as user inputs, network requests, or real-time updates, reactive programming can simplify the management of these streams.

- **Event-driven architectures (EDAs)**: For systems that rely on EDAs, such as microservices or serverless applications, reactive programming can help manage the flow of events and responses in an efficient manner.

- **Real-time applications**: Applications that rely on low latency, or **Internet of Things (IoT)** systems, can greatly benefit from reactive programming. The ability to handle high-frequency data updates and propagate changes efficiently is a key advantage.

In the following section, we will explore practical examples that demonstrate the use of reactive programming with TypeScript, starting with asynchronous data flows and propagation of changes.

Asynchronous propagation of changes

In practical terms, reactive programming represents a paradigm where we use declarative code to describe asynchronous communications and events. This means that when we submit a request or a message to a channel, it will be processed or accepted at a later time. As we obtain data as part of the response that we are trying to build, we send it back asynchronously. It then becomes the responsibility of the consumer to react based on those changes.

Before implementing this communication, it is important to establish the format in which data will be transmitted, whether it is sent in chunks or returned in a single response. This predefined structure helps ensure that both producers and consumers can effectively handle the data exchange.

Next, we will describe a few of the most popular communication techniques and patterns that you can use when developing reactive programming systems.

The Pull pattern

With the **Pull pattern**, the consumer of the data needs to proactively query the source for updates and react based on any new information. This means that the consumer must periodically poll the producer for any changes in values.

Figure 8.1 illustrates the Pull pattern, where the consumer actively requests data from the producer when needed:

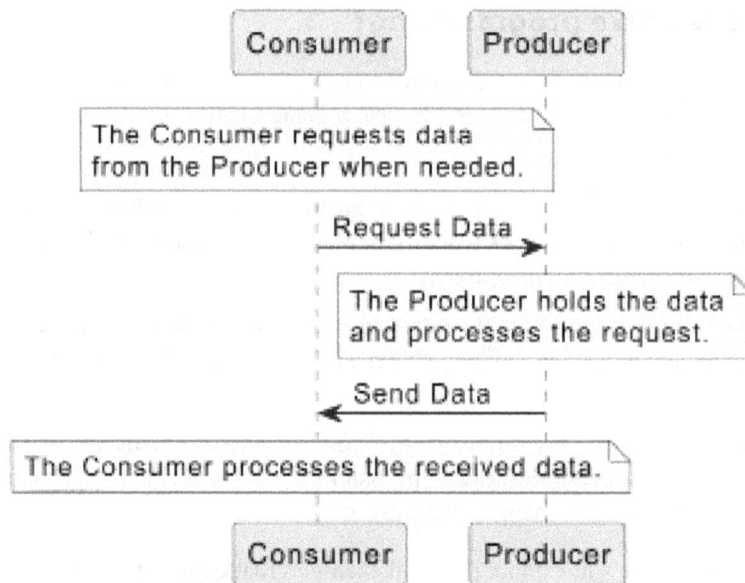

Figure 8.1 – Diagram of the Pull pattern

In this diagram, the consumer sends a request to the producer, indicating that it requires specific data. The producer, which holds the requested data, processes the consumer's request and responds by sending the data back to the consumer. Once the consumer receives the data, it proceeds to process the information according to its requirements.

To understand how polling works in code, we refer to the example described by David Walsh in his 2015 article, *JavaScript Polling*, which is available at `https://davidwalsh.name/javascript-polling`. This tutorial demonstrates how to create a function that takes a function returning a Promise and checks its result periodically. If the request is successful, it resolves with the data; otherwise, it continues polling until either success is achieved or a timeout is reached:

patterns.ts

```ts
export interface AsyncRequest<T> {
  success: boolean;
  data?: T;
}

export async function asyncPoll<T>(
  fn: () => PromiseLike<AsyncRequest<T>>,
  pollInterval = 5000,
  pollTimeout = 30000,
  abortSignal?: AbortSignal
): Promise<T> {
  if (abortSignal?.aborted) {
    throw new Error("Polling aborted");
  }

  const endTime = new Date().getTime() + pollTimeout;

  const condition = (resolve: (value: T) => void,
    reject: (reason?: any) => void): void => {
      if (abortSignal?.aborted) {
        reject(new Error("Polling aborted"));
        return;
      }

      Promise.resolve(fn()).then((result) => {
        const now = new Date().getTime();
        if (result.success) {
          if (result.data === undefined) {
            reject(new Error("Successful response
              must include data"));
            return;
          }
          resolve(result.data);
        } else if (now < endTime) {
          setTimeout(condition, pollInterval,
```

```
            resolve, reject);
        } else {
            reject(new Error("Reached timeout. Exiting"));
        }
    })
    .catch(reject);
};


return new Promise(condition);
}
```

In the preceding code, the `asyncPoll` function accepts another function parameter named `fn`, which will be periodically called to resolve its results. If the result is something that the client is interested in, then the Promise resolves with the data. Conversely, if the polling exceeds the specified timeout, the Promise rejects, indicating that no relevant updates were received within the allotted time.

You can inspect the result by resolving the Promise and reading the `data` property:

---

patterns.ts

```
const result = asyncPoll(async () => {
  try {
    const result = await Promise.resolve(
      { data: "Value" })
    if (result.data) {
      return Promise.resolve({
        success: true,
        data: result,
      })
    } else {
      return Promise.resolve({
        success: false,
      })
    }
  } catch (err) {
    return Promise.reject(err)
  }
})
result.then((d) => {
  console.log(d.data) // Value
})
```

This example demonstrates how to retrieve information asynchronously and then halt the process.

However, you might encounter scenarios where you need to periodically pull data from an `iterator`. Here's a simple illustration of that:

patterns.ts

```
const source = [1, 3, 4];
const iter = new ListIterator(source);
function pollOnData(iterator: ListIterator<number>) {
  while (iterator.hasNext()) {
    console.log("Processing data:", iterator.next());
  }
}
// Producer
setTimeout(() => {
  source.push(Math.floor(Math.random() * 100));
}, 1000);
// Consumer
setTimeout(() => {
  pollOnData(iter);
}, 2000);
```

In this example, we have a list `source` that is wrapped in an `iterator`. The `producer` adds new integers to the `source`, while the `consumer` polls the `iterator` to process these new numbers. It's important to note that the `producer` and `consumer` operate at different rates, which introduces the risk that the `producer` may generate more data than the `consumer` can handle in a timely manner.

The Pull pattern employed here is straightforward and does not necessitate significant architectural changes. However, one drawback of this approach is the increased amount of code required to manage the process, which can lead to unnecessary resource consumption. This version maintains the original information while enhancing readability and coherence.

The Push pattern

In the **Push pattern**, the consumer receives new values from the producer as soon as they become available. This is the opposite of the Pull pattern and can lead to better efficiency in terms of communication overhead since the responsibility now rests with the producer to push the relevant values to consumers. The producer may also offer additional features, such as replays or persisted messages.

Figure 8.2 illustrates the Push pattern, where the producer actively sends data to the consumer as soon as it becomes available:

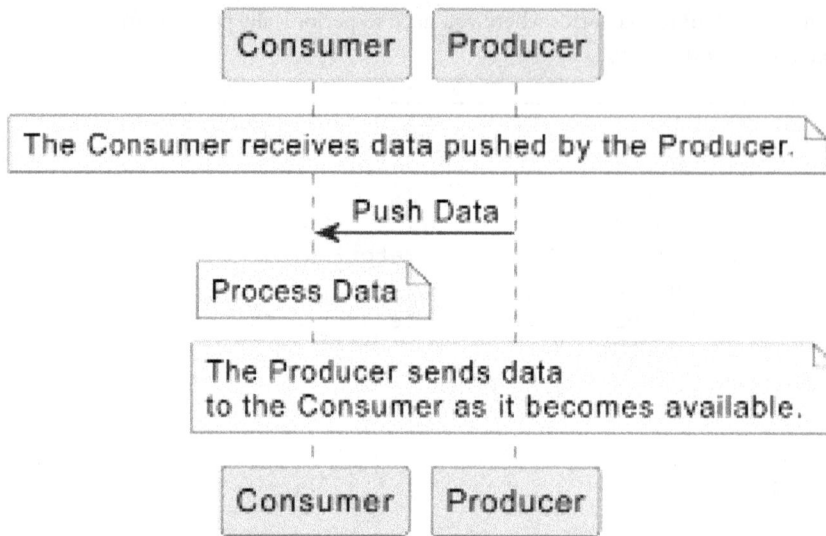

Figure 8.2 – Diagram of the Push pattern

In this diagram, the producer initiates the communication by pushing data to the consumer, eliminating the need for the consumer to request updates actively. Upon receiving the data, the consumer processes it immediately, which is particularly beneficial in scenarios requiring timely updates, such as notifications in messaging applications or live data feeds.

The Push pattern is similar to the *Observer pattern* we learned about in *Chapter 5*. Here's an example of how to implement the Push pattern using the Observer pattern:

patterns.ts

```typescript
import {Subject} from 'rxjs';
class Producer {
  private subject = new Subject<number>();
  sendData(data: number) {
    this.subject.next(data);
  }
  subscribe(callback: (data: number) => void) {
    this.subject.subscribe(callback);
  }
}
```

In this example, the `Producer` class contains a `Subject` class from the RxJS library. When the `Producer` class has new data to send, it calls the `sendData` method, which updates the internal state and notifies all subscribed consumers.

Here's how you can use the Push pattern with the Observer pattern:

patterns.ts

```ts
// Create a producer instance
const producer = new Producer();
producer.subscribe((data) => {
  console.log('Subscriber 1 received:', data);
});
producer.subscribe((data) => {
  console.log('Subscriber 2 received:', data);
});

// Send some data
producer.sendData(42);
producer.sendData(100);
```

In this example, we create a `Producer` instance and add two subscriber callbacks. Whenever the producer has new data to send, it calls the `sendData` method, which updates the state and notifies all subscribed consumers.

Real-world uses of the Push pattern

The Push pattern is used in the following scenarios:

- **Using WebSockets**: A common implementation of the Push pattern is through **WebSockets**, which allow for two-way communication between a client and a server.

- **Notifications in mobile apps**: Mobile apps often utilize push notifications to inform users of new messages, updates, or alerts. This ensures that users are informed without needing to open the app continuously.

- **Streaming services**: In media streaming applications, the Push pattern allows for real-time updates of available content or live broadcasts, enhancing user engagement and experience.

- **IoT devices**: IoT devices often use the Push pattern to send data back to a central server or application. For instance, a smart thermostat might push temperature data to a user's smartphone app, allowing on-the-fly adjustments.

The main benefit of the Push pattern is that consumers receive data as soon as it becomes available, without the need to constantly poll for changes. This can lead to more efficient communication and better responsiveness in real-time scenarios.

The Pull-Push pattern

The **Pull-Push pattern** is a hybrid approach for detecting changes and propagating them to consumers. Instead of the producer sending the actual data directly, as seen in the Observer pattern, it sends a message containing the endpoint or path that the consumer can use to retrieve the latest data.

The Pull-Push pattern is particularly useful when the producer cannot send large payloads to the client due to security or performance concerns. Instead, it instructs the consumer to query a different source that the producer has consistently updated.

In *Figure 8.3*, we illustrate how data flows using this pattern:

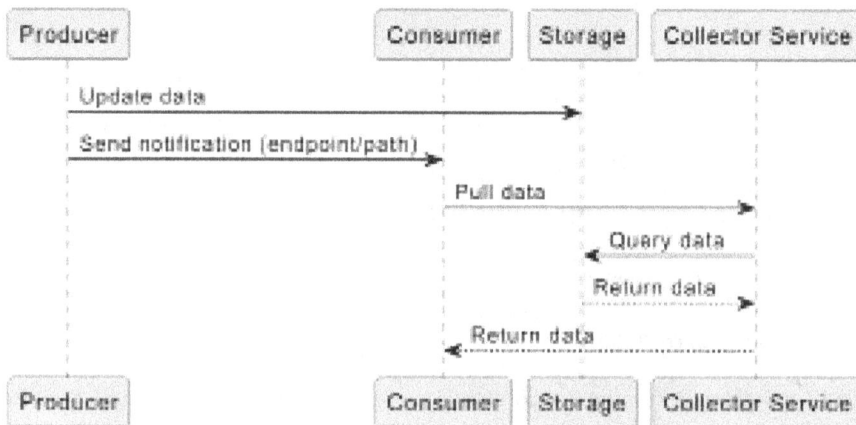

Figure 8.3 – Diagram of the Pull-Push pattern

In this flow, the producer first updates the storage with new data and sends notifications to the consumer. Upon receiving these notifications, the consumer then pulls the data from the collector service, which knows how to query the data from storage.

The main advantage of this asynchronous communication flow is that it reduces the burden on the producer, eliminating the need to store messages for the consumer. This pattern is particularly beneficial in scenarios where the consumer does not have direct knowledge of the producer but still needs access to relevant information.

Here's a simplified example in TypeScript that demonstrates the Pull-Push pattern (please see the full code of the respective classes in the file mentioned; see the *Technical requirements* section for the link to the GitHub repo):

pull-push.ts

```typescript
class Producer {
  private storage: Storage
  ...
}
class Consumer {
  private collector: Collector
  ...
}
class Storage {
  private data: any[] = []
  ...
}
class Consumer {
  constructor(private collector: Collector) {}

  async *pullDataStream() {
    while (await this.collector.hasMoreData()) {
      const data = await this.collector.pullData();
      for (const item of data) {
        yield item;
      }
      await new Promise(resolve =>
        setTimeout(resolve, 1000));
    }
  }
}
// Example usage
async function example() {
  const storage = new Storage();
  const producer = new Producer(storage);
  const collector = new Collector(storage);
  const consumer = new Consumer(collector);

  // Producer adds data
  await producer.updateData({ id: 1,
    value: "First Data" });
  await producer.updateData({ id: 2,
```

```
      value: "Second Data" });

    // Consumer pulls data using async generator
    for await (const item of consumer.pullDataStream()) {
      console.log('Received:', item);
    }
  }
}
example();
```

In this example, the `Producer` class updates the `Storage` class with new data and notifies the `Consumer` class to pull the data from the `Collector` class. The `Collector` class retrieves the data from the `Storage` class, demonstrating the Pull-Push pattern in action.

Before we continue learning about Promises and Futures, we can check out some important strategies for testing the Pull-Push pattern.

Testing strategies of the Pull-Push pattern

When it comes to testing the Pull-Push pattern, we can write tests that ensure accurate data saving and retrieval. That includes unit testing both the `Producer` and the `Consumer` classes and their ability to pull data from storage. Then, we also need to test the integration between them to ensure that they handle all the use cases and that the entire flow from data production to consumption works as expected.

We provide sample unit tests located in the project source code folder (see the *Technical requirements* section) that showcases the preceding strategies. You can run them locally by using the following command:

```
$ npm run test --pull-push
```

Again, feel free to review the test cases to get an idea of how this is implemented, what is being tested, and how. You will now learn how you can use Promises and Futures to perform asynchronous computations.

Understanding Promises and Futures

This section expands into the fundamental concepts of **Promises** and **Futures**, two key abstractions in reactive programming that help manage asynchronous operations and data flows. These constructs are essential for creating responsive, non-blocking applications that can efficiently handle concurrent tasks.

Promises and Futures both represent the eventual results of an asynchronous operation. They provide a way to reason about and manipulate values that may not be immediately available, allowing developers to write cleaner and composable code. We start by exploring the familiar concepts of Promises, and then we look at Futures.

Promises

Promises are a fundamental concept in modern JavaScript and TypeScript for handling asynchronous operations. The way that Promises work is by creating a container that can either resolve to a value in the future or reject with a message.

Simply speaking, a **Promise** is when you call a function, and instead of returning an actual value, it returns an object that promises you that a value will be returned at some point. The creator of the `Promise` object will have to get this value by checking on the outcome of this computation at a later time, be it successful by *resolving* or unsuccessful by *rejecting*.

Let's start with a typical example of how you might use Promises in the real world:

promises.ts

```
import fetch from "node-fetch"
interface Todo {
  userId: number;
  id: number;
  title: string;
  completed: boolean;
}
const pullFromApi = new Promise<Todo>(async
  (resolve, reject) => {
    try {
      const response = await fetch(
        'https://jsonplaceholder.typicode.com/todos/1');

      // Check if the response is ok (status in the range 200-299)
      if (!response.ok) {
        throw new Error(`HTTP error!
          status: ${response.status}`);
      }

      const json = await response.json();
      resolve(json as Todo);
    } catch (err) {
    reject(err instanceof Error ?
      err : new Error('Unknown error occurred'));
  }
});
```

```
(async () => {
  await pullFromApi
}) ()
```

In this example, you create a new `Promise` object that accepts an executor function with two parameters – `resolve` and `reject`. The former is the callback function that you need to use when you want to return a successful response, while the latter is the callback function that you need to use when you want to return a failed response.

The Promise API offers several helper methods for working with Promises:

- `Promise.all`: Waits for all Promises in an array to resolve and returns an array of their resolved values

- `Promise.race`: Returns a Promise that resolves or rejects as soon as one of the Promises in an array resolves or rejects

- `Promise.allSettled`: Returns a Promise that resolves with an array of objects containing the Promise result regardless of whether they were fulfilled or rejected

Here's an example using `Promise.race` and `Promise.all`:

patterns.ts

```
function delay(ms: number = 1000) {
  return new Promise((resolve) =>
    setTimeout(resolve, ms))
}
function failAfter(ms: number = 1000) {
  return new Promise((_, reject) =>
    setTimeout(reject, ms))
}
const races = Promise.race([delay(1000), failAfter(500)]);
const all = Promise.all([delay(1000), failAfter(1500)]);
(async () => {
  races
    .then((value) => {
      console.log(value)
    })
    .catch((_) => {
      console.log("Error")
    })
}) ();
(async () => {
  all
```

```
    .then((value) => {
      console.log(value)
    })
    .catch((_) => {
      console.log("Error")
    })
}) ()
```

The code defines two functions, `delay` and `failAfter`, which return Promises that resolve and reject after a specified timeout, respectively; it then uses `Promise.race` to log the result of the first Promise to settle (which will be an error due to `failAfter` rejecting after a delay) and `Promise.all` to log the results of both Promises (which will also result in an error since `failAfter` rejects before delay resolves).

If you want to check out the `Promise.allSettled` method added as part of the ECMAScript 2020 standard, you will have to add the following declaration package to the `lib` section in `tsconfig.json` to use it:

tsconfig.json

```
"lib": [
  "dom",
  "es2015",
  "es2020"
],
```

Then, you can use it as follows:

promises.ts

```
const settled = Promise.allSettled([delay(1000),
  failAfter(500)]);
(async () => {
  settled
    .then((value) => {
      console.log(value)
    })
    .catch((_) => {
      console.log("Error")
    })
}) ()
```

When you run this code, you will see that it will resolve with the following values:

```
[
  { status: 'fulfilled', value: undefined },
  { status: 'rejected', reason: undefined }
]
```

When you use `allSettled`, the Promise will collect all results from all Promises passed on the list. In this case, the first Promise was resolved and the second was rejected. This is very useful for triggering asynchronous tasks that do not depend on each other.

We will continue discovering Futures next and how they differ from Promises.

Futures

Futures are a way to represent asynchronous computations, similar to Promises. They provide a way to chain and compose asynchronous operations, with some key differences compared to Promises:

- **Laziness**: Futures are lazy, meaning they don't start executing until you explicitly call a method such as `fork` or `run`. Promises, on the other hand, are eager and start executing as soon as they are created.

- **Cancellation**: Futures provide a way to cancel an ongoing asynchronous operation, while Promises do not have built-in cancellation support.

- **Execution context**: Futures store the execution context of an asynchronous operation, which is a function that takes `resolve` and `reject` callbacks. This function returns a `cancel` function that can be used to abort the operation.

TypeScript does not offer a native implementation of a Future, but we can create a simple one for our purposes. We start with some definitions first:

futures.ts

```
type Reject = (reason?: any) => void
type Resolve<T> = (value: T) => void
type Execution<E, T> = (resolve: Resolve<T>,
  reject: Reject) => () => void
```

These definitions are for the task that represents the Future computation. The main difference here with Promise is that it returns the `() => void` function from `thunk`, which is used for cancellation purposes.

Let's see the remaining code for the Future:

futures.ts

```
class Future<E, T> {
  private fn: Execution<E, T>
  constructor(ex: Execution<E, T>) {
    this.fn = ex
  }
  fork(reject: Reject, resolve: Resolve<T>): () => void {
    return this.fn(resolve, reject)
  }

  static success<E, T>(value: T): Future<E, T> {
    return new Future((resolve) => {
      resolve(value)
      return () => {}
    })
  }
  static fail<E, T>(error: E): Future<E, T> {
    return new Future((_, reject) => {
      reject(error)
      return () => {}
    })
  }
  then<U>(f: (value: T) => Future<E, U>): Future<E, U> {
    return new Future((resolve, reject) => {
      return this.fn((value: T) => f(value)
        .fork(reject, resolve), reject)
    })
  }
}
```

In the highlighted section, you can see that the Future class encapsulates an asynchronous computation that can be chained and executed lazily. It stores a function (fn) that represents the computation. The fork method triggers the execution of this function, passing in resolve and reject callbacks. The success and fail static methods create pre-resolved or pre-rejected Futures. The then method allows for the chaining of operations, creating a new Future that will execute the original computation and then apply the given function to its result.

We show here an example of a Future using the `then` method:

futures.ts

```
const delayedTask = new Future<Error, string>(
  (resolve, reject) => {
    const timerId = setTimeout(() =>
      resolve("Hello, Future!"), 1000)
    return () => clearTimeout(timerId) // Cancellation function
})
const uppercaseTask = delayedTask.then((value) =>
  Future.success(value.toUpperCase()))
    const cancelTask = uppercaseTask.fork(
      (error) => console.error("Task failed:", error),
      (result) => console.log("Task succeeded:", result),
  )
// cancelTask();
```

We create a Future task in a similar way to a Promise by passing `resolve` and `reject` callbacks. We also chain one call to perform an uppercase conversion of the result of the previous Future. Once saved in the `task` variable, it's not executed immediately. You will need to call the `fork` method to pass the callbacks for the error and the successful results.

You will get back a `cancellation` function that you can use to abort the Future task. This is handy as native Promises do not offer the possibility to cancel tasks altogether. Overall, both Future and Promise objects deal with the asynchronous execution of tasks, and they fit nicely in a reactive programming model.

Open source implementation of Futures

While Futures are not natively supported in TypeScript, developers can implement them using third-party libraries or custom implementations. The **Fluture** library at `https://github.com/fluture-js/Fluture` provides a robust implementation of Futures. This library allows you to create and manipulate Futures with various combinators, making it easier to work with asynchronous computations. Here is an example:

```
import { Future } from 'fluture';
const futureValue: Future<number> =
  Future((reject, resolve) => {
    setTimeout(() => resolve(42), 1000);
});
```

```
futureValue.fork(
    error => console.error('Error:', error),
    value => console.log('Value:', value)
);
```

In this example, a `Future<number>` instance is instantiated, which represents an asynchronous computation that will eventually resolve to a `number` type. The `Future` constructor takes a function with two parameters: `reject` and `resolve`. Inside this function, `setTimeout` is used to simulate an asynchronous operation that resolves with the value `42` after 1 second. This approach allows for a functional programming style where asynchronous computations are handled more predictably than with traditional Promises and have control over execution flow.

Testing strategies for Futures

When testing Futures, it's essential to ensure that the asynchronous nature of calls does not introduce unnecessary side effects. Once you have a stable set of Future implementations, you can proceed to write unit tests for that library.

Regarding Promises, they are inherently supported in the ES6 runtime, making additional testing for them generally unnecessary.

We provide sample unit tests in the project's source code folder (see the *Technical requirements* section) that demonstrate these strategies. You can run them locally using the following command:

```
$ npm run test --futures
```

We will now continue our exploration of reactive programming structures by learning more about Observables.

Exploring Observables

An **Observable** represents a sequence that can be invoked and produces Future values or events. The idea is to create an Observable object to receive Future values. Once the observable pushes a value, the observers will receive it at some point.

Observables build upon the fundamental concepts of the Observer pattern discussed in *Chapter 5*. However, the Observer pattern was specific to classes and had a limited scope. Observables aim to expand the idea of composing asynchronous and event-based programs that react to changes.

In the context of reactive programming, Observables represent the producers of Future values, while observers represent the consumers. By default, communication occurs as soon as the observable has any observers. It waits to be invoked (subscribed) before it can emit any data. The association between the producer and the consumer is decoupled, as they do not need to know the details of how the values are produced or consumed.

Figure 8.4 illustrates how an observable produces values, how observers consume those values, and the relationship between them:

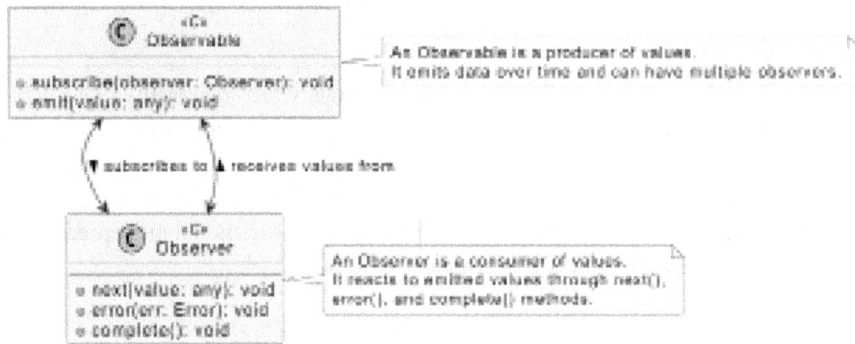

Figure 8.4 – Representation of Observables

To understand a bit better how to use Observables using code, we are going to introduce the ReactiveX library in TypeScript.

ReactiveX, commonly known as **RxJS** in the JavaScript/TypeScript ecosystem, is a comprehensive library for reactive programming. It leverages Observables to simplify the composition of asynchronous data streams.

To start, you create a `producer` object that invokes future streams of data. There are several ways to do this, starting with the `observable` object:

observables.ts

```
import { Observable, of, from } from 'rxjs';
of(1, 2, 3, 4, 5);
of({ id: 1, data: "value" });
from([1, 2, 3, 4, 5]);
from(Promise.resolve("data"));
function* getNextRandom() {
  yield Math.random() * 100;
}
const randomValues = new Observable<number>
  ((subscriber) => {
    subscriber.next(1);
    subscriber.next(2);
    subscriber.next(3);
```

```
    setInterval(() => {
      subscriber.next(getNextRandom().next().value);
    }, 1000);
});
```

In the provided code, you can see various ways to create observable producers from different sources. You can use the `of` operator to create one from a list of parameters. The `from` operator is similar but takes a collection of values. It can also detect if the source is a Promise and will convert it to an observable.

Finally, you can see a more customized approach using the `Observable` constructor. It accepts a function with one parameter called `subscriber`, which represents the sink that the producer will push Future values to. Using the `subscriber.next` method, you push those values into the subscriber list.

By default, these Observables are inactive and won't produce any values. They are lazy by nature. Once you add a subscriber to the list, it will activate. Using the `subscribe` method on an existing observable initiates this process:

observables.ts

```
let origin = from([1, 2, 3, 4, new Error("Error")]);
origin.subscribe({
  next: (v: any) => {
    console.log("Value accepted: ", v);
  },
  error: (e) => {
    console.log("Error accepted: ", e);
  },
  complete: () => {
    console.log("Finished");
  }
});
of([1, 2, 3]).subscribe({
  next: (values) => console.log("Values:", values),
  complete: () => console.info("Completed")
});
```

The `subscribe` method accepts an object that contains three callback functions. The first one is the callback used to accept a new value from the producer stream. Because we used the `from` operator, it will send the items in the list one by one. *Figure 8.5* shows how the values are emitted:

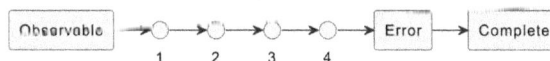

Figure 8.5 – Observable values

The subscriber will receive the values one by one. Since the last value is an `Error` object, it will trigger the second callback passed into the `subscribe` method. This will not interrupt the flow of communication because the observable is not closed. Once the observable has run out of values, it will trigger the `finalize` or `complete` function, which is the third callback in the `subscribe` method. If a new subscriber tries to subscribe at a later time, it will still get the same stream of events:

observables.ts

```
setTimeout(() => {
  origin.subscribe(
    (v: any) => {
      console.log("Value accepted: ", v);
    }
  );
}, 1000);
```

The new subscriber will receive the same values as the first subscriber at a later time. This feature is particularly useful in scenarios where you want to ensure that all subscribers receive the same sequence of events, regardless of when they subscribe.

In the next section, we'll explain how to compose operators on top of Observables, further expanding operator capabilities.

Composable operators

Reactive programming gains significant power from incorporating functional programming concepts such as *composability* and *purity*. This fusion has led to the term *FRP*. In the context of RxJS, this means utilizing operators – composable functions that take an observable and return another observable.

The fundamental idea is to take familiar functional programming building blocks such as `map`, `reduce`, and `filter` and adapt them to work with Observables. Instead of operating on concrete values, these operators work on streams of data.

RxJS provides a rich array of operators designed to handle various aspects of data stream manipulation. Here are a few examples:

observables.ts

```
import { of, from, interval } from "rxjs"
import { filter, take, share, map } from "rxjs/operators"
interval(1000).pipe(
  take(5),
  map((v: number) => v * v),
  tap(v => console.log(`Squared value: ${v}`))
```

```
    // Side effect moved to tap
).subscribe();
// Output: Squared value: 0, 1, 4, 9, 16
of(1, 2, 3, 4, 5, 6, 7, 8, 9, 10).pipe(
    tap(v => console.log(`Processing value: ${v}`)),
    // Log before filtering
    filter((v: number) => v % 3 === 0),
    tap(v => console.log(`Divisible by 3: ${v}`))
    // Log after filtering
).subscribe();
// Output: Divisible by 3: 3, 6, 9
from([
    { id: 1, name: "Alice", age: 30 },
    { id: 2, name: "Bob", age: 25 },
    { id: 3, name: "Charlie", age: 35 },
])
    .pipe(map((user) => user?.name))
    .subscribe((name: string) => console.log(
      `Name: ${name}`))
// Output: Name: Alice, Name: Bob, Name: Charlie
```

The code uses `interval` to create a stream of numbers emitted every second, `take` to limit it to five emissions, and `map` to square each value.

Next, it employs the `of` operator to create a simple observable of numbers, then uses `filter` to emit only those divisible by 3, illustrating how to create and filter data streams.

Lastly, it utilizes `from` to create an observable from an array of objects, and `map` with optional chaining to extract the `name` property from each object.

The `pipe` operator accepts a list of FRP operators that work on the stream of data and applies them as a chain. For example, if you have three operators, `op1`, `op2`, and `op3`, then `of(1).pipe(op1, op2, op3)` is equivalent to `op1().op2().op3()`, using the value 1 as the initial parameter.

There are dozens of operators in RxJS that deal with creation, manipulation, filtering, combining, or error handling. Each chain of operators will run in turn, generating a new observable for the following chained item. The main benefit of using them is that you can store those transformations in code and have the consumers receive only the most relevant data, thereby avoiding putting some business logic into their side.

We will next explore one more concept in Observables, which is the difference between cold and hot Observables.

Cold versus hot Observables

In our previous discussion, we highlighted how subscribers receive values from an observable immediately upon subscribing, regardless of when they join. This characteristic defines **cold Observables**, where the producer replays the entire sequence of values for each new subscription. Consequently, subscribers can enjoy the complete history of emitted values without missing any, even if they subscribe later.

In contrast, we have **hot Observables**. With hot Observables, the producer emits data at specific intervals, independent of whether there are any subscribers present. You can think of this as a live broadcast: the producer starts emitting data regardless of the audience's presence. Subscribers who join later will only receive the current stream of values, missing any values emitted before they subscribed.

In the context of the RxJS library, it's important to note that at least one subscription is required to initiate the stream. Once the stream is active, it can be shared among multiple subscribers. Any new subscribers will only receive values emitted after they join.

Here's how you can create a hot observable using RxJS:

observables.ts

```typescript
import { interval } from "rxjs";
import { take, share } from "rxjs/operators";
const stream$ = interval(1000).pipe(take(5), share());
stream$.subscribe((v) =>
  console.log("Value accepted from first subscriber: ",
    v)
);
setTimeout(() => {
  stream$.subscribe((v) => {
    console.log("Value accepted from second subscriber: ",
      v);
  });
}, 3000);
```

In this example, we use the `interval` operator to create an observable that emits sequential numbers (0, 1, 2, 3, ...) at 1-second intervals. The `pipe` operator allows us to compose multiple operators together. We utilize the `take` operator to limit the stream to the first five emitted values. The `share` operator then enables the observable to be shared among all subscribers, effectively multicasting the original observable and its current values.

When you run this program, you will see output similar to the following:

```
Value accepted from first subscriber: 0
Value accepted from first subscriber: 1
Value accepted from first subscriber: 2
```

```
Value accepted from second subscriber: 2
Value accepted from first subscriber: 3
Value accepted from second subscriber: 3
Value accepted from first subscriber: 4
Value accepted from second subscriber: 4
```

In this scenario, the first subscriber receives the initial value of 0. Because we shared the observable stream, subsequent subscribers will only receive the latest values. In our case, the second subscriber joins after 3 seconds, receiving the current value of 2 while missing the earlier values. Once all five values have been emitted, the stream concludes, and all subscribers automatically unsubscribe.

Schedulers in RxJS

Schedulers are an essential part of RxJS that determine when a subscription starts and when notifications are delivered. Those are basically functions that queue tasks that will be resolved based on certain criteria, such as the type of scheduler. Currently, there are four types of schedulers:

- `null`: If no scheduler is provided in an `Observable` constructor, then the `null` scheduler will be provided by default. This scheduler executes tasks synchronously.

- `AsyncScheduler`: Executes tasks asynchronously using `setTimeout`.

- `QueueScheduler`: Executes tasks on a queue that runs on a trampoline scheduler. So, instead of executing it immediately, it will run after all preceding tasks have finished.

- `AsapScheduler`: Executes tasks using `setTimeout(task, 0)`.

While the choice of the scheduler is important, in practical terms, the `null` scheduler (default) is most commonly used, and the others are suitable for specialized use cases such as executing asynchronous tasks, long-running tasks, and so on.

Backpressure handling in RxJS

Backpressure is an effect when a producer emits values more rapidly than a consumer can process them. RxJS offers some operators that aid in controlling the flow of data:

- `buffer/bufferTime/bufferCount`: These operators buffer emitted values until the consumer is ready to process them.

- `throttle`: The `throttle` operator limits the number of emitted values over time, ensuring that the consumer is not overwhelmed. This is useful in scenarios where rapid emissions occur, such as user input events.

- `debounce`: This operator ensures that values are only emitted after a specified period of inactivity. This is particularly useful for scenarios such as search input, where you want to wait until the user has stopped typing before making an API call.

Using these operators effectively helps manage backpressure by controlling the rate at which data is emitted and processed. They improve user experience by preventing issues such as unresponsive interfaces and during high-frequency events such as scrolling or typing. Additionally, they can reduce network calls and unnecessary computations, saving bandwidth and improving efficiency across the system.

Example using WebSocket and RxJS

A common use case for RxJS is a *live chat feature*, where users can send and receive messages instantly. By using WebSockets, we can establish a persistent connection between the client and server, enabling seamless message exchange. RxJS operators will be utilized to manage the flow of incoming messages efficiently, ensuring that the chat interface remains responsive and user-friendly. Here is a small snippet:

Websockets.ts

```
import { webSocket } from 'rxjs/webSocket';
import { throttleTime, bufferTime, map, tap }
  from 'rxjs/operators';
import { Observable } from 'rxjs';
const chatSocket = webSocket<string>
  ('ws://localhost:8080/chat');
const messageStream$: Observable<string> =
  chatSocket.pipe(
  tap(message => console.log('New message received:',
    message)), // Debugging/logging
  throttleTime(100),
  bufferTime(1000),
  map(messages => messages.join('\n'))
);
messageStream$.subscribe({
  next: bufferedMessages => {
    console.log('Buffered messages:', bufferedMessages);
    updateChatUI(bufferedMessages);
  },
  error: error => console.error('WebSocket error:', error)
});
function updateChatUI(messages: string) {
    // Update the chat UI with the new messages
    console.log('Updating chat UI with:', messages);
}
```

This example establishes a WebSocket connection to a server at ws://localhost:8080/chat, creating an observable, messageStream$, that listens for incoming messages. Then, it uses RxJS operators to process messages efficiently. Then, the UI is updated to reflect the new changes as they are being pushed through the pipeline.

Testing strategies for observable pipelines

When testing Observables, it's important to ensure the observable pipelines do not introduce unexpected behavior. To achieve consistent results, it's essential to test the entire observable pipeline, from the source to the final emissions.

One testing aspect is to handle errors gracefully. By testing the error-handling capabilities of your observable pipelines, you can ensure that errors are propagated correctly. Another aspect is the accuracy of streamed values. If the values are not pushed in the correct order or they are not pushed in the right format, you will encounter runtime errors.

Additionally, when testing hot Observables, `TestScheduler` from RxJS provides precise control over time-based operations. `TestScheduler` allows you to simulate time passage without actual delays, making tests faster and more reliable. Here's an example:

```
import { TestScheduler } from 'rxjs/testing';
const scheduler = new TestScheduler((actual, expected) => {
  expect(actual).toEqual(expected);
});
scheduler.run(({ cold, expectObservable }) => {
  const source$ = cold('a-b-c|', { a: 1, b: 2, c: 3 })
    .pipe(shareReplay(1));
  expectObservable(source$).toBe('a-b-c|',
    { a: 1, b: 2, c: 3 });
});
```

While `share()` creates a basic multicast observable, `shareReplay(n)` adds a replay buffer of size n, making it particularly useful for testing scenarios where you need to verify that late subscribers receive the correct sequence of values.

Another useful testing technique is using **marble testing**. This technique allows you to visualize the timing and behavior of Observables using marble diagrams. Here is how it is done using `TestScheduler`:

```
import { TestScheduler } from 'rxjs/testing';
const testScheduler = new TestScheduler((actual,
  expected) => {
    expect(actual).toEqual(expected);
});
testScheduler.run(({ cold, expectObservable }) => {
    const source$ = cold('---a---b---c|');
    expectObservable(source$).toBe('---a---b---c|');
});
```

In this example, inside the `testScheduler.run` method, a `source$` cold observable is created, which emits values over time, represented by the `---a---b---c|` marble diagram. The `expectObservable` function is then used to assert that the emitted values from `source$` match the expected marble diagram, ensuring that the observable behaves as intended during testing.

For your understanding, we provide sample unit tests in the project's source code folder (see the *Technical requirements* section) that demonstrate these strategies. You can run them locally using the following command:

```
$ npm run test --observables
```

That concludes our exploration of Observables using RxJS. This library offers a wealth of features for managing Observables. You can customize subscription start times and notification delivery using different schedulers or by employing subjects to multicast values to multiple observers.

> **Tip**
> If you're eager to explore the topic of RxJS Observables further, be sure to check out the recommended books and resources in the *Further reading* section.

Summary

In this chapter, we explored fundamental concepts of reactive programming and their usage in the real world.

We started by explaining the fundamental concepts of reactive programming. We explored in detail alternative ways of change propagation, including Push, Pull, and the hybrid model. Then, we learned more about Promises and Futures and their key differences. Finally, we spent some time understanding Observables, FRP operators, and cold versus hot Observables.

Utilizing these concepts will encourage you to create composable, cleaner, and readable code that scales well as your application grows over time. In the following chapter, we will shift gears and focus on the most recommended practices and techniques when developing large-scale TypeScript applications.

Q&A

Feel free to review the following questions and their corresponding answers to address any concerns or gain additional insights:

1. How does reactive programming differ from object-oriented programming (OOP)?

    Answer: *OOP* deals with how objects are created and used and how they manage their state and behavior. An object represents an entity of the real world and can interact with the rest of the program via methods. *Reactive programming*, on the other hand, deals with data and how it is propagated into other parts of the system.

2. How do Observables compare to the Observer pattern?

   Answer: Both are similar, but they work on a different level. With an *Observer pattern*, you add and dispose of observers in the list and notify the subscriber list of any state changes using methods and encapsulation. *Observables*, on the other hand, are more flexible as they are built on top of the concepts of the Observer pattern and can be composed in a functional way. You can think of Observables as an extension of the Observer pattern, managing sequences of data and composable operators.

3. How does reactive programming compare with functional programming?

   Answer: *Functional programming* deals with functions, immutability, and the purity of computation. *Reactive programming*, on the other hand, is concerned with asynchronous data streams and the propagation of change. Their common point is that reactive programming borrows several concepts of functional programming in terms of the propagation of change in a composable and pure way.

Further reading

- A good, in-depth book about reactive programming is *Mastering Reactive JavaScript*, by *Erich de Souza Oliveira*. It is available at `https://www.packtpub.com/en-ie/product/mastering-reactive-javascript-9781786463388`.

- The *Reactive Manifesto* can be found at `https://www.reactivemanifesto.org/`.

9

Developing Modern and Robust TypeScript Applications

So far in this book, we've explored classical design patterns, functional programming, and reactive methodologies. As we enter the final three chapters, our focus will shift to practical techniques for building real-world TypeScript applications, highlighting best practices and efficient strategies.

In this chapter, we'll examine how to combine various design patterns to create robust applications while leveraging TypeScript's powerful utility types and functions to make your code cleaner and more maintainable. We'll also introduce **domain-driven design** (**DDD**), a methodology that emphasizes matching your application's structure with business needs.

Then, we'll look at the **Model-View-Controller** (**MVC**) architecture, a widely used pattern that improves code organization by separating concerns. Additionally, we'll cover the SOLID principles, which provide a clear guide for writing clean, maintainable, and scalable code.

In this chapter, we'll cover the following main topics:

- Combining design patterns effectively
- Leveraging TypeScript's utility types
- Implementing DDD
- Embracing SOLID principles
- Applying the MVC architecture

By the end of this chapter, you'll have gained valuable knowledge and insights for developing real-world TypeScript applications, especially the best practices that work well together.

Technical requirements

The code bundle for this chapter is available in this book's GitHub repository: `https://github.com/PacktPublishing/TypeScript-5-Design-Patterns-and-Best-Practices/tree/main/chapters/chapter09_Best_practices`.

Combining design patterns effectively

Design patterns are powerful tools in software development, but their true potential is often realized when they're combined strategically.

Here are some key principles to keep in mind:

- **Purpose and fit**: Assess whether the combination of design patterns matches your specific project requirements. Not all combinations yield beneficial outcomes; prioritize those that address your unique challenges effectively.

- **Flexibility versus complexity**: Consider the implications of added complexity against the desired flexibility. Use design patterns that complement each other and streamline system architecture rather than complicate it.

- **Testability**: Analyze how the combination of patterns makes it easier to write and maintain unit tests. Patterns should facilitate easier testing processes, rather than complicating them.

So, let's explore some effective combinations of design patterns in TypeScript, along with improved examples and additional clarifications.

Combining Singleton with other patterns

The Singleton pattern is highly flexible and can be combined with many other patterns without much effort, so long as it's implemented correctly. We'll look at some common and effective combinations in the subsequent sections.

Singleton with the Builder pattern

The `Builder` object is usually a single instance and should only be used for creating a new object. However, before each use, the client should reset the `Builder` object to clean up any internal state that it may have from previous usage. The simplest way to provide a builder Singleton is by using a default export:

```
export class PremiumWebsiteBuilder {
  private state: State = initialState;
  reset(): void {
    // Reset internal state
    this.state = initialState;
  }
```

```
    // Other builder methods...
}

export default new PremiumWebsiteBuilder()
```

Here, we used a default export for this module that exports a single instance of `Builder`. Now, any part of the code that imports this default export will receive a Singleton instance tied to the package version.

Singleton with the Façade pattern

The combination of the Singleton and Façade patterns is particularly powerful when you need to provide a simplified, unified interface for a complex subsystem while ensuring that only one instance of this interface exists throughout the application.

The Singleton aspect facilitates lazy initialization, meaning the Façade pattern is only created when it's first needed. This combination proves especially useful in various scenarios, such as managing connections to external services or databases, providing a unified API for diverse backend services, and coordinating actions across multiple subsystems in large applications.

Here's an example implementation:

Singleton-facade.ts

```
interface ServiceA {}
interface ServiceB {}
class SystemFacade {
    private static instance: SystemFacade;
    private constructor(
        private serviceA: ServiceA,
        private serviceB: ServiceB
    ) {}

    static getInstance(serviceA: ServiceA,
      serviceB: ServiceB): SystemFacade {
        if (!SystemFacade.instance) {
            SystemFacade.instance =
                new SystemFacade(serviceA, serviceB);
        }
        return SystemFacade.instance;
    }
    performComplexOperation(): void {
    }
}
class ConcreteServiceA implements ServiceA {}
class ConcreteServiceB implements ServiceA {}
```

```
// Usage
const facade = SystemFacade.getInstance(
  new ConcreteServiceA(), new ConcreteServiceB());
facade.performComplexOperation();
```

In this example, `SystemFacade` acts as both a Singleton and a Façade. It provides a simplified interface (`performComplexOperation`) to coordinate actions between `ServiceA` and `ServiceB` while ensuring only one instance of `SystemFacade` exists. This approach centralizes the control of these services and provides a consistent interface for other parts of the application to interact with them.

However, a potential drawback of this design pattern combination is that centralizing too much complexity into a Singleton-Façade can create a bottleneck. As the subsystem grows, this can lead to performance issues and hinder scalability, making it difficult to manage and modify the system effectively.

Singleton with the Factory Method and Abstract Factory patterns

The factory method is a key component of both the Factory Method and Abstract Factory design patterns. In the context of the Abstract Factory pattern, the factory methods don't maintain any internal state, making them suitable for implementation as Singletons. This would prevent the unnecessary creation of multiple factory instances. However, using Singleton factories can have implications when combined with dependency injection.

When factories are implemented as Singletons, they can limit flexibility in testing because the Singleton pattern can't provide mocks or stubs easily. This makes it challenging to isolate components during unit tests as the same instance is shared across tests. Consequently, if a test requires a specific state or behavior from the factory, it may not be possible to achieve this without modifying the Singleton instance itself or resorting to more complex workarounds.

Singleton with the State pattern

As you may recall, the State pattern (see *Chapter 6*) is created when you have the `Originator` object accept a `State` object and can alter its behavior when the internal state object changes. Because you can create a `State` object once and share it with the `Originator` object, you can make it a *Singleton* so that all `Originator` objects will only share one instance of it at the same time.

Generally, any pattern that requires a single instance of an object to be present throughout the life cycle of the application should be exported as a Singleton.

Next, we'll look at some combinations of the Iterator pattern.

Iterator with other patterns

Let's explore how the Iterator pattern can be combined with other design patterns to achieve specific criteria, such as enhancing flexibility, promoting separation of concerns, and improving code maintenance.

Iterator with the Composite pattern

The combination of the *Iterator* and *Composite* patterns offers a nice approach to managing complex hierarchical structures. The Composite pattern enables the creation of tree structures that represent part-whole hierarchies of objects. In contrast, the Iterator pattern offers a way to access the elements of an aggregate object in sequence without exposing its internal representation.

When these two patterns are combined, you can traverse the complex structure created by the Composite pattern, regardless of the tree's depth or complexity.

Now, let's look at a TypeScript implementation that demonstrates this combination:

Iterator-composite.ts

```typescript
const root = new Composite("Root")
root.add(new Composite("Child1"))
root.add(new Composite("Child2"))

const iterator = root.createIterator();
while (iterator.hasNext()) {
    const component = iterator.next();
    if (component) {
        console.log(component.getName());
    }
}
```

First, we create a `Composite` object named `Root` and add two child `Composite` objects to it, forming a simple tree structure. Then, we create an iterator by calling the `createIterator()` method on the root `Composite` object. We iterate over the components in the tree structure by repeatedly calling the `hasNext()` and `next()` methods of the iterator. This shows how the Iterator pattern allows us to traverse the Composite structure uniformly.

Note that when implementing this combination, especially for deep structures, it's beneficial to consider caching or memoization strategies to improve efficiency.

Caching allows you to store previously accessed components, reducing the need to traverse the same paths in the hierarchy repeatedly. This can significantly enhance performance when you're dealing with large or deeply nested structures. **Memoization** can also be applied to store the results of expensive function calls, enabling quicker access to elements during traversal.

Iterator with Visitor

The Iterator with Visitor pattern allows you to perform operations on elements of a collection without having to modify the collection classes themselves. This approach is particularly useful when you want to execute various operations on a collection without cluttering its interface. Here's a small code example that illustrates this concept:

Iterator-visitor.ts

```
const collection = new ElementCollection();
collection.add(new ElementA("Element A1"));
collection.add(new ElementB("Element B1"));
collection.add(new ElementA("Element A2"));

const visitor = new ConcreteVisitor();
const iterator = collection.createIterator();

while (iterator.hasNext()) {
    const element = iterator.next();
    if (element) {
        element.accept(visitor);
    }
}
```

In this example, we added two instances of `ElementA` and one instance of `ElementB` to the `ElementCollection` instance. Next, we instantiated `ConcreteVisitor`, which implements the operations to be performed on each element. We created an iterator for the collection using the `createIterator()` method. The `while` loop iterated through the elements in the collection and used the `accept` method while passing the `visitor` instance. This shows the combined use of the Iterator and Visitor patterns to traverse a collection and apply operations without having to modify the element classes as it's a very flexible combination.

Overall, when trying to combine design patterns, you should adjust them carefully to see whether they're fit for purpose first and don't become harder to test or understand. Careful and accurate naming would help if the intent weren't immediately apparent.

Let's continue by exploring some recommended ways we can use utility functions and custom types.

Leveraging TypeScript's utility types

TypeScript provides a rich set of **utility types** that can help you perform common type transformations. Understanding and using these utility types effectively can significantly enhance your TypeScript code's type safety and expressiveness. Let's explore some advanced use cases and create custom utility types.

Composing utility types

One of the most powerful aspects of TypeScript's utility types is their *composability*. You can combine multiple utility types to create more complex type transformations. Here's an example of removing a `readonly` modifier from object properties:

Utilities.ts

```
type Mutable<T> = {
  -readonly [K in keyof T]: Mutable<T[K]>;
};

interface UserState {
  readonly name: string;
  readonly age: number;
  readonly address: {
    readonly street: string;
    readonly city: string;
  };
}
const mutableUserState: Mutable<UserState> = {
  name: "Alice",
  age: 24,
  address: {
    street: "123 Main St",
    city: "Wonderland"
  }
};
mutableUserState.age = 31;
mutableUserProfile.address.city = "New Wonderland";
const newUserState: UserState = { ...mutableUserState };
```

The `Mutable` type is a TypeScript utility that maps all properties of a given type, T, recursively and removes their read-only properties. The `-readonly` modifier that's applied to each property, P, in T also includes nested objects. Recall that a mapped type allows a new type to be created by transforming the properties of an existing type.

For example, the `Mutable<UserState>` type creates `mutableUserState`, where every property, including the address field, is mutable. Consequently, it will allow nested updates to be made to its object properties with a simple assignment.

Creating custom utility types

While TypeScript provides many useful utility types out of the box, you'll often need to create custom ones for your specific use cases. The following example demonstrates a more advanced usage of mapped types that can be used to create custom utilities:

Utilities.ts

```
type OptionalKeys<T> = { [K in keyof T]-?: {}
  extends Pick<T, K> ? K : never }[keyof T];
type RequiredKeys<T> = { [K in keyof T]-?: {}
  extends Pick<T, K> ? never : K }[keyof T];
interface User {
  id: number;
  name: string;
  email?: string;
}

type UserOptionalKeys = OptionalKeys<User>; // "email"
type UserRequiredKeys = RequiredKeys<User>; // "id" | "name"
```

The `OptionalKeys` and `RequiredKeys` types are custom TypeScript utilities that are designed to extract optional and required keys from a given type, T. The `OptionalKeys<T>` type iterates over all keys, K, in T. It checks whether an empty object (`{}`) can be assigned to the property, K, of T using `Pick<T, K>`. If it can, K is optional; otherwise, it's excluded. The result is a union of all optional keys.

Similarly, `RequiredKeys<T>` also iterates over the keys in T, but it includes K in the result if an empty object can't be assigned to K. This identifies all required keys.

> **Important note**
>
> It's important to note that using complex mapped types with large interfaces can lead to performance trade-offs. Recursive type-checking may slow down compile times in TypeScript, especially in projects with extensive type definitions.

For example, in the user interface, `email` is an optional property, while `id` and `name` are required. Thus, `UserOptionalKeys` evaluates to `email`, and `UserRequiredKeys` evaluates to `"id" | "name"`.

> **Additional resources**
>
> A lot of open source libraries, such as **ts-toolbelt** (`https://millsp.github.io/ts-toolbelt/`), provide large collections of similar utility types and helpers. We suggest taking a look at their implementation to understand how they work.

Leveraging mapped types with utility types

Previously, we saw some examples of how mapped types can be used to create utility types since they're a powerful technique in TypeScript that allows for flexible type transformations. By combining mapped types, which transform types based on their keys, with utility types, which encapsulate common type operations, we can create reusable type transformations.

The following example shows this concept in action:

Utilities.ts

```ts
type Mutable<T> = {
  -readonly [P in keyof T]: T[P]
}
type FunctionPropertyNames<T> = {
  [K in keyof T]: T[K] extends Function ? K : never
}[keyof T]
type FunctionProperties<T> = Pick<T,
  FunctionPropertyNames<T>>
interface Calculator {
  readonly value: number
  add: (n: number) => void
  subtract: (n: number) => void
}
// Using FunctionPropertyNames to extract method names
type Names = FunctionPropertyNames<Calculator>;
// " subtract" | "add"
type MutableCalculator = Mutable<Calculator>
type CalculatorMethods = FunctionProperties<Calculator>
const calc: MutableCalculator = {
  value: 0,
  add(n) {
    this.value += n
  },
  subtract(n) {
    this.value -= n
  },
}
calc.value = 10 // This is now allowed
```

The Mutable type is a mapped type that transforms a given type, T, by removing the readonly modifier from all its properties. This is achieved by iterating over each key, P, in T using a mapped type and assigning the original property type, T[P], to each key. Using the readonly syntax removes the readonly modifier, making the properties mutable.

The `FunctionPropertyNames` type is a utility type that extracts the names of function properties from a given type, `T`, and uses a mapped type to iterate over the keys, `K`, in `T`. The `FunctionProperties` type is another utility type that leverages `FunctionPropertyNames` to create a new type by picking only the function properties from `T` using the `Pick` utility.

In the example provided, the `Calculator` interface represents an object with a read-only value property and two function properties, and the `CalculatorMethods` type, created using `FunctionProperties`, extracts only the function properties from `Calculator`.

Now that we have a good understanding of the capabilities of mapped types for creating utilities, let's explore the basic concepts of DDD.

Implementing DDD

DDD represents an approach to software development that allows us to translate complex domain business logic into software components that match their meaning and purpose. It's a way that we can design applications that speak the same language as the problems they're solving.

The core focus of DDD circles around answering questions such as *"How do you organize business logic?"* and *"How can you manage complexity when the application grows over time?"*

Those are valid questions, and the answers aren't definite. A central pattern in DDD is the **bounded context**. This concept represents a logical boundary between the separate sub-domains of the organization. Think of it as boxes that contain all the information on a particular domain, such as the user authentication domain, the logistics domain, and the shopping cart domain. For example, in a shopping cart domain, the relevant entities are **Cart**, **Cart Item**, **Shipping**, **Price**, **Adjustment**, and so on.

In the context of microservices, each service can be viewed as a bounded context, encapsulating its own domain logic, data models, and rules. This approach helps in creating modular and independently deployable units by establishing clear boundaries around each service's responsibilities. Each microservice can be developed, tested, and deployed independently, which accelerates the development life cycle.

The building blocks of DDD are related to having a *clear* and *ubiquitous* language. This is a common vocabulary that we define so that when we're talking to stakeholders and domain experts, they have the same understanding. For example, when we're in the domain of financial trading, an *instrument* represents an asset that can be traded or seen as a package of capital that may be traded. In a different domain, an *instrument* could represent something completely different.

We'll discuss three key concepts related to DDD:

- **Bounded contexts**: For defining a logical boundary between the separate sub-domains of the organization
- **Common language**: For establishing a shared vocabulary among stakeholders and developers

- **Entities and value objects**: For understanding how these building blocks represent core aspects of the business domain

---

Additional resources

If you want to delve deeper into this subject, we recommend reading the book *Implementing Domain-Driven Design*, by Vaughn Vernon. It's available at `https://www.amazon.com/exec/obidos/ASIN/0321834577/acmorg-20`.

The building blocks of DDD

Let's discuss the key concepts related to DDD and how they come together to form this methodology.

Bounded contexts

Bounded contexts are crucial in DDD as they define clear logical boundaries within which a specific domain model is applicable. This helps to isolate different sub-domains and keep a consistent and relevant set of models for that particular area of the organization.

A quick example of bounded contexts can be seen through an e-commerce platform. Within this platform, the Order Management subdomain can be divided into several bounded contexts:

- **Shopping cart context**: This context manages the items a user intends to purchase, including operations such as adding or removing products and calculating totals
- **Payment processing context**: This context handles all aspects related to payment transactions, such as credit card processing and payment gateway integration
- **Shipping context**: This context oversees the logistics of delivering products, including tracking shipments and managing delivery addresses

Each of these bounded contexts has specific models, language, and rules that are distinct from one another.

Common language

Common or **ubiquitous language** is another crucial concept in DDD. It involves creating a shared vocabulary that's understood by all stakeholders, including developers, domain experts, and business analysts.

Once this common language framework is established, everyone involved in the project can communicate effectively about the domain, reducing misunderstandings and aligning expectations. For example, in an e-commerce context, terms such as **Cart, Checkout, Order, Product,** and **Customer** would have specific meanings that everyone understands. Outside of this context, the meaning would be different.

In practice, establishing this terminology involves creating a documentation site of terms used within the project that defines each term's meaning based on the domain context and is accessible to all team members.

Entities

Entities are objects that are part of the domain and stored in a persistence layer. For example, a learning management system might have the following entities:

- `Author`: Represents the course author
- `Course`: Represents a course students can enroll in
- `Enrollment`: Represents a student's enrollment in a course
- `Student`: Represents a student attending courses
- `Group`: Represents a group of students coordinating to complete a course

These objects within the domain possess a unique identity and are typically mutable. They often encapsulate business logic, enforce invariants, and have life cycles that include creation, modification, and potential deletion.

Entities can form relationships with other entities or value objects, playing crucial roles in the domain model. They usually include persistence-related fields such as `id`, `created_at`, and `updated_at`. In practice, entities are often managed through the **Repository pattern** and may serve as aggregate roots.

> **The Repository pattern**
>
> The Repository pattern is a design pattern that acts as an abstraction layer between the domain logic of an application and its data access layer. It provides a collection-like interface for accessing domain objects, acting as a mediator between the domain and data mapping layers. If you want to learn more about this pattern, we've provided a great reference link in the *Further reading* section at the end of this chapter.

Value objects

A **value object** is another key concept in DDD that represents an aspect of the domain without a conceptual identity (no `id` parameters). Value objects are immutable and considered equal if they have the same attributes, regardless of their identity, and they typically validate their own state upon creation. Additionally, they encapsulate related attributes and behaviors that form a representation of data within the domain model.

Here are some examples:

- `AddressField`: It encapsulates the aspect of an address within a business domain and contains relevant logic to handle addresses within that domain

- `EmailField`: Represents a valid email string field

- `AmountField`: Represents a price in decimal format

Here's an example of a value object implementation for `Money` that represents currency:

Ddd.ts

```typescript
class Money {
  private readonly amount: number
  private readonly currency: string
  constructor(amount: number, currency: string) {
    this.amount = amount
    this.currency = currency
    this.validate()
  }
  private validate(): void {
    if (this.amount < 0) {
      throw new Error("Amount cannot be negative")
    }
    if (this.currency.length !== 3) {
      throw new Error("Currency must be a 3-letter
        ISO code")
    }
  }

  private ensureSameCurrency(other: Money): void {
    if (this.currency !== other.currency) {
      throw new Error("Cannot perform operations on
        different currencies");
    }
  }
  public equals(other: Money): boolean {
    return this.amount === other.amount &&
      this.currency === other.currency;
  }
  public add(other: Money): Money {
    this.ensureSameCurrency(other);
    return new Money(this.amount + other.amount,
      this.currency);
  }

  public subtract(other: Money): Money {
    this.ensureSameCurrency(other);
```

```
    const resultAmount = this.amount - other.amount;
    if (resultAmount < 0) {
      throw new Error("Resulting amount cannot be
        negative");
    }
    return new Money(resultAmount, this.currency);
  }
  public equals(other: Money): boolean {
    return this.amount === other.amount &&
      this.currency === other.currency
  }
}
```

Here, the Money class represents a value object by encapsulating two related attributes: amount and currency. This class is immutable since both properties are declared as readonly. The validate method checks whether the amount or currency field is valid.

Additionally, the equals method allows for attribute-based equality comparison, enabling two Money instances to be considered equal if they have the same amount and currency. Note that there are no id fields since there's no point in adding unique identifiers for currency values.

You can use this value object when you want your application to deal with comparing Money instances in a composable way.

Domain events

Domain events are indicators of something that has happened in a domain, and we want other parts of the application to respond to them. You create and dispatch events in response to an action. Here are some examples:

- When the user is registered, send a confirmation email

- When a post model is saved, send a message to PostSocialService to promote it on social media

Domain events are an excellent way to decouple business logic without sacrificing clarity. You can implement domain events using familiar design patterns that you've learned about, such as the Mediator and Observer patterns.

Here's a quick example of a simple web application that illustrates the usage of domain events when a new user registers on the platform:

ddd.ts

```
const dispatcher = new EventDispatcher()
const userService = new UserService(dispatcher)
```

```
async function sendWelcomeEmail(event: UserRegisteredEvent)
{
  const maxRetries = 3;

  for (let attempt = 1; attempt <= maxRetries; attempt++) {
    try {
      // Simulating sending an email that can fail
      await sendEmail(event.email);
      console.log(`Successfully sent welcome
        email to ${event.email}`);
      return;
    } catch (error) {
      console.error(`Attempt ${attempt} failed to send
        email to ${event.email}:`, error);
      if (attempt === maxRetries) {
        console.error(`Failed to send welcome email after
          ${maxRetries} attempts.`);
      }
    }
  }
}
async function notifyAdminOfNewUser(
  event: UserRegisteredEvent) {
    console.log(`Notifying admin of new user:
      ${event.userId}`);
  }

dispatcher.addListener(sendWelcomeEmail)
dispatcher.addListener(notifyAdminOfNewUser)

userService.registerUser("user123", "user@example.com")
```

In this example, we have a basic EventDispatcher that adds listeners and dispatches events. Here, UserService uses EventDispatcher to dispatch UserRegisteredEvent when a user is registered. Then, we create two simple event handlers – sendWelcomeEmail and notifyAdminOfNewUser – and add them to the EventDispatcher instance. When userService.registerUser() is called, it triggers the event, which then calls both handlers. The code also includes an example of a simple retry mechanism that tries to re-send the email if the operation fails.

The use of domain events, as demonstrated here, allows for loose coupling between different parts of the system, enabling easier evolution and maintenance of the code base. The principles of DDD often complement other software design practices and architectural patterns, contributing to more robust and adaptable software systems.

Before you consider applying DDD in your project, you must also consider its drawbacks.

Current disadvantages of DDD

DDD isn't perfect and isn't the only solution for the large-scale development of software products. Here are some drawbacks of DDD:

- **Needs considerable time and resource investment**: Implementing DDD can be time-consuming and resource-intensive, especially when developing a ubiquitous language and refining domain models. This can be challenging for projects with tight deadlines or limited resources.

- **No size fits all**: DDD is most beneficial in complex domains where business logic is intricate. For simpler applications, applying DDD principles could complicate development unnecessarily.

- **Dependency on domain experts**: Successfully implementing DDD relies heavily on access to domain experts. If these experts are unavailable or communication is poor, it can hinder the development process considerably.

Overall, while DDD has the potential to scale well due to its modularity and suitability with modern architectural practices such as microservices, its effectiveness largely depends on how well it's implemented.

In the next section, we'll discuss the SOLID principles.

Embracing SOLID principles

SOLID is an acronym for the first five **object-oriented programming (OOP)** design principles:

- Single Responsibility Principle
- Open-Closed Principle
- Liskov Substitution Principle
- Interface Segregation Principle
- Dependency Inversion Principle

These principles were coined by Robert C. Martin in his 2000 paper *Design Principles and Design Patterns*, which is available at `https://staff.cs.utu.fi/~jounsmed/doos_06/material/DesignPrinciplesAndPatterns.pdf`. These principles exhibit a strong correlation with OOP languages and how to structure your programs with maintenance and extensibility in mind. Adopting these practices can contribute to producing code that's easier to refactor and reason about.

To start, we'll take a deep dive into these principles while looking at some representative examples in TypeScript. We'll make some conclusions after.

Single Responsibility Principle

The **Single Responsibility Principle** states that *a class should only have one reason to change*. In terms of functionality, a *class* represents a type that supports OOP principles such as encapsulation, polymorphism, inheritance, and abstraction. If we put too many responsibilities in classes, then they become what we call **God objects** – that is, objects that know too much or do too much. The real challenge is finding a balance between responsibilities.

Let's look at a simple example with a class that represents a `User` model in an application. You capture some information about the user, such as their `name`, `email`, and `password`:

Soild.ts

```
class User {
  constructor(
    private name: string,
    private email: string,
    private password: string,
  ) {}
}
```

Now, you have a requirement to get a `slug` field, which is a field that we use to store and generate valid URLs from a `User` model. It's a good idea to add the following method inside the model since it's related to it:

Solid.ts

```
class User {
...
    generateSlug(): string {
        return kebabCase(this.name)
      }
}
```

Next, you have a requirement to perform a `login` operation for the user and to send emails. You might be tempted to add these methods in the same model:

Solid.ts

```
class User {
...
    login(email: string, password: string) {}
    sendEmail(email: string, template: string) {}
}
```

At this point, the Single Responsibility Principle has been violated. Here, the Single Responsibility Principle advises us not to do this as it gives too many responsibilities to the User model. Instead, what you should do is create two different services that log in and send the emails for the User model:

solid.ts

```
class UserAccountService {
    login(user: User, password: string) {}
}
class EmailService {
    sendEmailToUser(user: User, template: string) {}
}
```

Now, each class has one reason to change. If we were to change the way emails are sent to users, we would have to modify EmailService. The same would happen for the login operation, where we would have to change UserAccountService.

The benefits you gain by separating those concerns with this principle are mostly obvious:

- **Testing**: It's easier to test a single feature or branch instead of multiple branches

- **Organization**: Smaller classes can be located more easily when given a proper name and core functionality can be discovered faster

Naturally, you must consider that splitting those methods into classes creates multiple objects that may have to be consolidated if needed or used as part of a Façade design pattern. This is because directly invoking 100 services in a function to perform a business workflow isn't ideal.

Open-Closed Principle

The **Open-Closed Principle** states that *when you define software entities, you should be able to extend their functionality, but you shouldn't be able to modify the existing entity.*

Instead, you should just add a new mapping or configuration that allows the right strategy to be applied when it's run.

For the User model we defined previously, we want to extend the behavior based on the account status. Suppose we have a new field for capturing the account type of the User class. Initially, we have two account types: Normal and Premium. We leverage single responsibility to create a new class for sending vouchers based on the user account type:

Solid.ts

```
type AccountType = "Normal" | "Premium"
class User {
```

```
  constructor(
    private name: string,
    private email: string,
    private password: string,
    private accountType: AccountType = "Normal",
  ) {}
  isPremium(): boolean {
    return this.accountType === "Premium"
  }
}
class VoucherService {
  getVoucher(user: User): string {
    if (user.isPremium()) {
      return "15% discount"
    } else {
      return "10% discount"
    }
  }
}
```

The preceding code would work, but consider a case where you must add another user account type with a different voucher offer. You would have to modify both the User class and the VoucherService class:

Solid.ts

```
type AccountType = "Normal" | "Premium" | "Ultimate";
class User {
...
  isUltimate(): boolean {
    return this.accountType === "Ultimate";
  }
  getVoucher(user: User): string {
    if (user.isPremium()) {
      return "15% discount";
    }
    if (user.IsUltimate()) {
      return "20% discount";
    }
    else {
      return "10% discount";
    }
  }
}
```

This principle dictates that you should make the `getVoucher` method more resistant to change by modification. Instead of calling the respective `user` methods, you should abstract the way you generate vouchers based on the user account type. Here's one way to do this:

Solid.ts

```
type Voucher = string
const userTypeToVoucherMap: Record<AccountType,
Voucher> = {
  Normal: "10% discount",
  Premium: "15% discount",
  Ultimate: "20% discount",
}
class VoucherService {
  getVoucher(user: User): string {
    return userTypeToVoucherMap[user.getAccountType()];
  }
}
```

This looks like the Factory Method pattern or Strategy pattern. Instead of querying the type of the user, you provide a factory of vouchers based on the user account type mapping. Now, if you want to extend or modify the voucher, you can do so by changing the mapping instead of `VoucherService` in one place. The main benefit here is that for any similar future changes, you'll have to change the code in a few places in a more predictable way.

Liskov Substitution Principle

The **Liskov Substitution Principle** concerns passing objects or interfaces as parameters. It states that *given an object parameter, we should be able to pass subclasses of that object without changing the behavior of the program*. In that case, the client won't see any difference in the expected results and should be able to work without any breaking changes.

You can think of this concept as the principle of least astonishment. If you allow an entity that represents a model and allows inherited models, then you shouldn't break this specialization. If your inherited models do a different thing, such as returning a different representation or type, then when the client leverages the polymorphic call, it will break and return incorrect results. Clients don't have to change if some of the subtypes don't inherit from parent types properly.

There are several ways that a subtype can violate this principle:

- Returning an incompatible object with the parent class
- Throwing an exception that's not thrown by the parent class
- Introducing side effects that the parent class doesn't handle

Let's look at an example with collections. Here, Bag represents a container of values where you should be able to put values in and retrieve them in any order:

Solid.ts

```
interface Bag<T> {
  push(item: T): void
  pop(): T | undefined
  isEmpty(): boolean
}
```

This interface represents a generic stack-like container, so you could be tempted to implement it using a stack:

Solid.ts

```
class Stack<T> implements Bag<T> {
  constructor(private items = []) {}
  push<T>(item: T) {}
  pop(): T | undefined {
    if (this.items.length > 0) {
      return this.items.pop()
    }

    return undefined
  }
  isEmpty(): boolean {
    return this.items.length === 0
  }
}
```

You should have realized that stacks are more constrained than bags as they return an item in **first in, first out** (FIFO) order. If you rely on the expectation that the order of items doesn't matter, then you can use a stack in any place where a bag is expected. Now, you must provide a different subtype that violates one principle, as shown in the following example:

Solid.ts

```
class NonEmptyStack<T> implements Bag<T> {
  private tag: any = Symbol()
  constructor(private items: T[] = []) {
    if (this.items.length == 0) {
      this.items.push(this.tag)
    }
}
```

```
  }
  push(item: T) {
    this.items.push(item)
  }
  pop(): T | undefined {
    if (this.items.length === 1) {
      const item = this.items.pop()
      this.items.push(this.tag)
      return item
    }
    if (this.items.length > 1) {
      return this.items.pop()
    }
    return undefined
  }
  isEmpty(): boolean {
    return this.items.length === 0
  }
}
```

This bag implementation introduces a side effect as it makes sure that it always contains one last element. Thus, isEmpty() will always return false. Clients expecting standard stack behavior – where an empty stack should return true for isEmpty() – will encounter unexpected results. This breaks the assumption that any subclass of a stack should behave like a standard stack, leading to potential bugs and confusion in client code.

Therefore, when using inheritance to create specialized implementations such as NonEmptyStack, it's important to consider the set of expectations that have been set by their supertype to maintain substitutability and prevent client assumptions from being broken.

Interface Segregation Principle

The **Interface Segregation Principle** applies to interfaces. It states that *when you define interfaces, you should make them as thin and as small as possible*. If you want more extensibility, you can create new interfaces that derive from existing ones.

A typical use case with this principle is when you're defining new interfaces and you end up adding more methods to it. In this case, all classes that implement this interface will have to implement the new methods to satisfy the interface contract. Let's look at an example that considers the `Collection` interface, which represents a container of values:

Solid.ts

```typescript
interface Collection<T> {
  pushBack(item: T): void
  popBack(): T
  pushFront(item: T): void
  popFront(): T
  isEmpty(): boolean
  insertAt(item: T, index: number): void
  deleteAt(index: number): T | undefined
}
```

The more methods you include in this interface, the more difficult it is to implement all of them. With TypeScript, you can mark some properties as optional with the question mark operator (?), but this doesn't hide the fact that this interface is very generic. If you ever want to provide more flexibility for the classes when implementing this `Collection` interface, you should break it apart into smaller interfaces:

Solid.ts

```typescript
interface Collection<T> {
  isEmpty(): boolean
}
interface Array<T> extends Collection<T> {
  insertAt(item: T, index: number): void
  deleteAt(index: number): T | undefined
}
interface Stack<T> extends Collection<T> {
  pushFront(item: T): void
  popFront(): T
}
interface Queue<T> extends Collection<T> {
  pushBack(item: T): void
  popFront(): T
}
```

Now, these interfaces are easier to extend and you can choose to extend only the most relevant interfaces. For example, for the implementation of a bag data structure that represents a container that you just push or pop items to and from, you can use the `Stack` interface. The methods you need to implement are `isEmpty`, `pushFront`, and `popFront`; there are no other irrelevant methods for this data structure.

> **Note on performance implications**
>
> Different data structures have varying access patterns that can significantly affect performance. For instance, using an *array* allows for efficient random access but can incur high costs for insertions and deletions in the middle. In contrast, a *stack* that's implemented with an array may perform well for push and pop operations at the end, but using `pushFront` and `popFront` could lead to linear complexity due to element shifting. Similarly, *queues* implemented with arrays may suffer from inefficiencies when items are removed from the front.

Of course, this would require some initial designing of which methods go on which interface, but overall, it keeps the code clean and with minimal change requirements.

Dependency Inversion Principle

The **Dependency Inversion Principle** states that *when you use modules in your entities, you should pass them as abstractions instead of directly instantiating them*. You can understand what we mean by looking at the following program:

Solid.ts

```typescript
type User = {
  name: string
  email: string
}
class UserService {
  constructor() {}
  findByEmail(email: string): User | undefined {
    const userRepo = UserRepositoryFactory.getInstance()
    return userRepo.findByEmail(email)
  }
}
class UserRepositoryFactory {
  static getInstance(): UserRepository {
    return new UserRepository()
  }
}
class UserRepository {
```

```
  users: User[] = [{ name: "Theo",
    email: "theo@example.com" }]
  findByEmail(email: string): User | undefined {
    const user = this.users.find((u) => u.email === email)
    return user
  }
}
```

This program contains three entities. First, `UserService` is a top-level component that calls the `UserRepositoryFactory` class to get an instance of the `UserRepository` service. The violation of this principle happens here within the highlighted code section.

We import `UserRepositoryFactory` directly inside the function, which makes it a hard dependency. If the `UserRepositoryFactory` class changes, we'll have to change the `UserService` class as well. Additionally, we can't test the method in isolation easily, so we'll have to mock the whole `UserRepositoryFactory` module to do so.

The solution to making it less dependent and more testable is to pass the instance in the constructor and make it implement an interface instead:

Solid.ts

```
class UserService {
  constructor(private userQuery:
    UserQuery = UserRepositoryFactory.getInstance()) {}
  findByEmail(email: string): User | undefined {
    return this.userQuery.findByEmail(email)
  }
}
class UserRepository implements UserQuery {
  users: User[] = [{ name: "Theo",
    email: "theo@example.com" }]
  findByEmail(email: string): User | undefined {
    return this.users.find((u) => u.email === email);
  }
}
class MockUserQuery implements UserQuery {
  private users: User[] = [
    { name: "Alice", email: "alice@example.com" },
    { name: "Bob", email: "bob@example.com" },
  ];

  findByEmail(email: string): User | undefined {
    return this.users.find((u) => u.email === email);
```

```
    }
  }
// Unit test for UserService
describe("UserService", () => {
  let userService: UserService;
  let mockUserQuery: MockUserQuery;

  beforeEach(() => {
    mockUserQuery = new MockUserQuery();
    userService = new UserService(mockUserQuery);
    // Injecting the mock
  });
  // Test cases
});
```

By following this principle, the UserService class now depends on the UserQuery abstraction instead of the concrete UserRepository implementation. This decoupling allows for easier testing since you can provide a mock implementation of UserQuery during testing. It also makes the code more flexible and maintainable as you can easily swap out different implementations of UserQuery without modifying the UserService class.

The preceding code also shows how to create test mocks via the MockUserQuery class, which implements the UserQuery interface and provides a predefined set of users. This mock can simulate various scenarios without relying on actual database access.

Using **dependency injection (DI)** frameworks such as InversifyJS or Angular's DI container provides several significant benefits for managing dependencies in TypeScript applications. These frameworks promote loose coupling between components by allowing dependencies to be injected rather than hard-coded, which enhances flexibility and maintainability.

Is using SOLID the best practice?

One fundamental mistake you can make when learning about these principles is to look at them as the final solution or something that will magically make programs better. The truth is that they won't. The main reason is that we don't know when and how things will change, and we can't predict that consistently.

Let's say you have one feature that you're working on, and you've decided to use specific design patterns. You design and implement the solution using the best-understood practices for your current tooling. Then, you go and work on another feature, and at some point, the business requires some radical code changes to be made to the first feature. No matter what principles you used back then, you'll have to refactor or completely rewrite part of the application to accommodate the new changes.

Conceivably, now, you will have to replace some patterns with different ones, such as Memento with Observer, Factory Method with Abstract Factory, and so on. However, back then, your decision-making process was based on a different set of requirements, so there was no need to follow all the principles under the sun to get the job done.

You must consider other patterns and principles such as **Don't Repeat Yourself** (**DRY**) or **Keep It Simple, Stupid** (**KISS**) and how they relate to the SOLID principles. With DRY, you aim to reduce the repetition of software blocks, replacing them with abstractions, whereas with KISS, you aim to favor simple over complex and convoluted patterns. All three principles (DRY, SOLID, and KISS) are hard to satisfy altogether and can't be applied consistently.

Sometimes, applying SOLID principles can make the code more complicated; you must create more classes to do a single thing, you'll have to give them proper names – sometimes longer ones – or you'll have to sacrifice cohesion. You should think of the SOLID principles as valuable tools in your toolbox, together with DRY, that you can use when needed to create highly composable software components.

With that concept covered, let's take a closer look at the MVC pattern, a software architecture pattern that helps us develop medium to large-scale applications.

Applying the MVC architecture

MVC refers to a software architecture design that organizes software modules into three interconnected components: the model, the view, and the controller. Each component adheres to the **separation of concerns principle**, which dictates that each component should have a specific role and responsibility within the application.

The following sections will provide detailed explanations of each component and understand how they interact, specifically using TypeScript.

Model

The **model** in MVC represents the core data that maps a particular entity in your system. The model is responsible for encapsulating all the business logic for managing the data it represents, including validation, integrity, and data retrieval. In a TypeScript application, models can be defined as classes or interfaces that encapsulate the properties and methods related to a specific entity.

Here's an example of how you would create a model that represents a Todo item:

Mvc.ts

```
interface TodoModel {
    id: number
    title: string
    completed: boolean
```

```
    toggleCompletion(): void
}
class Todo implements TodoModel {
  constructor(
    public readonly id: number,
    public title: string,
    public completed: boolean = false,
  ) {}

  toggleCompletion(): void {
    this.completed = !this.completed
  }
}
```

In this example, the `Todo` class serves as the model for a to-do item, encapsulating its properties and behavior. It contains the necessary properties and methods to update its state.

In terms of enhancing the model, we can apply a few patterns here. The Singleton and Factory Method patterns, both of which we explored in *Chapter 3*, are suitable for being used with models since they allow objects to be created without the need to specify the exact class of object that will be created. The Builder pattern can also be used to create complex view models that are used by controllers to interact with the view since they allow you to construct these objects in a clear and manageable way.

Now, let's check out the view component.

View

The **view** component represents the presentation layer, which defines how the model or data is presented to the user. This layer also handles user interactions that may trigger the controller to perform specific logic.

In the context of TypeScript, views are often implemented using frameworks such as **Angular**, **React**, or **Vue**, where components are used to render UI elements.

It's important to note that the **model** is typically associated with the Domain layer. Meanwhile, the **controller** is associated with the Application layer, managing user input and coordinating interactions between the **view** and the **model**.

Here's a small example of how to use a view that presents a `TodoModel` list that prints its contents to the console:

Mvc.ts

```
class TodoList {
  private todos: TodoModel[] = []
```

```
    private nextId: number = 1
    addTodo(title: string): void {
      const newTodo = new TodoModel(this.nextId++, title)
      this.todos.push(newTodo)
    }

    getTodos(): TodoModel[] {
      return this.todos
    }
}

class TodoView {
  constructor(private model: TodoList) {}
  displayTodos() {
    console.log("Todo List:")
    this.model.getTodos().forEach((todo, index) => {
      console.log(`${index + 1}. ${todo}`)
    })
  }
  promptAddTodo() {
    const readline = require("readline").createInterface({
      input: process.stdin,
      output: process.stdout,
    })
    readline.question("Enter a new todo: ",
    (todo: string) => {
      console.log("Todo added successfully!")
      readline.close()
    })
  }
}
```

Here, TodoView handles the current list of to-dos and prompts the user for input to add new todos. The displayTodos method retrieves the list of to-dos from the TodoList model and outputs them to the console in a numbered format. Then, promptAddTodo accepts a Todo item from the console and prints its contents.

Now, where does the controller fit into this? Well, the controller's job is to sit between the view and the model and handle their interactions. When the model changes, the controller must arrange an update for the view to reflect the new changes. We'll explain this process next.

Controller

The **controller** acts as the *glue* between the model and the view components. It's supposed to be the piece of code that listens for interactions (user input, click events, and actions). After, it processes those inputs and uses the model methods to retrieve new versions of the model data. Then, with the process of propagation, it would update the view based on the new model data.

Therefore, the controller plays a crucial role in providing up-to-date resolution and reflection of the model data. A common way to do this is by binding both the view and the model inside the controller, as shown in the following code example:

Mvc.ts

```typescript
class TodoController {
    constructor(private  model: TodoList,
    private view: TodoView) {}
    addTodo(title: string): void {
        this.model.addTodo(title);
        console.log("Todo added successfully!");
        this.view.displayTodos();
    }
    promptAddTodo(): void {
        this.view.promptAddTodo();
    }
}
const todoList = new TodoList();

const todoView = new TodoView(todoList);
const todoController = new TodoController(todoList,
  todoView);
todoController.promptAddTodo();
```

Here, `TodoController` has been initialized with instances of both `Model` and `View`, allowing it to access and manipulate the to-do data. The `addTodo` method takes a title for a new to-do item, adds it to the `TodoList` model, and then calls the `displayTodos` method on `TodoView` to refresh the displayed list of to-dos, ensuring that users see the most current information. The `promptAddTodo` method delegates the task of prompting the user for input to `View`.

Overall, the MVC architecture offers numerous benefits that significantly enhance software development processes. It supports the creation of multiple views for a single model, reducing code duplication and enhancing the user experience across various platforms. Furthermore, the MVC architecture makes it easier to test as each component can be tested independently, improving overall code quality and reliability.

Incorporating TypeScript into your MVC architecture further enhances these benefits by leveraging strong typing to enforce model consistency across views and controllers. With TypeScript, you can define interfaces or types for your models, ensuring that both the view and controller adhere to a consistent structure. This reduces the likelihood of runtime errors caused by type mismatches since TypeScript catches these issues at compile time.

With these benefits in mind, we can say that adopting an MVC architecture for your projects is a viable first step toward creating scalable, maintainable, and efficient applications.

Summary

In this chapter, we provided a list of recommendations and best practices when developing large-scale TypeScript applications. Those practices stem from a combination of experience, traditional patterns, industry best practices, and recommended modern architectural practices. Making use of multiple design patterns makes those abstractions more flexible and dynamic.

Utility types provide several common and very useful type transformations to help us avoid code duplication when writing types. Understanding when and how to use DDD offers a robust architectural approach for how to design software applications. Additionally, leveraging the concepts of the SOLID principles can help create easier software designs to understand, maintain, and extend when implemented correctly.

Adopting the MVC architecture can greatly improve the organization and maintainability of your applications. MVC allows for a clear separation of concerns by dividing the application into three interconnected components: the model, which manages data and business logic; the view, which handles the user interface and presentation; and the controller, which manages user input and interactions between the model and view.

The next chapter will look at the most important caveats and gotchas when developing applications in TypeScript. Using what you learned in this chapter, you'll learn how to produce the most appropriate and accurate abstraction for your software requirements.

Q&A

Feel free to review the following questions and their corresponding answers to address any concerns or gain additional insights:

1. What are the benefits of combining design patterns?

    Answer: When you combine design patterns, you generally want to use the best traits of each pattern. For example, you may leverage the Singleton pattern with any other pattern that needs to exist only once in the application life cycle. In other cases, you want to leverage their similarities, for example, with the Observer and Mediator patterns.

2. What's the difference between the Omit and Pick utility types?

    Answer: The Omit<U, T> type lets you pick all properties from the existing type, U, and then remove the specified keys of the T type. This will create a new type consisting of the properties, T, that have been omitted from the U type. On the other hand, Pick<U, T> does the opposite. You specify the parameters you want to extract from U without checking for any relationship with T. This will create a new type consisting of the selected properties, T, of the U type.

3. How is DRY different from SOLID?

    Answer: Both are basic engineering principles. With DRY, you avoid excessive code duplication by extracting common code into functions or classes. With SOLID, you attempt to create code abstractions that are easier to change, do a single thing at a time, and are more flexible when testing. Off-and-on SOLID can introduce code duplication and sometimes DRY can violate some of the rules of SOLID. Their usage depends on the level of complexity you want to maintain.

Further reading

- A good reference for mastering TypeScript beyond the basics is *Mastering TypeScript, Fourth Edition*, by Nathan Rozentals. It's available at: `https://www.packtpub.com/product/mastering-typescript-fourth-edition/9781800564732`.

- An introduction to the Repository pattern is available at `https://www.umlboard.com/design-patterns/repository.html`.

- A good hands-on book about TypeScript combining lots of elements is *Full-Stack React, TypeScript, and Node*, by David Choi. It's available at: `https://www.packtpub.com/product/full-stack-react-typescript-and-node/9781839219931`.

Get This Book's PDF Version and Exclusive Extras

UNLOCK NOW

Scan the QR code (or go to `packtpub.com/unlock`). Search for this book by name, confirm the edition, and then follow the steps on the page.

Note: Keep your invoice handly. Purchase made directly from packt don't require one.

10
Anti-Patterns and Workarounds

Just as there are good design patterns and best practices when using TypeScript, there are some anti-patterns as well. When working on large-scale applications, you will inevitably come across some patterns or parts that look problematic, are hard to read and change, or promote dangerous behavior. This happens because as the application grows, you will need to write more code that fits the existing code base, and quite often, you will have to make some compromises.

Over time, as more people contribute to the same code space, you will see many inconsistencies – things such as **god objects**, inconsistent use of patterns, or even the excessive use of any types. God objects refer to classes or objects that know too much or do too much, thereby violating the **Single-Responsibility Principle** (**SRP**) and introducing complexity. In this chapter, we will look at approaches to work around these problems.

In this chapter, we will explore several important aspects of TypeScript's type system and best practices for maintaining code quality. We will analyze the pitfalls of class overuse and inheritance and provide strategies to avoid these common issues. Then, we will discuss the dangers of using permissive or incorrect types that can lead to runtime errors, as well as the challenges associated with using idiomatic code from other languages.

Additionally, we will list type inference gotchas, highlighting its limitations and how misunderstandings can lead to brittle types or incorrect type-checking behavior. Finally, we will identify how complicated generics can make code harder to read and maintain, along with best practices for their effective use.

Here is a list of topics that will be covered in this chapter:

- Class overuse
- Permissive or incorrect types
- Using idiomatic code from other languages
- Type inference gotchas
- Generic gotchas

By the end of this chapter, you will be able to recognize the most important anti-patterns and provide workarounds for them when required.

Technical requirements

The code bundle for this chapter is available on GitHub here: `https://github.com/PacktPublishing/TypeScript-5-Design-Patterns-and-Best-Practices/tree/main/chapters/chapter10_Anti_patterns`.

Class overuse

Object-Oriented Programming (OOP) principles and design patterns encourage modeling real-world entities using classes. While the benefits of OOP are well recognized, it often leads to an overabundance of classes. This can create complications in your code structure.

To explain what we mean, when you try emulating a system using classical OOP techniques such as **inheritance** and **encapsulation**, you inevitably have to carry over the whole hierarchy. In the next section, we'll examine an analogy to emphasize this issue at hand.

The jungle problem

When you attempt to emulate a system using classical OOP techniques such as inheritance and encapsulation, you often end up carrying over entire class hierarchies. This is exemplified by the *banana, monkey, jungle* problem. For instance, if you want to use a Banana object, you might need to import a `Jungle` object that contains a `Monkey` instance, which exposes the `getBanana()` method:

```
new Jungle().getAnimalByType("Monkey").getBanana();
```

This illustrates how your class structure can become convoluted, leading to unnecessary dependencies and complexity in your code.

A good solution for the jungle problem is to consider favoring *composition* over *inheritance*. The `Jungle` object could represent an environment or context where various animals and fruits exist, instead of being tightly coupled with specific animal behaviors (such as retrieving bananas).

Unlike inheritance, composition allows for greater flexibility by combining behaviors at runtime, thus reducing class dependencies and enhancing reusability. With inheritance, you often create a hierarchy that can lead to tightly coupled classes, making it difficult to modify or extend functionality without affecting multiple parts of your code base.

Composition, on the other hand, enables you to build complex behaviors by combining simpler components, which can be easily swapped or modified without changing the entire structure.

This is what the interaction would look like:

```
class Jungle {
  constructor(private animal: Animal,
    private fruit: Fruit) {}
  feedAnimals() {
    this.animal.eat(this.fruit);
  }
}
const jungle = new Jungle();
const monkey = new Monkey();
const banana = new Banana();
jungle.addAnimal(monkey);
jungle.addFruit(banana);
jungle.feedAnimals(); // Outputs: The monkey eats a banana.
```

The Jungle object now serves as a container for animals and fruits and triggers interactions for the elements it contains. For instance, the feedAnimals method within the Jungle class can traverse the compositional chain of animals and invoke their respective eat() methods, passing in a fruit from its collection.

While this works for that particular use case, you can easily apply its concepts to any similar piece of software code.

Example of class overuse

Consider a scenario where we have a CSV class that implements two interfaces – Reader for reading from a CSV file and Writer for writing to a file:

Class-overuse.ts

```
interface Reader {
  read(): string[]
}
interface Writer {
  write(input: string[]): void
}
class CSV implements Reader, Writer {
  constructor(private csvFilePath: string) {}
  read(): string[] {
    // Logic to read CSV
    return ["data1", "data2"]
```

```
  }

  write(input: string[]): void {
    // Logic to write to CSV
  }
}
```

In the preceding code, the `Reader` interface defines a `read()` method, which is responsible for reading data from a CSV file, and the `Writer` interface writes it to a CSV file using the `write()` method. The CSV class constructor accepts a file path as a parameter, which is used in the implementation of both the `read()` and `write()` methods. Initially, this setup works well. However, as we define new classes that only partially reuse the functionality of the CSV class, we introduce tight coupling:

Class-overuse.ts

```typescript
class ExcelToCSV extends CSV {
  constructor(
    csvFilePath: string,
    private excelFilePath: string,
  ) {
    super(csvFilePath)
  }
  read(): string[] {
    // Logic to read from Excel file
    return ["excelData1", "excelData2"]
  }
}
class ExcelToPDF extends ExcelToCSV {
  constructor(
    csvFilePath: string,
    excelFilePath: string,
    private pdfFilePath: string,
  ) {
    super(csvFilePath, excelFilePath)
  }
  write(input: string[]): void {
    // Logic to write to PDF
  }
}
```

In the preceding code, the `ExcelToCSV` class uses the `write` method from the superclass and overrides the `read` method to read from an Excel file. The `ExcelToPDF` class extends the `ExcelToCSV` interface so that it uses the `read` method from the parent and overloads the `write` method to write to PDF. Both classes reuse part of the base class methods.

The problem is now that this partial dependency creates a tight coupling between all classes and breaks the SRP (see *Chapter 9* for details) as well. You will have to include both the `CSV` and `ExcelToCSV` classes if you want to use functionality from the base classes. One way to improve this is when you extend the behavior of classes, it's preferred to use *composition* over *inheritance*. Instead of inheriting from a base class, just implement a single well-defined interface for each of the functionalities you want to provide. Using the previous code for the `CSV` class, you can redefine it as follows:

Class-overuse.ts

```
class CSVReader implements Reader {
  constructor(private csvFilePath: string) {}
  read(): string[] {
    // Logic to read CSV
    return ["data1", "data2"]
  }
}

class CSVWriter implements Writer {
  write(input: string[]): void {
    // Logic to write to CSV
  }
}
class ExcelReader implements Reader {
  constructor(private excelFilePath: string) {}
  read(): string[] {
    // Logic to read from Excel file
    return ["excelData1", "excelData2"]
  }
}
class PDFWriter implements Writer {
  write(input: string[]): void {
    // Logic to write to PDF
  }
}
```

Here, we broke the `CSV` class into `CSVReader` and `CSVWriter` classes. We also dispersed the `ExcelToCSV` and `ExcelToPDF` classes to inherit from the `Reader` and `Writer` interfaces, respectively.

Now you can combine both the `reader` and `writer` classes in a more abstract way:

Class-overuse.ts

```ts
class ReaderToWriters {
    constructor(private reader: Reader,
      private writers: Writer[]) {}
    perform() {
        const lines = this.reader.read();
        this.writers.forEach(writer =>
          writer.write(lines));
    }
}
```

In the preceding code, the `ReaderToWriters` class operates on only the `Reader` and `Writer` types, so there is no hardcoded dependency involved. You just pass on an instance of their types and it will work as expected.

This style of reuse is called **black-box reuse** and it's useful as it follows SOLID principles and makes code easier to understand and extend.

Using interfaces for models

When defining new models or entities in TypeScript, consider using interfaces instead of classes. For example, consider a `configuration` interface that declares a list of API paths:

Class-overuse.ts

```ts
interface Configuration {
  paths: {
    apiBase: string
    login: string
  }
}
const applicationConfig: Configuration = {
  paths: {
    apiBase: "/v1",
    login: "/login",
  },
}
function updateEmployee(employee: Employee,
  updates: Partial<Employee>): Employee {
  return { ...employee, ...updates };
}
```

Here, `applicationConfig` is typed as `Configuration`, allowing TypeScript to enforce type checking without the overhead of a class. You can further improve this by using `Readonly` and `Partial` to enforce immutability and optional updates, as per the following example:

Class-overuse.ts

```
interface Project {
  id: number;
  name: string;
  description?: string;
}
type ReadonlyProject = Readonly<Project>;
type PartialProject = Partial<Project>;
const initialProject: ReadonlyProject = { id: 1,
  name: "TypeScript Guide" };
const updatedProject: Project = { ...initialProject,
  description: "An updated TypeScript guide" };
```

In this code, `ReadonlyProject` prevents modifications and `PartialProject` allows partial updates. The code showcases how to create an initial project object and update it with additional properties while maintaining type safety and immutability.

Overall, type composition over classes works better in the aforementioned contexts, and this is one of the reasons TypeScript is considered a very flexible language. This approach not only adheres to best practices but also leverages TypeScript's flexibility effectively. Next, we'll discuss the dangers of using overly permissive or incorrect types.

Overly permissive types

When integrating a library that lacks TypeScript declarations or developing new features from scratch, you might be tempted to take shortcuts with type definitions. This often leads to using permissive or incorrect types, which can undermine TypeScript's type-checking capabilities. In this section, we will explore common pitfalls associated with these types and provide examples to illustrate their implications.

Common pitfalls

Here, we will explain the most obvious uses of permissive or incorrect types:

- **Using the any type**: The any type essentially opts out of type checking. When you declare a variable or parameter as any, TypeScript will not enforce any constraints on it, which can lead to runtime errors that are difficult to debug.

The most common use case is declaring function arguments without declaring their type (in that case, TypeScript will infer them as any):

Permissive-types.ts

```
function processValue(value) {
   console.log(value.toUpperCase()) // This will throw an error
if value is not a string
}


processValue("hello") // Works fine
processValue(123) // Runtime error: value.toUpperCase is not a
function
```

In this example, the processValue function accepts any type of input. If a number is passed instead of a string, it results in a runtime error, demonstrating why using any is discouraged.

> **Note**
>
> As an alternative to any, TypeScript provides the unknown type, which is safer because it enforces type checking. When you declare a variable as unknown, you must perform some form of type checking before performing operations on it. This helps prevent runtime errors and encourages better coding practices.

* **Using the Function type**: The Function type is a generic container that can represent any function signature. However, this permissiveness comes at the cost of losing specific input and output types. Let's look at an example:

Permissive-types.ts

```
interface Callback {
    onEvent: Function; // Permissive type
}
const callback1: Callback = {
    onEvent: (a: string) => a.toUpperCase(),
};
const callback2: Callback = {
    onEvent: () => "Hello",
};

const callback3: Callback = {
    onEvent: () => 1,
};
```

In this example, all three `onEvent` properties pass the type check because they are considered valid `Function` types. However, this is problematic because the first `callback` expects a string but could be called with any type and the second `callback` returns a string, while the third returns a number. This lack of specificity can lead to unexpected behavior when these callbacks are invoked. To maximize the benefits of TypeScript's type-checking features, it's essential to invest time in defining accurate and representative types for your objects and interfaces. Instead of using `any` or `Function`, you can define more specific types:

Permissive-types.ts

```ts
interface Callback<T> {
    onEvent: (arg: T) => void;
}
const stringCallback: Callback<string> = {
    onEvent: (a) => console.log(a.toUpperCase()),
};
const numberCallback: Callback<number> = {
    onEvent: (n) => console.log(n * 2),
};
stringCallback.onEvent("hello"); // Works fine
numberCallback.onEvent(5);       // Works fine

// stringCallback.onEvent(5);       // Error: Argument of type
'number' is not assignable to parameter of type 'string'.
```

In this example, the `Callback` interface now accepts a generic type parameter, `<T>`, allowing you to specify what type the `onEvent` method should accept, which enforces stricter type checking and enhances code readability and maintainability.

By taking the time to define precise types for your variables and functions, you leverage TypeScript's full potential for catching errors at compile time rather than runtime.

In the next section, we will discuss why borrowing idiomatic code from other languages can introduce further complications in your TypeScript projects.

Using idiomatic code from other languages

When developers transition to TypeScript from other languages, they often bring coding patterns and idioms that may not be ideal in TypeScript. Although many programming concepts are shared between many languages, such as control loops, classes, and functions, there are many other concepts particular to one language that cannot be used in a different language.

In the next subsections, we show some obvious cases where using some idiomatic constructs from other languages will not work well with TypeScript, starting first with the Java language.

From the Java language

Java developers often use **Plain Old Java Objects (POJOs)** or **JavaBeans**. Let's look at how this pattern might be inappropriately applied in TypeScript and then how to improve it.

POJO is a naming convention for creating a class that follows some rules, especially in the context of Java EE where object serialization is crucial for some operations. The more standardized version of POJOs is the JavaBean naming convention. When following this convention, you will need to adhere to the following rules:

- **Access levels**: We mark all properties as `private` and we only allow `getter` and `setter` methods for access or modification.

- **Method names**: When defining `getters`, you will need to prefix the method with `get` – for example, `getName()` or `getEmail()`. When defining `setters`, you will need to prefix the method with `set` – for example, `setName()` or `setEmail()`.

- **Default constructor**: You need to use a constructor with no arguments and it must be `public`.

- **Serializable**: The class needs to implement the `Serializable` interface.

To understand why using POJOs in TypeScript is not ideal, we'll show an example class in TypeScript for a typical `Employee` model:

Idiomatic-code.ts

```
class Employee {
  constructor(private id: string, private name: string) {}
  getName(): string {
    return this.name
  }
  setName(name: string) {
    this.name = name
  }
  getId(): string {
    return this.id
  }
  setId(id: string) {
    this.id = id
  }
}
```

If you attempt to declare more than one constructor in TypeScript, then you will find that it's not allowed, so you cannot provide both a no-argument constructor and another one with arguments. Additionally, TypeScript will complain if you provide a no-argument constructor as the property's name and ID may have not been initialized.

You will see the following errors:

```
Property 'name' has no initializer and is not definitely assigned in the
constructor. ts(2564)
(property) Employee.name: string
class Empl  View Problem (⌃F8)   Quick Fix... (⌘.)   Fix using Copilot (⌘I)
  private name: string;
  private id: string;
  constructor(
  ) {}
```

Figure 10.1 – TypeScript compiler message when it complains when you use a no-argument constructor

The concept of serialization applies to Java only, so it's not relevant to TypeScript. However, you can serialize plain TypeScript objects using the JSON.stringify method as follows:

```
console.log(JSON.stringify(new Employee("Theo", "1")));
//{"id":"Theo","name":"1"}
```

You will find that this works only for basic cases and does not handle polymorphism, object identity, or when containing native JavaScript types such as Map, Set, or BigInt. However, in most cases, you can implement a custom object mapper or use a Factory Method to convert an object to JSON and vice versa.

The use of get/set methods is overly verbose and not needed most of the time. If you want to provide encapsulation, you can only have getter methods and if you want to modify an existing Employee class method, you just create a new Employee instance with the updated field name instead:

```
const theo = new Employee("Theo", "1");
new Employee(theo.getName(), "2");
```

Finally, you may opt out of using classes altogether as you can work with types, type assignments, and object de-structuring, as follows:

Idiomatic-code.ts

```
interface Employee {
    readonly id: string;
    readonly name: string;
    readonly department: string;
}
function createEmployee(id: string, name: string,
  department: string): Employee {
    return { id, name, department };
```

```
}
function updateEmployee(employee: Employee,
  updates: Partial<Employee>): Employee {
    return { ...employee, ...updates };
}
const emp = createEmployee('1', 'John Doe', 'IT');
console.log(emp.name); // John Doe
const updatedEmp = updateEmployee(emp,
  { department: 'HR' });
console.log(updatedEmp.department); // HR
```

This approach uses an interface instead of a class for simple data structures and provides factory functions for creation and updates, promoting immutability. This form is more idiomatic TypeScript and is the preferred way to work with types.

Now let's look at some of the idiomatic constructs from the **Go language**.

From the Go language

With Go, there is an idiomatic way to handle errors. Go code uses error values to indicate an abnormal state. When a function call results in an error, then it declares the returns as an error type in a multiple-return statement. It's not unusual for a function to return a result and an error together:

Idiomatic-code.ts

```
function divideNumbers(a: number, b: number):
  [number | null, Error | null] {
    if (b === 0) {
        return [null, new Error("Division by zero")];
    }
    return [a / b, null];
}
const [result, err] = divideNumbers(10, 2);
if (err !== null) {
    console.error("Error:", err.message);
} else {
    console.log("Result:", result);
}
```

For every operation like this, the programmer will check that the `err` object is not `null` and then proceed with the happy path. Otherwise, they will abort.

This approach mimics Go's multiple return values and explicit error checking, but it's not idiomatic TypeScript. A more idiomatic TypeScript approach is by using exceptions:

Idiomatic-code.ts

```
function divideNumbers(a: number, b: number): number {
    if (b === 0) {
        throw new Error("Division by zero");
    }
    return a / b;
}
try {
    const result = divideNumbers(10, 2);
    console.log("Result:", result);
} catch (error) {
    console.error("Error:", error.message);
}
```

Here, we use a `try/catch` statement to capture the error condition and to print the error into the console. Go does not offer this mechanism; it relies on plain error checking, which has its pros and cons. For example, one good advantage is **explicitness**, which requires developers to check for errors explicitly after each operation that can fail. This makes it clear where errors can occur and encourages developers to handle them immediately. On the other hand, **error propagation** is a challenge when using this pattern. Go developers would have to consider ways to propagate errors to higher layers of abstraction without losing context. This can lead to more cumbersome code when dealing with nested function calls.

In any case, the main rule is to consistently try to use the available error-handling facilities and language options with the use of promises and `async/await` functions. This is because those features offer a nicer abstraction layer over error handling and async control flow in general.

Next, we explain some common type inference gotchas.

Type inference gotchas

TypeScript's **type inference** is a powerful feature, but it can sometimes lead to unexpected results. Understanding these gotchas can help you write more robust and type-safe code. Let's explore some common anti-patterns related to type inference and how to avoid them.

Anti-pattern – relying too heavily on implicit typing

In TypeScript, you can declare types for variables or instances either explicitly or implicitly. Here is an example of explicit typing:

```
const arr: number[] = [1,2,3]
```

On the other hand, implicit typing is when you don't declare the type of variable and let the compiler infer it:

```
const arr = [1,2,3] // type of arr inferred as number[]
```

If you declare and do not assign any value within the same line, then TypeScript will infer it as any:

```
let x; // fails with noImplicitAny flag enabled
x = 2;
```

This will fail to compile with the noImplicitAny flag, so in this case, it's recommended to always declare the expected type of variable.

Not using const assertions for literal types

When working with object literals, TypeScript might infer a wider type than intended:

Type-inference.ts

```
const colors = {
  red: "#FF0000",
  green: "#00FF00",
  blue: "#0000FF"
};
function getColor(color: "red" | "green" | "blue") {
  return colors[color];
}
```

Here, while the color parameter in getColor is valid, the return type is of type string, which is a wider type than the available kinds of color types .

A better approach is using **const assertion**, which narrows down the type of the response:

Type-inference.ts

```
const colors = {
  red: "#FF0000",
  green: "#00FF00",
```

```
  blue: "#0000FF"
} as const;

function getColor(color: keyof typeof colors) {
  return colors[color];
}
// return type is of type "#FF0000" | "#00FF00" | "#0000FF"
```

The return type is now more accurate, and it allows TypeScript to provide stricter type checking and autocompletion in IDEs, reducing the likelihood of errors.

Next, we'll explain some pitfalls of generics.

Generics gotchas

While **generics** in TypeScript are a very powerful language feature, they tend to be more complex in nature and they come with their own set of challenges. In this section, we'll explore some common **gotchas** to watch out for when using generics in TypeScript.

Confusing naming of multiple generic types

If you are using more than a single generic type, then having single-letter names such as T or K might improve readability. For example, instead of using K and V, consider using TKey and TValue in key-value pairs. Using something more descriptive is always beneficial.

For example, consider this type:

```
interface KeyValuePair<T, K> {
    key: T;
    value: K;
}
```

It could better be defined as follows:

```
interface KeyValuePair<TKey, TValue> {
    key: TKey;
    value: TValue;
}
```

Here is another example:

```
interface ApiResponse<T, K> {
    data: T;
    error?: K;
}
```

Instead of this, you can refactor it as follows:

```
interface ApiResponse<TData, TError> {
    data: TData;
    error?: TError;
}
```

This makes it clear what each type represents: `TData` is for the data type and `TError` is for the error type.

In addition, consider declaring types explicitly in complex code bases, even when TypeScript can infer types, for maintainability and readability:

```
const items: number[] = [1, 2, 3]; // Explicit type for clarity
```

While not strictly necessary (as TypeScript can infer that `[1, 2, 3]` is a number array), explicit typing improves code readability and maintainability, especially if the code is part of a public API.

Overly permissive default generic types

Providing default types for generics can simplify usage but may lead to confusion if not documented clearly. Additionally, it may allow very permissive values, which provide less type safety. Take the following example:

Generic-types.ts

```
type Config<T = {}, U = {}> = {
  ctx?: T
  data?: U
}
const t: Config = {
    ctx: {color: 'red'},
    data: {}
}
```

Here, the `Config` type has the default parameters `T` and `U`, both defaulting to an empty object type (`{}`). When you declare `const t: Config`, you are using the default `{}` type.

When you assign `{ color: 'red' }` to `ctx`, TypeScript allows this because the object literal can have any shape. However, it infers that `ctx` is still of type `{}` due to the use of default types. So, confusion arises when you try to access `t.ctx.color`. Since `ctx` is inferred as `{}`, TypeScript raises an error stating that a `color` property of type `{}` does not exist.

To resolve this issue and avoid similar confusion, you should provide a more explicitly specific type for default generic types or constraints:

Generic-types.ts

```
type WithColor = { color: string };
type Config<T extends WithColor, U = {}> = {
  ctx?: T
  data?: U
}
const t: Config<WithColor> = {
    ctx: {color: 'red'},
    data: {}
}
if (t.ctx) {
  t.ctx.color = 'blue'
}
```

The `Config` type is now defined to require a type parameter, `T`, that extends `WithColor`, ensuring that the `ctx` property must include a `color` attribute. This explicit constraint enhances both the readability and maintainability of the code, as it clearly shows the expected structure of the generic types.

Using constraints in generics can also clarify intended usage in other contexts. Take the following example:

Generic-types.ts

```
type FetchOptions<T extends { url: string }> = {
    params: T;
};
const options: FetchOptions<{ url: string;
  queryParams?: string }> = {
    params: { url: "/api/data", queryParams: "id=123" }
};
```

The `FetchOptions` type requires a generic parameter, `T`, which must have a `url` property. This constraint ensures that any object passed as the `params` property will include a valid URL.

Ignoring newer features of TypeScript

This is more of a general reminder about the importance of utilizing the latest TypeScript features to enhance type safety. TypeScript 5 offers a wealth of tools and utilities designed to improve type safety, but failing to leverage these features can lead to a suboptimal coding experience with insufficient safety nets.

For instance, consider the `NoInfer` utility type introduced in TypeScript 5.4. This feature allows developers to mark certain type parameters as *not eligible for inference*, which helps enforce stricter type checks. Consider the following function that demonstrates an example:

Generic-types.ts

```
function find<T extends string>(heyStack: T[],
  needle: T): number {
  return heyStack.indexOf(needle);
};
console.log(find(["a","b","c"],"d"))
```

This implementation of the `find` function passes the type-checking phase without any issues. However, if you inspect the inferred type of the `find` function, you will see that it is inferred as follows:

```
function find<"a" | "b" | "c" | "d">
  (heyStack: ("a" | "b" | "c" | "d")[],
  needle: "a" | "b" | "c" | "d"): number
```

This occurs because both the array and the string used as the second argument are utilized to infer the type `T`, so the final type of `T` is widened to be `"a"` | `"b"` | `"c"` | `"d"`. Is there a way to provide a more accurate type for the `needle` parameter so that the type checker would flag it as an error when we pass a character not in `heyStack`?

Let's see what happens when we use TypeScript 5's `NoInfer` utility type to wrap the second parameter:

Generic-types.ts

```
function find<T extends string>(heyStack: T[],
  needle: NoInfer<T>): number {
  return heyStack.indexOf(needle)
}
// Argument of type '"d"' is not assignable to parameter of type '"a"
| "b" | "c"'
// Incorrect usage:
const invalidResult = find(["a", "b", "c"], "d");
// Type error due to NoInfer constraint
```

With `NoInfer`, we instruct the compiler to ignore type inference at that point. This would make the type of `needle` as `'a'` | `'b'` | `'c'`, allowing TypeScript to explicitly raise an error when passing `"d"` as an argument.

This simple change significantly enhances type-checking capabilities by leveraging the latest features of TypeScript. As general advice, regularly reviewing your existing code base for such improvements is good practice, as it can help catch potential issues early and ensure that your code remains robust and maintainable.

As a rule of thumb, when defining generic types, make sure to specify constraints clearly and use more specific types whenever possible. By being explicit about the expected types, you reduce ambiguity, making your code more robust and easier to maintain in the long run.

Summary

In this chapter, we explored some of the most important caveats and anti-patterns when working with TypeScript. In general terms, TypeScript is very adaptive as a language and accepts alternative programming models. However, you should strive to avoid confusion when developing with types, prefer plain functions and types over classes, and leverage type inference when needed.

In the last chapter of the book, we are going to carry out a detailed exploration of the usage of design patterns and best practices within two popular TypeScript frameworks: tRPC and Apollo Client. By studying these frameworks, we will gain valuable insights into how they have been designed to work using idiomatic TypeScript.

Q&A

Feel free to review the following questions and their corresponding answers to address any concerns or gain additional insights:

1. What is the purpose of the `NoInfer` utility type in TypeScript?

    Answer: The `NoInfer` utility type, first introduced in TypeScript 5.4, is used to prevent type inference at specific points in a function or type definition, which allows for stricter and more accurate type definitions.

2. How do you understand black-box reuse in the context of object composition?

    Answer: **Black-box reuse** means that you use a component without knowing its internals. All you possess is a component interface. At that time, you test it without knowing or expecting a particular library or function to trigger because this is concealed. With black-box reuse, you can debug and test code many times and in alternative scenarios, and it closely follows the Liskov Substitution Principle.

Further reading

For a comprehensive overview of code smells, see this resource: `https://refactoring.guru/refactoring/smells`.

Get This Book's PDF Version and Exclusive Extras

UNLOCK NOW

Scan the QR code (or go to `packtpub.com/unlock`). Search for this book by name, confirm the edition, and then follow the steps on the page.

Note: Keep your invoice handly. Purchase made directly from packt don't require one.

11

Exploring Design Patterns in Open Source Architectures

In this final chapter, we'll explore the practical application of design patterns and best practices within two popular TypeScript frameworks: **Apollo Client** and **TypeScript Remote Procedure Call** (**tRPC**).

Throughout this chapter, you'll develop skills in identifying how design patterns are used in Apollo Client and tRPC to optimize application architecture. You'll learn how to read and identify patterns in source code and understand the reason why they're used in that way.

This chapter covers the following main topics:

- Introduction to Apollo Client and tRPC
- Design patterns in Apollo Client
- Design patterns in tRPC

By the end of this chapter, you'll have gained valuable insights into how design patterns are used in real-world open source technologies. This practical understanding will enable you to follow similar approaches when you're designing your own projects.

Technical requirements

The code bundle for this chapter is available in this book's GitHub repository: `https://github.com/PacktPublishing/TypeScript-5-Design-Patterns-and-Best-Practices/tree/main/chapters/chapter11-Open_source_patterns`.

Introduction to Apollo Client and tRPC

In this section, we'll provide a brief overview of two popular open source projects that utilize TypeScript under the hood: **Apollo Client** and **tRPC**. While they have competing functionality, both aim to simplify the process of connecting the frontend to the backend.

In this section, we'll explore these technologies and understand their unique strengths.

Apollo Client

Apollo Client is a powerful client for GraphQL APIs, with a built-in state management and caching strategy. It offers a rich set of features for fetching, caching, and updating data in your application.

> **A note regarding Apollo caching strategies**
>
> Apollo offers four cache strategies: **Cache-First**, **Network-Only**, **Cache-and-Network**, and **No Cache**. The *Cache-First strategy* prioritizes cached data by checking for existing entries before making a network request. In contrast, the *Network-Only strategy* always fetches fresh data from the server, ensuring users receive the most up-to-date information, though at the cost of potentially increased latency. The *Cache-and-Network* strategy returns cached data immediately while simultaneously fetching updated data from the network, allowing for quick responses and fresh content. Lastly, the *No Cache option* disables caching altogether.

This client is used in both server-side and client-side scenarios and offers a comprehensive set of tools for easier debugging via a Dev Tools extension. Let's take a look at the reasons to use Apollo Client compared to a regular fetch, for example.

Why use Apollo Client?

You'll want to use Apollo Client for the following reasons:

- **GraphQL backend**: If you're serving your APIs using GraphQL, then Apollo Client is an excellent tool for that use case

- **Complex single-page applications (SPAs)**: It's useful when you're dealing with complex requirements and state management needs and you want complete control over the caching strategies for both client-side and server-side data

- **Debugging experience**: If you want a solid developer experience out of the box, then Apollo Client offers a plethora of tools to make that happen

- **Solid documentation**: Apollo Client offers comprehensive documentation and tons of examples of usage

- **TypeScript support**: The source code is written in TypeScript and it offers fully typed clients and integration with **graphql-codegen**

Of course, depending on your requirements, you may need to extend and configure Apollo Client so that you can handle more advanced scenarios. In that case, you're also covered since the client offers ways to extend the functionality of the client itself using multiple configuration options.

Next, we'll take a look at how to use Apollo Client.

Basic usage

Here's a basic example of how to set up and use Apollo Client in a React application:

1. To set up Apollo Client, you need to install the necessary dependencies:

    ```
    $ npm install @apollo/client graphql
    ```

    These packages include @apollo/client, which is the main client code, and graphql, which is the core GraphQL JavaScript implementation.

2. The next step is to create the client with the API configuration:

---

apollo/src/client.ts

```ts
import { ApolloClient, InMemoryCache, gql }
  from "@apollo/client/core"
const client = new ApolloClient({
  uri: "https://countries.trevorblades.com/",
  cache: new InMemoryCache(),
})
```

In this code snippet, we're importing the necessary components from Apollo Client and creating a new ApolloClient instance with two main configurations: uri is the URL of our GraphQL API and cache is Apollo's normalized in-memory cache. This helps in storing and retrieving data efficiently.

3. Once we have our client set up, we can use it to query the API. Here's an example of how to do that:

---

apollo/src/client.ts

```ts
type Country = {
  name: string
  capital: string
  currency: string
}
client
  .query<Country>({
    query: gql`
      query {
        country(code: "IE") {
          name
          capital
          currency
        }
```

```
        }
        `,
    })
    .then((result) => {
        // Type guard to ensure result.data.country is defined and
    matches expected structure
        if (result.data && result.data.country) {
            console.log(result.data.country.name);
        } else {
            throw new Error("Unexpected API
                response structure");
        }
    })
    .catch((error) => {
        console.error("Error fetching country data:",
            error);
    });
```

We use the `client.query()` method to send a query to our GraphQL API. We're using TypeScript generics (`<Country>`) to type the result of our query. The query itself is defined using the `gql` tagged template literal. After sending the query, we simply log the result to the console.

This example demonstrates a basic query, but Apollo Client supports more complex operations, including mutations, subscriptions, and advanced caching strategies. In a real-world application, you'd typically use Apollo Client within your React components, often with hooks such as `useQuery` for a more declarative approach to data fetching.

Now, let's check out the usage of the tRPC framework.

tRPC – a TypeScript-first RPC framework

tRPC is a lightweight framework that's designed to streamline the process of building end-to-end typesafe APIs. It's particularly well-suited for TypeScript monorepos and full-stack TypeScript projects.

tRPC isn't a replacement for GraphQL but rather a different approach to building APIs that focuses on leveraging TypeScript's type system to ensure type safety across your entire application stack.

Why use tRPC?

It's important to understand some of the reasons to use tRPC compared to other frameworks. tRPC shines in several scenarios:

- **Full-stack TypeScript projects**: When both your frontend and backend are written in TypeScript, tRPC provides seamless integration and type safety across the entire stack

- **Monorepo architectures**: tRPC is ideal for projects where frontend and backend code live in the same repository, allowing for easy sharing of types and schemas
- **Rapid prototyping**: Its minimal boilerplate and automatic type inference make tRPC excellent for quickly building and iterating on APIs

Since it's a rather recent framework and offers a unique approach to building type-safe APIs, you may find some of the concepts harder to understand when you work with this framework initially. However, once you've understood its benefits, it can be very flexible and powerful. Let's compare this to Apollo.

When to consider Apollo Client

While tRPC has its strengths, there are scenarios where Apollo Client might be a better fit for your project's needs:

- **Non-TypeScript projects**: If your project isn't primarily written in TypeScript, Apollo Client can still be easily integrated into JavaScript applications, providing a robust solution without requiring TypeScript's type system. While tRPC would still work fine using JavaScript, you'll miss the benefits of type checking.
- **Rich ecosystem and support**: Apollo Client benefits from a large community and extensive documentation, providing numerous resources, tools, and integrations.

In summary, while tRPC offers seamless TypeScript integration and is ideal for monorepo setups, Apollo Client offers several caching mechanisms and a rich feature set, making it a compelling choice when working with GraphQL APIs.

We'll look at how to use tRPC in the next section.

Basic usage

Here's a basic implementation of tRPC in a full-stack TypeScript project:

1. To set up tRPC, you need to install the necessary dependencies:

   ```
   $ npm install @trpc/server@next @trpc/client@next
   ```

   These packages include `@trpc/server@next`, which is the main server code, and `@trpc/client@next`, which is the main client code.

2. Next, set up the server code, which contains a simple endpoint that responds with a greeting message:

Trpc/src/server.ts

```
import { initTRPC } from "@trpc/server"
import { createHTTPServer } from
  "@trpc/server/adapters/standalone"
```

```
const t = initTRPC.create()
const appRouter = t.router({
  hello: t.procedure
    .input((val: unknown) => {
      if (typeof val === "string") return val
      throw new Error("Invalid input: expected
        string")
    })
    .query((req) => {
      return `Hello, ${req.input}!`
    }),
})
const server = createHTTPServer({
  router: appRouter,
})
server.listen(3000)
export type AppRouter = typeof appRouter
```

In this server setup, we initialize tRPC and create a router. Then, we define a simple greeting procedure that takes a string input and returns a greeting. Finally, we create an HTTP server that uses our tRPC router. The type definition of our API is exported so that it can be used on the client side.

3.   Then, set up the client code, which contains a fully type-safe client that can interact with the router endpoints:

Trac/src/client.ts

```
import { createTRPCClient, httpBatchLink }
  from '@trpc/client';
import type { AppRouter } from './server';
const trpc = createTRPCClient<AppRouter>({
  links: [
    httpBatchLink({
      url: 'http://localhost:3000',
    }),
  ],
});
async function main() {
  try {
    const response = await trpc.hello
      .query('tRPC User');
    console.log(response);
  } catch (error) {
```

```
        console.error('Error:', error);
    }
}

main();
```

In this client setup, we create a tRPC client by using the type definition exported from our server. We provide the HTTP link to connect to our server and then we can call the exported greeting procedure defined on our server, with full type safety.

Looking at the usage of this framework, we can see that it demonstrates the implementation of the Factory Method pattern through the createTRPCClient function. Recall that with this pattern, we encapsulate the object creation logic.

Additionally, notice the use of generics: createTRPCClient<AppRouter>. The AppRouter type, which is imported from the server, defines the shape of your API. The client code uses async/await syntax to work with the asynchronous nature of API calls in a synchronous-looking code style. This is how modern TypeScript is used in many open source projects.

Before we dive into the design patterns that are used in tRPC and Apollo Client, it's important to understand how to review and identify design patterns in open source projects effectively.

Techniques for reviewing design patterns in open source projects

Popular and widely used open source projects often utilize one or more design patterns within their code architecture. However, detecting them isn't obvious unless their documentation resources mention the usage of those patterns. Therefore, when you review the code implementations, you must be able to recognize patterns by looking at certain patterns.

Apply these techniques so that you can analyze other open source projects and learn about their architecture:

- **Start with the documentation**: Most well-maintained open source projects provide comprehensive documentation. This is often the best place to start your review.

- **Examine architecture overviews**: Look for sections that describe the overall architecture or design philosophy of the project. For example, a lot of projects use **architectural decision records (ADRs)**, which are often committed to version control.

- **Check API references**: These can give insights into the public interfaces and how the project is intended to be used. Look for API reference material sections in their documentation site.

- **Read contributing guidelines and READMEs**: These often contain information about code organization and design principles. Many projects also utilize **GitHub wikis** and **discussions**, which could contain valuable insights into how the projects are structured and how they work.

- **Analyze the project structure**: The way a project is organized can reveal a lot about its design patterns. Look at how the code is organized into directories. Common patterns often have specific folder structures (for example, MVC, feature-based, or layer-based organization). Additionally, consistent naming can indicate the role of different components in the overall design. If, for example, a file is named `CarFactory.ts`, this suggests that the author uses a Factory Method pattern in that file.

- **Look for common design pattern implementations**: Some patterns are more common than others and are easier to detect:

  - **Creational patterns**: Look for the Factory Method pattern, Singleton implementations, or Builder patterns

  - **Structural patterns**: Identify the use of the Adapter, Decorator, or Façade pattern

  - **Behavioral patterns**: Observe implementations of the Observer, Strategy, or Command pattern

- **Analyze dependencies and imports**: The way different parts of the project depend on each other can reveal a lot about the design:

  - **Dependency injection**: Look at how dependencies are managed and injected. Are there many classes that accept interfaces as parameters? Are there any usages of dependency injection frameworks such as Inversify.js?

  - **Module dependencies**: Analyze import statements to understand the relationships between different parts of the code base. Usually, relevant module dependencies are bundled together in the same package as `utils`, `common`, and others.

- **Study the test cases**: Tests often provide insights into how the code is designed to be used and extended:

  - **Unit tests**: These can reveal the expected behaviors of individual components. Look for test case names that check for similar behaviors in design patterns.

  - **Integration tests**: Show how different parts of the system are intended to work together.

- **Mock objects**: The use of mocks can indicate key abstractions and interfaces in the systems.

By applying these techniques, you can uncover and understand the design patterns that are used in open source projects, gaining valuable insights on how to adapt them to meet your specific needs.

Now that we've had a quick overview of both projects, let's delve into their code and explore their usage of design patterns and best practices. We'll start with Apollo Client.

Design patterns in Apollo Client

This section explores the usage of design patterns and the practices of the Apollo Client project. The Apollo Client project is hosted on GitHub at: `https://github.com/apollographql/apollo-client`.

> **Note**
>
> A cloned version of the Apollo Client repository is also provided inside the project's repository, inside the `external-repos` folder: `https://github.com/PacktPublishing/TypeScript-5-Design-Patterns-and-Best-Practices/tree/main/external-repos/apollo-client`.

First, we'll take a look at the project structure and file organization. Then, we'll get into the code that runs this client.

Project structure

The Apollo Client project is organized into several key directories. Let's take a brief look at them:

- `src/`: Contains the core source code
- `cache/`: Implements caching mechanisms
- `core/`: The core functionality of Apollo Client
- `link/`: Contains the network layer and request pipeline
- `react/`: Features React-specific implementations
- `utilities/`: Houses helper functions and utilities
- `config/`: Contains configuration files for the build process, testing, and other development tools
- `docs/`: Houses the project documentation
- `integration-tests/`: Contains integration testing cases, allowing the library to be tested thoroughly in various scenarios
- `patches/`: Includes patches that have been applied to dependencies to ensure compatibility with the project
- `scripts/`: Contains useful codemods and scripts for development and maintenance tasks
- `eslint-local-rules/`: Contains custom ESLint rules specific to the project

Apollo Client is structured as a single project, with all its core functionality, utilities, and framework-specific implementations contained within one package. This is evident from the project structure you've shared, where all the code is under a single `src` directory and there's a lack of multiple folders containing `package.json` files.

> **Monorepo versus multi-repo projects**
>
> **Monorepos** consolidate multiple projects into a single repository, facilitating easier code sharing, unified versioning, and consistent tooling across projects. This approach works well in environments with highly interdependent projects and frequent cross-project changes. However, it can become unwieldy as the code base grows, potentially slowing down operations, especially when there are build errors.
>
> On the other hand, **multi-repo strategies** separate projects into individual repositories. This approach offers clearer boundaries between projects, granular access control, and the flexibility to use different tools and workflows for each project. The trade-off comes in the form of increased complexity in managing dependencies and ensuring consistency across projects.

The benefits of this project structure are *cohesion* and *ease of development* – the inclusion of configuration, documentation, and testing directories creates a self-contained development environment. Having the `docs` folder in the main repository ensures that documentation is versioned alongside the code. The separate `integration-tests` folder allows for comprehensive testing without the need to clutter the main source code. Finally, this structure hints at a modular design that separates concerns and promotes maintainability.

However, this architecture can become unwieldy if you're not careful. The additional folders and files can make the project structure more complex for newcomers to navigate. If it's not actively maintained, folders such as `docs` and `scripts` might become outdated or not used at all. Additionally, the need to manage multiple aspects (docs, tests, and scripts) in the build process can make the build process more complex and fragile.

So, as a rule of thumb, when structuring your future TypeScript projects, you should consider the following aspects:

- **Project scope and scale**: For simple projects, a single package would work sufficiently. As your project grows in scope or complexity, consider transitioning to a monorepo structure or a multi-repo approach.

- **Testing strategy**: Separate unit tests (often alongside source files) from integration tests and consider a dedicated `integration-tests/` or `e2e-tests/` folder for more complex test scenarios.

- **Build and maintenance scripts**: Create a `scripts/` folder for custom build, maintenance, and developer productivity tools.

- **Documentation**: Include a `docs/` folder in your main repository to keep documentation in sync with the code. For larger projects, consider using a documentation generation tool that pulls from source code comments.

- **File naming**: Maintain consistent file naming conventions across the project. This consistency significantly enhances searchability and navigation within the code base, especially as the project scales. For instance, all React component files could end with `.component.tsx`, while utility functions could use `.util.ts`.

- **Dependency patches**: Use a `patches/` folder to make temporary fixes to dependencies. However, whenever possible, aim to contribute these fixes upstream when possible.

This set of guidelines will help you get a good grasp of how TypeScript projects are structured in the wild. Of course, the ideal structure can vary based on specific needs, team size, and project goals. Regularly reviewing and refactoring your project structure as it evolves is important to maintaining a healthy, manageable code base.

Now, let's dive into the code to see which design patterns are being used here.

Observed design patterns

Because the full code of the Apollo Client project spans many files and it's quite extensive, we're only going to focus on the main client code located in `src/core/ApolloClient.ts`. This file contains the main exported class for Apollo Client and is a good entry point for reviewing the code. The following is a list of the observed design patterns that are used in this class, along with some explanations of their usage:

- **Observer pattern**: The Observer pattern is used throughout the client code, especially within the `ObservableQuery` and `QueryManager` classes. The `ObservableQuery` class is designed to manage the state of a query and notify subscribers about changes. When a query is executed, it returns an instance of `ObservableQuery`, which can be subscribed to for updates.

  Here's the code snippet:

  ```
  public watchQuery<
    T = any,
    TVariables extends OperationVariables =
      OperationVariables,
  >(options: WatchQueryOptions<TVariables,
    T>): ObservableQuery<T, TVariables> {
      ...
  }
  ```

The watchQuery method in Apollo Client is designed to observe changes in a specific GraphQL query's results by returning ObservableQuery. This allows components to subscribe to the observable and receive updates whenever the relevant data in the cache changes. For example, if a query fetching a person's details is executed and later modified by another query, all subscribers to the original query will automatically receive the updated data.

A great reason to use this pattern is when you expect multiple queries to run asynchronously but you want a reliable way of receiving actual changes from the cache.

- **Strategy pattern**: The Strategy pattern is employed in Apollo Client to allow developers to specify different fetching strategies for queries, such as cache-first, network-only, and cache-and-network. These are used in the watchQuery and query methods' accept options, which include fetchPolicy. This option determines how the client should fetch data when executing a query:

```
if (this.disableNetworkFetches && (options
  .fetchPolicy === "network-only" ||
  options.fetchPolicy === "cache-and-network")) {
    options = { ...options, fetchPolicy:
      "cache-first" };
}
return this.queryManager.watchQuery<T,
  TVariables>(options);
```

The if statement checks whether network fetches have been disabled (which can occur during server-side rendering or when a delay is specified) and whether the requested fetch policy is set to network-only or cache-and-network. If both conditions are true, it modifies the options object to change the fetch policy to cache-first. This changes the fetch strategy based on the provided policy configuration.

- **Composite pattern**: The Composite pattern is utilized in Apollo Client by chaining ApolloLink instances, allowing multiple links to be combined into a single cohesive link. Although it isn't immediately obvious in this code, when HttpLink is instantiated, it can be combined with other links (such as authentication links or error handling links) to create a more sophisticated network layer. The chaining can be achieved by using the ApolloLink.from() method, which takes an array of links and returns a single link that executes them in sequence. For example, the code for ApolloLink.from() is located at src/link/core/ApolloLink.ts:

```
public static from(links: (ApolloLink |
  RequestHandler)[]): ApolloLink {
    if (links.length === 0) return ApolloLink.empty();
    return links.map(toLink).reduce((x, y) =>
      x.concat(y)) as ApolloLink;
}
```

The `from` method takes an array of links and combines them into a single link. It maps each input to a link using the `toLink` function and then reduces the array using the `concat` method to create a composite link.

Each `ApolloLink` can intercept, modify, or delay requests and responses individually. For example, you might have an `AuthLink` link that adds authorization headers to requests and an `ErrorLink` link that handles errors globally:

```
const link = ApolloLink.from([errorLink,
  authLink, httpLink]);
const client = new ApolloClient({
  link,
  cache: new InMemoryCache(),
});
```

Each link can be modified or replaced independently without impacting others, making it easy to adapt to changing requirements. So, in essence, it allows you to compose multiple links into a single link structure, enabling complex request handling without complicating the client's core logic.

- **Memento pattern**: The Memento pattern is utilized in Apollo Client primarily through the `extract` and `restore` methods of the cache. This pattern allows the client to save and restore the state of the cache. After a server-side render, the extracted cache can be sent to the client, allowing it to start with a pre-populated state, thus improving performance and the user experience.

Of course, these design patterns are just a few of the many that can be found throughout the Apollo Client library. As Apollo Client continues to evolve, it's likely to incorporate additional design patterns and considerations that enhance its capabilities. We encourage you to explore the source code (see the *Technical requirements* section) to discover and analyze other design patterns that may not be immediately apparent.

Now, let's take a look at the design patterns used in tRPC.

Design patterns in tRPC

This section explores the usage of design patterns and the practices of the tRPC project. The tRPC project is hosted on GitHub at: `https://github.com/trpc/trpc`.

> **Note**
>
> A cloned version of the tRPC repository is also provided in the project repository, inside the `external-repos` folder: `https://github.com/PacktPublishing/TypeScript-5-Design-Patterns-and-Best-Practices/tree/main/external-repos/trpc`.

Let's take a look at the project structure and file organization before we examine the code that powers up this architecture.

Project structure

The folder structure of the tRPC project reveals a well-organized layout. The following are the key directories:

- `www`: This folder houses the documentation site, providing resources for **React Query** and guides for users and developers to understand and utilize tRPC effectively

- `examples`: This directory contains example boilerplate projects that demonstrate how to implement tRPC in various scenarios, serving as practical references for developers

- `scripts`: This folder includes pipeline and deployment scripts

- `packages`: This is a monorepo structure containing the core packages of tRPC, including the following:

  - `client`: The client-side library for interacting with tRPC

  - `next`: Integrations for using tRPC with Next.js applications

  - `react-query`: A package that integrates tRPC with react-query library for enhanced data fetching capabilities

  - `server`: The server-side implementation of tRPC

- `tests`: Contains test suites for ensuring code quality and compliance

This structure allows you to easily manage dependencies and versioning across different packages, thus making it simpler to maintain and update individual components without affecting the entire system. The inclusion of example boilerplate projects helps developers quickly understand how to implement tRPC in real-world scenarios.

Compared to Apollo Client, this project offers a more modular approach. It uses a monorepo approach with a clear separation of concerns across different packages (`client`, `server`, and so on). Apollo Client generally has a more centralized structure.

The presence of a dedicated `react-query` package in tRPC allows you to seamlessly integrate with React Query for data fetching, which isn't a primary focus in Apollo Client. Also, regarding type safety, it emphasizes type safety throughout its API, leveraging TypeScript to ensure that both client and server types are in sync. While Apollo Client also supports TypeScript, it doesn't enforce type safety as diligently in its core API in general.

With those observations in mind, let's take a closer look at the design patterns that are implemented in tRPC.

Observed design patterns

Compared to Apollo Client, the source code of tRPC is a bit more organized and has better naming conventions. A quick inspection of the `server` package shows that it employs several design patterns:

- **Observable pattern**: tRPC contains a custom implementation of the Observable pattern inside the `server/src/observable` folder. The exported observable utilities are `isObservable`, `observable`, and other related operators. For example, the Observables are used throughout the application as a means to propagate subscription errors:

  ```
  observer.error(TRPCClientError.from(error));
  ```

  If an error occurs during the subscription process, it can be captured and reported back to the observer. Additionally, `behaviorSubject` is used to manage and emit connection state changes (for example, connecting, connected, and error states). This allows clients to update their UI reactively based on the current connection status:

  ```
  const connectionState = behaviorSubject<
          TRPCConnectionState<TRPCClientError<any>>
      >({
        type: 'state',
        state: 'connecting',
        error: null,
      });
      const connectionSub = connectionState
      .subscribe({
        next(state) {
          observer.next({
            result: state,
          });
        },
      });
  ```

  The preceding code snippet initializes a `behaviorSubject` object named `connectionState`, which is used to track and manage the connection status of a tRPC subscription. The `connectionState` subject allows observers to subscribe to changes in the connection state. The `connectionSub` variable holds the subscription to this `behaviorSubject`, where it listens for state updates. Upon receiving a new state, it calls `observer.next()` to emit the updated connection state to any subscribers.

- **Adapter pattern**: In tRPC, the Adapter pattern is designed for different frameworks through its various adapters, such as **Express** and **Next.js**. These adapters serve as intermediary functions that translate tRPC's internal API into a format that's compatible with the specific framework's request and response handling mechanisms. Those adapters are located in the `server/src/` `adapters` folder. Here's an example of the `createNextApiHandler` function, which is tailored for Next.js:

```
import { createNextApiHandler }
  from '@trpc/server/adapters/next';
import { createContext }
  from '../../../server/trpc/context';
import { appRouter }
  from '../../../server/trpc/router/_app';
export default createNextApiHandler({
  router: appRouter,
  createContext,
});
```

This adapter wraps `appRouter` and the context that was exported from the tRPC server so that the developer can export this as a Next.js route handler. Similar adapters are provided for popular frameworks such as **Express.js**, **Fastify**, and **node-http**, enabling them to implement tRPC in existing applications with minimal changes needing to be made to their existing code base.

This allows developers to add middleware for authentication, logging, or any other custom requirements. Here's an example illustrating how to extend `createContext` so that it includes custom authentication logic:

```
import type { CreateNextContextOptions }
  from '@trpc/server/adapters/next';
import { getSessionFromCookie, type Session }
  from './auth';
interface CreateInnerContextOptions extends
  Partial<CreateNextContextOptions> {
  session: Session | null;
}
export async function createContextInner(opts?:
  CreateInnerContextOptions) {
  return {
    session: opts?.session || null,
  };
}
export async function createContext(opts:
  CreateNextContextOptions) {
  const session = getSessionFromCookie(opts.req);
  // Get session from cookie
  const contextInner = await createContextInner(
  { session });
  return {
```

```
    ...contextInner,
    req: opts.req,
    res: opts.res,
  };
}
export type Context = Awaited<ReturnType<typeof
  createContextInner>>;
```

The `createContext` function serves as the outer context. This is invoked with `CreateNextContextOptions`, which includes the Next.js request (`req`) and response (`res`) objects. It retrieves the user's session from cookies using the custom `getSessionFromCookie` function and then calls `createContextInner`, passing the session as an option. The `createContextInner` function constructs the inner context, which always includes the session and can be extended with additional properties as needed.

- **Proxy pattern**: In tRPC, the Proxy pattern is utilized so that procedure calls can be handled more abstractly. This pattern enables the creation of proxy objects that can intercept method calls and provide additional functionality, such as input validation, error handling, and context management. As an example, take a look at the RPC proxy implementation located at `server/src/unstable-core-do-not-import/createProxy.ts`:

```
return createRecursiveProxy<ReturnType
  <RouterCaller<any, any>>>(
  async ({ path, args }) => {
    const fullPath = path.join('.');
    // Rest of logic to resolve the procedure and execute it
  }
);
```

The `createRecursiveProxy` function implements the Proxy pattern. It creates a proxy object that intercepts calls to procedures defined in a tRPC router. When a method is called on this proxy, it dynamically resolves the appropriate procedure based on the path provided. The proxy intercepts calls to methods and can perform operations before or after invoking the actual procedure. Here's an example:

```
const basic = createRecursiveProxy((opts) => {
  return opts; // This function typically handles the resolution
logic
});

const queryResult = basic.foo.bar.query();
console.log(queryResult); // Output: { path: ['foo', 'bar',
'query'], args: [] }

const queryWithArgsResult = basic.foo.bar.query(
  { id: 1 });
```

```
console.log(queryWithArgsResult); // Output: { path: ['foo',
'bar', 'query'], args: [{ id: 1 }] }

const mutateResult = basic.foo.bar.mutate();
console.log(mutateResult); // Output: { path: ['foo', 'bar',
'mutate'], args: [] }
```

The `createRecursiveProxy` function creates a proxy that allows developers to call methods on a nested structure, such as `basic.foo.bar.query()`, without having to explicitly define each method in advance. Instead, the proxy intercepts these calls and captures the method name and any arguments provided, returning an object that includes the resolved path and arguments.

This is one key feature that makes the proxy pattern look like something *magical* is happening behind the scenes!

To explore additional patterns and their implementations within tRPC, I encourage you to dig into the source code. Start by examining the adapters, middleware, and procedure directories since they contain various implementations of existing patterns. Look for areas where functionality is being extended or modified as these may provide insights into how new patterns could be integrated.

Hopefully, by reading actual TypeScript code, you'll develop a good grasp of how to leverage these patterns in your projects and adopt better practices and more efficient development workflows.

Summary

This chapter explored the design patterns that are utilized within the Apollo Client and tRPC open source projects. Regarding Apollo Client, we discussed various key patterns, including the Observer pattern, which enables reactive data updates through subscriptions to query results; the Factory pattern, which facilitates the creation of network links; the Composite pattern, which allows us to chain multiple links to manage complex request handling; and the Memento pattern, which supports saving and restoring cache states for improved performance and state management. Then, we looked at tRPC and its significant patterns. This includes the Proxy pattern, which allows dynamic method resolution for procedure calls; the Adapter pattern, which allows you to integrate with various frameworks, such as Express and Next.js; and the Observer pattern, which is used to propagate changes to subscribers. Each pattern contributes to a modular, maintainable code base, making both projects fairly robust and type-safe.

As you consider your next steps, I encourage you to review more complex design patterns and their applications. For instance, exploring patterns within the Redux ecosystem can provide insights into state management strategies that complement what you've learned about the Proxy and Observer patterns. Additionally, studying advanced use cases for these patterns in reactive architectures can enhance your understanding of how to implement them effectively in larger systems.

As a concluding piece of advice, I wish to remind you that understanding design patterns is just the beginning. You have the tools and knowledge to apply these patterns creatively in your projects. Embrace the challenges ahead with confidence! Go forward and apply what you've learned and ultimately contribute to building better applications with TypeScript.

Q&A

Feel free to review the following questions and their corresponding answers to address any concerns or gain additional insights:

1. How does the Observer pattern enhance the functionality of Apollo Client?

    Answer: The Observer pattern allows components to subscribe to changes in query results. This means that when data in the cache is updated, all subscribed components automatically receive the new data.

2. Can you give an example of how the Composite pattern is implemented in Apollo Client?

    Answer: The Composite pattern is implemented through methods such as `ApolloLink.from`, `concat`, and `split`, which allow multiple `ApolloLink` instances to be combined into a single link. This enables complex network request handling as you can chain various links together.

3. What role does the Proxy pattern play in tRPC?

    Answer: In tRPC, the Proxy pattern is used for method resolution for procedure calls. It allows you to intercept calls to procedures and allows functionalities such as input validation and centralized error handling without the need to alter the core logic.

12

Unlock Your Exclusive Benefits

Your copy of this book includes the following exclusive benefit:

- ⌂ Next-gen Packt Reader
- ⊡ DRM-free PDF/ePub downloads

Follow the guide below to unlock them. The process takes only a few minutes and needs to be completed once.

Unlock this Book's Free Benefits in 3 Easy Steps

Step 1

Keep your purchase invoice ready for *Step 3*. If you have a physical copy, scan it using your phone and save it as a PDF, JPG, or PNG.

For more help on finding your invoice, visit `https://www.packtpub.com/unlock-benefits/help`.

> **Note**
> If you bought this book directly from Packt, no invoice is required. After *Step 2*, you can access your exclusive content right away.

Step 2

Scan the QR code or go to `packtpub.com/unlock`.

On the page that opens (similar to *Figure 12.1* on desktop), search for this book by name and select the correct edition.

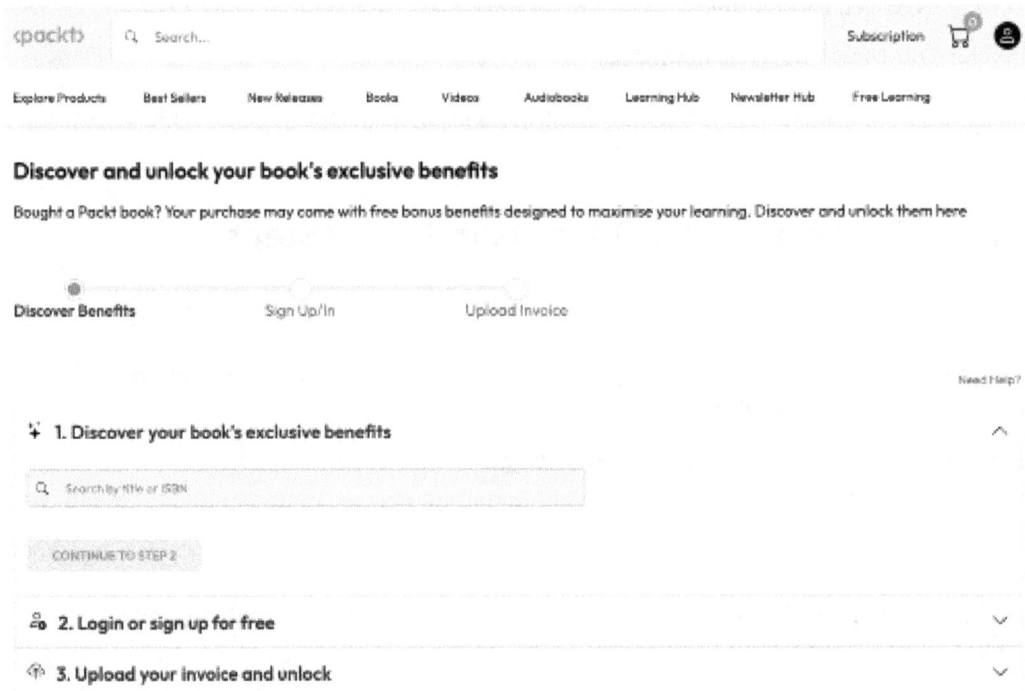

Figure 12.1: Packt unlock landing page on desktop

Step 3

After selecting your book, sign in to your Packt account or create one for free. Then upload your invoice (PDF, PNG, or JPG, up to 10 MB). Follow the on-screen instructions to finish the process.

Need help?

If you get stuck and need help, visit https://www.packtpub.com/unlock-benefits/help for a detailed FAQ on how to find your invoices and more. This QR code will take you to the help page.

Note

If you are still facing issues, reach out to customercare@packt.com.

Index

‹packt›

packtpub.com

Subscribe to our online digital library for full access to over 7,000 books and videos, as well as industry leading tools to help you plan your personal development and advance your career. For more information, please visit our website.

Why subscribe?

- Spend less time learning and more time coding with practical eBooks and Videos from over 4,000 industry professionals

- Improve your learning with Skill Plans built especially for you

- Get a free eBook or video every month

- Fully searchable for easy access to vital information

- Copy and paste, print, and bookmark content

At www.packtpub.com, you can also read a collection of free technical articles, sign up for a range of free newsletters, and receive exclusive discounts and offers on Packt books and eBooks.

Other Books You May Enjoy

If you enjoyed this book, you may be interested in these other books by Packt:

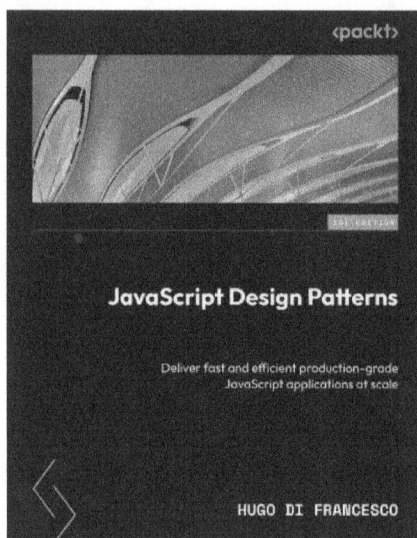

JavaScript Design Patterns

Hugo Di Francesco

ISBN: 978-1-80461-227-9

- Find out how patterns are classified into creational, structural, and behavioral
- Implement the right set of patterns for different business scenarios
- Explore diverse frontend architectures and different rendering approaches
- Identify and address common asynchronous programming performance pitfalls
- Leverage event-driven programming in the browser to deliver fast and secure applications
- Boost application performance using asset loading strategies and offloading JavaScript execution

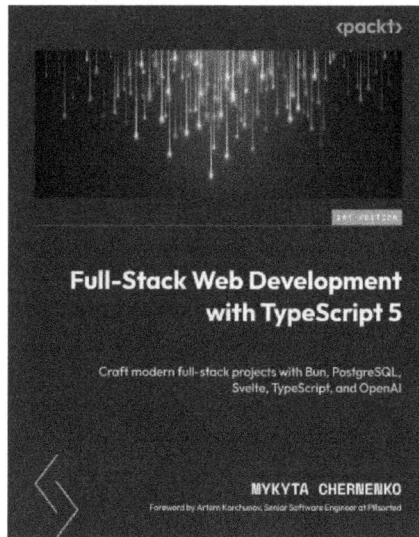

Full-Stack Web Development with TypeScript 5

Mykyta Chernenko

ISBN: 978-1-83588-558-1

- Develop a chat application by implementing frontend and backend features effectively
- Build powerful backends using PostgreSQL
- Write unit tests efficiently for cleaner and more reliable apps
- Understand full-stack application architecture for better scalability and maintainability
- Create dynamic and responsive UIs with Svelte
- Use debugging, testing, and logging tools in web applications to quickly detect and minimize errors

Packt is searching for authors like you

If you're interested in becoming an author for Packt, please visit `authors.packtpub.com` and apply today. We have worked with thousands of developers and tech professionals, just like you, to help them share their insight with the global tech community. You can make a general application, apply for a specific hot topic that we are recruiting an author for, or submit your own idea.

Share Your Thoughts

Now you've finished *TypeScript 5 Design Patterns and Best Practices*, we'd love to hear your thoughts! Scan the QR code below to go straight to the Amazon review page for this book and share your feedback or leave a review on the site that you purchased it from.

https://packt.link/r/1835883230

Your review is important to us and the tech community and will help us make sure we're delivering excellent quality content.